Conversion table

Liquid measures

1000 ml = 1 liter
1000 ml = 10 dl
1000 ml = 100 cl

	(US)	(UK)
1 cup =	240 ml	295 ml
=	2.4 dl	2.95 dl
3/4 cup =	180 ml	220 ml
=	0.8 dl	2.2 dl
2/3 cup =	160 ml	197 ml
=	1.6 dl	1.97 dl
1/2 cup =	120 ml	148 ml
=	1.2 dl	1.48 dl
1/3 cup =	80 ml	89 ml
=	0.8 dl	8.9 dl
1/4 cup =	60 ml	74 ml
=	0.6 dl	7.4 dl

1 tbsp = 15 ml
1 tsp   = 5 ml

Weight measures

1000 g	=	1 kg
4 oz	=	1/4 lb
	=	112 g
8 oz	=	1/2 lb
	=	224 g
12 oz	=	3/4 lb
	=	336 g
16 oz	=	1 lb
	=	448 g
32 oz	=	2 lb
	=	896 g

Length measures

1/4 inch = 0.6 cm
1/2 inch = 1.2 cm
1 inch   = 2.5 cm

Oven temperatures

122°F	=	50°C
167°F	=	75°C
300°F	=	150°C
350°F	=	175°C
392°F	=	200°C
482°F	=	250°C
572°F	=	300°C

The art of home cooking

THE ART OF HOME COOKING

Recipes Leif Mannerström *Guest chef* Ola Andersson

Photography, food and still-lifes Tomas Yeh

Photography, settings Lisa Nestorson

Stylist Sarah Bergh

English translation Roger Tanner

prisma

Swedish food – a lifelong love affair!

After 50 years at the stove in Sweden and abroad, my relationship to food is both simple and uncomplicated. Good food is one of the most vital ingredients of our lives. My love of food is passionate and dedicated, especially where traditional Swedish home cooking – *husmanskost* – is concerned. Now people in other countries have also begun discovering Swedish food. We must be very glad of that, because food makes an important difference to a country's international image. In our chill Nordic latitudes we have access to fantastic raw materials which can be turned into equally fantastic culinary, gustatory experiences. A national treasure!

During my time as cook and restaurant worker, Swedish cooking has won a worldwide reputation, though perhaps not primarily on account of *husmanskost*. Which is a pity, because traditional home fare, carefully and lovingly prepared, is among the best and healthiest food obtainable.

Thirty-odd years ago I played a part in introducing the French *nouvelle cuisine* in Sweden. Big deal. It was an incredibly happy time in my life, and I venture to claim that in this way my colleague and friend Crister Svantesson and I paved the way for the many new trends that have put Swedish cooks and Swedish cooking on the world map.

This book can be seen as a long-overdue tribute to my old colleague Tore Wretman, the Grand Old Man of the Swedish restaurant industry. I have no hesitation in saying that it was his efforts 40 or more years ago that saved traditional Swedish home cooking from oblivion.

Now I would like to add something to the legacy of past generations. In this cookbook I share with you the knowledge and hints I've gathered over the years about what I love and always have loved most of all.

The recipes chosen are the ones I like. The ones I think are tastiest and best. My own favourites, with neither frills nor furbelows. Here you will find what you need to know about familiar delicacies of the traditional Swedish dinner table.

By all means look ahead, but remember to look back. Our forefathers also "knew their onions", and now it's books like this one that can pass on the tradition to the next generation and the one after that. By passing on the zest and happiness of good cooking to our children and grandchildren, we'll be doing them the good turn of a lifetime!

Göteborg, May 2006
Leif Mannerström

My Twelve Commandments

1. Always start your cooking with the kitchen clean and shining and everything in order. Make sure the washing-up is out of the way, so that you can wash things up as you go instead of filling the sink.

2. Hygiene in the kitchen means everything! Worktops clean and thoroughly wiped, chopping boards properly washed up and bowls and pans intact is the golden rule as far as I'm concerned.

3. Get out all the ingredients you will be needing, unless they have to be kept cold. Clean, cut, chop and put them into small bowls or onto chopping boards, so as to have them handy the moment they are needed. That way you keep things running smoothly.

4. Get proper, high-quality equipment – think of it as an investment. Always make sure the knives are sharp and everything else in working order.

5. Plan your shopping, especially if you're an occasional cook and don't have everything at your fingertips or in your head.

6. Always buy the best possible raw materials. Don't compromise on quality. Meat that looks pale and lifeless will probably taste that way. Vegetables that have withered are past redemption. And with good-quality raw materials you can keep things simple. Good quality shows, and poor quality can't be hidden.

7. Always be ready to experiment with flavours which you like and believe can go well together. For my own part I make up new concoctions almost daily, working out new combinations by trial and error and sometimes coming up with something that has the makings of a real hit.

8. Favourite music and a glass of good red wine beside the chopping boards are very good for job satisfaction.

9. Practise your skill at peeling, trimming, shredding and chopping, and work will come easier. Neatly cut raw materials make food a delight to both eye and palate.

10. Think of all cooking as a form of enjoyment. Make a feast of it, together with the family or the friends you have invited in. If possible, go for food that partly looks after itself and won't mind a bit of trotting to and fro between kitchen and reception room.

11. A few words about herbs and spices, too … Use fresh ones wherever possible.

12. So off you go! Think of your kitchen as a fun workshop, both for culinary classics and for successful experiments with new raw materials and new flavours.

9

Last but not least.

Have fun with your food! Experiment! Gamble!
Think of recipes as advice, not always to be slavishly adhered to.
Enjoy yourself in the kitchen, and you simply can't go wrong!

Classified index

10

11

Collops serves 6

There is little argument about the standing of collops in traditional Swedish cooking. Stewing steak is the ideal cut, but brisket will do, though it needs rather more cooking time to get tender. Collops is first-rate winter food, just the thing on a snowbound day with a howling winter wind outside.

Ingredients:
2 kg stewing steak or brisket
2 onions
2 carrots
butter for frying
1/2 tbsp flour
6 bay leaves
10–15 allspice corns
4-5 cloves
2 tbsp "anchovy" liquor
salt and pepper

Serve with:
boiled floury potatoes
pickled beetroot

Procedure
Cut the meat into cubes of about 4 cm. Peel the onion and carrot and cut up large. Brown the meat well all round in the cast iron pot. Season. Sprinkle with a little flour, stir well and add enough water to cover the meat and vegetables. Now add all the herbs and the "anchovy" liquor.

Simmer gently for about 1 1/2 hours, stirring occasionally to make sure nothing sticks.

Season to taste before serving straight from the pot, together with potatoes and plenty of pickled beetroot.

Pickled beetroot

Fresh, boiled beetroot with chopped red (Spanish) onion and sheep's milk cheese in vinaigrette sauce are unbeatable in summertime. But if the harvest is good, perhaps you will feel like pickling a few. There are, of course, many recipes for pickled beetroot. Personally I use basically the same 1–2–3 pickling liquid as for herring, to give the beetroot just the right degree of sting.

Ingredients:
2 kg beetroot
horse radish
preserving agent (optional)

Pickling liquid
2 dl Swedish distilled vinegar, ättika (12 % strength)
4 dl caster sugar
6 dl water
5–6 white peppercorns
5–6 allspice corns
10–15 cloves
2 bay leaves
a pinch or two of salt
Atamon or sodium benzoate

Procedure:
Wash the beetroot with a soft brush and rinse thoroughly. Leave about 2 cm of the haulm and take care not to damage the root tips, otherwise the beetroot will lose colour. Put the beetroot in a casserole and pour on enough water to cover. Bring to the boil and then cook over a medium flame until they are done. Smallish beetroot will generally be ready in 30 or 35 minutes, large ones can take up to an hour.

Meanwhile set the oven to 100–1250. Wash up some big glass jars with undamaged lids, and put them on a wire rack in the oven for at least 10 minutes.

Bring all the pickling liquid ingredients to the boil. Stir till the sugar dissolves. Keep the liquor warm under cover. Peel the horse radish and cut up into small cubes.

Pour off the cooking water and quickly rinse the beetroot in cold water. You might care to put a pair of rubber gloves on before removing the peel. Slice the beetroot or leave them whole.

Add the preserving agent, if any, to the warm liquor. Transfer the beetroot to hot jars and pour on the liquor. Add a few cubes of horseradish on top. Screw on the lids immediately and tightly. After an hour or so the lids will say "click". The beetroot are ready for sampling after a week.

13

Swedish steamboat steak   serves 4

This is usually a staple item on the many regular boat services in the Stockholm archipelago, and in Swedish restaurants too. But – always serve it medium! Swedish beef, of course, but a touch of French mustard works wonders.

Ingredients:
4 sirloin steaks (200 g each), well marbled
4 yellow or red onions
butter and oil for frying
a pinch of sugar
1 tbsp Kikkoman soy
2–3 tbsp gravy sauce (see p. 121)
salt and pepper

Serve with:
fried, boiled or riced potato
salt gherkin
French mustard

Procedure:
Peel and slice the onion and fry in butter and oil till golden brown. Season lightly and sprinkle with a pinch of sugar towards the end. Set aside and keep warm.

Pound the steaks lightly, then season them. Heat a large frying pan, a cast iron one if possible. Put in a few tbsp oil and a large knob of butter. Fry the steaks for a couple of minutes on each side. They must be pink in the middle. Transfer them to a warm dish.

Fry up the onion again, quickly, and arrange it neatly on or beside the steaks.

Deglaze the pan with a few tbsp water, add soy and gravy sauce. Pour the sauce to one side of the steaks and serve instantly with fried, boiled or riced potatoes, salt gherkins and French mustard.

Beef Stroganov   serves 4

Needless to say, this dish was named after a Russian – Alexander Stroganoff, famed for his magnificent banquets. His kitchen was staffed by French maîtres de cuisine and French chefs.

Even so, beef Stroganov is nothing to make a fuss about, though in Sweden especially it has been transformed beyond recognition – roughly speaking, into Falun sausage in tomato sauce. Perish the thought! No, only the best of beef will do for Stroganov. Either that or nothing at all, as far as I'm concerned. Strictly speaking, it should be served with Russian smetana, a mild-flavoured sour cream, but good old Swedish gräddfil does the job quite creditably.

Ingredients:
600 g fillet of beef or marbled steak
1 large onion
1 clove of garlic
200 g ceps, button mushrooms or some other tasty kind
butter and oil for frying
1 tsp paprika powder
1 tbsp tomato purée
1 beef stock cube
5 dl milk with the top on (4 dl milk, 1 dl cream)
salt and pepper

Serve with:
rice or riced potatoes
salt gherkins
gräddfil (Swedish sour cream)

Procedure:
Cut the meat into centimetre-thick strips. Peel the onion, chop it quite roughly, peel and chop the garlic. Trim the mushrooms and cut up small. Brown the meat quickly all round in butter and oil in a frying pan. Set aside (reserve the juices). Fry the onion and mushrooms in the pan. Add the garlic, paprika powder and tomato purée. Fry for another minute or so before crumbling in the stock cube and diluting with the milk-and-cream mixture.

Reduce the sauce until it thickens, then season to taste. Add the juices from frying the meat. Put in the meat and heat everything thoroughly. Serve with boiled rice or riced potatoes, sticks of salt gherkin and gräddfil.

15

Swedish "anchovies" and vodka serves 4

This is a quickly made appetiser and just the thing with vodka if the right sort of people just drop in but the conversation dries up.

Almost any excuse – even bad company! – is welcome for getting this wonderful dish of genuine Swedish "anchovy" and a glass or two of vodka to go with it – or is it the other way round?

Ingredients:
2 tins of filleted Swedish "anchovies" (125 g each)

Marinade:
1 red onion
1 clove of garlic
2 tbsp olive oil
1/2 tbsp red wine vinegar
pepper

Garnish:
dill sprigs

Serve with:
toast made with white bread or crisp bread (see p. 50)
butter
matured cheese

Procedure:
Reserve the liquor from the anchovies, for spicy duties to come.

Peel and chop the red onion and garlic. Mix the olive oil and vinegar together and season with pepper. Add the red onion and garlic and pour this marinade over the anchovies. Stir a little and garnish with dill sprigs. Leave to stand while you are getting the other trimmings ready.

Hint:
Should, contrary to all expectation, something be left over, you can very well mash the leftovers with a fork and use them for flavouring meat cakes or meatballs. Believe me, it'll make your day.

Chicken wings in garlic butter serves 4

Chicken wings have steadily gained popularity in recent years. For this recipe you don't use the whole wing, all the way out to the tip, but just the two innermost joints. Otherwise there won't be much of a meat ration. A glass of light red wine goes very well with this one – a cool Beaujolais, for example.

Ingredients:
16 chicken wings
olive oil
salt and pepper

Garlic butter:
200 g butter at room temperature
1 bunch of parsley
a couple of sprigs of thyme
5–6 cloves of garlic
a few drops of Worcester sauce
salt and pepper

Procedure:
Set the oven to 200 or 2250. Part the wings, cutting away the outermost joint. Carefully pull down the flesh on the thickest part, exposing the bone. Brush with olive oil, add salt and pepper. Upend the wings in a greased oven-proof dish, with the bones pointing upwards. Roast them in the middle of the oven for about 15 minutes till crisp.

Meanwhile prepare the garlic butter. Chop the parsley and thyme small. Crush the garlic. Mix everything together.

Brush or daub the wings generously with butter. Keep roasting till the butter has melted, the chicken is thoroughly cooked and the whole thing is bubbling.

Serve steaming hot, e.g. with fresh-baked white bread.

Skåne "egg cake" with pork serves 4

What would a farmhouse cookbook be without Skåne "egg cake"? And what could be more natural than my very likeable guest cook, Ola Andersson, a great lover of Skåne specialities, undertaking to pass on the great tradition? To make it extra good he even made a detour to his butcher for the best of dry-salted pork. Basically, though, believe me, it will turn out just as well with ordinary bacon or gammon. The only thing about the "egg cake" is that you have to keep an eye on it all the time, so start by frying the pork, which you then put by in a warm place.

Here the "egg cake" itself is the star turn, so to drink you need nothing more expensive than ice-cold beer.

Ingredients:
8 eggs
3 dl white flour
7 dl milk
1 1/2 tsp salt
butter for frying

Serve with:
800 g salt pancetta
uncooked, stirred lingonberry jam (see p. 25)

Procedure:
Slice the pork, fry it and keep warm.

Beat the batter ingredients together. Heat a frying pan to a high temperature. Put in a generous knob of butter and wait until it is nut brown. Reduce the heat by half. Pour in the batter and begin stirring it slowly and gently with a wooden spoon. Detach and lift up whole sheets of it from the bottom of the pan. Now stir in the middle, but not outwards towards the edges, until the batter is looking creamy; the edges have to remain in position to stabilise the cake. Turn the heat full on again, and push the edges down to shape them.

Take a saucepan lid or a large, not too heavy dish and rinse it in cold water. Put the lid or dish on the frying pan and wait for about a minute. Now turn the pan over quickly, so that the cake lands bottom up on the dish. Put in a fresh knob of butter and slide the cake back into the frying pan again, with the temperature still high. Smooth the edges if necessary. Shake the pan a little and fry for another minute or so. Put the lid on and quickly turn everything out. Serve instantly, with the crisp-fried pork and uncooked lingonberry jam.

19

Fish and shellfish burger serves 4

Never buy shop burgers – make your own! Using minced beef, minced game or, as here, minced fish.

Ingredients:
400 g minced cod or mince of some other white fish
200 g minced salmon
1 bunch of chives, chopped small
2 egg yolks
1 tbsp sweet chilli sauce
butter for frying
salt and pepper

Serve with:
4 hamburger buns or similar bread
lettuce leaves or young beetroot leaves
1 small red onion
tomato
shrimp salad

Procedure:
Stir all the ingredients together into a smooth mixture. Shape four large burgers. Fry them in a generous knob of butter in a frying pan for 3–4 minutes on each side until they are a nice colour and look ready.

Grill the bread very quickly and top it with lettuce leaves, fish burgers and rings of red onion. Finish off with a generous dob of shrimp salad and either put together or arrange as pictured.

Shrimp salad serves 4

A really good, home-made shrimp salad is what, in my opinion, goes best with fish burgers – you'll find the recipe for fish burgers in this book – but also with other minced fish recipes. And of course, it also goes excellently with fried fish.

Ingredients:
100 g peeled shrimps
1 dl mayonnaise
1 dl gräddfil (soured cream)
1 tsp Dijon mustard
2 tbsp fine-chopped dill
2 tsp fine-chopped chives
salt and pepper

Procedure:
Mix the dressing first, by carefully blending all the ingredients except the shrimps. Divide the shrimps if they are big ones, and fold them into the sauce. Leave in a cold place for a few hours before serving.

Cabbage pudding serves 6

Cabbage pudding may sound a little ordinary and tubby, but if prepared in the somewhat more elegant way I suggest, it's a treat to look at. So I usually bake my cabbage pudding in a tin with a detachable rim. Before serving I carefully transfer it to a warm dish, and then when carving it you can clearly see the fine stratification of cabbage leaves and farce.

Ingredients:
800 g mixed beef and pork mince
1 cabbage – Savoy or wild cabbage/kale
1 onion
butter for frying
1 cold boiled potato or the corresponding quantity of mash
2 dl milk
1 dl dried breadcrumbs
2 eggs
6 tbsp Kikkoman soy
2 tbsp golden syrup
2 tbsp concentrated veal stock
2 tbsp melted butter
1 tbsp brown sugar
salt and pepper

Sauce:
3–4 dl gravy sauce (see p. 26)
uncooked, stirred lingonberry jam

Procedure:
Cut the stalk out of the cabbage head and parboil it in lightly salted water for 10–15 minutes (15 minutes for white cabbage). Remove with a slotted spoon and carefully detach the good leaves. Cut away the hard central vein in each leaf, then put the leaves aside for the time being.

 Set the oven to 200°C. Peel the onion and chop small, chop the remains of the cabbage small and fry everything in a little butter. Mash the potato with a fork. Mix milk and dried bread crumbs with the mashed potato and the fried onion and cabbage mixture. Leave to swell for about 10 minutes. Blend this mixture with the mince, eggs, soy, treacle and concentrated veal stock. Add salt and pepper. Stir quickly to a loose batter. Test-fry a small dob of the mixture to check the seasoning.

 Brown the cabbage leaves quickly in a little butter. Grease a tin with a detachable rim thoroughly, and then put in alternate layers of cabbage leaves and farce, starting and finishing with cabbage. Brush with butter, season with pepper, sprinkle with a pinch of salt and the brown sugar.

 Bake in the middle of the oven for 40–45 minutes. It is a good idea to put a roasting pan underneath, in case some of the stock seeps out of the tin. Give the pudding a few minutes to settle before you remove the rim. Carefully transfer the pudding to a warm serving dish. Pour a little of the hot gravy round it. Serve immediately with boiled potatoes, the rest of the gravy in a gravy boat, pressed cucumber and uncooked, stirred lingonberry jam.

Uncooked, stirred lingonberry jam
makes 2 1/2 kg

As you will already have noticed, I personally think that uncooked, stirred lingonberry jam goes well with many of the recipes in this book. So I might as well give you a dependable recipe for that too. Uncooked lingonberries will not keep as long as cooked jam, though on the other hand they usually get eaten up quickly. With the extra sugar included, the jam will at any rate keep for 3 months or so if stored in a cold, dark place, because lingonberries contain a natural preservative of their own.

25

Ingredients:
1 kg lingonberries, topped and tailed
5–7 dl caster sugar

Procedure:
Rinse the lingonberries if you didn't pick them yourself. Make sure they dry reasonably well. Mix them with the sugar in a mixing bowl and keep stirring till the sugar stops crunching on the wooden spoon. The jam will then be ready for pouring into absolutely clean glass jars with lids intact. The jars will be cleanest if, after washing them up, you put them in the oven for 10 minutes at 1250. Leave the jars to cool before filling them.

Hints:
For a more durable but equally good jam, find a cooked jam with high lingonberry content, mix roughly equal parts and store in jars.

Pressed cucumber

Pressed cucumber goes well with any number of things – meatballs, mince hazel-hens, roast spring chicken and leg of pork, to mention but a few. This is how my grandmother, Cecilia, used to make it, and so do I, with the addition of a few rings of chilli.

Ingredients:
1 cucumber (200–250 g)
1 bunch of parsley
pepper

Dressing:
1 dl Swedish distilled vinegar, ättika (12%)
2 dl caster sugar
3 dl water
10–12 slices of chilli pepper
salt

Procedure:
Shave the cucumber into very thin slices. Put these on a dish and salt them lightly; the salt will extract some of the moisture. Leave for about 15 minutes and then drain well in a colander. Pat gently with kitchen tissue. Chop the parsley small. Put alternate layers of sliced cucumber, parley and a little pepper in a glass bowl. Mix the ingredients for the dressing, check for seasoning – sweet'n-sour is what you want. Pour the dressing over the cucumber. Sprinkle plenty of parsley on top and store cold for at least an hour before serving.

Meat cakes with onion serves 4

This and meatballs are about as Swedish as it gets. And it cannot be said too often that mince is far and away the noblest raw material of the Swedish kitchen. Everyone loves it, and the scope for variation is almost infinite. No variation this time, however: simply a juicy meat cake with onion and no nonsense. But put a bottle of Aalborg snaps and a few beers in the fridge before you go out to shop.

Ingredients:
300 g minced beef
300 g mixed (beef and pork) mince
2 medium-large onions
butter and oil for frying
3 boiled potatoes
1 dl milk with the top on (1/2 dl milk, 1/2 dl cream)
1 egg
1 dl dried breadcrumbs
1 dl water
1 tbsp concentrated veal stock
1 tbsp Kikkoman soy
salt and pepper
2 large onions
butter for frying
a pinch of sugar

Serve with:
fried or boiled potatoes
pressed cucumber or Asian cucumber (see p. 42)
gravy sauce (see p. 121)

Procedure:
Peel the medium-large onions. Grate one of them, chop the other one small and fry it in butter. Mash the potatoes with a fork. Mix the cream and milk, the egg, the grated and the fried onion, the potato, the breadcrumbs and the water in a mixing bowl. Leave the mixture to swell for a while.

Now mix it with the mince, veal stock and soy. Add salt and pepper and stir thoroughly till you have a smooth mixture. Test-fry a little to check the seasoning. Put to one side.

Peel the large onions and slice them thinly. Fry them in butter till golden brown, sprinkle with a pinch of sugar and put to one side.

Shape four nice big meat cakes and fry them slowly in butter and a little oil until they are crisp and golden brown; give them about 4–5 minutes on each side.

Meantime, fry the onion once more and then put a thick layer of it on top of the finished meat cakes.

Pea soup with pork serves 6

It's no more than a slight exaggeration to say that Sweden's Age of Greatness in the 17th and 18th centuries was founded on pea soup. And it's no exaggeration at all to say that pea soup nowadays comes pretty well top of the dining room pops, with Swedish arrack punch as its indispensable concomitant, not forgetting beer or mineral water. So let's do it. The meat and sausages can be got ready a day in advance.

Soup ingredients:
500 g dried yellow peas
stock from boiling the pork
1 tsp thyme
2 tsp marjoram
pepper
salt (if needed)

Side plate ingredients:
500 g salt loin/shoulder of pork
500 g salt pancetta
1 pork sausage
1 meat sausage

1 large onion
2 carrots
1/2 leek (the white part)
3 bay leaves
10 white peppercorns
10 allspice corns
1/2 tbsp salt per litre of water

Serve with:
toasted crisp bread (see p. 50)
matured seed-spiced cheese (*kryddost*)
strong sweet mustard
warm Swedish arrack punch

Procedure:
Put the pork in a casserole, pour on water and bring to the boil. Remove the pork with a slotted spoon, rinse it under the tap and put it in fresh water, again bringing to the boil. Meanwhile, peel and trim the vegetables, cutting them up small. Add the vegetables and spices to the pot. Cook for 1–1 1/2 hours, until the meat is ready. With about 10 minutes still to go, put in the sausages, after first pricking them carefully to stop them bursting. Leave everything to cool in the liquid.

Soak the peas overnight in plenty of cold water. Rinse them and transfer to a large casserole. Pour on most of the pork stock. Bring to the boil and add the spices. Cook the peas over a low flame for at least 1 hour, probably somewhat longer. Skim a few times and remove the peel floating to the surface; it will rise easiest if you stir the pot with a balloon whisk. Season to taste when the peas are done. I don't like my pea soup to be too thick. If it is, add a little more water and check the seasoning.

Heat the pork and sausages for about 5 minutes. Serve the soup piping hot with the pork to one side, on a warm side plate, and the indispensable accessories.

Griddle snaps serves 4

After pea soup and pork, most people prefer, I think, to round off the feast with pancakes or griddle snaps served with jam and whipped cream. This is also just the thing after a good meat soup with winter at its coldest. For my own part I find griddle snaps a tad more sophisticated, but that of course is a matter of individual preference.

With a mob of starving kids at the table, waiting, I suppose there's nothing for it but bumper pancakes. But then you'll need a different and slightly bigger mixture than mine, the sort of thing you'll find in any cookbook. I suggest that, time permitting, and if you're a bit of an artist, you should try making some really good-looking griddle snaps. As a nice added touch, squirt the cream on from an icing bag with a fluted nozzle fitted.

Batter ingredients:
3 eggs
1 1/2 dl white flour
2 dl cream + 1 dl water or 3 dl milk
a pinch of salt
a tbsp sugar
1/2 dl melted butter
butter for frying

Serve with:
raspberry or "Queen's Jam" (raspberry and blueberry)
2 dl whipped cream

29

Procedure:
Beat the eggs and flour to a smooth mixture in a mixing bowl. Dilute with the cream and water or milk, add salt and sugar. Stir in the melted butter just before frying. Melt a little butter in a griddle and fry 16–20 snaps golden brown on both sides. Leave to cool a little.

Whip the cream hard enough to be squeezed from the icing bag. Squirt it round the edge of the first griddle snap. Put a little jam in the middle, put the next snap on top of this. Repeat the procedure until you have four snaps on top of each other. Finish off with a round of cream and jam on top.

Meatballs à la Lilian   serves 10

Lilian, my wife, is of course very well fed, but there have also been occasions when she has had to get dinner for herself and the children – meatballs, for example. The following recipe is your chance of making the best meatballs in Sweden. As a professional cook I find you can save time by first putting the mixture into a plastic icing bag. I then cut the right-sized hole at the bottom of the bag so as to squeeze out meatballs of exactly the same format.

Ingredients:
800 minced beef
800 mixed pork and beef mince
2 dl milk with the top on (1 1/2 dl milk, 1/2 dl cream)
2 dl dried breadcrumbs
2 eggs
1 dl water
4 medium-large boiled potatoes
2 large onions
1 tsp brown sugar
2 tbsp "anchovy" liquor
4 tbsp. concentrated veal stock
2 tbsp Kikkoman soy
butter for frying
salt and pepper

To Serve:
mashed potato (see p. 103)
uncooked, stirred lingonberry jam (see p. 25)

Procedure:
Blend the creamy milk, dried breadcrumbs, egg and water into a loose batter. Leave to swell for a while. Mash the potatoes carefully with a fork. Peel the onions. Grate one of them, chop the other one small and fry it golden brown. (This way you get a tastier farce with two kinds of onion flavour.)

Blend all the ingredients quickly into a smooth batter. Add salt and pepper. Fry a small dob to test the seasoning.

Shape the roundest meatballs you can and fry them golden brown in butter, a number at a time. Serve with mashed potato and the lingonberry jam.

Salmon pudding   serves 4–5

Salmon pudding is something in a class of its own and one of the best possible ways of cooking this quintessentially Swedish party fish. Salt salmon is perhaps not so easy to get hold of nowadays, but smoked salmon or gravlax will also do. Or why not a mixture of all three? Otherwise salting your own salmon is really no hassle.

Buy a whole side of salmon, cut out as many thin slices as you need and put the rest in the freezer for another time. Salt the slices lightly on both sides and store them cold for a couple of hours. Then you're ready to go. A full-bodied lager or a glass of cool Chardonnay will set it off very nicely.

Ingredients:
800 g sliced salmon
2 onions
butter for frying
800 g firm, cold boiled potatoes
1 bunch of dill
4 eggs
3 dl milk
1 dl cream
salt and pepper

Serve with:
about 150 g butter
2 tsp Swedish caviar
1 tbsp "anchovy" liquor
1 bundle of green asparagus
a sprig of dill

Procedure:
Set the oven to 2000. Peel and shred the onion, fry it golden brown in butter over a low flame. Peel the potatoes and slice them thinly. Cut up the dill but save a couple of sprigs for garnish.

Grease a tin with a detachable rim and line it with a layer of salmon. Let the slices hang over the edge. Now add alternate layers of potato, onion, dill and salmon, seasoning lightly in between. Fold the salmon slices over the top later and press down a little. Beat the eggs, milk and cream together, season lightly and pour the mixture into the tin. Bake in the middle of the oven for about 40 minutes. Test with a skewer to see if it's done.

Brown the butter in a saucepan and add caviar and "anchovy" liquor to taste. Boil the asparagus. Cut it up and put the pieces on top of the salmon pudding. Garnish with one or two sprigs of dill. Serve everything piping hot with the butter to one side.

Shrimp Crêpes Prince Bertil and salmon crêpes serves 4 (8 crêpes)

Crêpes, sad to say, have become somewhat of a forgotten delicacy in the Swedish cuisine. In the 1960s every self-respecting restaurant had crêpes of various kinds on the menu, and so I have to admit that asking you now to try a couple of almost forgotten classics does feel just a teeny bit retro.

Prince Bertil was a gourmet, and shrimp crêpes were among his absolute favourites. Perhaps, given the current debate on diet, they are a little on the fat side, but it's a sad life if you can't bend the rules once in a while. Two crêpes per person, plus a fresh green salad, adds up to the perfect lunch. At a pinch you can get the hollandaise sauce from a bag, if you find making your own too finicky.

Ingredients:
3 eggs
3 tbsp white flour
1 1/2 dl whipping cream
1 1/2 dl milk
4–5 cl soda water
1 pinch of sugar
2 pinches of salt
butter and oil for frying

Shrimp filling:
1 batch of hollandaise sauce
1 bunch of dill
300 g peeled shrimps
melted butter
freshly grated parmesan or Västerbotten cheese

Salmon filling:
200 g smoked salmon
2 hard-boiled eggs
1 bunch of dill
1 bunch of chives
1 tbsp butter
1 tbsp white flour
3 dl milk with the top on (2 1/2 dl milk, 1/2 dl cream)
melted butter
newly grated parmesan or Västerbotten cheese
salt and pepper

Procedure:
Beat the eggs fluffy and fold down the other ingredients to make a fine, smooth batter. It will be smoothest if you don't add all the liquid at once. Fry eight thin pancakes in oil and butter in a crêpe pan or an ordinary frying pan. Put them to one side when ready – singly, to keep them from getting stuck together.

Shrimp crêpes: Make the hollandaise sauce. Chop the dill small. Mix the shrimps and dill into the hollandaise sauce and distribute between the pancakes. Fold them over and pack them closely into a greased oven dish. Brush with melted butter and sprinkle with grated cheese.

Salmon crêpes: Cut the salmon into small pieces and chop the eggs. Chop the dill fine and cut the chives very small. Melt the butter in a saucepan, add the flour and wait for the two to amalgamate a little. Add the creamy milk, whisking all the time, reduce for a few minutes until it thickens slightly. Season to taste. Fold the salmon, egg, chives and dill into the mixture. Distribute this filling between the pancakes. Fold them over and pack them closely into a greased oven dish. Brush with melted butter and sprinkle with grated cheese.

Set the oven to 2500, top heat only. Bake the crêpes on a high shelf until they are hot and a nice shade of brown.

Hints:
Shrimp shells can be used to make concentrated shrimp stock, which is an excellent flavouring for fish and au gratin sauces. Personally I usually freeze the shells as they are, but of course you can make the concentrated stock the same day as you peel the shrimps. (See p. 250.)

Hollandaise sauce serves 4

My guess is that a lot of good cooks in the home do most things in the kitchen but perhaps not hollandaise sauce, which is rather a pity, because making your own isn't really all that tricky, and the result is far better than the powder-based version. Try it, and afterwards you and the family won't accept anything but your home-made hollandaise with boiled or fried fish or a lovely spread of spring vegetables. The cooking oil is added to stop the sauce curdling. And be sure to use a steel saucepan.

Ingredients:

200 g butter	1 tbsp water
1/2 dl neutral oil	1 tsp lemon juice
4 egg yolks	1/2 pinch of cayenne pepper
	salt and pepper

Procedure:
Melt the butter over a low flame, so that the whey (the white stuff) sinks to the bottom. Transfer the now clarified butter to another saucepan, but don't discard the whey. Stir the oil into the butter and keep warm, about 50°C.

Mix the egg yolks and water together in a steel saucepan and heat very slowly, whisking all the time, until the yokes are creamy and a little frothy. Remove from the heat and beat in the mixture of butter and oil in a narrow jet. If the sauce seems too thick, you can whisk in a little of the whey residue. Season with the lemon juice, a little cayenne pepper and salt and pepper.

The sauce must not boil on any account, but you can keep it at the right temperature over a bain-marie.

Hints:
This is a good basic sauce which can be varied several ways. Flavour it, for example, with truffle or 1 tsp highly aromatic truffle oil. It is also a good idea to stir in herbs of different kinds, such as fine-chopped dill, fresh tarragon, fine-chopped flat-leaf parsley or chives. Chopped shrimps or crayfish tails are another possibility, or 1 dl Dijon mustard.

Cod with parsley sauce serves 4

Cod with parsley sauce has a very long history and is among the real heavyweights of Swedish traditional cooking, especially, of course, on the west coast of Sweden. Cod is tasty and nourishing.

It is tastiest in winter, when the liver is fine and soft and the females are full of roe – two outstanding delicacies in themselves. I venture to say that cod liver, properly treated, is in no way inferior to duck or goose liver.

Ingredients:
1 1/2 kg cod (cut from the middle if possible)
300 g cod roe
300 g cod liver
1 slice of onion
2–3 whole cloves
1 carrot
1/2 bunch of parsley
4 leaves of Savoy cabbage
salt

Cooking liquid:
8 dl water
1/2 dl Swedish distilled vinegar, ättika (12% strength)
1 slice of onion
5 white peppercorns
5 allspice corns
5 whole cloves
1/2 bunch of dill
1 bay leaf
1/2 tbsp salt

Sauce:
1 bunch of parsley
3 tbsp butter
1 tbsp white flour
4 dl fish stock (roe/liver cooking liquid + 1 stock cube)
1 dl milk with the top on (1/2 dl milk, 1/2 dl cream)
1 tbsp lemon juice
salt and pepper

Serve with:
boiled floury potatoes

Procedure:
Start by rinsing the roe and liver. Mix the cooking liquid in a saucepan and bring it to the boil. Put in the roe and simmer over a low flame for 30 or 25 minutes, depending on how thick it is. Put in the liver at half time. Remove from the heat and cover. Now it's the cod's turn. You can cook the roe and liver a day in advance if you like.

Gut or clean the cod, making sure the black membranes in the stomach are removed completely. Trim the edges of the belly. Rinse the fish and cut it into slices 4–5 cm wide. Salt on both sides and leave in a cold place for a few hours.

Now the sauce. Pick the parsley leaves and cut them up small. Melt 2 tbsp of the butter in a saucepan and stir in the flour. Dilute with the fish stock and creamy milk, and whisk until you have a smooth sauce. Add lemon juice, salt and pepper to taste, then stir in the parsley. Keep the sauce warm and glaze with 1 tbsp butter just before serving.

Bring the water to the boil, after adding 1 tbsp salt per litre. Peel and cut up the carrot. Put the pieces, the slice of onion, the cloves and parsley into the water. Simmer for about minutes, then put in the cod. Simmer for another 5 or 6 minutes, depending on the thickness of the cod. Turn off the heat and leave the fish in its liquor for at least 10 minutes.

Blanche the Savoy cabbage in lightly salted water for a few minutes, until it is soft and manageable. Heat the roe and liver in the rest of the cooking liquid. Now wrap them in cabbage leaves and fold into nice round packages.

Cut these packages into slices 4–5 cm thick, using a sharp knife, and arrange them attractively together with the fish, on a warm serving dish. Serve with the sauce and boiled floury potatoes to absorb it.

Potato dumplings with pork serves 4

There are any number of recipes for these dumplings. In the old days, when country folk ran out of pork they sometimes filled their dumplings with herring, Baltic herring or eel instead. At Sjömagasinet we make a rather unconventional dough, using no flour … It never fails to catch on.

In my book on herring I filled the dumplings with matjes herring, which is also incredibly good.

Ingredients:
700 g potatoes, King Edward preferably
1 1/2 dl potato flour
3 egg yolks
50 g browned butter
1 tsp salt

Filling:
400 g salt pancetta
1 large onion
butter for frying
2 tsp freshly crushed allspice

Serve with:
400 g salt pancetta
uncooked, stirred lingonberry jam (see p. 25)
browned butter

Procedure:
Peel and boil the potatoes. Rice them (through a ricer) into a mixing bowl and leave to cool a little. Stir in the potato flour, the egg yolks, the butter and salt, blending into a smooth dough.

Cut the pork for the filling into half-centimetre cubes. Peel the onion and cut into pieces the same size. Heat the butter and fry the pork and onion till golden brown. Mix in the allspice, then remove from the heat.

Bring plenty of lightly salted water to the boil in an amply sized saucepan. Roll the potato dough into a loaf and cut it into slices about 2 cm thick. Make small wells in the middle and put the filling in them. Fold into balls round the filling. Flatten slightly.

Crisp-fry the extra pork, putting a little butter in the pan to start with, to keep it from burning. Drain on kitchen tissue. Keep warm.

Boil the dumplings a few at a time for 5–6 minutes, until they float to the surface. Serve instantly with the pork, lingonberry jam and browned butter.

Sautéed kidney serves 4

This recipe dates from a time when slaughtering on the farm was common practice and nothing could be wasted. In those days too we ate more offal, which is very good for you. Kidney and liver are today to be found at least in well-stocked food stores. Sautéed kidney is a delicacy I can thoroughly recommend. Other offal (not awful!) delights I recall are liver in cream sauce, calf liver Anglais, huckster's hash and sausage cake. Whatever the offal, a cold beer completes it.

Ingredients:
800 g kidney of sucking lamb or white (milk-fed) veal
2 red onions
200 g button mushrooms
1 apple
butter for frying
2 tbsp brandy
3 tbsp concentrated veal stock
3 dl whipping cream
1 tsp Dijon mustard
salt and pepper

Serve with:
boiled or riced potatoes

Procedure:
Peel and shred the onion. Dice the mushrooms. De-core the apple and cut into segments. Cut up or slice the kidneys. Add salt and pepper.

Brown the kidneys quickly in butter in a fairly hot pan, flambé with a dash of brandy (not too close to the cooker fan!). Connoisseurs prefer their kidney a little pink on the inside. When the flames have died down, remove the meat and fry the other ingredients very quickly. Dilute with veal stock and cream, adding mustard and seasoning to taste. Return the meat to the pan and simmer for 4–5 minutes. Serve immediately with boiled or riced potatoes.

Parsley-flavoured roast chicken serves 4–5

This is one of the basic ways of doing chicken, an excellent foundation for recipes of several different kinds and, what is more, goes a long way. The leftovers from a really big corn-fed chicken can form the ingredients of a good chicken soup, a tasty salad or a satisfying lunchtime sandwich using dark bread, a bed of lettuce and slices of tomato. Practical and economical traditional home cooking at its best, in other words.

Ingredients:
1 corn-fed chicken (1.2–1.4 kg)
2 bunches of flat-leaf parsley
1 lemon
1 whole bulb of garlic
olive oil
1 dl chicken stock (optional)
1 bunch of thyme
salt and pepper

Serve with:
mashed potato (see p. 103)
mixed salad with blue cheese dressing
gravy sauce (see p. 121)
1 dl chicken stock (optional)

Procedure:
Set the oven to 175°C. Pick the parsley stalks and leaves separately. Shred the leaves fine, and do the same with some of the thyme leaves. Put the parsley stalks, one or two sprigs of thyme and the garlic halves in the cavity. Rub the chicken all over with lemon, add salt and pepper and sprinkle with chopped thyme.

Roast the chicken in the middle of the oven for just over 60 minutes, basting every now and then with the juices formed. Pour 1 dl chicken stock into the roasting tin if it's looking parched. Remove the chicken with about 15 minutes oven time still to go. Brush it with a little olive oil and roll it in the chopped parsley. Return it to the oven and baste until ready. It's ready if, when you pierce the thickest part of it with a sharp knife, a clear liquid emerges.

Serve the chicken nicely carved together with mashed potato, a large bowl of lovely lettuce and a warm gravy sauce flavoured with 1 dl chicken stock.

Blue cheese dressing serves 4–5

Blue cheese dressing goes best with a fresh, newly cut green salad, but it also does credit to grilled steaks and entrecote or as a dip sauce – thick and creamy – for young vegetables.

Ingredients:
100 g blue cheese, preferably Roquefort or some comparable type
1 clove of garlic
2 tsp white wine vinegar
2 tbsp mayonnaise
1 1/2 dl gräddfil (soured cream)
salt and pepper
1 tsp lemon juice

Procedure:
Cut the cheese into small pieces. Peel and crush the garlic clove. Put all the ingredients into a blender and run them to a creamy sauce. Season to taste. For a thinner sauce, add a little more gräddfil.

41

Skåne mustard steak serves 6–8

I love steaks and stews of every conceivable kind. This is substantial fare for all ages and something for the family to gather round. It is also food that takes care of itself while you concentrate on chatting and being sociable or perhaps on preparing a really nice dessert to finish off with.

Aunt Astrid's Skåne mustard steak, as recalled from the days of my youth, beats all records in terms of memorable Sunday dinners. And perhaps the memory is made all the more vivid by the fact that she always combined her speciality with a good creamy sauce, tasty green vegetables and spicy pickles from summer and autumn harvest.

Uncork, well in advance, a powerful red wine that can stand up to all these wonderful fragrances and flavours. Give the children black currant squash, preferably home made, on the rocks.

Ingredients:
1 1/2–2 kg marbled stewing steak
3.4 tbsp Colman's mustard powder
3 onions
3 carrots
butter for frying
1 bottle of pale ale (33 cl)
1 l beef stock
5–6 Swedish "anchovy" fillets
3 bay leaves
2 allspice corns
10 white peppercorns
1 sprig of thyme
3 dl whipping cream
salt and pepper

Serve with:
boiled green vegetables, turned in butter
boiled floury potatoes
pickled gherkin (see p. 119)
Asian cucumber
pickled green tomatoes
pickled pearl onions
black/red currant jelly

Procedure:
Rub the meat carefully with mustard powder, season all over. Peel the onion and carrots and cut up small. Brown the meat all over in a generous knob of butter in a cast iron casserole. Remove the meat and brown the vegetables. Return the meat to the pot and pour on the beer and stock. Add the "anchovy" fillets, the allspice and white peppercorns, thyme and bay leaves. Cover and simmer for about 1 1/2 hours until the meat feels really tender.

While the meat is cooking, prepare the vegetables you are going to serve with it.

Set the oven to 75°C. Remove the meat from the pot when it is done, wrap it in aluminium foil and put it in the oven to keep warm. Strain the stock and reduce to 1/3. Pour in the cream, reduce further and season to taste.

Remove the steak and carve slices 1/2–1 cm thick. Arrange the vegetables neatly round them on the serving dish. Serve immediately with the trimmings and with floury potatoes to absorb the glorious gravy.

Asian cucumber

I think Asian cucumber is one of the nicest trimming imaginable, for example with a fine Sunday joint or the spicy fragrance of a good stew. It often figured on the table when I was young and learned to appreciate well-cooked dinners in the bosom of my family.

Grandma Cecilia, on my father's side, and gourmandising Aunt Astrid on my mother's, in Helsingborg, did roughly as described here. Divide the cucumbers into smaller pieces if you don't have a clay pot and cellar to store them in. Otherwise your best plan is to cut it up and store the pieces in glass jars which you have sterilised in the oven for a good ten minutes at 100–1250.

Ingredients:
2 kg white cucumber
2 l water
2 tbsp salt
8–10 dill crowns
preservative, e.g. (in Sweden) Atamon

Pickling liquid:
two handfuls of button onions
3 dl Swedish distilled vinegar, ättika (12% strength)
7–8 dl caster sugar
9 dl water
10–15 black peppercorns
1–2 tbsp yellow mustard seeds
a few pieces of mace

Procedure:
Peel the cucumbers and split them down the middle. Scoop out the seeds with a spoon. Put the cucumbers into a big pot or plastic bucket. Bring the water, with the salt added, to the boil and pour it over the cucumber halves. Put a heavy weight on top to hold the cucumbers down. Leave overnight.

Remove the cucumbers and dry them a little. Peel the onions. Bring all the pickling liquid ingredients to the boil, stirring well so as to dissolve all the sugar. Test the sweetness, which must be really pronounced.

Fill the jars with alternate layers of cucumbers and dill crowns. Retrieve the onions and bits of mace and distribute them evenly between the jars. Stir in the preservative and pour it onto the hot pickling liquid. Close the lids and leave to cool. After an hour or so you can hear the jars clicking. Sample after one week, if you can wait that long.

Leg of pork in aspic   serves 4

Leg of pork is a wonderful joint of pork that, sadly, has been relegated to comparative obscurity in recent years. Apart from leg of pork and mashed root vegetables, there are lots of good things to be done with this cut of the pig and a modicum of skill. Try this aspic recipe, and you'll find you have a lunchtime recipe that has nothing to be bashful about when served with fried new potatoes and home-pickled beetroot. Or a spicy, attractive-looking spread for a satisfying late-night sandwich. It's a good idea to cook the meat a day earlier, so as to give it time to absorb all the goodness from the cooking liquid.

Ingredients for boiling the pork:
2 salted legs of pork, about 1 kg each
2 onions
1 carrot
1/5 celeriac bulb (about 100 g)
3 bay leaves
1 tsp allspice corns
1 tsp white peppercorns
4–5 cloves
1 pinch of dried thyme
1/2 tsp salt per litre of water

Aspic ingredients:
the pork
about 150 g button onions
5–6 baby carrots
1 bunch of flat-leaf parsley
6 sheets of gelatine
1 tbsp "anchovy" liquor
10 crushed allspice corns
salt and pepper

Serve with:
mixed green salad

Procedure:
Peel and slice the onions. Peel and cross-cut the carrots. Clean and cut up the celeriac. Blanche the meat by boiling it hard for a minute or so. Remove it and rinse under the tap. Return the meat to the pot and pour on enough fresh water to cover it. Bring to the boil again and add the vegetables and herbs. Simmer for about 2 hours, until the meat starts to come away from the bone. Remove from the heat and leave to cool in its own liquor.

Carefully remove the meat from the pot. Remove and strain about a litre of the pork stock and reduce it slowly until half is left. Peel the onions and carrots. Dice the carrots small and quarter the onions. Simmer them for about 10 minutes in a little of the remaining stock and then strain. Shred the parsley leaves fine and soak the gelatine leaves in cold water.

Pick the meat off the bones, discarding fat and rind, and cut up into 1/2 cm cubes. Put these in the reduced stock together with the boiled vegetables, the parsley leaves and the gelatine (wrung dry). Add the "anchovy" liquor and allspice and test for seasoning. Pour the aspic into a suitably sized, cold tin which you have rinsed.

Leave in a cold place overnight.

45

Dill meat my way serves 6

Boiled veal or lamb with dill sauce is one of my "top five" in traditional Swedish home cooking. Where dill meat is concerned,
the sauce is really the star of the show. Boiling meat and making
a good job of it isn't really all that difficult. The meat for this
recipe can actually be cooked a day in advance, leaving you time
to concentrate on the sauce. I can't think of anything to drink
with dill meat other than beer or mineral water.

Ingredients:
1 1/2 kg veal, lamb or elk calf, e.g. back, shoulder or ribs
1 large onion
1 leek
2–3 carrots
1 parsnip
salt
6–8 white peppercorns
8–10 allspice corns
4 whole cloves
4 bay leaves
the dill stalks from the sauce
1 tsp thyme
6–8 whole white peppercorns

Dill sauce:
3 bunches of dill
1 tbsp flour
1 tbsp butter
5 dl thick stock from cooking the meat
1–2 veal stock cubes (optional)
2 dl milk with the top on (1/2 dl milk, 1 1/2 dl cream)
2 tbsp Swedish distilled vinegar, ättika (12% strength)
4 tbsp sugar
salt and pepper

Serve with:
boiled floury potatoes

Procedure:
Peel the onion and cut it up into large pieces. Clean the leek and
cut it up diagonally. Peel the carrots and parsnip and cut them the
same way.

Put the meat in cold water in a big casserole and bring to the
boil. Boil for one minute at the most, then lift the meat out with a
slotted spoon and rinse it quickly under the tap. Clean the pot
and bring the meat to the boil again in fresh water (remember
you'll need room for the vegetables too). Measure how much
water you pour in. Add salt, beginning with a tsp per litre of
water; check the seasoning later on.

When the meat has come to the boil, add the onion, the green
vegetables, the dill stalks and the herbs and simmer for an hour
at most. If the meat is on the bone, it will be done when it starts
coming away from the bone, otherwise you can test with a skewer.
Remove the carrots and parsnip with a slotted spoon after half an
hour; they will be served with the meat in due course. If the meat

is being served the same day, you can add 15 minutes more cooking time. For serving the next day, just let it cool in it liquor.

Remove the meat and skim the stock for the sauce. Cold stock
is easy to skim, whereas with warm stock the fat tends to float
about. But try anyway. If you boiled the meat a day early, heat it
in the stock you won't be needing for the sauce. Cut up the meat
into pieces.

Chop the dill for the sauce reasonably small. Fry the flour in
the butter in a saucepan. Dilute with strained stock and creamy
milk. Season the stock to taste, and if it is too watery, add 1–2
stock cubes. The sauce must be right on the borderline between
opaque and thick. Start flavouring with 1 tbsp ättika and 2 tbsp
sugar. Season to taste. Point up if necessary with a very, very little
more ättika.

When you are satisfied with the balance, fold in the dill. There
must be plenty of it. Lastly, put the meat into the sauce together
with the vegetables reserved from the boiling, and make sure
everything is thoroughly heated. Serve piping hot with potatoes.

Hints:
Dill is practically the only herb or spice you can never have too
much of. Dill sauce, for example, tastes of dill no matter whether
you use one bunch or three, but the flavour will be much more
pronounced if you are generous in this respect.

Bœuf à la Lindström serves 4

Bœuf à la Lindström must surely be a Swedish invention? Well, yes and no, because it comes from Russia. It was a man called Henrik Lindström, born and bred in St Petersburg, who walked into Hotell Witt, Kalmar, with some good friends on 4th May 1862, thereby introducing the recipe in Sweden.

Lindström ordered all the ingredients, whereupon the party mixed a big steak each and sent it out to the kitchen to be fried in butter. The result was hugely appreciated, and Hotell Witt has had Bœuf à la Lindström on its menu ever since.

My father, Gösta, loved Bœuf à la Lindström, so much so that he improved on the original recipe by adding Dijon mustard, chopped anchovy fillets or Swedish "anchovy" liquor to the customary ingredients, plus a dash of HP Sauce. I still get a kick out of his version.

Ingredients:
500 g minced beef
100 mixed (pork and beef) mince
1 onion
2 tbsp capers
3 tbsp pickled beetroot
1 small boiled potato
1 tbsp (real!) anchovies
5 egg yolks
1 tbsp Dijon mustard
1 tbsp HP Sauce
butter for frying
salt and pepper

Serve with:
4 fried eggs
fried potato
salt gherkin
browned butter

Procedure:
Peel the onion and chop small. Rough-chop the capers (for more flavour). Dice the beetroot and potato small. Chop the anchovies small as well. Mix the farce thoroughly with all the other ingredients. Add salt and pepper. Fry a small test piece and check the seasoning. Make four big patties and fry them in butter over a medium flame for 4–5 minutes on each side.

Serve with carefully fried eggs, fried potato, browned butter and (for me) salt gherkin cut in sticks.

Hints:
Remember that Bœuf à la Lindström can also be made on a small scale, or else round like ordinary meatballs. Just the thing for the Christmas table, for some other special buffet or as a late-night snack.

Fried, lightly salted herring with onion sauce   serves 4

As many people know already, I am so enamoured of herring and Baltic herring that I've written a whole book about them. And I still go round trying to think up new ways of varying and improving the cooking of this typically Swedish delicacy.

Here is a method I've used a few times, and there is no doubt that you get better results with fresh, lightly salted herring than with salt herring put to soak.

Ingredients:
12 large, fresh herring fillets
1 tbsp salt
2 tbsp rye flour
3 tbsp dried breadcrumbs
oil and butter for frying
pepper

Onion sauce:
1 red onion
1 (yellow) onion
1/2 leek
butter for frying
1 tsp white flour
2 dl whipping cream
2 dl milk
1 tbsp Kikkoman soy
1 pinch of sugar
salt and pepper

Serve with:
jacket potatoes
toasted crisp bread

Procedure:
Bone the fillets as completely as possible. Pull away the skin, salt them and store in a cold place overnight.

Boil the peeled potatoes and add quite a lot of coarse salt. Meanwhile make the onion sauce. Peel the onions and slice them neatly, clean the leek and cut into rings on the diagonal. Brown the onion in the butter, just sufficiently for it to change colour a little. Sprinkle with the flour and dilute with the cream and milk. Put a little colour into the sauce with the soy. Sprinkle with a pinch of sugar. Season lightly. Simmer over a low flame for about 5 minutes.

Mix the rye flour and sifted breadcrumbs together and dredge the herring fillets in the mixture. Pat the mixture a little, to keep it in place. Add a little pepper. Heat a frying pan with butter and oil in it and fry the fillets for a few minutes on each side till they are golden brown and crisp. Serve immediately, with plenty of onion sauce, boiled potatoes in their jackets and toasted crisp bread.

Toasted crisp bread

Now let me tell you what I think about toasted crisp bread. Such is my fondness for it that I never – but never – eat crisp bread that isn't toasted.

Believe me, if you make an art of toasting, the family's crisp bread consumption will escalate quite vertically. For maximum crispness, of course, the bread has to cool first. When it has cooled, spread it with plenty of butter, put a thick slice of matured Swedish hard cheese on that and you'll have a sandwich that takes one heck of a lot of beating.

Procedure:
Crisp bread can be toasted either in a toaster or in the oven. For day-to-day consistency of quality, a toaster with a thermometer is a sound investment. Either way, the crisp bread has to be toasted at a low temperature. You can very well toast for a couple of days ahead, if you have storage space for such a quantity. If using the oven, put the bread out on a baking sheet about 10 cm from the grill element. Set the oven to grill and 175°C, toasting the bread for not more than 2 minutes on each side.

Danish roast with red cabbage serves 4

I call it Danish because I think it must have originated in Skåne or Denmark. And, Skåne now having been Swedish for centuries, it is of course only meet, right and proper to cull treasures from the traditional Scanian cuisine, no matter whether they are of Danish descent or not.

The Swedish name of this roast means both "Palings" – because after roasting the rind looks like that kind of fence – and "Rib Steak", because that's the part of the pig the meat should come from. Well, a joint by any other name … and don't be surprised if fights break out over the crackling!

Ingredients:
1–1.2 kg "rib steak" of pork, with the rind still on
4 tsp whole caraway seeds
two handfuls of button onions
8–10 baby carrots
700 g small potatoes
salt and pepper

Serve with:
red cabbage
2–3 dl stewed apple (see p. 85)
2–3 tbsp grated horseradish
gravy sauce (see p. 121)

Procedure:
Set the oven to 200°C. Cook the red cabbage, if you want it home-cooked.

Rub the sides of the meat with salt, pepper and caraway. Make very sure no salt or spices come near the rind, because then your crackling won't crackle. Leave the steak to rest for a while before putting it in the oven.

Put the steak, rind downwards, in a roasting tin and pour in about 2 cm water. Put the tin on he middle shelf of the oven for about 30 minutes or until nearly all the water has been absorbed. Turn the steak and lower the temperature to 175°C. Add a dash of water if things look like charring. Return to the oven again for about 1 1/2 hours, basting frequently with juices from the steak.

Bake the vegetables in the pot direct. Peel the onions and carrots. Peel and slice the potatoes. Put the vegetables round the steak about 30 minutes before the end of roasting time. When the crackling begins to swell up, your mouth can begin to water.

Heat the red cabbage so that it will be warm when the meat is done. Mix the horse radish and stewed apple together. Slice the steak, season the carved surface and serve with red cabbage, stewed apple and the gravy sauce to one side.

Red cabbage serves 4–6

With all respect to tinned red cabbage, the home-made variety, in my opinion, is a cut above it. Red cabbage goes with any number of dishes and best of all with different kinds of pork – steak, ham and spare ribs – but it also makes an excellent companion to goose and pork sausage.

Try this recipe, in which, basically, the cabbage takes care of itself once you've got it started. Red cabbage benefits from being made a day in advance, to be heated before serving.

Ingredients:
1 small red cabbage head (3/4–1 kg)
1 medium-sized red onion
4 sharp apples
2–3 tbsp neutral oil
1–2 pinches ground cloves
4 newly crushed allspice corns
1 bay leaf
1 small piece of cinnamon stick
1 dl caster sugar
1/2 dl red wine
2 tbsp red wine vinegar or lemon juice
1–2 tbsp black current jelly or undiluted squash
1/2 dl water or pork stock
1 tsp salt

Procedure:
Rinse the cabbage and remove any damaged leaves. Now cut in half and remove the thick centre stalk. Shred fine. Peel the onion and slice it thinly. De-core and shred the apples. Heat the oil in a big saucepan or casserole and put in alternate layers of cabbage, apple and onion. Stir-fry everything for a few minutes, without it changing colour. Add the spices and sugar, red wine and vinegar. Stir well, then cover and simmer on a low flame for at least an hour.

Sample when the cabbage starts to feel soft; I don't think it should be *al dente*. Stir in the Kelly or squash with about 15–20 minutes of the cooking time to go. Dilute with a little water as well, to keep the cabbage from boiling dry. Check the sweetness and acidity before serving the cabbage piping hot with pork or as one of several trimmings.

53

Boiled salt leg of pork with mashed root vegetables and creamed mustard serves 4

Boiled salt leg of pork and mashed root vegetables has its appointed place on my personal list of top-ranking Swedish home-cooking recipes. It has a centuries-long ancestry, steeped in the traditions of an agrarian society, but nowadays it makes regular appearances in posh restaurants and in the gourmet cuisine of contemporary urban society.

This is something to treat your friends to, especially those who are not as fond of or accustomed to cooking as yourself or else more inhibited about what to give people.

Ingredients:
4 legs of pork
1 onion
10 allspice corns
4 bay leaves
2 sprigs of fresh thyme

Creamed mustard:
1 bunch of chives
1 dl crème fraîche
1 tsp Colman's mustard powder
2 tsp Dijon mustard

Mashed root vegetables:
1 large swede
2–3 carrots
3–4 potatoes
2 tbsp butter
salt (if needed)
crushed allspice and crushed cloves

Serve with:
strong mustard (optional)

Procedure:
Put the pork in the pot, cover with cold water and bring to the boil. Keep it boiling briskly for a minute or so. Remove the pork with a slotted spoon and rinse it under the cold tap. Clean the pot, return the meat and cover with fresh water. Peel and cut up the onion. Add this and the herbs and spices when the water with the pork in has come to the boil. Turn down the heat and simmer till the pork is tender, say for 1 1/2 or 2 hours or until the meat is coming away from the bone.

Chop the chives for the creamed mustard small. Stir all the ingredients together and store in a cold place.

Peel and cut up the root vegetables for the mash. Boil the swede and carrot in a little of the pork sock (after checking the saltiness). Boil for 1/2 hour. Add the potatoes and cook till soft. Now put the whole lot through a potato ricer. Brown the butter and stir it into the mash. Season to taste with salt, crushed allspice and crushed cloves.

Heat the pork and serve it piping hot with the mash and creamed mustard. Strong mustard also goes well with this one.

A home-made mustard

A lot of people, myself included of course, like making their own mustard at Christmas. Tastes differ a great deal where mustard is concerned. Many people like a mustard to make your hair curl, while others prefer a very sweet one. This one is of the former kind. Assuming that most people do not have an iron trough and cannon ball, I suggest you run your mustard in the blender.

Ingredients:
1 dl brown mustard seed
2 dl water
2 tbsp sweet Swedish mustard
1 dl caster sugar
2 tbsp Swedish distilled vinegar, ättika (12% strength)
a dash of cream (optional)

Procedure:
Put the mustard seeds in the blender and run it at top speed till they are crushed. Dilute with water and the other ingredients. Run the blender until the sugar dissolves. Scrape the sides a few times, so nothing gets left out. Add more sugar to taste or else a dash of cream if the mustard is too strong.

55

Restaurang Gourmet's potato au gratin serves 4-6

Restaurang Gourmet in Stockholm was my first favourite restaurant. It had everything: lovely food, a wonderful atmosphere and friendly service. I remember very often thinking to myself that one day I would like to own a restaurant of the same quality. It was run by Peter Schück, together with Tore Wretman the best restaurateur in Stockholm at that time.

The list of ingredients calls for Swiss gruyere or Emmenthaler, but a well-matured Swedish Grevé will do fine.

Ingredients:
1 kg firm potatoes
2 cloves of garlic
butter to grease the tin with
2–3 dl grated cheese – gruyere, Emmenthaler or Grevé
a few scrapes of nutmeg
2 dl dry white wine
4 dl whipping cream
salt and pepper

Procedure:
Set the oven to 175°C. Peel the potatoes and cut them into 1/2 cm thick slices. Don't' rinse them. Peel the garlic and chop small. Grease an oven-proof dish with quite a lot of butter. Put in alternate layers of sliced potato, grated cheese, chopped garlic, nutmeg and seasoning. Pour the wine over carefully, so as not to send all the other flavours to the bottom. Bake in the middle of the oven for about 20 minutes.

Remove from the oven and carefully pour on the cream. Bake for another 1 1/2 hours or so until it has set, the top is nicely browned and the potato has just the right creamy texture.

Johanna's potato au gratin serves 4

We used to serve this easy but delicious potato au gratin with different kinds of meat at Restaurang Johanna, Göteborg, in the 1970s. Although thoroughly uncomplicated, it was always highly appreciated. It goes really well with grilled fillet of beef, tournedos, entrecote, lamb chops and roast lamb.

By all means double the quantity, but in that case use a wider oven dish, to make sure everything is thoroughly cooked and of getting a nicely browned surface. It's incredible, really, the number of wonderful things that you can make with just ordinary, plain spuds.

Ingredients:
4–5 large, firm potatoes or 8–10 smaller ones
butter to grease the dish with
11/2 dl milk
11/2 dl whipping cream
salt and pepper

Procedure:
Set the oven to 175°C. Peel the potatoes and quarter them lengthwise if they are big ones, otherwise just halve them lengthwise. Cut these segments into millimetre-thin slices. Whatever you do, don't rinse the potatoes or the starch will be lost, and you need it in order to achieve the right, creamy consistency.

Grease an oven-proof dish with quite a lot of butter. Put in layers of sliced potato with seasoning in between. Mix the milk and cream and pour it over the potato. Stir a little with a spoon and smooth the surface. Bake in the middle of the oven for about 1 1/2 hours, until the top is nicely browned and the consistency is firm but still creamy.

Lightly salted fresh herring with brown butter serves 4

On the west coast of Sweden at least, you can often get hold of really fat, freshly caught herring, silvery-glittering whoppers that are just the thing, both for good weekday fare and more advanced experiments in the culinary workshop. Try this extra-tasty version at lunchtime, in the company of a freezer-dewy drop of the creature and a frothy lager, for example after a morning constitutional or when you get back from the shops. Your herring, though, must be shopped a day earlier, to give it that indispensable, alluring salty tang.

Ingredients:
8 fresh, fat herring fillets
1 1/2 tbsp flake salt or 1 1/2 tsp fine salt

Garnish:
8 boiled new potatoes
2 hard-boiled eggs
2 medium-large red onions
2 bunches of chives, chopped fine
2 bunches of dill, chopped fine
200 g butter

Serve with:
toasted crisp bread (see page 50)
matured cheese

Procedure:
Day 1: Skin the fillets, removing any remaining bones. Put them on a dish and salt them on both sides. Cover with plastic foil and store cold overnight.

Day 2: Set the oven to 125⁸. Slice the potatoes thinly. Shell and chop the eggs. Peel the onions and chop small. Grease an oven-proof dish. Arrange the potatoes in the middle of it. Get out the herring, rinse it quickly and pat it with kitchen tissue. Cut it up and arrange the egg and herbs as pictured. Bake in the oven for about 15 minutes, till the herring is just lukewarm.

Brown the butter nut brown and drizzle it, still simmering, onto the dish of herring. Serve immediately with toasted crisp bread and a good matured cheese.

Saithe marinated in Swedish anchovies and fried in butter, with cauliflower stewed in red onion serves 4

Saithe (alias coley) is an excellent member of the Gagidae (cod) family which has come to be undeservedly neglected in Swedish kitchens. Is that perhaps going to change now that we are having to husband the cod stocks in our coastal waters?

The relative cheapness and excellent flavour of saithe have also made it popular of late in high-class restaurants, among cooks with high aspirations. Try it yourself, and the family could well acquire a new favourite.

Ingredients:
800 g saithe fillets
butter for frying

Marinade:
1 bunch of dill, chopped fine
8 "anchovy" fillets
2 tbsp of the "anchovy" liquor
2 tbsp oil
salt and pepper

Creamed cauliflower:
béchamel sauce (see page 203)
1 cauliflower
2 red onions
butter for frying
a few scrapes of nutmeg
salt and pepper

Procedure:
Cut the fish into manageable pieces. Mix the ingredients for the marinade and fold the pieces of fish into it. Store cold for a few hours.

Make the béchamel sauce for the creamed cauliflower.

Pick the cauliflower into small florets. Blanche these in lightly salted water for 2–3 minutes. Strain in a colander. Peel and shred the onion. Fry the onion in butter in a saucepan until it starts to soften. Add the cauliflower and fry for another minute or so. Grate nutmeg over this and pour on the béchamel sauce. Mix thoroughly and simmer over a low flame for a few minutes.

Remove the fish from the marinade. Heat plenty of butter in a frying pan and fry the fish golden brown on both sides. Transfer to a warm serving dish and drizzle with a little of the marinade. Serve immediately, with the creamed cauliflower.

61

Filbunke serves 4-5

For some of us over-50s in Sweden, the taste of filbunke is one of our vividest childhood memories. Creamy filbunke was a standard breakfast treat in summertime. You can't make it today the way people used to – it doesn't turn out well. And, to my knowledge, you won't find proper filbunke in the shops either. But with the following recipe you can start a filbunke that will look nice and taste nice, using your favourite brand of cultured milk (filmjölk). To be honest, I haven't tried yoghurt, but here as ever, no experimental holds are barred in the noble art of traditional home cooking.

Ingredients:
1 dl whipping cream
1 l milk
1 dl filmjölk (3% fat content)

Serve with:
caster sugar
cinnamon or ginger
ginger snaps (optional)

Procedure:
Mix the cream and milk together in a saucepan. Heat the mixture to just under boiling point – it mustn't actually boil. Remove from the heat and cool the mixture, e.g. by putting the saucepan in cold water in the sink.

When the mixture is down to room temperature, i.e. 22-230, beat in the filmjölk. Pour into bowls, preferably glass ones. Cover with a dish or plastic foil and leave to stand in room temperature for about 24 hours.

Transfer to the fridge for 2-3 hours. Serve with sugar and cinnamon or ginger. Ginger snaps make a nice accompaniment as well.

Brisket of beef Flamande   serves 4

Why "Flamande" I honestly don't know. All I do know is that for
years it has been served in restaurants with a taste for the tradi-
tionally Swedish. It's just the thing for one of those days when
the last autumn leaves are flying in all directions and indoors you
fancy lighting the first fire of the season.

Vegetables can be chosen according to preference – whatever
you fancy out of whatever's going. The stock is so delicious, I
suggest laying the table with soup plates and a spoon as well as
knife and fork. Serve a cold, full-bodied beer, to match all the
good flavours.

Ingredients for cooking the meat:
1 1/2 kg lean brisket of beef
500 g salt pancetta
1 onion
1 leek (the green part)
1 carrot
a few parsley stalks
2 bay leaves
10 white peppercorns
3 whole cloves
5–6 allspice corns
salt

The pot:
brisket
pork
vegetables according to preference and season, e.g.
8–10 potatoes
8–10 button onions
2 carrots
2 parsnips or parsley roots
1 leek (the white part)
1 handful of sugar snap peas or string beans
1 small cabbage
2 apples

Sauce:
3 dl crème fraîche
1 apple, grated but not peeled
1 tsp Swedish distilled vinegar, ättika (12% strength)
1/2 tsp caster sugar
1–2 tbsp grated fresh horseradish

Garnish:
grated fresh horseradish

Procedure:
Put the brisket and pork in a pot, pour on water, bring to the boil
and keep boiling briskly for a few minutes. Meanwhile, peel and
slice the onion. Clean and slice the green part of the leek. Peel
and cut up the carrot. Remove the meat and rinse in cold water.
Clean the pot, return the meat and pour on enough water to
cover the meat and the vegetables to be added.

Add 1 tsp salt per litre of water to begin with, and check the
seasoning later on. Bring to the boil and add the vegetables and
the herbs and spices. Cover and simmer for 1 1/2–2 hours or until
the meat starts to feel tender. Remove from the heat and leave the
meat to cool in the stock. Remove the beef and pork and store
cold, under pressure if possible, till next day. Strain the stock and
store in a cold place.

Mix the sauce ingredients together and store in a cold place.

Heat the stock, after carefully removing any congealed fat from
the surface. Meanwhile, trim the vegetables for the pot. Peel the
potatoes and onions. Peel the carrots, parsnips or parsley roots.
Cut them into sticks. Clean and cut up the white of the leek. Top
and tail the sugar snap peas or string beans. Clean and quarter
the cauliflower. De-core the apples and cut them into segments.

Put in the vegetables, but remember that some need more or
less cooking than others: potatoes, cabbage and onion need
longest, peas shortest. Slice the beef, and the pork too if it isn't
sliced already. Put the meat in the stock for about 5 minutes
before serving. Remove the cauliflower if you like and slice the
florets.

64

Oxtail ragout, Daddy Gösta's way serves 4

Gösta, my father, was a professional cook who loved seeing his big family assembled round a glorious Sunday dinner of seductively fragrant stews and other substantial home fare.

This, for example, is how he would prepare a familiar classic like oxtail ragout – a satisfying, spicy dish that leaves nobody unmoved. He would marinate the meat a day in advance to bring out all the flavours properly. The aromas of the ragout itself are admirably supplemented by a full-bodied, full-flavoured red wine.

Ingredients:
12 good pieces of oxtail, from the thick part
flour for dredging
butter for frying
12 button onions
200 g fresh button mushrooms
100 g lean salt pork
baby carrots
1 dl Madeira
salt and pepper

Marinade:
2 onions
3 cloves of garlic
2 carrots
1 piece of celeriac (about 150 g)
1 sprig of thyme
4 bay leaves
1/2 bottle of red wine (about 3 1/2 dl)
1 dl balsamic vinegar
1 dl olive oil
1 dl strong beef stock

Serve with:
boiled potatoes

Procedure:
Day 1: Peel the onion, garlic, carrots and celeriac for the marinade and dice them small. Mix the herbs, wine, balsamic vinegar, olive oil and stock in a stainless mixing bowl to make a thick marinade. Store in the fridge overnight.

Day 2: Remove the meat but reserve the marinade. Dredge the pieces in white flour. Heat a large casserole and put in the butter. When it stops fizzing, brown the pieces of oxtail thoroughly, a few at a time, all round. Return the meat to the pot and pour the marinade over it. Dilute with a little water. Bring to the boil and then cook slowly for 1–1 1/2 hours. The ragout is done when the meat starts to come away from the bone.

Towards the end of the cooking time, peel and fry the onions and the button mushrooms, either whole or halved. Dice the pork. Scrape the carrots and leave them with a cm or so of the tops. Fry everything in butter and stir a few times. Add salt and a few twists of the peppermill. Remove from the heat.

Remove the meat from the pot and strain the vegetables and herbs. Pour the strained sauce back into the pot. Return the meat, add the fried vegetables and Madeira and simmer together for 5–10 minutes. Test the seasoning.

Serve either straight from the pot or on a warm serving dish. Boiled floury potatoes go well with this recipe.

67

Daddy Gösta at Restaurang Anglais,
Stockholm, early 1940s

Buckling au gratin serves 4

All along the east coast of Sweden there are as many recipes for buckling au gratin as there used to be fishing harbours. The recipes live on, whereas the fishing harbours are disappearing one after another as fishing grows more and more industrialised. However one may feel about that, the main thing is that the tradition and the recipes are surviving.

This au gratin is perfect for lunch or late supper, combined perhaps with toasted crisp bread (see page 50), matured cheese and a nicely balanced lager.

Ingredients:
6 bucklings
4 shallots
butter for frying
6 boiled potatoes
6–8 cherry tomatoes
1 bunch of dill
2 dl whipping cream
salt and pepper

Procedure:
Set the oven to 200°C. Peel the onion, cut it in rings and fry these gently in butter without their changing colour. Slice the potatoes thinly (no need to peel them if they are nice ones). Slice the tomatoes.

Clean the bucklings and pick out as many bones as you can. Chop the dill and mix it with half the cream. Put alternate layers of potato, onion, buckling pieces, tomato slices and dill cream in a greased oven-proof dish, starting with the potato. Pour on the remaining cream, then season. Bake in the middle of the oven for about 30 minutes. Garnish if you like with a little dill. Serve immediately.

Perch casserole serves 4

My favourite pursuit as a boy was running around on the landing stages and fishing for perch outside the stone caissons. Perch is rated a bony fish, but if you cut out the fillets to make a "wallet" it will usually be bone free. Perch pin bones radiate straight out from the spine, but if you make a "wallet cut" along half the fillet just under the centre line and discard the little strip just where the pin bones radiate outwards, you will get rid of them.

Take good care of the roe if there is any. It's a delicacy, and you bread and fry it just like the fillets, but over a slower heat. If you can't get hold of perch, then fresh whitefish, Arctic char, salmon, mackerel or pike-perch will do just as well.

Ingredients:
8–12 boneless perch fillets
dried bread crumbs and flour for breading
1 onion
1 bunch of dill
1 bunch of chives
1 small tin of Swedish "anchovies"
butter and oil for frying
3 dl cooking cream
salt and pepper

Garnish:
"anchovy" fillets
1 tomato

Serve with:
potatoes boiled with dill

Procedure:
Season the perch fillets. Mix the dried breadcrumbs and flour and dredge the fillets in the mixture.

Peel the onion, dill and chives and cut them up small. Mash the "anchovies" lightly (saving a few for garnish). Divide and de-seed the tomato for the garnish, cutting the flesh into thin strips for the same purpose.

Fry the fish golden brown in butter and oil for 2–3 minutes on each side. Remove and keep warm. Put in another knob of butter and fry the onion in the same pan, add the cream, the "anchovies" (or their liquor) and most of the dill and chives. Season the cream sauce to taste. Return the fillets to the pan and simmer gently for a few minutes. (Fry the roe, if any, and role it in the chopped dill and chives.)

Garnish with a few "anchovy" fillets and strips of tomato. Serve immediately, straight from the pan, with potatoes boiled with dill.

68

Boiled calf's tongue with a caper and parsley sauce serves 4

Boiled calf's tongue is a tasty, tender classic that used to be much more commonly seen on dinner tables than it is now – those were the days when we put quite a different value on inexpensive raw materials and there were plenty of butchers selling this particular delicacy.

If you can get hold of tongue nowadays from one of the surviving butchers' shops, I recommend, for its freshness, the following recipe, ideal for both lunch and dinner.

Boil the tongue the same way as for meat soup.

Ingredients:
1 salted calf's tongue
1 onion
1 carrot
1/2 leek
parsley stalks from the sauce
10 white peppercorns
2 bay leaves
salt

Sauce:
3 tbsp butter
1 tbsp white flour
2–3 dl stock from boiling the tongue
3–4 tbsp capers
1 bunch of parsley

White root vegetable purée
about 1 kg white root vegetables, e.g.:
about 1/2 kg potatoes
navet (French turnip)
parsley root
butter
nutmeg
salt and pepper

Service with:
Vegetables according to season, e.g. baby carrots and spring onions, as pictured, of sugar snap peas, broccoli or runner beans.

Procedure:
Immerse the tongue in water in a saucepan, bring to the boil and cook for a few minutes. Remove, rinse in cold water and return to the pot. Cover with water and bring to the boil again. Peel and cut up the onion and carrot. Clean and cut up the leek. Put the vegetables and parsley stalks into the saucepan with the tongue. (Reserve the parsley leaves for the sauce.) Cover and cook for about 1 1/2 hours. Test with a skewer to see if the meat is done. It must be really tender. Leave it to cool a little in the cooking liquid, then remove it with a slotted spoon, leaving it to cool completely in its cooking liquid. Everything this far can be done a day beforehand.

Melt 2 tbsp of the butter for the sauce in a saucepan. Fry the flour in the butter and dilute with stock. Cook slowly till you have a suitably thick sauce. Transfer to a food processor and put in the parsley. Run the food processor till the parsley is chopped fine. Strain the sauce back into the saucepan. Season to taste, then remove from the heat.

Peel and trim the root vegetables for the purée. Cut them up small. Boil them gently for about 10 minutes in the stock from the tongue, until they have softened. (Reserve the stock.) Rice the potatoes to a mash, finishing off with a knob of butter and a few scrapes of nutmeg. Season to taste. Dilute with a little more stock if the purée is too stodgy. Keep warm.

Peel and clean the vegetables to be served with the tongue. Boil the carrots in the stock from the tongue for about 25 minutes, adding the onion with about 5 minutes to go.

Slice the tongue thinly and heat it in the stock. Heat the sauce and glaze with the rest of the butter. Stir in the capers. Serve straight on hot plates or else neatly arranged on a serving dish with the meat on a lake of the sauce and the purée and vegetables neatly arranged round about.

Hints:
For a slightly more elegant, but also more ordinary presentation, you can make an ordinary, well-flavoured round of mashed potato au gratin. Stir 2 egg yolks into the mash and squeeze it out along one side of a greased oven-proof dish. Put the mash in the oven at 225°C until it is nicely browned, then arrange the meat, vegetables and sauce as already described.

Warm-smoked mackerel serves 4

This is lazy man's food, easy to prepare and really tasty, just the thing for warm summer's days when new potatoes throng the vegetable counter or you have just harvested your own. This recipe also works with warm-smoked salmon or buckling. The result will be somewhat different, mackerel having a taste all of its own, but it will be scrumptious all the same. Vodka and beer make a worthy accompaniment.

Ingredients:
2 smoked mackerel (about 600 g) or
the same quantity of warm-smoked salmon or buckling
butter to grease the dish

Garnish:
4 eggs
1 red onion
1 leek (the white part)
1 bunch of chives, chopped fine
1 bunch of dill, chopped fine
3 tbsp capers
2 tbsp grated horseradish
2 tomatoes
salt and pepper

Serve with:
new potatoes
100 g browned butter
2 dl gräddfil

Procedure:
Set the oven to 150°C. Boil the eggs for 8 minutes then put them to cool. Skin the mackerel and bone them carefully, so as to keep the fillets as intact as possible. Place the fillets in a greased oven-proof dish and bake in the middle of the oven for 5 minutes.

Meanwhile prepare the garnish. Peel and chop the red onion. Clean the leek and slice it finely. Mix the red onion, leek, chives, dill, capers and horseradish together. Cut the eggs into fairly large pieces. Dice the tomatoes.

Garnish the fish with egg, tomato and chopped vegetables. Return it to the oven for about 5 minutes. Meanwhile brown the butter, and I mean brown.

Remove the dish from the oven, drizzle the butter over it and serve immediately with new potatoes steamed in dill and with gräddfil.

75

Huckster's hash serves 4

This is a classic from the days when much more livestock was slaughtered on the farm or when there was a local butcher. I believe housewives in those days preferred fresh side pork and shiny pig's kidneys for their huckster's hash, but my own preference is for hind loin and white veal kidney.

Don't lift the lid until the guests have taken their places and the pot is on the table. The weird and wonderful fragrance exuded across the table is an appetiser in itself. The best drink to go with this one is a cold lager or a fresh table water.

Ingredients:
1 white veal kidney
800 g hind loin
2 large onions
1 kg large potatoes
butter for frying
3 bay leaves
3 dl pale beef stock
1 bottle of lager (33 cl)
one or two sprigs of thyme
1 carrot
1/2 leek
salt and pepper

Service with:
toasted crisp bead (see page 50)
butter
matured seed-spiced cheese

Procedure:
Trim away surplus fat before cutting the kidney into slices about 1 cm thick. Boil it quickly in lightly salted water. Peel and slice the onions. Peel the potatoes and cut them into slices about 1 cm thick. Cut the hind loin into slices of equal thickness.

Heat the butter in a frying pan and brown the potatoes, kidney, onion and meat in that order. Put all the ingredients in layers in a large casserole, beginning and ending with the potatoes. Insert the bay leaves in between layers. Season. Pour on the stock and the beer and "plant" the sprigs of thyme. Cover and simmer gently for about 1 hour. Shake the pot every now and then but do not lift the lid except when testing the seasoning and spices.

Peel the carrot and cut up small. Clean and slice the white of the leek. Distribute the vegetables in the pot and go on cooking for a few minutes. Serve with toasted crisp bread, butter and a matured seed-spiced cheese.

Swedish casserole serves 4

Swedish casserole is a genuine Swedish restaurant classic, but an endangered species. Take the chance of making it whenever you find good veal kidney at the meat counter. Swedish casserole used to be very common on the menus of large and small restaurants alike at both lunchtime and dinnertime. It is based entirely on genuine Swedish raw materials and the beer and other spices give is a deliciously composite flavour.

It will be best of all if you can prepare it a day beforehand and store it in the fridge overnight. That way the flavours will blend even better. Toasted crisp bread, matured cheese and a cold, bitter lager are the ideal companions.

Ingredients:
600 g pork off the bone or veal from the hind loin
2 small veal kidneys or 1 big one
600 g potatoes
1 large onion
1 leek
4–5 bay leaves
1 sprig of thyme
5 dl veal stock
1 bottle of light beer (33 cl)
salt and white pepper

Serve with:
1 bunch of parsley
toasted crisp bread (see page 50)
matured cheese

Procedure:
Trim the meat if necessary. Cut both meat and kidney into cm-thick slices.

Peel the potatoes and cut into slices 7–8 mm thick. Peel the onion and slice it quite thinly. Clean and slice the leek.

Put the meat and kidney in a casserole and pour in enough water to cover them, salting lightly. Bring to the boil and blanch for not more than 1 minute. Remove the meat with a slotted spoon and rinse it under the cold tap.

Clean the pot and put in alternate layers of potato, meat, kidney, onion and herbs and spices. Pour on the stock and beer and simmer for 30–35 minutes.

Cut up the parsley – not too small – and sprinkle it over the contents of the casserole.

Serve straight from the pot, preferably with toasted crisp bread and matured cheese.

Stewed burbot with the roe and liver serves 4

This is a classic Swedish fish recipe, served mainly in winter, burbot being at its best between December and February.

Burbot (alias lawyer or eelpout) is a long, slim freshwater member of the cod family. It is lean but tasty and properly treated, as in this recipe, a superb delicacy.

Buy ready-boned fillets at the fishmongers and you can start immediately on your cultural mission of handing down this lovely dish to future generations. And don't forget to include the roe and liver – both of them delicacies – in your purchase.

Ingredients:
1 kg burbot fillet with the roe and liver
1 onion
1 piece of celeriac
1 carrot
1/2 leek (the white part)
20 g runner beans
6 dl fish stock
2 dl dry white wine
1 tbsp lemon juice
1 tbsp white wine vinegar
1 mace
1 bay leave
3 dl whipping cream
2 tbsp green peas
1/2 tbsp flour for thickening (Sw. *Idealmjöl*)
2 egg yolks at room temperature
a pinch of sugar (optional)
salt and pepper

Serve with:
4 slices day-old white bread
butter for frying
1/2 bunch of chives, chopped fine
small dill flower heads
boiled floury potatoes

Procedure:
Clean the fish fillets more if necessary. Rinse the roe and liver under the cold tap. Peel the onion and chop fine. Peel the celeriac and carrot and dice them small. Clean the leek and cut into thin slices. Slice the beans.

Cut the bread into neat triangles and fry these quickly in butter. Dip one side of the bread instantly in the chopped chives, then put aside for the time being.

Bring the stock to the boil and add the wine, lemon juice, vinegar, mace, bay leaf and a little salt. Simmer the fish, liver and roe separately for 10–15 mm in the stock. Remove with a slotted spoon and keep warm.

Strain the stock and reduce by half. Add the cream, the diced vegetables and the peas and cook for another 5 minutes. Thicken the sauce with the flour and egg yolks. Season to taste with salt and pepper and perhaps a pinch of sugar. After this the sauce must not be allowed to boil again, but it must be served really warm.

Pour the sauce over the fish and garnish with the liver and roe sliced and with the croutons dipped in chives, plus a few dill flower heads.

Boiled floury potatoes to mix with the creamy sauce are the perfect accompaniment.

Mustard-coated pork chop with coleslaw

serves 2

Now I must say a few words in earnest about the pork chop, an often deplorably neglected raw material in Sweden. A lot of products nowadays masquerade as pork chops, but as loyal food lovers we will have none of it. The only cut that is worthy of the name of pork chop is the meat from the thickest part of the pig's hind loin. And the layer of fat must be left *in situ*, With pork, it is the fat that carries the flavour, and those not wishing to eat the fat can cut it away at table.

That said, we can get down to business – the business of a feast for two on a Saturday evening.

Ingredients:
2 pork chops on the bone (200 g each)
1 egg
1/2 tbsp Dijon mustard
1/2 tbsp Swedish mustard
grated day-old white bread or dried breadcrumbs
white flour
butter for frying
1/2 dl oil for frying
salt and pepper

Coleslaw:
1 segment of a normal-sized cauliflower
1 segment of a normal-sized Savoy cabbage
1 red onion
100 g spinach leaves
1/2 tsp whole caraway seeds
1 tbsp lemon juice
1 tsp grated lemon zest
2 dl crème fraîche
salt and pepper

Garnish :
a few parsley or rosemary sprigs
2 wedges of lemon

Service with:
crisp-fried bacon
grilled potato halves or boiled potatoes
browned butter

Procedure:
Beat the egg and mix it with Dijon mustard and Swedish mustard in a deep plate. Mix day-old white bread or dried breadcrumbs with salt and pepper on another plate. Pour flour onto a third plate. Dip the chops in flour, shake a little, then dip them in the egg mixture and finally in the breadcrumbs. Now put them to one side.

Next the coleslaw. Peel the red onion and shred it fine. Cut the cabbage, Savoy cabbage and spinach into extremely narrow strips. drip with lemon juice and stir in the lemon zest. Pound the caraway in a mortar and sprinkle it on. Mix everything with the crème fraîche. Season to taste, then put away in a cold place.

Shred and crisp-fry the bacon, then put it between layers of domestic tissue. Keep it warm afterwards.

Heat butter and oil in a big frying pan. Fry the chops golden brown and crisp, 5–6 minutes on each side. Place them on a layer of domestic tissue for a minute or so.

Arrange neatly on a warm serving dish or warm plates, with potatoes, bacon and coleslaw round the chops. Garnish with a few sprigs of parsley and a segment of lemon.

81

Hints:
Just for a change, you can use small potatoes and split them down the middle. Turn the pieces in oil and grill them to a nice chequer pattern in a griddle. Transfer them to an oven-proof dish and roast them in the oven at 200°C for about 20 minutes until they are done.

National Baltic Herring serves 4

At the beginning of this century I took part in the annual Sweden's National Dish competition, the content and design of which are meant to tie in with Swedish culinary tradition. My entry was the recipe given below, and the jury liked it so much that they voted me the winner. Aptly enough, the dish was christened National Baltic Herring, and those days when we have it on the menu at Sjömagasinet there isn't usually a single Baltic herring left by the time we finish. I had made a simple sauce to go with my entry, and I topped the herring with battered dill. Try it yourself!

You get extra points for serving straight on warm plates and squeezing the mashed potato attractively from an icing bag, though you need almost blacksmith's hands to do it, I don't mind admitting.

Beer and a wee drop of the creature go down very nicely with this one.

Ingredients:
24 Baltic herring
4 eggs
1 onion
1/2 bunch of dill
1/2 bunch of chives
8 Swedish "anchovy" fillets
rye flour
dried breadcrumbs
butter and rapeseed oil for frying
salt and pepper

Sauce:
2 dl crème fraîche
2 tbsp butter
1 tbsp chives, chopped fine
1 tbsp Slotts caviar (bleak roe)
salt and pepper

Mashed potato:
800 g potatoes
3 dl milk with the top on (2 1/2 dl milk, 1/2 dl cream)
1/2 bunch of dill, chopped fine
2 tbsp butter
a couple of scrapes of nutmeg
salt and pepper

Garnish:
deep-fried dill (optional)

Procedure:
Make the mashed potato fairly loose. Peel and boil the potatoes. Rice them, through a potato ricer, into a serving bowl or saucepan. Heat the creamy milk and stir. Add the dill, butter and nutmeg. Season to taste. Keep warm.

Soft-boil the eggs (4–5 minutes). Peel the onion and chop it very fine. Cut the dill and chives equally small. Mash the onion, egg, dill, chives and "anchovies" into a firm batter. Distribute and spread out this mixture evenly on half the herring fillets. Season lightly, then put the remaining fillets on top. Press together gently and dredge the moist fillets in a mixture of rye flour, dried breadcrumbs, salt and pepper.

Heat a saucepan with a generous knob of butter and a tablespoonful or so of rapeseed oil in it. Fry the herring a few at a time for 3–4 minutes on each side. Keep them warm, or else use two frying pans.

Melt the crème fraîche in a saucepan. Stir in the butter, chives and caviar. Season to taste, if necessary.

If you fancy trying deep-fried dill as a garnish, start by heating ordinary cooking oil to about 180°C in a wide pan. Deep-fry whole dill flower heads for, at most, 10 seconds, and fish them out again, for example, with a slotted spoon.

Stewed apple makes about 3 kg

One of the nicest and most rewarding of autumn preserves is your own stewed apple, and all the more so, of course, if you have had the privilege of growing your own apples or at least picking them. A fairly sharp kind of apple gives the best results.

Ingredients:
2 kg sharp apples
800 g caster sugar
3 dl concentrated apple juice
juice of 1 lemon
sodium benzoate or some other preservative (Sw.: Atamon)

Procedure:
Set the oven to 100–125°C. Peel the apples and put them whole into water with lemon juice, to keep them from darkening. When you've peeled them all, quarter them, de-core and remove the tails and stalks.

Pour the sugar, apple juice and lemon juice into a big casserole or preserving pan. Bring to the boil over a low flame, stirring occasionally to melt the sugar. Cut the apples into smaller pieces and add these to the mixture. Cover and cook slowly for 30–45 minutes, depending on the kind of apple you have chosen. Stir occasionally – apples burn easily.

Meanwhile carefully wash up some glass jars with lids intact and put them in the oven for at least 10 minutes to sterilise them.

Check the stewed apple for sweetness. Add preservative. Personally I like stewed apple best if there are a few small bits of apple in it, but tastes vary. For a firmer product, replace half the sugar with the corresponding amount of jam sugar. Use less preservative in that case, because jam sugar contains both that and pectin.

Pour the stewed apple into hot jars without spilling down the sides, and screw the caps tight immediately.

After an hour or so you will hear a distinct click from the lids, which tells you that you have made a very durable preserve that does not require a cold storage space. Of course, you can store it in the freezer as well.

Apple compote serves 4–5

Apple compote is a plain but superb accompaniment to meat recipes of various kinds – beef, for example, but pork as well. Try it with potato cakes and pork. Apple compote taste best when slightly acidulous.

Ingredients:
2 sharp apples
juice of 1/2 lemon
2 tbsp caster sugar

Procedure:
Peel the apples and cut them in small pieces. Put them in a saucepan and pour on the lemon juice. Simmer over a low flame for about 20 minutes. Add the sugar carefully towards the end of the cooking time.

Coiled Sausage Special serves 4

I have vivid memories of Coiled Sausage Special from my youth onwards, and also from the time when I was pretty green in the kitchen. In those days a whole gang of us hungry young cooks could gather round the kitchen table at Daddy Gösta's in the Södermalm district of Stockholm.

We tried spinning yarns from the short time we'd clocked up in kitchens, but, striplings that we were, every time Dad put us in our places with more or less tall stories about stuck-up celebrity chefs and eccentric cold-buffet manageresses.

To keep the conversation going, Dad use to fry Coiled Sausage Special, for which we had an unlimited appetite. There was a time when every butcher sold this type of sausage, but nowadays it's harder to come by. Covered markets, though, can usually run to it.

Ingredients:
800 g coiled sausage
800 g boiled firm potatoes
1 large onion
butter for frying
salt and pepper (optional)

Serve with:
fried eggs
pickled beetroot (see page 13)
toasted crisp bread (see page 50)

Procedure:
Peel the potatoes and cut them into squares a little over 1 cm. Peel and rough-chop the onion. Remove the skin from the sausage and cut it into 2–3 cm pieces.

Fry the potato and onion golden brown in butter in a frying pan, add the pieces of sausage and lower the heat. Turn and mix into a kind of hash, frying till the sausage is thoroughly warmed. Season to taste, if you want to.

Meanwhile fry the eggs in another frying pan.

Serve the sausage with fried eggs, pickled beetroot and toasted crisp bread.

Potato cakes with pork serves 4

Now we come to the part – the serious department of the Swedish cuisine – where we have to roll up our shirtsleeves and clean our glasses. Potato cakes with pork are a restaurant classic and a veritable table-turner when we serve them at Sjömagasinet in Göteborg.

This is definitely a dish for the finest dinner tables. At least I think so, devotee as I am of these glorious Swedish delicacies.

Trying serving apple compote with it.

Potato cake ingredients:
1 kg potatoes
1 egg

1 tbsp flour
butter and pork dripping for frying
salt and pepper

Garnish:
800 g salt pancetta, sliced
butter and oil for frying

Serve with:
uncooked, stirred lingonberry jam (see page 25)
apple compote (see page 85)

Procedure:
Peel the potatoes and coarse-grate them. Wring out the liquid if necessary. Beat the eggs and flour together and fold the grated potato into the mixture. Mix everything together quickly, adding salt and pepper.

Fry the pork till it is crisp and golden brown, but not too long, because that will make it tough and dry. Start the frying operation with a little oil and butter in the pan. When the pork is done, pour off the fat but reserve it for frying the potato cakes. Keep the pork warm.

Brown the butter and a little pork dripping in a large frying pan, put in blobs of the batter and pat them as thin as possible. Fry the potato cakes crisp and golden brown on both sides. Serve piping hot with the pork, uncooked, stirred lingonberry jam or perhaps apple compote. Though I need hardly add that both together is if anything even better.

Roast lamb with baker's potatoes serves 4–6

A lot of the things we eat in Sweden are of French origin. Nothing strange about that – food can immigrate and settle, just like people.

I haven't a clue why this recipe is called "roast lamb with baker's potatoes" but that's the literal translation of its French name, Gigot à la boulangère. Perhaps it's because, in the old days, while the bake oven was still hot the bakers would put food in it for the end of the working day.

Whatever the etymology, the result is good eating, especially when autumn storms and rain are tearing at the treetops and you fancy an extra tasty, full-bodied red wine to go with all the other seductive aromas.

Ingredients:
1 1/2–2 kg leg of lamb, on the bone but with the knuckle removed
6–8 cloves of garlic
2 sprigs of rosemary
thin strips of lemon peel
olive oil
coarse salt
pepper

Baker's potatoes:
1 kg floury potatoes
2 onions
4 cloves of garlic
2 tbsp butter
1/2 tbsp caster sugar
3–4 sprigs of thyme
3 bay leaves
1 bottle of light beer (33 cl)
1 1/2 dl white wine
2 dl chicken stock
salt and pepper

Garnish:
a handful of watercress

Serve with:
crisp green lettuce or
tomato salad with red onion

Procedure:
Set the oven to 175°C. Peel the garlic cloves and cut them lengthwise. Cut a pocket along the bone of the lamb or at other points. Lard with garlic and a few sprigs of rosemary. Rub the meat with olive oil, grated lemon zest, coarse salt and pepper. Insert a roasting thermometer in the thickest part of the joint. Place the joint on a wire rack and put this on the middle shelf of the oven with a roasting tin underneath. Remove the steak at 55°C for underdone or 65–70°C for well done.

Cut the potatoes into slices about 1/2 cm thick. Peel the onion and garlic, slice them thinly and fry them golden brown in butter in a frying pan. Add sugar, salt and pepper to taste. Transfer the potato to a deep gratin dish, alternating with layers of onion, thyme, bay leaf and seasoning. Pour the beer, wine and stock. Position the tin underneath the joint in the oven, so that the juices from the lamb will drip down onto the potatoes. The potatoes should be done in about 1 hour, after which the joint will need another 15–30 minutes. If the potatoes look like getting overdone, cover them with aluminium foil to trap the meat juices. These can be poured onto the potatoes afterwards.

Remove the joint from the oven and wrap it in aluminium foil. Cover with a tea towel and leave for 20–30 minutes. Carve neat slices and put these, either onto a warm serving dish with the rest of the joint or, quite simply, neatly on top of the potatoes. A handful of watercress will make a nice garnish.

Serve, for example, with crisp lettuce or a salad of tomato and red onion.

89

Pike mince balls au gratin with Parmesan

serves 4

Sweden's lakes and watercourses abound with top-quality pike – just the thing for grinding to farce for making these fish balls or a fish pâté. Enquire after minced pike at your fishmonger's, or else buy a whole fish and fillet and mince it yourself. If there is no pike available, haddock will do.

The fastest and easiest way of preparing the mixture for pike mince balls is in a food processor, but of course you can do the job by hand if you want to. The mixture might seem to contain overmuch cream, but it has to in order to achieve the right consistency.

It's important to begin by preparing fish stock before getting to work on the fish balls themselves.

Pike mince balls au gratin with Parmesan are well worth a top-end wine – say a Chablis or a sauvignon blanc.

Ingredients:
400 g minced pike or haddock
2 egg yolks
4 dl whipping cream
salt and pepper

Sauce:
5 dl fish stock (see page 250)
1 shallot
2 dl white wine
3 dl milk with the top on (2 dl milk, 1 dl cream)
1 tbsp butter
1 tbsp flour
1 dl concentrated fish stock
1 tbsp butter
3 dl Parmesan cheese, grated fine
salt and pepper

Garnish:
1/2 leek (the white part)
butter for frying
1/2 bunch of chives, chopped fine

Service with:
riced potato, rice or mashed potato (see page 103)

Procedure

Start by preparing the concentrated fish stock, doing it by the book. Peel the shallot and chop fine. Pour the concentrated fish stock into a steel saucepan, adding the wine and shallot. Bring to the boil and reduce to about 1 dl.

Now make the sauce. Heat the creamy milk in a saucepan. Melt the butter in another saucepan and stir the flour into it without the flour changing colour. Beat in the creamy milk and concentrated fish stock, stirring to a smooth sauce. Season to taste and simmer gently for about 10 minutes. Strain the sauce and remove from the heat.

Peel and boil the potatoes, or cook the rice, keep warm.

Set the oven to 175°C. Mix the fish farce, making sure all the ingredients are equally cold – this is important! Transfer the farce, egg yolks, salt and pepper to the food processor. Run it for about 30 seconds. Stop to scrape the sides with a rubber or plastic spatula, then run the machine for another 30 seconds or so. Add the cream and run for another minute or so, until the farce is looking smooth and even.

Make large oval balls of the mixture using a big table spoon dipped in lukewarm water. Put the balls on a greased baking tray. Cover with oven-proof foil and bake in the middle of the oven for about 15 minutes.

Clean the leek and slice thinly. Fry it in a little butter in a frying pan for about 1 minute, then remove from the heat.

Set the open to 225o and top heat. Transfer the fish balls to a large oven-proof dish. Heat the sauce and stir about 1 dl of the Parmesan into it. Drizzle the sauce over the fish balls and sprinkle them with the remaining cheese. Bake on a fairly high shelf for about 10 minutes, till the surface bubbles and looks well done. Meanwhile make the mashed potato, if you are serving it. Garnish the dish with the chives and leek round the edges.

Hints:

A food processor is one of the most fantastic kitchen machines in existence. If you haven't already got one, buy one as soon as possible, and it will be one of your best kitchen investments ever. Why not make this recipe its maiden voyage?

Breast of chicken with Parmesan, prosciutto and basil serves 4

I dedicate this recipe to Robert Maglia, who worked for me at Sjömagasinet. He is one of my absolute favourite chefs and in recent years has done brilliantly in Stockholm.

Robert Maglia uses a lot of chicken, and I think this recipe for stuffed breast of chicken would appeal to his sophisticated taste buds. And what better accompaniment to this than a bottle of full-bodied, well-tempered Italian wine?

Ingredients:
4 chicken breast with the skin on
4 slices of prosciutto
about 100 g sliced, matured Parmesan cheese
1 pot of basil
4 toothpicks
butter and olive oil for frying
salt and pepper

Sauce:
2 shallots
1 clove of garlic
8 small tomatoes
1/2 red paprika
1/2 yellow paprika
100 g button mushrooms
1 tsp tomato purée
10 basil leaves, chopped fine
grated zest of 1/2 lemon
juice of 1/2 lemon
about 2 tbsp white wine
a little water (if needed)
2 tbsp olive oil for frying
salt and pepper

Garnish:
basil leaves

Serve with:
rice or tagliatelle
toasted farmhouse bread

Procedure:
Set the oven to 175°C. Prepare all the ingredients of the sauce. Peel the shallot and chop fine. Peel and crush the garlic. Scald and peel the tomatoes, then halve them. De-seed the paprika and cut in pieces. Slice the button mushrooms. Put everything aside for the moment.

Slit a wide pocket in each of the chicken breasts, and fill it with ham, Parmesan shavings and basil leaves. Season before closing the pockets with toothpicks. Brown the breasts all round in butter and oil in a sauté pan until they are a nice colour. Transfer the chicken and juices to an oven-proof dish and finish them off in the middle of the oven; given them 15–20 minutes to make sure they are cooked through. Baste several times.

Start cooking the rice, or put on the water for the pasta – whichever. If pasta, cook as per the instructions on the packet.

Now, back to the sauce. Heat a little more olive oil in the sauté pan you browned the chicken in. Sauté the onion and garlic for a minute or so. Add the tomato, paprika pieces and button mushrooms and sauté for a few minutes longer. Add the remaining ingredients and simmer, stirring continuously, for about 15 minutes. Season to taste. Add a little water if the sauce seems too thick.

Remove the chicken breasts from the oven and put them in the sauce. Simmer for another 5 minutes or so, basting repeatedly. Just before serving, remove the meat, carve diagonal, cm-thick slices, and return to the sauce. Garnish with basilica leaves. Serve with rice and pasta and, preferably, with toasted slices of farmhouse bread for soaking up the wonderful sauce.

95

Falun sausage au gratin serves 4

Believe it or not, but the records show Falun sausage – falukorv – that most Swedish of foods, to be a German invention. Apparently it was German miners in Falun who jibbed at the wastage of discarding the meat of clapped-out oxen employed on mining operations.

The Germans, who even in those days were known for the excellence of their sausage, began experimenting by chopping up the unchewable meat and making … Falun sausage. Still today, Falun sausage contains mostly beef, and the very name is now a protected trademark, combined with strict stipulations as to meat content.

Falun sausage is one of our very biggest favourites of the dinner table. Unfortunately, though, it is most often just fried. Try this recipe instead, and you will see what culinary potential resides within our best-known sausage. Taste your way forward. Rule number one: the better the sausage, the better the gratin.

Ingredients:
800 g Falun sausage
1–2 leeks
Swedish mustard
chilli sauce
paprika powder
1 onion
10–12 cherry tomatoes
2 salt gherkins
1 tsp fresh chopped thyme
2 dl whipping cream
150 grated matured Manor House cheese (herrgårdsost)
2 tbsp chopped parsley
salt and pepper

Serve with:
mashed potato (see page 103
sticks of salt gherkin (optional)

Procedure:
Set the oven to 175°C. Clean the leek and cut it into rings – not too thin. Cut the onion into half-rings – not too small.

Put the leek at the bottom of a well-greased oven-proof dish. Make a deep incision the full length of the Falun sausage. Part it carefully, but with the two halves still hanging together. Spread quite generously with mustard and chilli sauce. Transfer the sausage to the gratin dish, season and sprinkle with a little paprika powder. Halve the tomatoes and cut the salt gherkin into sticks. Garnish the sausage with onion, tomatoes, gherkin sticks and thyme. Drizzle with the cream. Sprinkle with the cheerse. Bake in the middle of the oven for about 30 minutes. Remove when the sausage is a nice colour and sprinkle with the chopped parsley.

Serve with your best mashed potato and perhaps more gherkin sticks.

Mackerel poached in court bouillon   serves 4

Lots of amateur fishing enthusiasts on the west coast of Sweden ask for nothing better in spring and early summer than to sail out in pursuit of this greenish-black delicacy. Poached mackerel, incidentally, is best one day after poaching.

Greta, my wonderful mother-in-law, was a wizard of the court bouillon. She had this fantastic sense of balance between acidity and salinity in the poaching liquid which is the real secret of cooking fish this way. Here is the recipe she used when fresh-caught mackerel entered her kitchen.

Ingredients:
1 kg fresh-caught mackerel

Poaching liquid:
1 1/2 l water
1 onion
2 carrots
1 dl white wine vinegar
10 white peppercorns
10 allspice corns
10 rosé peppercorns
2–3 whole cloves
1 bunch of dill
2 bay leaves
1/2 leek (the white part)
2 sheets of gelatine
2/3 tbsp salt
1/2 tbsp lemon juice

Serve with (e.g.):
new potatoes
dill
dill mayonnaise
pressed cucumber (see page 26)

Procedure:
Clean and rinse the mackerel thoroughly, scraping away any membranes with a knife. Cut up the fish in 4–5 cm thick pieces.

Peel and slice the onion and carrots. Bring all the poaching liquid ingredients to the boil in a saucepan and then simmer for about 5 minutes. Put in the mackerel and bring to the boil again. Simmer over a low flame for 2–3 minutes. Skim thoroughly. Remove from the heat and leave the fish to cool in the poaching liquid. Transfer to a cool place.

Boil the new potatoes. Chop the dill and roll the newly boiled potatoes in it. Serve the mackerel with the potatoes, dill mayonnaise and (for me!) pressed cucumber.

Dill mayonnaise   serves 4

Dill mayonnaise goes perfectly with different kinds of boiled fish if you can't be bothered to make any other sauce. It is easy to prepare and tastes wonderful.

Ingredients:
2 dl mayonnaise
1 dl soured cream (gräddfil)
1 tsp Dijon mustard
2 tbsp "anchovy" liquor
1 bunch of dill, chopped fine
salt and pepper

Procedure:
Mix all the ingredients except the dill thoroughly. Stir in the dill last of all, season to taste.

Hints:
The mayonnaise will taste fresher still if you add 1/2 grated shallot and the juice of a large lemon segment (about 1/2 tbsp).

99

Three kinds of herring

Herring – *sill* – of every kind has national treasure status where Swedish food is concerned. An invaluable asset. Here are three versions, manifestations of the culinary dignity of Swedish traditional home cooking, husmanskost. Appropriate drinks, in moderation, and a number of ditties from the Swedish drinking-song heritage are indispensable concomitants.

Spiced herring   serves 6–8

This is a year-round winner, but perhaps not all that common, due probably to its long marinating time. But believe me, it's well worth waiting for. You can double the proportions. Sandalwood powder is obtainable from well-stocked herb shops but can be dispensed with.

Ingredients:
10 medium-sized fat, fresh herring

Poaching liquid:
3 dl Swedish distilled vinegar, ättika (12% strength)
1 l water
1/2 dl salt

Dry marinade:
1 tbsp whole white peppercorns
1 1/2 tbsp whole allspice corns
10 bay leaves
1 tsp sandalwood powder (optional)
2 tsp ground ginger
1 tsp ground cloves
1 dl salt
2 1/2 dl caster sugar
1 dl of the poaching liquid (if needed)

Serve with:
boiled potatoes
toasted crisp bread (see page 50)
well-matured seed-spiced cheese

Procedure:
Day 1. Clean the fish and rinse it quickly under the cold tap. Leave the head on if you like. Mix the poaching liquid ingredients together in a mixing bowl. Put the fish in and store cold for about 48 hours.

Day 3. Remove the fish and drain it through a strainer. Reserve a few dl of the liquid.

A measuring spoon is best when adding the spices. Crush the white pepper and allspice, crumble the bay leaf. Mix all the spices, salt and sugar together for a dry marinade. Put alternate layers of fish and spices into a jar or glass bowl, with the dry ingredients at the bottom and top. Put a weight on top of the fish to hold it down in the mixture that forms. If this does not look like covering the fish, in spite of the weight applied, you can add a few dl of the reserved liquid.

Leave to marinate in a cold place for 3 weeks.

When the 3 weeks are up, cut the fish into 2 cm pieces for serving and up-end these on a glass serving dish. Serve with potatoes, toasted crisp bread and a well-matured seed-spiced cheese.

Pickled herring serves 4

With all respect to creativity and progress, this original recipe for pickled herring is one you readily return to, at least when the year's new potatoes, whether shopped or home-grown, demand attention.

Ingredients:
4 fillets of fat, salted Icelandic herring

Pickling liquid:
1 dl Swedish distilled vinegar, *ättika* (12% strength)
2 1/2 dl caster sugar
3 dl water
3–4 cloves
2 bay leaves
3–4 crushed white peppercorns
10–12 crushed allspice corns

Pickling solids:
1 onion
1 carrot
1 small piece of leek (the green part)
10–12 sprigs of dill
the pickling liquid

Garnish:
1 red onion
1 tsp crushed allspice

Serve with:
dill-fragrant new potatoes
dark rye bread – *kavring*
crisp bread
radishes
matured cheeses

Procedure:
Day 1. After removing any remaining bones, put the herring fillets in water and store them in the fridge for the night, for the salt to leech out.

Day 2. Mix the ättika, sugar and water in a steel saucepan and bring to the boil. Add the spices, cover and cook for 2–3 minutes. Remove the saucepan from the heat and leave the liquid to cool.

Peel the onion and slice thinly. Peel the carrot and slice it crosswise. Clean the leek and slice it thinly. Put alternate layers of fish, onion, leek and dill into a pot or glass bowl. Strain off the spices from the (now cooled) pickling liquid and pour it over the fish. Cover, e.g. with plastic foil, and store cold for 1–2 days.

Days 3–4. Remove the herring from the liquid and cut obliquely into neat slices. Up-end it so that the fillets look to be intact. Peel the red onion and slice it thinly. Put the rings of red onion on top, strain a little pickling liquid over the herring and, finally, sprinkle it with a little newly crushed allspice. Serve with dill-fragrant potatoes, *kavring*, crisp bread, radishes and one or two carefully matured cheeses.

Herring in mustard pickle serves 4

Herring – or rather, Baltic herring – in mustard pickle is many people's absolute favourite for a summertime buffet or yuletide spread. Here is my favourite recipe for the favourite.

Ingredients:
400 g Baltic herring fillets

Pickling liquid:
3 dl water
1 dl Swedish distilled vinegar, *ättika* (12% strength)
2 tbsp caster sugar
1 tbsp salt

Mustard sauce:
2 tbsp white wine vinegar
1/2 dl oil
1/2 crème fraîche
4 tbsp caster sugar or brown sugar
2 tbsp Slotts mustard
1 tbsp Dijon mustard
1 tbsp whipping cream
2 tbsp mayonnaise
1 pinch of salt
1/2 tsp crushed white pepper
1/2 medium-large onion
2 bunches of dill chopped fine, the stalks only
1 bunch of chives, chopped fine

Serve with:
white bread

Procedure:
Day 1. Skin the Baltic herring. Mix the pickling liquid ingredients together in a mixing bowl, immerse the herring in it and store cold overnight. Stir with a spoon once, to make sure of the pickling liquid getting round.

Day 2. Stir all the ingredients for the mustard sauce together in a bowl, except for the onion, dill and chives. Season to taste. Peel the onion and chop it fine. Stir the onion, dill and chives into the sauce.

Pour off the pickling liquid and put the Baltic herring fillets to drain in a strainer. carefully fold them into the sauce and store cold for 24 hours. Turn them and mix them once more, so that the sauce can get everywhere. This goes well with white bread.

Hints:
Roll the fillets together and top them with a little bleak roe. Drizzle the sauce all round.

Mashed potato serves 4–5

This is my standard recipe for mashed potato, the one I always take as my starting point. I often have occasion to flavour the mash different ways, to suit the main course, and I'm sure you can work out flavourings of your own which will suit your taste and the family's. But start off like this.

Ingredients:
1 kg floury potatoes
3 dl milk with the top on (2 1/2 dl milk, 1/2 dl cream)
2 tbsp butter
freshly grated nutmeg
salt and pepper

Procedure:
Peel the potatoes and boil them soft. Meanwhile, heat the milk and cream.

Drain the potatoes and leave them to steam for a minute or so. Rice or whisk them in the saucepan, add the butter and dilute with the hot creamy milk to make a fine, smooth mash. Hot - liquid saves the mash from getting cold, which gives it a more supple consistency and blends the flavours better. Season with a few scrapes of nutmeg, plus salt and pepper.

Hints:
You can upgrade the mash a bit by substituting celeriac for 1/3 of the potatoes and adding grated Västerbotten or some other strong cheese.

If serving with fried Baltic herring, 1 dl fine-chopped dill or 1 dl fine-chopped chives stirred into the mash will be just the ticket.

103

Blood pudding with a pork and onion sauce serves 4

My mother's parents had a farm, an old-fashioned one with live-stock husbandry, grain growing and ley farming. The end of November was pig-killing time, and along came Hugo the veteran butcher. Everything was ready and waiting for him, right down to the vodka. As he set to work, Granny stood next to him with a pail and a drop of *ättika* (distilled vinegar) at the ready. The pig's blood was collected in the pail, a teaspoon or so of ättika was added, and the blood then had to be whisked until it congealed. After Hugo had been paid, he was given a dram or two of the vodka. That was the custom. Granny and a few servant girls then got busy for a couple of hours, baking blood pudding, *paltbröd*. This "bread" had to last well into the winter. After it had cooled it was threaded onto a pole suspended from the bakehouse ceiling. There was enough blood for black pudding too. In those days nothing was wasted.

I don't remember what was served on the actual pig-killing day. It could have been huckster's hash. Be that as it may, the cast iron cauldron was put on the stove and one or two bits of pork were salted, fried and eaten there and then. There was a lot of work to be done before the pork not being used for sausage-making had been properly salted down for storage, the Christmas ham not least. Few homes had freezers in the 1940s.

Granny must have had her own blood pudding recipe, but if you are fond of blood pudding with a pork and onion sauce and would like to try making it some time, here comes my recipe. Blood has to be specially ordered from one of the few remaining butchers. Perhaps you think that saving blood and turning it into food is old-fashioned, but the French are good at it and some members of the talented young generation of chefs have also begun taking an interest in blood-based food.

To go with this recipe, I always serve a feisty beer and one or two drams of pure vodka – ice cold, of course.

Ingredients:
6 dl pig's blood
1 dl crushed ginger snaps (pepparkakor)
1 dl roasted onion
3 dl dark beer
50 g yeast
2 l rye flour
1/2 tsp thyme
1/2 tsp marjoram
1 tsp ground ginger
1/2 tsp ground allspice
1 tbsp brown sugar, 1 tsp salt

Pork and onion sauce:
12 slices salt pancetta
2 onions
butter for frying
1 tsp white flour
1 dl whipping cream
3 dl milk
1 veal stock cube
1 tbsp Kikkoman soy
salt and pepper

Procedure:
Pound the gingersnaps and the roasted onion to a fine powder in a mortar. Warm the pig's blood and beer to blood heat (!) in a saucepan. Dissolve the yeast in a little of the liquid in a spacious food processor or mixer. Add the remaining liquid and the other ingredients. Run the dough till it is supple and comes away from the sides. Transfer to a floured pastry board and knead slightly. Divide into twelve pieces and shape each of these into a ball with a circular motion of the palm of your hand or the ball of your thumb. Leave for 10 minutes before rolling into round cakes. Make a small hole in the middle of each one and transfer to well-greased baking sheets. Leave to rise in the warmest part of the kitchen for about 2 hours.

Set the oven to 225°C. Prick the cakes and bake them in the middle of the oven for about 25 minutes. Put them to cool between baking cloths, and then if possible hang them up on a pole. Blood pudding needs to be soaked for 4–5 hours before use. Then you boil it in lightly salted water in a big pot with a plate at the bottom and another on top (so as to keep the blood pudding from sticking to the bottom of the pot and also to keep it under the water). When the blood pudding feels soft, test with a skewer to see if it is done.

Cut cm-wide strips of pork for the pork and onion sauce. Peel and rough-chop the onion. Fry the pork and onion golden brown in a little butter in a frying pan. Remove the mixture and put to one side. Pour off most of the fat from the pan, then sprinkle the flour on and whisk in the cream and milk. Crumble the stock cube into the mixture and add the soy. Season, then simmer for about 5 minutes. Now return the pork to the frying pan and simmer the sauce for another 5 minutes.

Cut the blood pudding into big pieces and serve instantly with the pork and onion sauce.

Hints:
You can very well put the blood pudding to soak in a good stock or liquid from boiling ham, if available. You can boil it in stock too.

This pork and onion sauce is so good that for a change you can have it with boiled floury potatoes on their own.

Gravlax ("Head Waiter") sauce serves 6–8

You may have occasion to make this sauce now and then, so here's the recipe I generally serve at Sjömagasinet when there is gravlax or marinated Baltic herring on the menu.

Don't use olive oil, because it has a very distinctive flavour that won't fit in here. Head Waiter sauce goes well with marinated mackerel and whitefish too, I need hardly tell you, and of course with crab as well.

Ingredients:
2 tbsp Swedish mustard
1 tbsp dark Dijon mustard
3 tbsp caster sugar
juice of 1/2 lemon
1 tbsp red wine vinegar
1 tbsp Kikkoman soy
a dash or two of Worcester sauce
1/2 tsp ground white pepper
1 tbsp water
4 dl rapeseed or corn oil
1 bunch of dill, chopped fine

Procedure:
Mix together all the ingredients except the oil and dill until the sugar stops crunching. Pour on the oil in a thin jet, whisking all the time. If the sauce turns out too thick, dilute with a little more water.

Finally, stir in plenty of dill and put the sauce in a cold place for a few hours to "ripen". Stir in more chopped dill if you don't think you have enough already.

Chunky gravlax serves 4

Gravlax is another of my great favourites. The salmon must have at least 2 days in the marinade if it is to be served the old way, in chunks, which I think is tastiest. This marinating or "graving" of food goes back thousands of years to times when the possibilities of storing food for any great length of time were limited. In the past century, what used to be a counsel of necessity has become an up-market delicacy.

I add water to make the salmon tender all the way through, and I add brandy for the taste of it. To drink with gravlax I prefer a cold Moselle wine or an equally well-chilled Riesling.

Ingredients:
1 kg fresh salmon with the skin on (preferably from the middle of the fish)
2 dl caster sugar
1 dl salt (not mineral salt)
1 dl water
2 bunches of dill, rough-chopped
1 tbsp crushed white pepper
1 tbsp brandy

Garnish:
plenty of dill sprigs
wedges of lemon

Serve with:
toast and butter
Head Waiter sauce or dill-creamed potatoes

Procedure:
Scrape all the scales off the salmon if the fishmonger hasn't done so already. Make sure there are no bones left. Mix all the marinade ingredients to a paste. Rub this into the salmon all round and put the salmon in a deep bowl or a plastic bag. Pour the rest of the marinade over the fish, making sure it is evenly distributed. Store in a cold place for at least two days, turning the fish at least once to ensure the marinade reaches every part of it.

Remove the salmon and wipe it clean with kitchen tissue. Cut the flesh from the skin but leave a few mm behind. Divide the flesh into four or eight pieces. Cut the skin into eight strips; this is a delicacy in itself.

Arrange the salmon on a large serving dish or on plates direct. Heat a frying pan without any fat in it and grill the strips of skin till they are golden brown and crisp on both sides. Remove them, roll them up and insert a few dill sprigs. Arrange them decoratively on the serving dish. Serve immediately, with Head Waiter sauce and toast or creamed potatoes.

Hints:
Instead of dill you can use fine-chopped chives in the creamed potatoes. The gravlax too will be very tasty if you quickly grill it before serving.

Beef salad serves 4

Let's face it. Beef salad can be a purely leftover business, made using the remains of a Sunday joint, salt brisket or roast beef. But just as with Swedish hash (pyttipanna), properly thought through it can be a treat for the gods, given the right ingredients. There is plenty of scope here for your own imagination, and by way of encouragement I can reveal that no two of my own beef salads are ever alike. This, roughly speaking, is how one of them turned out.

Ingredients:
400 g cooked cold roast beef
1 onion
1 red onion
200–300 g cold boiled potatoes
2 tomatoes
1/2 cucumber
about 1 dl large capers or about 2 tbsp small ones
1 frisée lettuce (aka. curly endive)
about 1 handful of rocket
1 batch of vinaigrette sauce

Serve with:
fresh-baked coarse rye bread or a crisp baguette

Procedure:
Peel and shred the onions. Cut up all the ingredients nicely. Whisk the vinaigrette sauce together. Carefully fold the salad ingredients together, adding the sauce. Add a little pepper to taste.

Other possible ingredients, apart from those I have now mentioned, are iceberg lettuce, finely cut red paprika, strips of fresh radish, sticks of salt gherkin, and croutons fried in butter.

Vinaigrette sauce serves 4–6

Make a big batch of vinaigrette sauce while you're at it and store it in the fridge. You can use this vinaigrette for many different purposes – not only with green salads but also with chicken salad, Greek salad, ham and cheese salad and pasta salads, to mention just a few examples. And of course you can double the quantities.

Ingredients:
2 tsp Dijon mustard
1/2 dl red wine vinegar
1/2 dl water
3 dl olive oil
1 crushed clove of garlic
salt and pepper

Procedure:
Put all the ingredients in a bowl. Whisk till you have a fluffy, almost creamy vinaigrette, the way it goes when water and olive oil mingle. Taste carefully to see if you need more seasoning or more olive oil. Keep tasting from time to time, depending on what the vinaigrette is going to be used for.

109

Hints:
Chopped fresh herbs, flat-leaf parsley, chives, tarragon or capers cut small – depending on the end in view – will heighten the flavour of the vinaigrette.

And another thing. If you stir a hard-boiled egg chopped fine into a dl or so of vinaigrette, you get a very good sauce for putting on fresh-cooked cauliflower.

Danish roast beef with gravy potatoes

serves 4

For a number of years during my childhood the family lived in Helsingborg (spelt Hälsingborg in those days, but no matter). Sometimes we would catch the ferry and have Sunday dinner on the other side of Öresund, in Denmark. Then we would often order a great Danish roast beef with onions roasted whole and potatoes cooked in gravy. For a small boy, those were memorable excursions to a foreign land.

I believe this is more or less how the Danes went about preparing that seductive roast beef of theirs. As you see, I've included a really big piece of meat, but the leftovers can be used for several different things: beef salad, meat soup, *pyttipanna* or, quite simply, a number of good Swedo-Danish open sandwiches (*smørrebrød* in Danish).

Ingredients:
about 2 kg marbled sirloin
1 tsp thyme
plenty of medium-large onions
800 g potatoes
11/2 dl red wine
butter and oil for frying
salt and pepper

Gravy:
3 dl meat juices
3 dl water
2–3 tbsp concentrated veal stock (from a bottle)

Garnish:
a handful of cress

Procedure:
Set the oven to 225°C. Season the meat carefully and rub it with thyme. Brown the meat nicely all round in a frying pan. Transfer to a roasting tin or a big oven-proof dish and place on the middle shelf of the oven.

Peel the onions but leave the tops. Cut the potatoes into segments; no need to peel them if they are new. Deglaze the frying pan with 3 dl water. Stir together the ingredients for the gravy and bring to the boil.

Remove the roasting tin from the oven after about 20 minutes and place the onions and potatoes round the meat. Insert a roasting thermometer in the thickest part of the meat. Pour on the wine and gravy and return the roasting tin to the oven. When the inside temperature of the beef reaches about 60°C, it's done. Remove it from the roasting tin and wrap it in aluminium foil. Leave the onions and potatoes in the oven to finish roasting.

Leave the meat for about 30 minutes and then carve it in thin slices. Arrange it on a warm serving dish with the onions, potatoes and remaining gravy round it. Garnish with a generous handful of cress.

Hints:
This is how to make a really good Swedo-Danish *smørrebrød*:

Butter a slice of coarse rye bread. Put a big lettuce leaf on it, followed by a few slices of roast beef. Garnish with rings of red onion, pearl onions, roasted onion, slices of radish, red or black currant jelly, pickled gherkin and/or salt gherkin. Finish off with a little flake salt and pepper. Two sandwiches like this and a glass of beer make the perfect lunch for a male Viking, while one should do for his ladylove.

Cheeks of veal with mashed potato serves 4

There is absolutely no reason why posh restaurants should monopolise the best food made from slightly odd but first-class Swedish raw materials. Cheeks of veal with your very finest potato purée are a dinner treat that should be prepared two days in advance, because the meat has to be marinated and then, to make it really tender, needs to simmer in the oven for close on four hours.

If the meat is then left to soak in the good sauce for another 24 hours, it will improve still further. Invest in a full-bodied, full-flavoured red wine to go with it, and you will have feast for the gods.

Ingredients:
about 1 kg veal cheeks
3–4 tbsp white flour
2 veal stock cubes or 2 tbsp concentrated veal stock
butter for frying
water
salt and pepper

Marinade:
1 onion
1 carrot
1 tsp thyme
1 bottle of small (i.e. low-alcohol) beer – *svagdricka* (33 cl)
2 dl apple juice or cider
3 black peppercorns
1/2 shredded leek (the white part)
2 bay leaves
a few parsley stalks

Garnish:
1 handful of button onions
8–10 baby carrots
1 handful of sugar snap peas
1 handful of string beans
12 sage leaves
12 button mushrooms
300 g seedless grapes
butter for frying
pepper (if needed)

Serve with:
mashed potato (see page 103)

Procedure:
Day 1. Trim the meat carefully, removing any glands and membranes. Peel the onion and chop fine. Peel the carrot and slice thinly. Mix the marinade ingredients in a mixing bowl and put in the meat. Leave in a cold place to marinate for 24 hours.

Day 2. Set the oven to 150°C. Remove the meat from the marinade, drain it and then pat it with a little kitchen tissue. Reserve the marinade. Turn the meat in white flour, season all round. Brown the meat in butter in a frying pan until it is nicely coloured. Pour on the marinade, add the stock cubes or concentrated stock and bring everything to the boil. Skim carefully.

Transfer the meat to a roasting tin or some other oven-proof vessel. Pour on the marinade, diluting if necessary with a little water so as to cover the meat. Cover with grease-proof paper and a lid. Put in the oven for the better part of 4 hours. (Remember, this is a very powerful muscle and therefore needs a lot of time in the oven.) Test with a skewer when the meat starts to feel tender.

Remove the meat and skim the fat from the juices. Bring it briefly to the boil, season to taste. Now strain the sauce and return the meat. Thus far, everything can be done beforehand. It is a good idea for the meat to stand for 24 hours and soak up the good sauce.

Day 3. Prepare the garnish while the meat is being heated in the sauce. Peel the button onions. Brush and perhaps peel the carrots. Top and tail the sugar snap peas and string beans. Cook the vegetables in lightly salted water for, at most, 5 minutes, turn them in butter and, if you like, add a little pepper to taste. Halve the button mushrooms and grapes. Fry the mushrooms in butter in a frying pan. Add the grapes and sage. Add salt and pepper. Arrange the meat, mashed potato, sauce and trimmings nicely on warm plates and serve at once.

Hints:
To vary things, the small beer in the marinade can be replaced with just apple juice, genuine French cider, red wine or a full-flavoured white wine.

Nettle and spinach soup serves 4

Nettle soup with egg halves is a quintessentially Swedish spring special with a splendid characteristic flavour. It is good and satisfying, and above all proclaims the imminence of summer. But nettle soup can be a little tedious and pallid if simmered a few minutes too many.

So why not try this modern version, which keeps its colour better and can be combined with several tasty trimmings?

It is when you come to prepare a party soup like this one that you benefit from having some good stock put by.

Ingredients:
1 l young nettles
1/2 l fresh spinach
4 shallots
2 cloves of garlic
2 tsp whole aniseed
2 sprigs of thyme, chopped fine
1 bay leaf
1 dl dry sherry
1 l veal or chicken stock
1 slice of smoked pork
butter for frying
100 g butter at room temperature
1/2 tbsp lemon juice
salt and pepper

Garnish, e.g.:
4 boiled chicken or quails' eggs
1 bunch of lightly cooked fresh asparagus tips
boiled florets of broccoli
smoked eel
smoked salmon
crisp-fried bacon
chives

Procedure:
Clean and rinse the nettles and spinach. Remove the leaves but reserve the stalks. Blanche the nettle leaves and 2/3 of the spinach leaves in boiling water for about 30 seconds. Pour off the water and put the leaves in ice water for a couple of minutes, then take them out of the water and put them aside for the moment.

Peel and chop the shallots. Peel and chop the garlic. Sauté the onion, garlic, herbs and spices and spinach and nettle stalks in butter for a few minutes. Pour on the sherry and stock and simmer for about 30 minutes. Strain off the stock and discard the rest. Thus far the soup can be prepared in advance.

Put the blanched nettle and spinach leaves in a food processor together with the butter and lemon juice. Pour on the boiling stock and run the processor. Strain the soup and return it to the saucepan. Shred the remaining spinach leaves and put them in as well. Bring to the boil. Season to taste.

Serve, preferably, straightway in heated plates and with the garnish of your choice, e.g. triangles of white bread au gratin.

Hints:
The stock you make and strain also makes a good foundation for other soups, e.g. broccoli, parsley, ramson or spinach.

Calf's liver pâté with button mushrooms and bacon serves 4

Liver paste in all its forms is one of the biggest favourites of all, both on Swedish breakfast tables and as part of the now world-famous smorgasbord. Why not try making your own? It isn't difficult, and you can be certain of your pains being rewarded by the family's appreciation. This pâté can be garnished and supplemented in any number of different ways, e.g. as pictured.

Ingredients:
500 g calf's or pig's liver
3–4 dl milk
300 fat pork
6 Swedish "anchovy" fillets
1 onion
1 tbsp "anchovy" liquor
1 tbsp white flour
2 dl whipping cream
2 eggs
1 tbsp concentrated veal stock
1/2 tsp dried thyme
1 tsp dried marjoram
1/2 tsp ground ginger
1 tbsp Kikkoman soy
butter for frying
salt and pepper

Garnish:	*Serve with:*
100 g button mushrooms	rye bread, toasted crisp bread
140 g bacon	(se page 50) or farmhouse bread
some parsley leaves	pickled gherkins (see page 119)
1 onion	or salt gherkins
butter for frying	

Procedure:
Remove membranes and arteries from the liver and cut it into pieces about 2 cm large. Pour on milk and leave in a cold place for 4–5 hours, preferably overnight.

Set the oven to 175°C and put in a bain-marie. Cut up the pork. Grind the liver and pork together with the "anchovies". Chop the onion small and fry half of it in a little butter in a frying pan (the rest will be added raw). Mix all the ingredients together into a smooth, even paste. Fry a sample and test the seasoning.

Transfer the mixture to a greased 2-litre pâté tin or a Teflon mould, cover with oiled greaseproof paper or aluminium foil and bake for about 1 hour in the bain-marie. Test with a skewer to see when the pâté is done. It's ready when the needle comes out clean. Remove the greaseproof paper for the last 20 minutes, to give the pâté a nicely baked surface.

Peel and rough-chop the onion. Cut up the mushrooms and bacon. Brown them in butter in a frying pan until they start looking scrumpy. Strain off the surplus fat.

Serve the pâté warm or cold on rye bread, toasted crisp bread or fresh-baked farmhouse bread together with the "scrumped-up" mushrooms and bacon and pickled gherkin.

Pickled gherkin

Pickled Västerås gherkins are a very useful accessory, especially with roasts but also on liver paste sandwiches. I have two or three different recipes which I ring the changes with. Try this one, which is a little spicier. It might seem awkward, but it's well worth the trouble. For one thing, the gherkins come out nicer, and secondly, they are fully preserved and will keep for at least a year in a cool, dark cellar.

Ingredients:
3 kg Västerås gherkins
1 red paprika
2–3 onions
a piece of horseradish
dill crowns
1–2 tbsp yellow mustard seeds
20–25 black peppercorns

Pickling liquid:
8 dl water
5 dl Swedish distilled vinegar, ättika (12% strength)
1.1 l caster sugar
1 1/2 dl salt

Procedure:
Day 1. Soak the gherkins in water and brush them well. Rinse them under the tap and wipe them dry with a tea towel. Cut them diagonally into slices about 1/2 cm thick.

Divide the paprika, remove the white membranes and the seeds and cut up small. Peel the onions and cut them up quite large. Peel and dice the horseradish. Put alternate layers of sliced gherkin, onion, paprika and spices into a big jar, beginning and ending with dill crowns.

Bring the pickling liquid ingredients to the boil in a saucepan. Stir until the salt and sugar are thoroughly dissolved. Skim if necessary. Carefully pour the hot liquid over the gherkins. Put a plate or some other *ättika*-resistant weight on top of the gherkins to press them down. The gherkins will not be instantly submerged, but more liquid will gradually form as they are leeched out. Put them to stand for 24 hours.

Day 2. Set the oven to 100–125°C. Wash up sine glass jars and lids and rinse them thoroughly. Put in the oven on a newspaper for at least 10 minutes.

Pour the liquid from the gherkins into a saucepan and bring it to the boil. Meanwhile remove the gherkins from the oven and fill the jars with alternate layers of gherkins and spices. Fill up with boiling liquid and screw the caps tight immediately. After an hour or so you will hear a distinct click from the caps, signifying that your pickle is now an extremely durable preserve. Store the jars in a cool, dark place. Your gherkins will be ready for sampling after a week.

Cabbage dolmades serves 6

I love cabbage in any form and perhaps dolmades best of all. Sometimes you hear it said that dolmades are really Turkish, not Swedish, but considering they arrived here almost 300 years ago with those of Charles XII's warriors who made it back home, I think we can consider them naturalised.

Making good dolmades really is an art. Personally I don't like the farce to be too firm, and so instead of rice I always use cabbage leftovers chopped fine and a few mashed boiled potatoes. This brings out the cabbage flavour and heightens the experience. With this particular treat I find it hard to imagine drinking anything but vodka and beer.

Ingredients:
800 g mixed (pork and beef) mince
1 cabbage, Savoy cabbage or wild cabbage/kale
1 onion
butter for frying
1 cold boiled potato or the corresponding amount of mash
2 dl milk
1 dl dried breadcrumbs
2 eggs
4 tbsp Kikkoman soy
2 tbsp golden syrup
2 tbsp concentrated veal stock
2 tbsp melted butter
1 tbsp brown sugar
salt and pepper

Sauce:
6 dl gravy sauce
2 bay leaves
10 black peppercorns

Service with:
mashed or riced potato
pressed cucumber (see page 26)
uncooked, stirred lingonberry jam (see page 25)

Procedure:
Cut the stalk out of the cabbage head and parboil it in lightly salted water for about 15 minutes. Remove with a slotted spoon and carefully detach the good leaves. Cut away the hard central vein in each leaf, then put the leaves on a chopping board.

Set the oven to 200°C. Peel the onion and chop small, chop the remains of the cabbage small and fry everything in a little butter. Mash the potato with a fork. Mix milk and dried bread crumbs with the mashed potato and the fried onion and cabbage mixture. Leave to swell for about 10 minutes. Blend this mixture with the mince, eggs, soy, golden syrup and concentrated veal stock. Add salt and pepper. Stir quickly to a loose batter. Test-fry a small dob of the mixture to check the seasoning.

Dab the mixture onto the cabbage leaves, roll them up tightly into neat dolmades and put them in a greased oven-proof dish. Brush them with butter, and sprinkle them with pepper (from the mill), a pinch of salt and the brown sugar.

Bake on the middle shelf of the oven for about 30 minutes, until they are a nice colour all round, then add the gravy sauce and spices. Lower the heat to 150°C. Braise for another 30–40 minutes, basting frequently with the juices.

Serve piping hot with fluffy mashed potato or riced potato, pressed cucumber and uncooked, stirred lingonberry jam.

Gravy sauce

Gravy and gravy sauce hardly ever get made the same way twice. The secret is to capture and use all the flavours present in the meat juices, and this, you will appreciate, is not an exact science.

Your starting point, as the name suggests, is the gravy you get from a joint in the oven or by deglazing a frying pan with a little water after frying meatballs or steaks. Another method is that of browning and braising pork, veal or lamb bones in the oven and pouring water over them from time to time.

For a stronger flavour, the juices can then be blended with a couple of teaspoons of bottled concentrated beef or veal stock or home-made stock from braising meat, or again a small tub of concentrated meat stock stored in your freezer.

If you fancy a little thickening, start by melting 1 tbsp butter in a saucepan and stirring in a heaped teaspoon of flour before adding the gravy. You can also whisk in a couple of teaspoons of corn starch flour dissolved in a little water. Strain the gravy if you see fit, and then season to taste. Gravy can also be flavoured with butter, a herb, a tablespoon of "anchovy" liquor, a dob of black or red currant jelly or a few crushed juniper berries.

Cod fricassee with shellfish sauce

This is just the thing for a Saturday when you have extra time to spare for one of the finest fish in the sea. I like me, you think we should take all the warnings seriously and hold back on eating cod, you can get equally good results with haddock or hake. Serve a reasonable-quality dry or semi-dry white wine with it.

Ingredients:
600 g thick fillets of cod, haddock or hake
8 Norway lobster tails or 16 crayfish tails
200 g shrimps, unpeeled
1 1 net bag of mussels (about 1 kg)
2 carrots
1 leek (the white part)
1/2 kg potatoes
butter for frying
salt and pepper

Shellfish stock:
the shells of the crayfish and shrimps
1 onion
2 tbsp olive oil
1 dl white wine
the mussel liquid
3–4 dl water

Fricassee sauce:
1 tbsp butter
1 tbsp white flour
3 dl milk with the top on (2 1/2 dl milk, 1/2 dl cream)
2 dl reduced shellfish stock
salt and pepper

Garnish:
a few sprigs of parsley

Procedure:
If you have shopped whole crayfish, boil them and leave them to cool in the cooking liquid. Peel the shrimps and crayfish, reserving the shells.

Scrub the mussels in cold water, discarding the ones that don't clam up. Boil them in 2–3 dl water for 5–6 minutes, stirring several times. Remove them, e.g. with a slotted spoon, when they have opened. Leave them to cool a little before picking away the flesh. Reserve the cooking liquid.

Make the stock. Cut the heads and stomachs off the crayfish shells. Crush the shells into small pieces. Peel and slice the onion. Fry it in the oil in a saucepan for a couple of minutes without letting it change colour. Put in the crayfish and shrimp shells and pour on the wine, the mussel stock and the water. Bring to the boil, then simmer for 10–12 minutes. Strain the stock from the shells and reduce to about 2 dl.

Set the oven to 200°C. Peel the carrots and cut them into sticks. Clean the leek and cut it in rings. Fry the vegetables in a little butter for 2–3 minutes and remove from the heat. Peel the potatoes and pre-cook them for about 10 minutes before cutting them into thick slices. Clean the fish and cut it up neatly. Season the pieces, put them in a greased oven-proof dish with room for the other ingredients and bake in the oven for 10–12 minutes.

Meanwhile, make the sauce. Heat the cream and milk in a saucepan. Sauté the butter and flour quickly in another saucepan. Add the cream and milk to this and beat to a smooth sauce. Dilute with the shellfish stock and season to taste.

Remove the fish from the oven and add the potato, vegetables, crayfish tails, shrimps and mussels. Drizzle with the sauce and return to the oven for another 5–6 minutes. Garnish the fricassee with parsley leaves and serve piping hot.

123

Hints:
The mussels and stock will taste even better if you add 1 tbsp butter and 1 dl white wine when cooking them.

Leg of lamb with caper sauce, shredded leek and cheesy mashed potato serves 4

This is a lamb recipe with a difference, for which the legs of lamb can very well be cooked a day in advance, together with vegetables and herbs, and then left to soak in their own stock. Just the thing for a rough autumn day when the tempest is ripping the last leaves from the trees and you need something really warm inside you. Moreover, lamb is at its best in autumn and plentifully available at any meat counter worthy of the name.

Ingredients:
4 hind legs of lamb (about 1 1/2 kg)
1 leek (the green part)
2 carrots
2 bay leaves
1/2 bunch of parsley stalks
10 white peppercorns
2 tsp salt per litre of water

Cheesy mashed potato:
1 kg floury potatoes
2 dl lamb stock
a few scrapes of nutmeg
1 tbsp butter
1 1/2 dl grated Västerbotten or suchlike cheese
salt and pepper

Caper sauce:
2 dl reduced lamb stock
1 tbsp butter
1 tbsp white flour
2 dl whipping cream
1 tbsp liquor from the capers
1 tsp caster sugar
1/2 bunch of flat-leaf parsley, chopped small
3 tbsp capers
salt and pepper

Garnish:
1 leek (only the white part)
2 carrots (if required)
lamb stock

Procedure:
Put the meat in a large casserole with water and bring to the boil. Boil briskly for a few minutes, then remove and rinse the meat. Clean the pot and return the meat, pouring on fresh water. Clean and cut up the green of the leek. (Save the white for garnish.) Peel and cut up the carrots. Bring the lamb to the boil once more and put the other ingredients in with it. Simmer for about 1 1/2 hours until the meat starts to come away from the bone. Remove from the heat and leave the meat to soak up the stock.

Peel the potatoes and boil them in lightly salted water. Mash them roughly with an old-fashioned potato masher. Dilute to the right consistency with lamb stock from cooking the meat. Add nutmeg, butter, salt and pepper to taste. Keep warm.

Reduce 1/2 l of the lamb stock to about 2 dl. Sauté the butter for the sauce in a saucepan and whisk in the flour. Whisk in the reduced stock and cream, bring to the boil and simmer till the sauce starts to thicken. Add caper liquor, sugar and seasoning to taste. The caper liquor and sugar give the sauce a sweet-sour touch. Add the parsley and capers.

Clean the white of the leek and cut it in strips. Peel the carrots, if you are including them, and cut them crosswise. Simmer the vegetables for a minute or so in a little lamb stock and then remove them with a slotted spoon. Warm the meat and put the garnish on top. Serve immediately with the cheesy mashed potato and caper sauce.

Braised leg of veal serves 4

I love slow cooking of every kind, for a number of reasons. For one thing, the food takes care of itself most of the time, and for another, this way relatively simple raw materials can be turned into fragrant sensations. Braised leg of veal, whole or sliced, must have figured on the Swedish bill of fare from time immemorial.

Leg of veal done the Italian way is called osso bucco and is of far more recent origin. To catch the Italian ambience, serve the veal with a mild saffron risotto and a light Italian red wine.

Ingredients:
4 slices of leg of veal with the marrow bone (250 g each)
white flour for dredging
butter and olive oil for frying
about 1/2 dl water
1 onion
3 cloves of garlic
2 dl white wine
3 dl veal stock
2 dl tomato juice
1 tbsp tomato purée
2 lemons
1 bunch of flat-leaf parsley, the stalks
2 bay leaves
2 sprigs of thyme
1 carrot
1 parsnip, diced
a wedge of celeriac (about 150 g)
butter for frying
salt and pepper

Gremolata:
1 clove of garlic
grated zest of 1 lemon
about 1 dl shredded parsley leaves
2 tbsp olive oil

Saffron risotto:
3 dl avori rice
1 shallot, chopped small
2–3 tbsp olive oil for frying
1/2 g saffron
1 dl white wine
5 dl chicken stock
3 tbsp grated Parmesan cheese
1/2–1 tbsp lemon juice
2 tbsp butter
salt

Procedure:
Dredge the legs of veal in the flour, fry them golden brown in the oil and butter. Set aside, deglazing the pan with water if the fat has not burned. Reserve the pan juices.

Peel and chop onion and garlic, then sauté them in butter in a saucepan, pour on the wine and bring to the boil. Next pour in the veal stock, tomato juice, tomato purée and pan juices. Reduce for a few minutes by about half. Meanwhile grate the lemon zest and squeeze the juice from the lemons. Pick off the parsley leaves. Flavour the stock with lemon juice and zest, and put in the parsley stalks, bay leaves and sprigs of thyme. Season to taste.

Pour the stock over the meat in a sauté pan or suchlike and braise over a low flame for about 1 hour or until the meat is thoroughly tender.

Peel the root vegetables, cut them into cm cubes and add them with about 20 minutes cooking time left to go.

Prepare the ingredients for the gremolata. Peel the clove of garlic and chop small. Mix with the other ingredients.

Peel the shallot and chop small. Sauté rice, onion and saffron in the olive oil. Add salt. Gradually pour on the wine and stock and cook the rice until it is soft and creamy. Finally, stir in the Parmesan and lemon juice and glaze with the butter.

Serve the meat piping hot together with the gremolata and saffron risotto.

127

Fish soup serves 4

In coastal communities at least, fish soup has been a staple item on both the weekday and festive menu from time immemorial. Recipes vary, of course, depending on what is caught, but I hold it true whate'er befall that the quality of your fish soup stands or falls by a proper home-made fish stock. So if you want to excel in this field, I strongly recommend you to begin, a day in advance if you can, on page 250 by making a good fish stock, and then carry on from here.

Ingredients:
600 g cod, haddock, pike-perch or whitefish
6 Norway lobsters or 250 g peeled shrimps
1 onion
1 carrot
1 fennel bulb
1/2 dl olive oil for frying
2 cloves of garlic
1 tsp tomato purée
2 bay leaves
1 dl dry white wine
1 1/2 l fish stock (see page 250)
10 small tomatoes
1 handful of sugar snap peas
2 handfuls of string beans
12–16 fresh mussels
1 packet (1/2 g) of saffron
2 cl Pernod
1 bunch of spring onions (scallions)
salt and pepper

Service with:
1/2 bunch flat-leafed parsley, chopped small
toasted baguette, sliced
aïoli
grated Parmesan cheese

Procedure:
Make the fish stock, a day in advance if possible.

Get out a casserole big enough for all the ingredients to have plenty of room without breaking up. For the same reason, this soup must never be boiled fiercely.

Peel the onion and carrot and cut them up in strips. Clean and shred the fennel. Sauté in oil in a pot without it changing colour. Add the tomato purée, garlic, bay leaf, wine and fish stock. Add salt and pepper, then simmer gently for 5–6 minutes. Meanwhile cut up the fish and Norway lobsters into "mouthpieces". Divide the tomatoes. Top and tail the sugar snap peas and string beans and split them. Cut up the spring onion. Wash the mussels carefully in running water. Add the tomatoes, peas, beans, mussels, saffron, spring onion and Pernod to the pot. Put in the fish and simmer the soup for 5 minutes at most.

Add the pieces of crayfish or the shrimps 2 minutes before serving. Sprinkle with parsley immediately before serving. Serve together with toasted baguette, fresh-made aïoli and grated Parmesan. Put the soup in the middle of the table and serve straight from the pot, so that everyone round the table can see all the beautiful and wholesome ingredients floating about in the delicious bouillon.

Hints:
The bread will turn out extra crisp and good if you brush the slices or wedges with olive oil, dip them in grated Parmesan, sprinkle them with a few flakes of salt and grill them a nice colour in the oven.

Aïoli serves 4–5

Aïoli originated in Provence, where they really love the fragrance of garlic. But half a century of frequent foreign travel has also given us Swedes a fondness for the tempting flavour of garlic added to different kinds of cooking. Aïoli is a creamy sauce and an almost inseparable companion of good fish soup and boiled fish, but a good accompaniment to roast lamb, freshly cooked young vegetables and hard-boiled eggs. Get out the ingredients in time, so that they will all be the same temperature, otherwise the sauce is very liable to curdle.

Ingredients:
4 cloves of garlic
3 egg yolks
2 1/2 dl olive oil or rapeseed oil
1/2–1 tbsp water
1/2 pinch Cayenne pepper
salt and pepper

Procedure:
Peel and crush the garlic cloves and put them in a bowl together with the egg yolks. Drip the oil onto the egg segments, whisking all the time. Gradually the sauce will thicken and heavenly aromas will be wafted through the kitchen. Thin the sauce a little with water towards the end and season to taste with salt, pepper and a little Cayenne pepper.

Crisp-fried pork pancakes serves 4

This, in my opinion, is the best way of doing real crisp-fried pancakes. You fry them on the hob. The batter contains a lot of egg but not much flour. Soda water is the "secret" of the extra crispness. This batch should be enough for 8 pancakes, 2 per person, and the pancakes ought preferably to be served piping hot, straight from the griddle.

Ingredients:
400 g salt pancetta
5 eggs
2 dl sifted white flour
3 dl milk
2 dl cream
1/2 tsp caster sugar
1/2 tsp salt
1/2 tbsp butter for frying
1 dl soda water

Serve with:
uncooked, stirred lingonberry jam (see page 25)

Procedure:
Beat the eggs fluffy in a large mixing bowl. Sift over the flour and whisk together. Add the milk, cream, sugar and salt, beating to a smooth mixture. If small lumps remain, strain them through a coarse sieve. Put the bowl aside for the batter to swell a little.

Divide the pork into 2–3 cm pieces. Crisp-fry these in a little butter, then drain on kitchen tissue. Reserve the fat in the pan.

Stir the soda water into the batter. Heat a pancake griddle, put in 1 tsp dripping, a small knob of butter and a few bits of pork. Pour on just under 1 dl batter and spread over the griddle. Fry the pancakes nice and crispy and golden brown on both sides. Serve instantly with the uncooked, stirred lingonberry jam.

130

"Meadow food" vegetable soup serves 4

This is typical Swedish summertime fare at its very best. Take the opportunity of making it one day when the sun is beating down and not so much energy is needed. It's a soup for all kinds of seasonal vegetables, when they turn up in the shops or it's payback time in your garden. There's no meat in this soup, yet it still takes on a mild, distinctive flavour which goes well together with toasted crisp bread and a well-ripened cheese.

Ingredients:
4–5 potatoes, new if possible
2–3 carrots, young ones if obtainable
1 parsnip
1 onion
butter for frying
1–2 sticks of celery
a bunch of sugar snap peas
a bunch of broad beans
1/2 head of spring cabbage
1/2 leek
1 small head of broccoli
1 l chicken/pork/cube stock
2 dl whipping cream
1/2 bunch parsley
2 pinches dried thyme
a few scrapes of nutmeg
6 egg yolks
a knob of butter
salt
pepper

Garnish:
1/2 bunch parsley, chopped fine
4 egg yolks

Serve with:
toasted crisp bread (see page 50)
well-matured cheese

Procedure:
Peel and clean the root vegetables and cut them in small pieces. Peel and chop the onion and sauté everything in butter for about 5 minutes, stirring all the time and not letting it change colour.

Prepare the other vegetables. Shred the spring cabbage, top and tail the sugar snap peas. Needless to say, you use only the actual beans of the broad beans, not the pods, and if the beans are big ones you should peel them too.

Pour the stock over the sautéed mixture. Add the cream. Then add the vegetables – not all at once, because they have different cooking times – and the thyme. Save the broad beans, broccoli and fine-chopped rings of leek till last and put them in with the chopped parsley. Season with salt, pepper and a few scrapes of nutmeg.

Remove the soup from the heat when you think the vegetables are done, and thicken with the egg yolks, one by one. The soup mustn't boil again after this.

Finish off with chopped parsley and feel free to garnish with an extra egg yolk. Serve immediately with the proposed accessories or with something else you like better.

135

Mutton and cabbage stew   serves 6

This classic recipe has to be prepared in autumn, and preferably a day in advance, to give the different flavours time to blend properly and the meat to get even tastier.

Nowadays the "mutton" is usually lamb. You can use the left-over stock for making cabbage soup with veal mince balls, pork sausage or fried chipolatas – another autumn treat with a long ancestry. Bread, butter and well-matured cheese go very well with this dish, as well as spicy vodka and beer or mineral water.

Ingredients:
2–2 1/2 kg lamb (breast, shoulder or foreleg)
6–8 white peppercorns
8–10 pinches of allspice corns
3–4 whole cloves
4 bay leaves
salt
1 small turnip
1 kohlrabi
2–3 carrots
1–2 parsnips
1 kg potatoes
1 small head of cabbage
15–20 Brussels sprouts
1 leek
3–4 shallots
1–2 cloves of garlic
1/2–1 cauliflowers
1 small Savoy cabbage

Garnish:
flat-leafed parsley

Serve with:
toasted crisp bread (see page 20)
matured cheese
real butter

Procedure (roughly):
Cut the meat into chunks after first trimming away surplus fat. If you have bought legs they should be whole. Put the meat in a big casserole, pour on enough water to cover and bring to the boil. Continue boiling, gently, for not more than one minute. Remove the meat and rinse it under the cold tap. Clean the pot, return the meat. Pour on enough water to cover, measuring how much you use (and remember there will have to be room for all the vegetables too). Bring the meat to the boil. Skim it and add the spices, beginning with 1 tsp salt per litre of water.

Prepare the vegetables in the order you will be putting them into the pot. Turnip and kohlrabi are hard and need most cooking time. Peel and quarter them. Peel the carrots, parsnips and potatoes, cutting the carrots into sticks and the parsnips and potatoes into chunks. Cut the cabbage into fairly big wedges. Clean and halve the sprouts. Clean and cut up the leek, including some of the green if you like. Peel and divide the shallots, peel the garlic. Divide the cauliflower into large florets. Cut the Savoy cabbage into rough quarters.

Start putting in the vegetables when the meat has been cooking for 30 or 40 minutes, at the same time checking the seasoning. Add the vegetables in the following order: kohlrabi, turnip, carrots, parsnip, potatoes, cabbage sprouts, onion, leek, cauliflower and Savoy. Add more salt to taste.

After 1 1/2 hours at most, probably less, everything should be ready. The meat is done when it comes away from the bones. Garnish with flat-leafed parsley and put the pot on the table, or else carefully transfer everything to a thoroughly preheated serving dish.

Jansson's Temptation serves 4

This recipe is said to have been named after the opera singer Per Adolf "Pelle" Janzon (1844–1889) who invited some friends home one night, only to find that his larder was empty except for potatoes, Swedish "anchovies" onion and a dash of cream.

Personally I've experimented with several variants of Jansson. Try this one, made in individual tins with detachable rims. Remember, though, that for proper Jansson's Temptation, only genuine Swedish "anchovy" fillets, made from sprats, and whipping cream will do. Most people probably serve this delicacy with vodka and beer, and perhaps too toasted crisp bread.

Ingredients:
400 g potatoes
2 onions
butter for frying and brushing
"anchovy" liquor
2 tins (125 g each) of genuine "anchovy" fillets
2 dl whipping cream
salt and pepper

Procedure:
Set the oven to 175°C. Peel the potatoes and cut some of them into thin slices (to line the tins with). Shred the rest. Peel the onion and cut it into uniform strips, sautéing these golden brown in a saucepan. Add the strips of potato and the "anchovy" liquor, pour on the cream. Season to taste, stir and leave to bubble for about 5 minutes over a low flame.

Brush the tins well with butter at room temperature, then line the bottom and sides of each one with slices of potato. Fill up with alternate layers of the onion-and-potato mixture and "anchovy" fillets, ending with the mixture uppermost, topped with a few extra "anchovy" fillets if possible. Bake on the middle shelf of the oven for about 45 minutes or until golden-brown bubbles have formed on the surface.

Remove from the oven and leave for a minute or so. Remove the side and carefully transfer the Temptation to a plate; a wide frying spatula, for example, will come in useful for this purpose.

Ingredients:
1 red onion
2 hard-boiled eggs
2 tins (125 g each) of genuine Swedish "anchovy" fillets
1/2 bundle of chives, chopped small
1/2 bundle of dill, chopped small
butter for frying
salt and pepper

Serve with:
toasted crisp bread (see page 50)
butter

Procedure:
Peel the red onion and chop small. Shell and chop the eggs. Cut up the "anchovy" fillets. Begin by sautéing the onion in butter without it changing colour. Add the chopped egg and sauté for another minute or so. Add the other ingredients, fold everything in carefully and serve instantly, with bread and butter.

Warm gubbröra serves 4

Erik "Bullen" Berglund, an actor who was both gourmand and gourmet and whose portrait still adorns the label on a certain brand of tinned sausages, was good at this kind of extra treat, and his books of recipes are still sought after in Swedish antiquarian bookshops.

"Bullen" would have loved this quick recipe, especially if there had been a couple of ice-cold vodkas to go with it.

Two casseroles of Baltic herring serves 4–6

Believe it or not, but you can write a whole book about herring and Baltic herring and still have lots of wonderful variants missing.

Baltic herring roulades with "anchovy" were my grandmother's absolute favourite casserole, and she always made it at Christmastime.

Baltic herring roulades with Swedish anchovy

Ingredients:
20 Baltic herring fillets
butter for the dish

Marinade:
2 tins of "anchovy" fillets (125 g each) with the liquor
1 onion
1 bunch of chives, chopped small
one bunch of dill, chopped small
1 dl crème fraîche
1 dl whipping cream
1 tsp tomato purée
salt and pepper

Garnish:
dill

Procedure:
Set the oven to 175°C. Clean the fillets, carefully removing the dorsal fins. Chop the "anchovy" small or mash it with a fork. Peel the onion and chop small. Mix all the ingredients for the marinade thoroughly in a mixing bowl, including the "anchovy" liquor. Carefully fold in the Baltic herring fillets, mixing a little so that the marinade covers them properly. Leave in a cool place for a while, to give the fish time to absorb the flavour of the marinade.

Grease an oven-proof dish. Roll up the Baltic herring fillets, skin side outwards. Fill the dish with them and drizzle with what remains of the marinade. Grate a little butter over them and bake for 20–25 minutes, until they are nicely coloured.

Garnish with dill fronds and serve warm or lukewarm on a buffet. This casserole is best the day after, e.g. on a slice of toasted crisp bread with a cold beer.

Casserole of crayfish and tomato-flavoured Baltic herring

Ingredients:
16–20 Baltic herring fillets
butter for the dish

Marinade:
2 dl crayfish tails
1 dl tomato purée
2 dl "anchovy" liquor
1 heaped tsp crushed dill seeds
3 tbsp melted butter
1/2 dl oil
1 tbsp brown sugar
salt and pepper

Serve with:
new potatoes or rye bread
red onion chopped small

Procedure:
Set the oven to 200°C. Clean the Baltic herring fillets and carefully remove the dorsal fins. Rough-chop the crayfish tails. Blend the marinade ingredients in a mixing bowl. Carefully fold in the fillets, lifting and mixing them a little to make sure the marinade covers them properly. Put them in a cool place for a while, to give the fillets time to absorb the flavour of the marinade.

Grease an oven-proof dish. Roll up the Baltic herring fillets, skin side outwards. Pack the dish tight with them and drizzle with what remains of the marinade. Bake on the middle shelf of the oven for about 20 minutes, or until they are nicely coloured. Serve with dill-fragrant new potatoes or eat cold or lukewarm on rye bread with a little fine-chopped red onion.

Apple-glazed smoked pork with brown beans serves 4

Ola Andersson, my creative guest chef, whose track record includes captaincy of the Swedish National Cookery Team, is deeply rooted in the culinary traditions of Skåne.

This is how he likes to prepare pork and brown beans, and after sampling the result I found myself wondering why ever no one had thought of it before. So here you go. The art of home cooking at its noblest. Food for Scanians and for ordinary Vikings like you and me.

Ingredients:
700–800 g cold-smoked side of pork
500 g dried brown beans
water
1 l apple juice
liquid from cooking the pork (optional)
2 bay leaves
1 tbsp chopped thyme
2 cm cinnamon stick
2 tbsp Swedish distilled vinegar, *ättika* (12%)
1/2 dl golden syrup

Garnish:
1 apple
1/2 red onion
2–3 tbsp stewed apple (see page 85)
a few pinches of rosemary
salt and pepper

Serve with:
grated horseradish
fine-chopped chives

Procedure:
Put the beans to soak in water for a few hours, then pour off the water, transfer the beans to a casserole and pour on the apple juice. Put the whole piece of pork on top. Pour on enough water to cover (or alternatively liquid left over from cooking pork, if you happen to have it). Add salt and pepper, bay leaves, thyme and cinnamon stick. Boil the beans till they are soft, which will take about 1 1/2 hours.

Set the oven to 200°C. Remove the pork and put it to one side. Extract the bay leaves and cinnamon too. Season the beans to give the right balance between sharpness and sweetness, using the *ättika* and syrup. Check the seasoning. Keep warm.

Carefully cut away the rind from the pork, but leave the layer of fat where it is; those not wishing to eat it can cut it away at table. Cut the pork into four equal-sized pieces. Put these into a greased oven-proof dish and season them lightly. De-core the apple and dice it small. Peel the red onion and chop small. Spread the stewed apple on the pork, followed by the diced apple and the red onion. Sprinkle with rosemary and bake on the middle shelf of the oven for about 20 minutes.

Transfer the pork straight onto warm plates and garnish with grated horseradish and chives, or else do the same on a large serving dish. Enjoy it with the reheated beans.

143

Navarin of lamb serves 4

This is a dark, strong-flavoured lamb stew of French origin which has been a classic standby of equally classical Swedish restaurants for many years now.

Take the opportunity of preparing this recipe in autumn, when the meat counters are almost overflowing with fresh Swedish lamb. And autumn too is the time when we have any amount of newly harvested vegetables to feast on. The stage is set for your own imagination and talent.

Ingredients:
1 kg shoulder of lamb, off the bone, in pieces
2 onions
1 carrot
1/2 celeriac bulb (about 200 g)
1 whole bulb of garlic
2–3 tbsp white flour
butter and oil for frying
3 tbsp tomato purée
1/2 bottle of white wine
1 l beef stock
juice of 1/2 lemon
salt and pepper

Bouquet garni:
1 leek
10 sprigs of parsley
3 bay leaves
3–4 sprigs of rosemary
cotton thread

Serve with:
vegetables according to season, e.g. sugar snap peas, string beans, button onions browned and cooked in stock, young or shredded carrots, wedges of cabbage cooked in butter
riced potatoes, rice or risoni pasta

Procedure:
Start by preparing a bouquet garni. Trim the leek and cut the white part lengthwise. Tie all the ingredients together with a cotton thread.

Peel the onion, carrot and celeriac. Cut them into chunks. Half the garlic. Turn the meat in the flour and brown it all round in butter and oil in a frying pan. Remove it from the pan and brown the onion, carrot and celeriac in the same fat. Transfer the meat and vegetables to an iron casserole, adding the tomato purée, the wine and the stock. Put in the garlic and bouquet garni. Season the stock with lemon juice, salt and pepper. Simmer over a low flame for at least 1 hour, till the meat feels tender and fine. Remove the meat and strain the stock. Discard the vegetables.

Reduce the stock while preparing the vegetables you will be serving. The button onions and carrots may need up to 15 minutes' cooking to acquire the right softness.

Return the meat to the stock and bring everything to the boil. Serve the stew with the vegetables and riced potato, rice or risoni.

Boiled salted spare ribs with Alsatian potato   serves 4

Alsace is an exciting culinary region of France which my colleague Crister Svanteson and I had the benefit of visiting for a tele-recording. We sampled our way through restaurants at both ends of the market.

With one of our lunches we had some tremendously good mashed potato which we instantly christened Alsatian potato and were convinced would also go very well on a Swedish menu. It can be served with boiled, salted spare ribs, as suggested here, but also with grilled sausage, pork sausage or fried fish.

I don't remember if we drank a Riesling wine or a bitter local beer with it, but both should do equally well. Order salted ribs from your butcher. Alsatian potato can also be served with boiled leg of pork or other salted, boiled meat.

Ingredients:
1 1/2 kg salted thick spare ribs
1 onion
1 carrot
6 white peppercorns
6 allspice corns
2 bay leaves
1/2 bunch of parsley sprigs

Alsatian potato:
500 g floury potatoes
400 g sauerkraut
liquid from cooking the meat
2 tbsp butter
2 dl warm milk
100 g grated gruyere cheese, Emmenthaler or well-matured Grevé
salt and pepper

Serve with:
boiled vegetables, e.g. carrot, fresh cabbage or string beans
French mustard
grated horseradish (optional)

Procedure:
Put the meat in a big saucepan and pour on enough cold water to cover it. Bring quickly to the boil and cook for a minute or so. Change the water and bring to the boil again. Peel the onion and carrot and cut them into large pieces. Add them and the spices to the saucepan and simmer everything for about 1 hour, until the meat feels tender and starts coming away from the bone. Thus far you can prepare everything a day beforehand. Leave the meat to cool in its juice and store in a cold place.

Peel and boil the potatoes. Sauté the sauerkraut in its own liquor, stirring continuously, until it is dry. Add a little of the liquid from cooking the meat and carry on sautéing till the cabbage has browned slightly. Rice the potatoes and stir in butter, a little cooking liquid and warm milk to make a fluffy mash. Fold in the sauerkraut. Season to taste. Keep the mash warm. Stir in the cheese just before serving.

Heat the meat in its own stock. Serve it piping hot with Alsatian potato, boiled vegetables and French mustard, which you may care to flavour with grated horseradish.

147

Minced meat hazel-hens serves 4

The hazel-hen proper is a game bird that thrives best in conifer woods. It resembles the black grouse but is smaller and slightly fusiform (spool-shaped), which I suppose explains why dishes like beef hazel-hens, veal mince hazel-hens and pork hazel-hens, egg-shaped meatballs, are called after it.

For this recipe you can use any minced meat whatsoever, serving with a cream sauce, a green garnish and something pickled.

Ingredients:
800 g minced meat, game if possible
1/2 dl dried breadcrumbs
1 dl milk
100 g dried fruit, e.g. apricots, prunes, raisins
1 onion
1/2 bunch of parsley
1 egg
3 dl whipping cream
1 tbsp Kikkoman soy
butter for frying
salt and pepper

Garnish, e.g.:
1 cucumber
1/2 chilli
1/2 bunch of parsley

Dressing:
1 tbsp golden syrup
1/2 tbsp white wine vinegar
1/2 tbsp water
pepper

Serve with:
boiled floury potatoes
creamy sauce
pickles

Procedure:
Set the oven to 175°C. Put the dried breadcrumbs to soak in the milk.

Buy the softest fruit you can get and cut it up small. Peel the onion and chop small. Chop the parsley small. Mix the minced meat with the dried breadcrumbs, the egg, the cream, half the parsley, the onion and the fruit. Season to taste with the soy, salt and pepper.

Wet one hand and a tablespoon in lukewarm water and shape eight fairly large oval patties of the mixture. Put these in a greased oven-proof dish and bake on the middle shelf of the oven for about 20 minutes, until they are a nice colour.

Make a cream sauce and keep it warm.

Mix all the dressing ingredients together. Shave the cucumber, chop the chilli small and mix these with the remaining parsley. Pour the dressing over the mixture and leave it to stand till the hazel-hens are ready.

Serve the hazel-hens with boiled floury potatoes, the cucumber salad the cream sauce and some good pickles.

Cream sauce serves 4

A juicy steak with no cream sauce is like love without kisses: it dozes and then falls asleep, as the Italian saying goes. A really well-made, creamy sauce lends added inspiration to even the most perfect of Sunday joints. Even when frying meatballs, hazel-hens or roulades, you always get pan juices that are just the thing for a creamy sauce. Game also works this way.

In other words, this is a basic sauce which can be developed in a variety of ways as follows.

Ingredients:
1 tbsp butter
1 tbsp flour
4 dl milk with the top on (3 dl milk, 1 dl cream)
2 dl pan juices from frying meat or game
2 tbsp concentrated beef or veal stock
1 tbsp Kikkoman soy
1/2 tbsp red or black currant jelly
salt and pepper

Procedure:
Warm the cream and milk. Melt the butter in a saucepan and beat in the flour. Dilute with the cream and milk before the mixture changes colour. Whisk to a smooth sauce and dilute further with pan juices and stock. Flavour with soy, jelly, salt and pepper. Simmer over a low flame for about 10 minutes, whisking all the time.

Add more jelly if you like that contrast. Et voilà! Bob's your uncle and it only remains to harvest the diners' compliments.

151

Hints:
When serving this sauce with game, use the pan juices and flavour them with a few crushed juniper berries, a dash of port, crumbled blue cheese or a knob of whey cheese (*messmör*).

Deep-fried fish fillets · serves 4

There is more to traditional home fare than boiling and frying. Fish of different kinds can very well be deep-fried and served with various tasty accessories – chips, for example, as in Denmark and England. Just remember to be a little careful with the deep frying, so that the oil doesn't get too hot. Always have a lid handy that fits the pan, just in case the oil overheats and ignites. Just put the lid on to extinguish the flames. Never use water – that only worsens things. It goes against the grain to be serious and cautionary like this, but now I've done it and one day someone may be glad of the warning. Though your very best plan, of course, is to use a deep fryer. You get better results that way, and it's safer.

Ingredients:
800 g fillets of plaice
1 bunch of parsley
juice of 1/2 lemon
a few drops of Worcester sauce
about 2 dl white flour
2 beaten eggs
about 2 dl panko or ordinary dried breadcrumbs
1 l oil (not olive oil) for deep frying
salt and pepper

Skagen Mix:
1/2 kg fresh shrimps
1 red onion
1/2 bunch of chives, chopped small
1 dl mayonnaise
1/2 dl cultured cream (*gräddfil*)
2 tsp grated horseradish
juice of 1/2 lemon
a few drops of Worcester sauce
salt and pepper

Serve with:
Skagen Mix
1/2 bunch parsley
lemon wedges
boiled potatoes or chips (French fries)

Procedure:
Begin by marinating the fish fillets for 1 hour. Chop the parsley small and mix it with the lemon juice and Worcester sauce to form quite a dry marinade. Put the fish and marinade into a leak-proof plastic bag, tie up and turn the bag carefully round so as to mix the fish and marinade.

Prepare the Skagen Mix. Peel the shrimps and part them if they are big ones. Peel the red onion and chop small. Mix all the ingredients in a bowl. Add salt and pepper, lemon juice and Worcester sauce to taste. Transfer to a cold place.

Heat the oil to 180o in a big saucepan and measure the temperature with a caramel thermometer – or with a little piece of white bread. If the bread turns brown in 60 seconds, the oil is just the right temperature. But as I say, using a proper deep fryer is a better idea. Double-bread the fillets of fish. Dredge them first in flour mixed with salt and pepper and then in beaten egg. Finish by dredging them in the dried breadcrumbs. Pat the breading gently to secure it in position. Deep-fry the fillets, 3 or 4 at a time, till they are golden brown. Drain them for a minute or so on kitchen tissue and then transfer them to a warm dish. Lastly, deep-fry the parsley for 10 or 15 seconds, making quite sure it is dry before you start.

Serve the fish immediately with the parsley, the Skagen Mix, lemon wedges and boiled potatoes or chips/French fries.

153

Hash Bellman with egg and cream sauce

serves 4

The secret of a tasty *pyttipanna* (Swedish hash) lies in the preparations. You have to have different kinds of meat, and the meat, onion and potato all have to be cut up very small – centimetre cubes won't do. Your hash is sure to turn out best using raw-fried potato

The cream sauce version is less common, but Bellman, the 18th century Stockholm troubadour, was fond of it, and sometimes I fancy it myself for a change. A cold vodka and your favourite lager make the perfect accompaniment.

Ingredients:
600 g assorted meat: beef, pork, ham, smoked pork, Falun sausage
1 large onion
800 g potato
butter for frying
Worcester sauce
salt and pepper

Cream sauce:
1 tbsp butter
1/2 tbsp white flour
1 dl strong veal stock
2 dl cream
1/2 tsp Kikkoman soy
salt and pepper

Serve with:
4 newly fried eggs
pickled beetroot (see page 13)
toasted crisp bread (see page 50)
HP sauce

Procedure:
Cut the meat into small cubes and store in the fridge till frying time. Peel the onion and chop it up equally small. Peel the potatoes and dice them into small cubes.

Now make the sauce. Sauté the butter in a saucepan and stir in the flour. Dilute with the veal stock and cream. Add soy, salt and pepper to taste and simmer gently for 7–8 minutes.

Start by frying the potato in butter, adding the onion after a few minutes. Fry for about 15 minutes over a moderate flame, stirring frequently to keep the potato from burning.

Put the meat in the pan when the potato is almost done and brown everything at once, carefully stirring the ingredients together. Add salt, pepper and a few dashes of Worcester sauce to taste. Keep this mixture warm while frying the eggs.

Serve everything piping hot with eggs, beetroot and cream sauce together with toasted crisp bread and HP sauce.

Fish au gratin   serves 4

It is easily forgotten that the food served in restaurants over the years has also become a part of Swedish culinary history, and it is through the restaurants that some of the foreign influences we like have entered our country and enriched our culinary heritage. Fish au gratin is an old classic which has figured in many different guises through the passing years. It has an unlimited potential for excellence and well deserves the accompaniment of a very good dry or semi-dry white wine.

Ingredients:
800 g halibut, haddock, flatfish, cod or pike-perch
2 shallots
2–3 dl white wine
salt

Pommes duchesse
800 g potatoes, King Edward
2 tbsp butter
1 tbsp oil
a few scrapes of nutmeg
2 egg yolks
salt and pepper

White wine sauce:
cooking liquid from the fish
1 dl reduced concentrated fish stock (see page 250)
100 g butter
1/2 tbsp corn starch flour (Idealmjöl)
3 dl cream
1/2–1 tbsp lemon juice
1 dl whipped cream
salt and pepper

Garnish:
e.g. tomatoes, shrimps, button mushrooms lightly fried in butter, mussels, asparagus and parsley perhaps grated matured Parmesan cheese or a matured Västerbotten cheese

Procedure:
Start with the pommes duchesse. Peel the potatoes, boil them soft and "dry them in their steam" – i.e. drain them and return them to the (low!) heat. Put them through a potato ricer, then flavour with the butter, the oil, a few scrapes of nutmeg and salt and pepper. Stir in the egg yolks and set aside.

Set the oven to 225°C. Peel the shallots and chop them fine. Put a layer of shallot into a greased oven-proof dish. Put the fish on top of this and pour the wine over it. Add a little salt and cover the dish with grease-proof paper. Cook the fish on the middle shelf of the oven for 15–20 minutes.

Turn the oven to top heat. Put the mashed potato into an icing bag, preferably one with a star-shaped nozzle. Squeeze out the mash in a neat line or strip along the edge of an oven-proof dish with room for the whole concoction. Put the gratin dish with the mashed potato in the upper part of the oven and leave it there till the mash starts to change colour.

Meanwhile make the sauce. Strain the cooking liquid from the baked fish into a saucepan, mixing it with the concentrated fish stock. Melt the butter and whisk in the flour. Dilute with the fish stock and the unwhipped crem. Beat to a smooth sauce, adding lemon juice, salt and pepper to taste. Simmer till reduced by half. Beat in the butter and the whipped cream.

Place the fish and your chosen garnish in the centre of the dish with piped mashed potato. Pour on the sauce and bake on the middle shelf of the oven for about 10 minutes, until the surface is a nice golden brown. Serve piping hot.

Hints:
To make your gratin tastier still, sprinkle it with grated Parmesan or Västerbotten cheese before putting it in the oven.

157

Browned cabbage soup with veal mince balls serves 4

Perhaps browned cabbage soup sounds like typical workhouse fare. Nothing could be further from the truth. Try this variant, using cabbage, Savoy cabbage, veal mince balls and small potatoes in their jackets.

Fresh-baked white bread with a proper crust goes well with this soup, as do cheese-gratin triangles with a whiff of Cayenne pepper. A true delight for gourmets and gourmands alike.

Ingredients:
1/2 head of cabbage
1/2 head of Savoy cabbage
1 onion
1 1/2 l chicken stock, veal stock (see page 250) or ham stock
butter for frying
1 tsp caster sugar or syrup
1 pinch of pounded caraway
10 allspice corns
2 bay leaves
10 small new potatoes
salt and pepper

Veal mince balls:
200 g fine-ground veal mince
mushroom, truffle if possible
2 egg yolks
1 dl whipping cream

Serve with:
freshly baked white bread or cheese-gratin triangles

Procedure:
Cut away the stalk in the middle of the cabbage and shred the leaves. Peel and chop the onion.

Brown the butter in a large pot, add the cabbage and onion. Sauté, stirring continuously, till the vegetables are golden brown. Pour on the stock. Add sugar or syrup, caraway, allspice corns, bay leaves and potatoes. Season to taste. Simmer until the cabbage is soft and the potatoes cooked.

Meanwhile prepare the veal mince balls. Chop the mushroom small and mix it with the mince, the egg yolks and the cream. Season to taste. Make small, oblong patties and add them carefully to the soup. Simmer gently for 5–6 minutes until they are cooked.

Serve immediately with one of the suggested accompaniments and your favourite beer.

Veal fricadelles in curry sauce serves 4

Minced meat is infinitely variable, and with different sauces you get a new gustatory experience every time.

Veal fricadelles in curry sauce are a superb weekend dish deriving its character from the mildness and freshness of the curry sauce. Blended (pork and beef) mince, minced lamb or game farce will do just as well, of course.

Ingredients:
600 g minced veal
1 onion
3 boiled potatoes
2 eggs
1/2 bunch chopped parsley
1 tbsp Dijon mustard
a few drops of Worcester sauce
5 dl veal stock
salt and pepper

Curry sauce:
3 dl veal stock
1 small onion
2 cloves of garlic
1 apple
1 tbsp good-quality curry powder
2 tbsp butter
1 tbsp flour
1 dl apple juice
2 dl whipping cream
2–3 dl mango chutney
1 tsp lemon juice
salt and pepper

Garnish:
1 leek
2 red and/or yellow carrots
1 handful of string beans
1 handful of sugar snap peas
1/2 bunch of chives, chopped small

Serve with:
rice
mango chutney

Procedure:
Heat the veal stock in a generously sized saucepan.

Peel the onion for the farce and chop small. Rice the potato. Mix all the ingredients for the farce thoroughly in a bowl. You may care to fry a small sample, to check the seasoning.

Make round or oval patties of the mixture and simmer for 7–8 minutes in the stock until thoroughly cooked. Keep warm.

Now for the curry sauce. Peel the onion and garlic and chop them up small. De-core and dice the apple. Sauté the curry, onion, garlic and apple in butter in a saucepan for a few minutes. Sprinkle with the flour. Dilute with the veal stock from cooking the fricadelles and with the apple juice. Cook the sauce gently for about 10 minutes. Stir in the cream, mango chutney and lemon juice, simmer for another 10 minutes or so. Season to taste. Cook the sauce for another minute or so before straining it off. Put the fricadelles in the sauce and cook gently for about 5 minutes.

Meanwhile prepare the garnish. Peel the carrots and cut them into thick rounds or sticks. Clean the leek and cut up small. Blanch the green vegetables in lightly salted water, starting with the carrot, which takes longest. Toss the vegetables in butter if you like.

Serve the fricadelles on top of the garnish, with boiled rice and mango chutney.

161

Salted Tafelspitz with green vegetables boiled in stock and a mustard vinaigrette sauce serves 4

This is really an Austro-German speciality, but, incorporating as it does the same raw materials as many Swedish recipes, it merits a place in this book.

Tafelspitz can be and is made with beef of all kinds, from fillet to brisket, but here I've opted for rump cap, a roast-beef cut from the hindquarters – juicy and full of flavour. The ideal, of course, is if your butcher can supply you with a salted piece.

Ingredients:
1 salted rump cap (about 1 kg)
1 onion
1 carrot
1 wedge of celeriac (about 200 g)
1 leek (the white part)
about 10 sprigs of parsley
a few sprigs of thyme
2 bay leaves
8–10 white peppercorns
salt (if necessary)

Salad:
3 hard-boiled eggs
1 red onion
2 tbsp capers
1 dl flat-leafed parsley, chopped small
1/2 salt gherkin
2 tbsp grated horseradish

Mustard vinaigrette:
1/2 dl Dijon mustard
1 tbsp honey
1 tbsp red wine vinegar
3 dl rapeseed oil
2 tbsp water or stock from boiling the meat
salt and pepper

Serve with:
green vegetables according to season, boiled in the meat stock together with potatoes

Procedure:
Cover the meat with water, bring to the boil and continue boiling briskly for a minute or so. Remove the meat with a slotted spoon and rinse it under the tap. Return it to the pot and pour on fresh water. Bring to the boil again. Meanwhile prepare the spices, herbs and vegetables. Peel and split the onion. Peel and slice the carrot. Cut up the leek. Add all the ingredients to the pot. After a while, check to see if the stock needs more salt. Cover the pot and simmer for 1 1/2–2 hours, until the meat feels really tender. Remove the meat and strain the stock, then return the meat to the pot and leave it to cool. After the meat has cooled, put it under pressure for a few hours. Reserve the stock. Thus far everything can be done beforehand.

Prepare the salad. Chop the onion small and chop the eggs. Dice the salt gherkin. Mix all the ingredients and leave to stand. Beat together the ingredients for the vinaigrette and put them to one side.

Trim the seasonal vegetables and put them in boiling stock together with the potatoes, so that everything will attain just the right softness at once.

Slice the meat quite thinly and put the slices on a dish together with the salad. Drizzle mustard vinaigrette and grated horseradish over everything. Serve with the seasonal vegetables and the potatoes, which you leave in the stock to keep them warm.

162

Fish lasagne serves 4

You're sure to have tried Italian beef mince lasagne, but of course these good sauces go well with other basic raw materials too. Here's a fishy version worth trying.

The list of ingredients is a long one, but the procedure isn't very complicated. Fish lasagne goes very well together with a cool, dry white wine.

Ingredients:
4 slices (about 300 g)of red fish, e.g. salmon
4 slices (about 300 g) of white fish, e.g. plaice or cod
12 lasagne sheets, preferably fresh
salt and pepper

Tomato sauce:
1 onion
2 cloves of garlic
olive oil for frying
1 tin of whole tomatoes
1/2 tin of water
1/2 tsp thyme
1 tbsp Italian dried salad herbs
1 tsp oregano
2 tsp vinegar
1 tsp sugar
salt and pepper

Parmesan sauce:
3 tbsp butter
2 tbsp flour
6 dl milk
3–4 scrapes of nutmeg
1 bay leaf
2 dl grated Parmesan
salt and pepper

Garnish:
grated cheese, e.g. matured Manor House (optional)

Serve with:
tomato salad

Procedure:
Start with the tomato sauce. Peel and chop the onion and garlic. Sauté this in olive oil in a saucepan. Add the other ingredients and cook gently for 15 minutes over a low flame. Season to taste. Mix and strain the sauce, then put it aside for the time being.

Now the Parmesan sauce. Sauté the butter in a saucepan and stir in the flour. Dilute with the milk. Add the nutmeg, followed by the bay leaf and cheese. Season to taste. Whisk thoroughly and simmer for about 5 minutes. Strain.

Set the oven to 200°C. Season the fish lightly on both sides. Grease a generously proportioned oven-proof dish. Spread a layer of Parmesan sauce over the bottom of it, followed by a covering of lasagne sheets. The lasagne does not have to be cooked in advance. Put in the red fish first, followed by Parmesan sauce, the tomato sauce, a layer of lasagne sheets, the white fish, tomato sauce again, Parmesan sauce again, more lasagne sheets and finally just a layer of Parmesan sauce. Sprinkle with grated cheese.

Bake on the middle shelf of the oven for about 25 minutes, until the surface bubbles and has turned a nice colour. Serve piping hot with tomato salad.

Japanese beef with onion serves 4

Exotic foods and flavours continue to impact on the Swedish cuisine. Given another half-century, things which are now interesting, outlandish novelties may come to be regarded as an important part of Sweden's own culinary tradition.

And let's not forget the triumphal progress of Swedish cooking in many other parts of the world, the USA and UK not least, but also Japan. Did you know, for instance, that the Japanese are immensely curious regarding our surströmming tradition?

But now we're going to prepare a Japanese-inspired Swedish beef which would undoubtedly appeal to the Japanese as well and with which a lukewarm sake is perfectly in order.

Ingredients:
600 g wafer-thin slices of marbled beef
1 large (yellow) onion
1 large red onion
1 piece of leek (the green part)
1 crushed clove of garlic
2 tomatoes
1 chilli, medium strong
1 piece of fresh ginger (2–3 cm)
oil for frying
1 tbsp sesame oil
1 dl Kikkoman soy
salt and pepper

Serve with:
rice

Procedure:
Peel and shred the onions. Clean and slice the leek. Peel and crush the garlic clove. Cut the tomatoes in wedges. Cut the chilli into thin rings. Peel the ginger and cut it into needle-thin sticks.

Heat the oil in a wok pan and start by frying the meat until it starts to change colour. Remove it and fry the onion, leek and garlic in the same fat. Return the meat to the pan when the onion starts to change colour. Season lightly. Add the tomatoes, chilli and ginger, followed by sesame oil and soy to taste.

Serve everything piping hot with rice and, as already suggested, perhaps a small glass of the Japanese creature.

Danish chicken salad serves 4

The new bridge notwithstanding, people in Helsingborg still adhere firmly to the tradition of catching a boat across to Helsingør (Hamlet's Elsinore) in Denmark, if it's only in pursuit of *smørrebrød* and a lager.

That little outing was perhaps even more common in the days of my Helsingborg youth, when Danish *smørrebrød* was the real McCoy, dished up with all manner of accessories. In particular I've never forgotten the curry-fragrant chicken salad which I'm now going to give you the recipe for.

Serve it as part of a summertime buffet or at lunchtime, any day of the week.

Ingredients:
1 small grilled chicken
1 large yellow paprika
1 large red paprika
1–2 bunches of radishes
1 juicy, full-flavoured pear
1 handful of mixed salad, rough cut
1 handful of rocket

Dressing:
1 clove of garlic
1 tbsp good-quality curry powder
2 tbsp red wine vinegar
1 tsp Dijon mustard
1 tbsp sweet chilli sauce
1 tbsp water
1 1/2 dl olive oil
1/2 tsp caster sugar
salt and pepper

Procedure:
Make the dressing first, a day early if possible, to given the flavours time to blend thoroughly. Peel and crush the garlic clove. Mix all the ingredients together and beat the dressing till creamy. Check the seasoning.

Joint the chicken and cut the meat into thick strips.

De-core the paprikas and cut them into strips. Cut the radishes into wedges. Divide the pear into four segments, removing the core, then cut the segments into wafer-thin slices.

Mix all the ingredients except the rocket in a beautiful glass bowl and drizzle with the dressing. Mix lightly and top with a handful of rocket. Give the whole thing a few extra twists of the peppermill if you like (recommended) and serve immediately with dark rye bread and real butter.

169

Hints:
Leftovers of parsley-flavoured roast chicken are of course just the thing for this salad, though perhaps then there will only be enough for two servings, unless your imagination fires you to make a rather different salad, e.g. by making up the shortfall with 200 g of peeled shrimps.

Salmon poached in court bouillon serves 4

I think poached salmon can safely be termed the most popular summer food in all Sweden, along with herring and new potatoes. You can leave the skin, but in that case every single scale must be scraped off. This salmon can very well be prepared a day in advance, to gather extra flavour.

Poached salmon deserves a really good white wine, e.g. a Sauvignon Blanc, a Riesling or – why not? – a Chablis.

Poached salmon with just a dob of mayonnaise on toasted crisp bread isn't so bad either. Perhaps the quantity of salmon given here is a bit on the stingy side …

Ingredients:
800 fresh salmon

Poaching liquid (court bouillon):
1 1/2 l water
1 onion
1 dl white wine vinegar
10 white peppercorns
10 allspice corns
1 bunch of dill
2 bay leaves
1/2 slice of lemon
2 sheets of gelatine
1/2 tbsp salt

Garnish:
hard-boiled egg
green asparagus tips
shrimps
baby carrots
scalded new tomatoes
rings of red onion
sprigs of dill

Serve with:
boiled potatoes
mayonnaise
pressed cucumber (see page 26)

173

Procedure:
Scrape the scales from the fish. Carefully remove any remaining bones. Cut the salmon into pieces 1 1/2 cm thick.

Peel the onion and slice thinly.

Bring all the court bouillon ingredients to the boil in a big saucepan, then simmer gently for about 5 minutes. Put in the pieces of salmon and bring to the boil again. Simmer for 5–6 minutes, until they are thoroughly cooked, skimming if necessary. Remove from the heat and leave the salmon to cool in the court bouillon.

Serve with freshly boiled dill-fragrant potatoes, some garnish and mayonnaise.

Herring balls with sugar snap peas and currant sauce serves 4

Herring balls with currant sauce are to me something associated with Granny Cecilia, my father's mother. In the old days, when we ate a lot more herring than we do now, she and others like her were forced to ring the changes, and herring balls with currant sauce were one way of occasionally varying the monotony.

Herring balls are a typical Monday meal, perhaps using leftovers from a Sunday joint or some other meat. I like a clear, cold vodka to drink with them.

Ingredients:
200 g salt herring
200 g pork and beef mince
50 g dried bread crumbs
1 dl water or milk
100 g meat leftovers, e.g. ham
2 small onions
1 eg
dried bread crumbs for breading
butter for frying
salt and pepper

Warm salad:
150 g sugar snap peas
2 scallions
butter for frying

Serve with:
jacket potatoes
1/2 bunch chives
currant sauce

Procedure:
Put the salted herring fillets to soak in cold water for 4–6 hours. Make the currant sauce and keep it warm. Boil the potatoes and chop the chives small.

Pour the dried breadcrumbs and water/milk into a mixing bowl, leaving them to swell for a while. Grind or cut up the meat leftovers and the herring very small. Peel the onions. Grind or fine-grate one of them, and chop the other one up small and brown it in a little butter in a frying pan. Quickly blend all the ingredients into a smooth mixture. Shape into large flat patties or balls and turn these in the breadcrumbs.

Top and tail the sugar snap peas and scallions. Cut the sugar snap peas lengthwise into narrow strips and cut the scallions into thin rings.

Brown some butter in a frying pan and put in the herring balls. Fry them golden brown – about 3 minutes on each side. Sauté the sugar snap peas and scallions lightly, then season them carefully.

Halve the boiled potatoes and dip them in the chives. Serve the herring balls piping hot with the warm salad, the currant sauce and the potatoes.

Currant sauce serves 4

Herring balls are a traditional Swedish recipe and have been part of the home-fare repertoire for ages past. They used often to figure on Swedish Christmas buffets.

A sweet-and-sour currant sauce is of course the inalienable traditional accompaniment. Just for a change, this sauce can also be served with fried salt herring or boiled tongue.

Ingredients:
1 dl currants
3 dl water
1 tbsp butter
1 tbsp flour
2 tbsp concentrated veal stock, bottled
1 tbsp Swedish distilled vinegar, *ättika* (12%)
2 tbsp brown sugar
2 tbsp Kikkoman soy
1 tbsp butter
salt and pepper

Procedure:
Rinse the currants well in tepid water, then cook them in water for about 5 minutes until they soften. Strain off the liquid but reserve it.

Sauté butter and flour in a saucepan and dilute with 3 dl of the liquid from cooking the currants. Add the veal stock. Stir the sauce and simmer gently for 10 minutes. Flavour with ättika, brown sugar, soy, salt and pepper to taste, perhaps adding a little water if the sauce is too thick. The sauce must have a distinct acidity, but with a balancing sweetness. Put in the currants and glaze with a knob of butter. Serve the sauce hot.

Meat soup with dumplings serves 6–8

Meat soup with dumplings is one of the nicest and most warming meals you could wish for on a cold winter's day. It has its appointed place in the husmanskost tradition and, all things considered, it's quite a cushy number.

   This is a big batch, enough for two meals. Second time round you can have it on the table in next to no time if someone's hurrying off elsewhere. The best and easiest way is to boil the meat a day beforehand, leaving it in its cooking liquid to soak up all the spicy flavours.

Ingredients:
1–1.2 kg chuck steak (on the bone
1 onion
1 carrot
1 leek
1 piece of celeriac
a few stalks of parsley
some sprigs of thyme
3 bay leaves
10–12 white peppercorns
salt

For the soup:
stock from cooking the meat
the meat
1 onion
1–2 potatoes
2–3 carrot
2 parsnips
1 piece of celeriac (about 150 g)
1 leek
a few florets of cauliflower
1 bunch of parsley (leaves only)

Dumpling:
3 dl milk
3–4 tbsp flour
2 egg yolks
a few scrapes of nutmeg
salt

Serve with:
toasted crisp bread (see page 50)
well-matured cheese

Procedure:
Put the meat and bones into a casserole, cover with water and cook for a few minutes until the scum has floated up. Remove the meat with a slotted spoon and rinse it quickly in cold water. Clean the pot and return the meat. Pour on fresh water, about 2 l. Start by adding 1/2 tbsp salt, checking the salinity again later. Bring to the boil. Meanwhile prepare the vegetables. Cut the onion into big wedges, peel and cut up the carrot and clean and cut up the leek. Add the vegetables, herbs and spices to the pot. Cover and simmer gently for about 1 1/2 hours. Test for the meat to be almost done. It will finish cooking when left to cool in the stock. Strain the stock, return the meat to the pot and store in a cold place.

   Prepare the vegetables for the soup. Peel the onion and root vegetables. Clean the leek. Cut the vegetables into convenient mouthfuls, pluck the cauliflower into smaller pieces and put aside for the time being.

   Now the dumpling. Heat the milk in a saucepan. Add the flour and stir until you have quite a firm, slightly stodgy mixture. Add salt and a scrape or two of nutmeg. Remove from the heat and allow the mixture to cool slightly. Stir in the egg yolks. Bring lightly salted water to the boil. Shape the mixture into tablespoon-sized, oval dumplings and put these into the simmering water. They are ready when they float to the surface. Remove them with a slotted spoon.

   Remove any fat from the stock, heat it up and put in the vegetables. Cut the meat into small cubes and put it in when the vegetables are starting to soften. Put the dumplings in as well. Add plenty of fine-chopped parsley leaves just before serving.

   Serve with toasted crisp bread and a well-matured cheese.

177

Boiled salted brisket with browned root vegetables serves 4

Boiled salted brisket is a recipe that is always having to be rescued for posterity. New generations must be taught how to cook even humbler cuts like brisket, and how good it can be.

This was one of Tore Wretman's absolute favourites. In fact he was so fond of it, he even named one of his yachts after it – Salta Biten. I haven't yet followed suit, but you never know.

It's a good idea to boil the meat a day in advance, because it needs a few hours to get tender and come away from the bone (which can perhaps be included in the cooking, for the quality of the stock).

Ingredients:
1 kg salted brisket
6–8 white peppercorns
2–3 carrots
1 turnip
2 kohlrabi bulbs
800 g potatoes
butter or margarine for frying
icing sugar
salt and pepper

Serve with:
grated or rasped horseradish

Procedure:
Put the meat into a generously proportioned casserole and pour on plenty of water. Bring to the boil, removing from the heat after 1 minute. Rinse the meat quickly and clean the pot. Bring to the boil again and put in the peppercorns. Simmer for about 2 hours. Check the salinity: nothing sissy about this recipe! Leave the meat to cool in its juices if you are preparing it in advance.

Peel and trim the root vegetables before cutting them into cubes about 2 cm large. Peel the potatoes and boil them in the stock from cooking the meat.

Boil the root vegetables in stock from the pot until they are soft. Strain off the stock (reserving it for a good green vegetable soup another time). "Steam dry" the root vegetables and then brown them slightly in butter in a frying pan. Season to taste. Sprinkle with a couple of pinches of icing sugar, which will caramelise them slightly.

Warm the meat in the stock. You can cut it into fairly thick slices while it is still cold if you find this more convenient. Grate or rasp plenty of horseradish in the meantime.

When the meat is ready, arrange it on a warm serving dish, with root vegetables and potatoes round about it and horseradish strewn over it. Serve the extra in a separate bowl. Alternatively you can dole everything out on warm plates in similar fashion.

Warm fish pâté with veal sweetbreads, shellfish sauce and shellfish salad serves 4

This delicious item has not been part of the Swedish home fare repertoire for very long, for the simple reason that I've just made it up. After 50 years in the kitchen, I have to leave some kind of legacy to posterity, to the best of my ability. I use pike mince for the pâté mixture, but cod or some other white fish would do just as well.

The shellfish salad accompaniment isn't absolutely necessary, but I really recommend it. Lobster claws and crayfish tails, as usual, are selected according to the stretch of your pocket. A well-chilled Sauvignon Blanc or Riesling goes down excellently.

Ingredients:
200 g veal sweetbreads
1 shallot

Fish mince:
2 shallots
400 g shrimps in their shells, or else crayfish tails
butter for frying
300 g fine-ground pike mince
2 egg yolks
4 dl whipping cream
salt and pepper

Shellfish salad
1/2 courgette
butter for frying
a handful of baby spinach
lobster claws
Norway lobster tails
about 1 dl peeled shrimps
a little dill

Serve with:
shellfish sauce

Procedure:
Peel and part the shallots. Put the sweetbreads and onion into a saucepan, pour on cold water and salt lightly. Bring to the boil, then simmer for 15–20 minutes. Remove the sweetbreads with a slotted spoon and put in a cold place to cool completely. Thus far you can prepare everything a day in advance.

Set the oven to 125°C and put in a large dish of water as a bain-marie. Pluck the sweetbreads apart and be sure to remove all the membranes. Peel and chop the onion. Peel the shrimps and cut them up into smaller pieces. (Don't discard the shells, they'll be the foundation of your shellfish sauce.) Sauté everything quickly, season lightly and put to one side.

Make the fish mince in a food processor. It is important that all the ingredients should be refrigerator temperature. Put in the pike mince and egg yolks first and run them for a minute or so until you have a smooth mixture. Add salt and pepper. Lastly pour in all the cream and run for another minute or so, but not

longer in case the mixture curdles. Take 1/2 of the fish mince and mix it thoroughly with the sweetbread and shrimp sauté.

Grease a 2-litre oblong loaf tin with cold butter and put in about 1/2 the fish mince. Level out, then transfer the mince with the sweetbreads and shrimps to an icing bag, cut a fairly large opening and squeeze everything out evenly into the loaf tin. Finally spread the rest of the fish mince over the top, level out and cover the tin with aluminium foil. Bake in the bain-marie for 1 hour or until the pâté feels firm.

Cut the courgette in strips and sauté lightly in butter. Cut the ingredients for the salad, mix them together and store in a cold place.

Prepare the shellfish sauce and keep it warm.

When the pâté is done, leave it to settle for 10 minutes before carefully tipping it out of the tin and cutting one broad slice for each person. Serve immediately with salad and sauce. If there is sauce to spare, serve it separately in a sauceboat.

Shellfish sauce serves 4

Shellfish sauce is a very useful sauce that goes well with any number of fish recipes. This one is a real winner and easy to make, even if you start off by making your own fish stock. I'm sure I've said this before, but it bears repeating: if you like the fish sauce and other good sauces you get served in restaurants, it's because they have home-made concentrated stock to base them on. That's the whole secret.

Ingredients:
1/2 fresh shrimps, unpeeled
1 onion
1 tbsp olive oil
1 tbsp tomato purée
5 dl fish stock
2 dl whipping cream
1 tsp corn starch flour
2 tbsp brandy (optional)
salt and fresh-ground pepper

Procedure:
Peel the shrimps and reserve the shells (they're the star of the show, just for once). Peel the onion and chop fine. Sauté the shells in oil in a saucepan for a minute or so. Add the onion and tomato purée and sauté for about another minute. Pour on the fish stock and cook slowly for 15 minutes. Pour off through a close-meshed strainer.

Pour the strained stock into a saucepan and reduce by half. Add the cream and thicken with corn starch flour. Simmer the sauce for about 10 minutes. Add salt and pepper to taste, and perhaps one or two tablespoons of brandy.

Hints:
The shrimps can either be divided into smaller pieces and put in the sauce, which must not be allowed to boil afterwards, or else they can be used for really tasty shrimp sandwiches by way of a starter.

Coq au vin serves 4

Now what? Is this a book about Swedish or French cuisine? But coq au vin is definitely part of the Swedish tradition too, for we have been cooking chicken, of one gender and quality or another, this way for goodness knows how long.

Any country's cuisine is a mixture of native inventions and borrowings from abroad, so by all means call it chicken in red wine. It will be best made with a fresh corn-fed chicken. A big-flavoured red wine makes the best drinking accompaniment.

Ingredients:
1 corn-fed chicken (about 11/2 kg)
1 large onion
butter and oil for frying
1 bottle of loud, inky red wine
2 tbsp of red wine vinegar
2 chicken stock cubes or 3 tbsp concentrated stock
4 dl water
1 bunch of fresh thyme
4 bay leaves
3–4 cloves of garlic
1 tbsp of tomato purée
200 g salted pancetta
200 g button mushrooms
200 g button onions
3 carrots
salt and pepper

Serve with:
boiled potatoes, rice or tagliatelle

Procedure:
Joint the chicken into large pieces and season them. Peel the onion and cut it into large pieces. Brown the pieces of chicken and the onion all round in butter and oil in a generously proportioned casserole. Crumble the stock cubes into this and pour on the red wine, vinegar and water. Put in the thyme, bay leaves, whole cloves of garlic and tomato purée. Stir gently till everything is mixed together, cover and simmer for about 30 minutes.

Remove the pieces of chicken, e.g. with a slotted spoon, and strain the stock. Pour the stock back into the pot and reduce for 7–8 minutes until it starts to thicken slightly.

Meanwhile cut the pancetta into strips. Cut the mushrooms into large pieces. Peel the button onions but leave the tops on. Peel the carrots and cut them into sticks. Crisp-fry the pancetta in a frying pan. Brown the mushrooms, onion and sticks of carrot in the pork fat in the same frying pan.

Return the chicken in the reduced juices. Add the pancetta and the sautéed vegetables. Let everything cook gently together for about 10 minutes. Season to taste, but remember that this pancetta is salt in itself. Serve piping hot with boiled potatoes, rice or tagliatelle.

182

Viennese meat farce serves 4

A rose by any other name … I have heard this wonderful recipe, made using my favourite ingredient, referred to as meat loaf and all sorts of other things. We are dealing here with a much-loved classic of the Swedish kitchen, served with potatoes and cream sauce or gravy.

Now I suggest you try making "Viennese meat farce" by way of a change. Dish it up on a Saturday or Sunday, with a little extra effort to beautify the filling.

A pungent red wine for the grown-ups and ice-cold black currant squash for the youngest diners go down well with this recipe.

Ingredients:
800 g mixed (pork and beef) mince
1 large onion
280 g bacon or 300 g pancetta, sliced thin
1 dl milk
1 dl dried bread crumbs
2 boiled medium-sized potatoes
2 dl whipping cream
2 eggs
1 pinch of brown sugar
1 tbsp "anchovy" liquor
1 tbsp Kikkoman soy
2 tbsp concentrated veal stock
butter for frying
salt and pepper

Filling:
green vegetables in every form, e.g.
wax beans
sugar snap peas
fennel
courgette
carrots
leek

Cream sauce (see page 151):
or gravy sauce:
2 dl veal stock
juices from the farce pan
salt and pepper

Serve with:
boiled floury potatoes
pickled gherkins (see page 119)
Asian cucumber (see page 42)
pickled tomatoes
pearl onions
red or black currant jelly

Procedure:
Set the oven to 150°C. Clean the vegetables for the filling and cut them into pieces of roughly equal length so that they can be placed lengthwise in the farce. Boil them for a few minutes in lightly salted water, then pour off the water and put the vegetables to drain between sheets of kitchen tissue.

Peel the onion and chop small. Sauté half of it in a little butter in a frying pan; the rest will be mixed in raw. Mix the milk and dried bread crumbs together. Leave to swell for 10 minutes. Mash the potato smooth and mix the farce together with all the ingredients except the bacon to form a smooth mixture. This has to be quite fluffy; add more cream if necessary. Season to taste; it is a good idea to fry a small knob of the mixture and check the seasoning. Line a tin of about 2 l capacity, Teflon if you have one, with slices of bacon or pancetta, hanging these over the side so that they can be folded back over the farce. Put about 1/3 of the farce into the tin, then line up the vegetables so that they will make a nice pattern when served. Add another 1/3 of the farce and a new layer of vegetable sticks, finishing off with the remaining farce. Press down a little before folding over the bacon or pancetta slices to seal the tin. Bake on the middle shelf of the oven for about 1 hour. Test with a skewer to see if the farce is done: it's ready when clear stock bubbles up. Set aside, covered over and still in the tin, for about 10 minutes.

Meanwhile, reduce the gravy sauce, preferably with a base of home-made concentrated veal stock, or else a strong stock cube or concentrated stock from a bottle, mixed with the strained stock from baking the farce in the oven. Season to taste.

Carefully turn the farce out of the tin and, using a really sharp knife, gently cut it into slices about 2 cm thick. Serve immediately with boiled floury potatoes, hot cream sauce or gravy and some of the accessories.

185

Salmon fricassee in curry serves 4

This rather unusual recipe originated with my very good friend Erik Lallerstedt, though he dubbed it Lax Carl XVI Gustav, after the King of Sweden.

Another thing I remember is that what makes it so tasty is the curry, an article which has come to be used more and more in Swedish cooking during recent years. This, more or less, is how Erik made it.

Ingredients:
800 g fresh salmon in large pieces
butter for frying
salt and pepper

Garnish:
1 onion
1 carrot
1 red paprika
1 fennel bulb
1 apple
1/2 courgette
100 button mushrooms
1 crushed clove of garlic
butter for frying

Curry sauce:
2 tbsp butter
1 tbsp good-quality curry powder
3 dl cooking cream
1 dl fish stock
salt

Serve with:
rice

Procedure:
Start with the vegetables. Peel and chop the onion, Peel and cut up the carrots. Clean the rest of the vegetables and cut them into smallish pieces. Sauté all the vegetables in butter in a frying pan till they start to soften but are still al dente. Put to one side for the time being.

Trim and season the pieces of salmon.

Carry on with the sauce. Heat the butter in a saucepan and quickly sauté the curry. Dilute with the cream and fish stock. Reduce the sauce until it starts to thicken slightly. Put in the garnish and let it simmer for a few minutes. Add salt to taste. Meanwhile fry the fish in butter in a frying pan for 5–6 minutes on each side, till it is golden brown. Carefully fold it into the sauce. Make sure everything is thoroughly warmed. Serve with boiled rice.

Cobbler's hotpot serves 4

This is a classic which comes in various guises, the reason doubt-less being that in days gone by there was hardly a *stadshotell* in the land which didn't have it on the menu for lunch.

Where the name comes from is anybody's guess, but one explanation as good as any is that a well beaten-out sirloin steak actually can look rather like the sole of a shoe, in which case the strips of pork would be the nails. Export beer and a vodka are standard accompaniments when I serve this one.

Ingredients:
4 well-hung, marbled sirloin steaks (about 200 g each)
butter for frying
150 g salt pancetta or bacon

Aroma butter:
100 g butter at room temperature
parsley, chopped fine
1 tsp lemon juice
1 tsp Worcester sauce
salt and pepper

Mashed potato:
about 1 kg potatoes
about 2 tbsp butter
about 2 dl milk with the top on (1 1/2 dl milk, 1/2 dl cream)
chives chopped fine
nutmeg
salt and pepper

Serve with:
salt gherkins
browned butter (optional)

Procedure:
Stir together the ingredients for the aroma butter and put in a cool place. Peel and boil the potatoes for the mash. Pound or whisk a fairly loose potato mash with butter, cream and milk, chives and a few scrapes of nutmeg. Season to taste.

Cut the pancetta/bacon into narrow strips and brown quickly. Keep warm. Cut up the salt gherkins.

Flatten the steaks thoroughly. Season them and fry them in butter in a hot pan, but not too long or the meat may go dry (it's meant to be a little bloody in the middle).

Serve immediately on warm plates with the pancetta/bacon and aroma butter on the meat and mashed potato and salt gherkins to one side. Serve with a little browned butter as well if you fancy the idea.

Frankfurter à la Greta serves 1

I honestly haven't a clue who Greta is or – more probably – was, but this is the perfect method for preparing a single portion of food either for lunch or as a quick dinner. Given that so many people like taking their lunch with them to work, scope for vari-ety is welcome.

The original recipe used fillet of beef, but here I've tried using Frankfurter. You can equally well use fillet of pork, beef or salmon, and in my book on herring and Baltic herring I tried using the latter; it turned out very well.

Ingredients:
3 Frankfurters
2 potatoes
1 small onion
2 egg yolks
1 tbsp Swedish mustard
1/2 tbsp Dijon mustard
1 tbsp chives, chopped small
butter for frying
salt and pepper

Procedure:
Peel the potatoes and cut them into centimetre cubes. Start by raw-frying them in butter in a frying pan. Add salt and pepper. Cut the Frankfurters into crescent-shaped pieces. Peel the onion and chop it quite small. Mix the sausage, onion, egg yolks, mus-tard and chives together. Add salt and pepper. Fry the mixture in butter in a frying pan, stirring it a little and shaping it into an omelette when it starts to set. Turn it carefully so as to colour it all over – either "chef's style", with a forward movement followed by a short twitch upwards and backwards, or else with a wide fry-ing spatula. Arrange the sausage mixture and the fried potato separately as pictured and eat at once, or else put them in your "bait tin" and reheat in the micro next day.

189

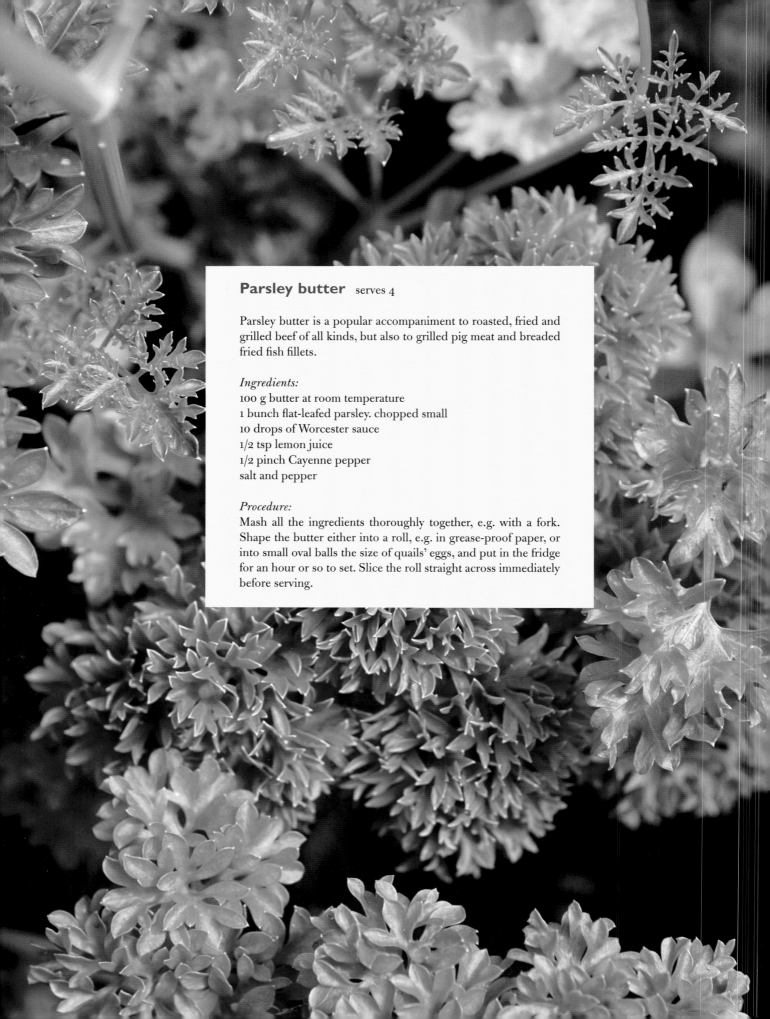

Parsley butter serves 4

Parsley butter is a popular accompaniment to roasted, fried and grilled beef of all kinds, but also to grilled pig meat and breaded fried fish fillets.

Ingredients:
100 g butter at room temperature
1 bunch flat-leafed parsley. chopped small
10 drops of Worcester sauce
1/2 tsp lemon juice
1/2 pinch Cayenne pepper
salt and pepper

Procedure:
Mash all the ingredients thoroughly together, e.g. with a fork. Shape the butter either into a roll, e.g. in grease-proof paper, or into small oval balls the size of quails' eggs, and put in the fridge for an hour or so to set. Slice the roll straight across immediately before serving.

Garlic butter serves 4

Garlic butter has been a popular classic ever since the modern-day grill restaurants began to appear in the 1960s. It heightens the flavour of fried, roast and grilled beef of ever kind, but also of grilled pig meat and lamb chops. Chips (French fries) can be served with it, for example. Garlic butter also makes a nice addition to baked potatoes served with meat.

Ingredients:
100 g butter at room temperature
4 cloves of garlic
2 tsp Kikkoman soy
3-4 drops of Worcester sauce
salt and pepper

Procedure:
Peel and crush the cloves of garlic. Mash all the ingredients thoroughly, e.g. with a fork, to make a smooth butter. Shape the butter either into a roll, e.g. in grease-proof paper, or into small oval balls the size of quails' eggs, and put in the fridge for an hour or so to set.
  Slice the roll straight across immediately before serving.

Hints:
Garlic butter can be varied by adding flat-leafed parsley or chives, chopped fine.
  A completely different variant of herb butter can be achieved by adding 2 tbsp finely grated Parmesan cheese instead of garlic. This goes indescribably well with pork chops or grilled schnitzel!

Sausage cake serves 4

This is an ancient, fine-flavoured recipe which, until at least the 1960s, used not to be an uncommon feature of Swedish dinner tables.

It deserves to be brought back into vogue, for sausage cake with melted butter and uncooked, stirred lingonberry jam is really good. Go easy on the herbs and spices. This cake should have a distinctive but mild flavour, and cloves especially are liable to get out of hand.

Test-fry a little of the mixture in some butter, on the principle of trial and error. And remember that you can't mix the raw materials, or your mixture will be an unmanageable mess.

Ingredients:
200 g pig's liver
150 salted, fat pork
2 dl pearl barley
1 dl rice
3 dl milk
1 dl beef or chicken stock
1 large onion
1 dl raisins
1/2 dl Madeira
3 eggs
1/2 golden syrup or treacle
1 tsp dried marjoram
2 pinches of ground ginger
2 pinches of ground cloves
4 bay leaves
salt and pepper

Serve with:
uncooked, stirred lingonberry jam (see page 25)
melted butter
potatoes or mashed potato (see page 103)

Procedure:
Set the oven to 175°C. Boil the pearl barley and rice in stock and milk in a saucepan for about 20 minutes, until they are barely soft.

Peel the onion and chop small. Put the raisins to soak in the Madeira until it's time to add them.

Mince the liver and pork. Blend them with the rice and pearl barley "porridge", the onion, raisins, Madeira and eggs to form a smooth mixture. Add the syrup/treacle, herbs and spices (except the bay leaves), salt and pepper. You may care to test-fry a small blob of the mixture.

Pour the mixture into a greased oven-proof dish holding about 2 litres. Arrange the bay leaves neatly on top.

Bake on the middle shelf of the oven for about 1 hour, until the cake has turned a nice colour and is done all the way through. Serve straight from the dish with the lingonberry jam and melted butter. In some parts of Sweden, potatoes or mashed potato are also included.

Grilled fresh salmon with buckling butter

serves 4

Salmon has always been a big number in Swedish eating, above all on festive occasions. Nowadays it is an inexpensive raw material, but it has kept its position as an outstanding delicacy.

Here it is the aroma butter and the fresh vegetables, perhaps culled from your own garden, that tickle the taste buds. The choice, of course, is yours, depending on what's available. A full-flavoured white wine completes the pleasure.

Ingredients:
4 pieces of fresh salmon (about 200 g each)
vegetables according to season, e.g.
  new potatoes, carrots, onion, radishes, wax beans, cucumber, sugar snap peas
lemon juice
1/2 bunch of chives, chopped small
a knob of butter
salt and pepper

Buckling butter:
1 small red onion
juice of 1 lemon
2 bucklings
2 tbsp capers
1/2 bunch of chives, chopped small
100 g butter at room temperature
Worcester sauce

Garnish:
wedges of lemon
sprigs of dill

Procedure:
Start with the butter. Peel the red onion and chop fine. Boil it with the lemon juice until the liquid is absorbed. Leave to cool. Clean and bone the bucklings carefully. Chop the capers up rough. Mix the butter and buckling together, with or without a blender, then add the red onion, the chives, the capers and a few drops of Worcester sauce. Season to taste. Use tablespoons to shape four oval balls of the mixture and store them cold.

Brush the potatoes carefully and slice them up. Trim the vegetables and cut them up neatly. Boil the potatoes and put in the vegetables successively, so that everything will be ready at the same time. Roughly in this order: carrots, onion, radishes, wax beans, cucumber and sugar snap peas (which only need a few minutes cooking time).

Meanwhile heat a grill pan or an outdoor grill. Season the pieces of salmon. Grill them for 3–4 minutes on each side, until they are thoroughly done. "Steam-dry" the vegetables, season them lightly and turn them in a knob of butter, the chives and little lemon juice in a pan to make them shiny.

Arrange the vegetables on a warm serving dish or put them straight onto warm plates with the salmon on top. Finish off with the buckling butter and serve instantly.

Blood pudding with crisp-fried pork and uncooked, stirred lingonberry jam serves 4

Blood pudding with crisp-fried pork is a memento of times past when diet needed to be varied and absolutely nothing could be wasted.

Nowadays, blood-based food is far commoner on the mainland of Europe than in Sweden. In France there is hardly a butcher who does not make and sell one or more different kinds of black sausage. The same goes for Germany and Belgium. The use of blood in cooking has in fact become quite trendy among the younger generation of chefs.

Ingredients:
1 l pig's blood
400 g lard
1 onion
1 sharp apple
butter for frying
1/2 dl concentrated apple juice
2 dl milk
20 g salt
pepper
1 tbsp concentrated beef or veal stock (bottled)
1 dl brown sugar
1 l rye flour
2 pinches of allspice
2 pinches of marjoram
1 pinch of cinnamon
1 pinch of ginger
3 dl white currants

Serve with:
800 sliced salt pancetta
uncooked, stirred lingonberry jam (see page 25)

Procedure:
Set the oven to 150°C and put in a bain-marie.

Cut the lard into small cubes. This will be a bit easier if the lard has spent 1/2 hour in the freezer first. Peel the onion and chop small, de-core and dice the apple. Sauté the lard, onion and apple in a little butter in a frying pan, diluting with the apple juice. Simmer gently for a minute or so.

Mix the blood and milk in a mixing bowl and add salt and pepper. Put in the sautéed mixture and other ingredients. Stir thoroughly till you have a smooth mixture. Fry a little of it to check the seasoning.

Pour the mixture into Teflon tins (in which case you won't need to line them with lard). Cover these with foil. Place them in the bain-marie and bake them slowly for about 2 hours. The blood pudding will be ready when it is no longer sticky inside: test with a skewer.

Serve with crisp-friend pork and uncooked, stirred lingonberry jam. Any leftovers can be used for a fry-up some other time.

Brisket of beef Lyonnaise serves 4

This doesn't sound exactly like traditional Swedish home cooking, but the raw materials are as Swedish as anything: brisket of beef, potatoes, red onion and parsley. Somewhat prosaically, this recipe could be described as hash made using brisket left over from a dinner earlier in the week. A perfect lunch recipe, in other words, though executed with a Gallic touch.

Ingredients:
600 g boiled beef brisket
600 g firm potatoes
2 onions
1/2 bunch flat-leafed parsley, chopped fine
2–3 tsp red wine vinegar
butter and oil for frying
a few dashes of Worcester sauce
salt and pepper

Serve with:
Dijon mustard

Procedure:
Set the oven to 175°C. Peel the potatoes and cut them into neat triangles 1/2 cm thick. Brown these all round in butter and oil and put them in the oven for about 15 minutes to finish them off.

Peel the onions and cut them into nice triangular leaves. Cut the meat in similar fashion to the onion and potato. Sauté the onion in butter and oil in a frying pan till it softens and changes colour a little. Retrieve it, then brown the meat quickly in the same fat at a higher temperature. Remove the potato from the oven and mix everything together in one pan. Season the mixture and add the parsley. Sprinkle with a few drops of vinegar and serve instantly with Dijon mustard.

198

Sautéed fillet of veal with button mushrooms and a tarragon and chive sauce serves 4

Sautéed fillet of veal is a star turn, just the thing for that special dinner in the bosom of the family. Good fillet of veal not always being that easy to come by, I've tried using fillet of pork in this recipe, and it turns out almost as well, but not quite. Keep the frying time short enough for the meat to stay pink inside. At any rate, that's the way I like it best.

In recent years we have sometimes been told that meat must not be seasoned before it is fried, and the same has been said concerning fish. But how are the raw materials to catch the flavour of the seasoning and develop their wonderful innate aromas if the spices aren't there at the frying? So I persist in seasoning before browning, and I recommend, as a counsel of perfection, that you do the same.

Ingredients:
600 g inner fillet of veal
1 large onion
1/2 leek (the white part)
100 g button mushrooms
1 veal stock cube
1 tbsp pale Dijon mustard
1/2 white wine
1 bunch of chives, chopped small
1 tbsp fresh tarragon, chopped small
3 dl cooking cream
butter for frying
salt and pepper

Serve with:
riced potatoes, ribbon pasta, rice or avorio rice

Procedure:
Cut the fillet of veal into cm-thick slices and season them. Peel the onion and chop small. Clean and slice the leek. Slice the button mushrooms. Heat butter in a pan and quickly fry the slices of veal on both sides to give them a nice colour but without frying them all the way through. Remove from the pan and keep warm.

Put in another knob of butter and brown the onion, leek and button mushrooms till everything has changed colour slightly. Crumble in the stock cube and add the mustard, wine, chives, tarragon and, lastly, the cream. Simmer the sauce for a few minutes. Put the meat back in and bring everything swiftly to the boil.

Serve piping hot together with riced potatoes, ribbon pasta, ordinary rice or avorio rice without saffron but otherwise cooked in the same way as for braised leg of veal (see page 127).

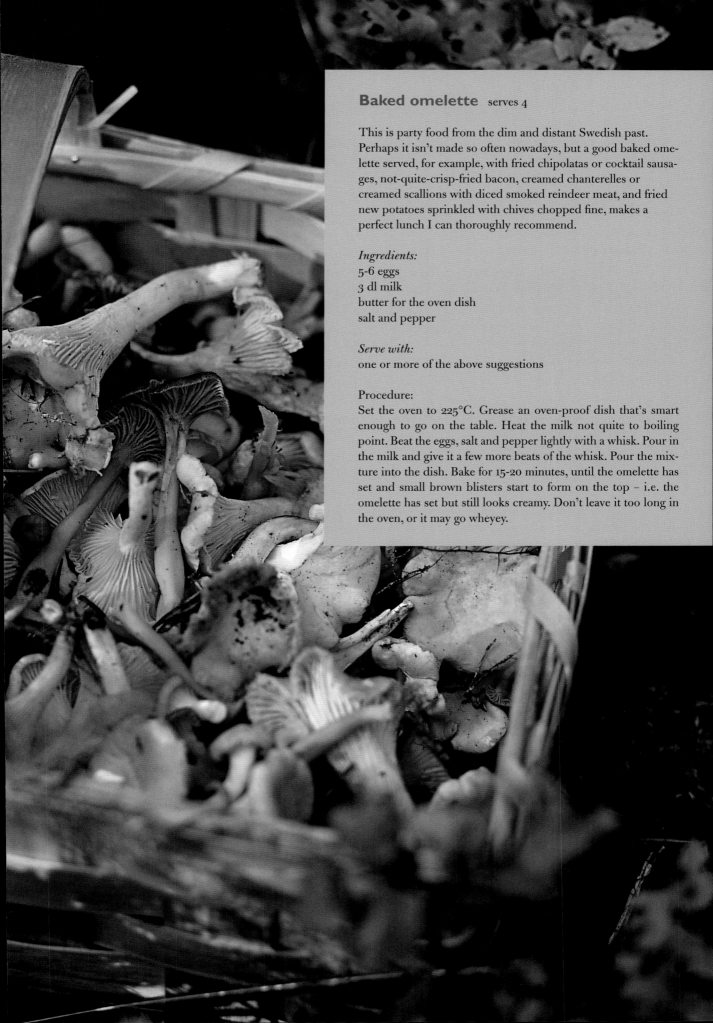

Baked omelette serves 4

This is party food from the dim and distant Swedish past. Perhaps it isn't made so often nowadays, but a good baked omelette served, for example, with fried chipolatas or cocktail sausages, not-quite-crisp-fried bacon, creamed chanterelles or creamed scallions with diced smoked reindeer meat, and fried new potatoes sprinkled with chives chopped fine, makes a perfect lunch I can thoroughly recommend.

Ingredients:
5-6 eggs
3 dl milk
butter for the oven dish
salt and pepper

Serve with:
one or more of the above suggestions

Procedure:
Set the oven to 225°C. Grease an oven-proof dish that's smart enough to go on the table. Heat the milk not quite to boiling point. Beat the eggs, salt and pepper lightly with a whisk. Pour in the milk and give it a few more beats of the whisk. Pour the mixture into the dish. Bake for 15-20 minutes, until the omelette has set and small brown blisters start to form on the top – i.e. the omelette has set but still looks creamy. Don't leave it too long in the oven, or it may go wheyey.

Boiled haddock with Skåne mustard sauce and glazed carrots   serves 4

Boiled haddock and mustard sauce is an ancient classic which my creative, wide-awake guest chef Ola Andersson has fished up out of the Scanian culinary heritage and put into modern clothing.

This haddock is a really sparky number, thanks to the salinity and the strong, distinct sauce, and so anything to drink but beer and mineral water is, I think, out of the question.

Ingredients:
1.4 kg haddock (the thickest part)

Salting:
20 g salt per litre of water

Cooking liquid:
1 onion
1 carrot
10 allspice corns
10 white peppercorns
2 bay leaves
10–12 dill stalks
2 tbsp salt per litre of water

Sauce:
about 35 g mustard seeds
1 batch of béchamel sauce
1–1 1/2 dl cooking liquid
water

Garnish:
4 carrots
2 shallots
1 tbsp butter
1 tsp crushed caraway seeds
1 pinch of caster sugar
1/2 bunch of flat-leafed parsley (not the stalks)
salt and pepper

Serve with:
boiled floury potatoes

Procedure:
Cleanse the fish of blood and membranes and cut it into pieces 7–8 cm wide. Pickle it in salt water in a mixing bowl or suchlike for about 2 hours; the pickling liquid must cover the fish. Pour off the pickling liquid afterwards.

Pound the mustard seeds for the sauce in a little water, to release their oils. A bowl and cannonball are the ideal method, but alternatively you can grind the seeds in a spice mill, mix them with water and run them in a food processor for 2–3 minutes until you get a fluffy cream and the oils are released.

Prepare the cooking liquid. Peel the onion and cut it in wedges. Peel and cut up the carrot. Put all the cooking liquid ingredients in a capacious saucepan. Bring to the boil and sim

mer for about 15 minutes. Put in the fish and simmer for another 5 minutes or so. Set aside and leave the fish in the liquid for about 10 minutes until the flesh comes away from the bones.

Meanwhile prepare the béchamel sauce, dilute it with the cooking liquid and keep it warm.

Prepare the glazed carrots. Peel the carrots and cut them diagonally into thick rounds. Peel the shallots and chop them up small. Cover the bottom of a saucepan with water. Bring this to the boil and put in the carrots, the shallot, the caraway and the sugar. Season to taste. Cover and simmer till the carrots are tender. Stir in the parsley.

Vigorously whisk the mustard into the béchamel sauce, which must not be allowed to boil again afterwards. Serve the fish immediately in its cooking liquid with the carrots, sauce and boiled floury potatoes.

Béchamel sauce   serves 4–5

Béchamel is a toothsome white basic sauce with a wide range of uses. It can be just sauce, or it can form the basis of all kinds of stews, for example. It was invented at the court of Louis XIV in the 17th century, but it is not too regal to be the indispensable concomitant of such plain but pleasurable fare as salt Baltic herring and jacket potatoes, which was still being eaten in Sweden long after World War 2 had ended.

Ingredients:
2 tbsp butter
2 tbsp flour
5 dl milk
salt and pepper

Procedure:
Heat the milk not quite to boiling point. Melt the butter in a steel saucepan and whisk in the flour. Pour on the milk and whisk to a fine, smooth sauce. Season to taste, but remember that too much salt in a smooth béchamel sauce will stick out like a sore thumb.

Hints:
For an effective contrast, you can simmer two or three cloves with the milk. A few slices of onion in the milk will also impart a slightly different touch. Strain off the cloves and onion before whisking in the milk.

For a thinner sauce, simply reduce the flour input.

Fillet of pork with stilton sauce serves 4

Here's another big party-time favourite. The fillet makes a nice change from other cuts of pork, but it tends to be less juicy, due to its being practically devoid of fat. For this reason, fillet of pork is usually cooked and served in a sauce with accessories of different kinds. Try this one, using stilton cheese, which personally I'm very fond of.

Ingredients:
2 fillets of pork (about 800 g)
1–2 tbsp butter for frying
salt and pepper

Sauce:
2 shallots chopped small
150 g well-ripened stilton in pieces
1 dl earthy, full-bodied red wine
4 cl whisky
2 tbsp concentrated veal stock (bottled)
1 1/2 dl whipping cream
salt and pepper

String beans:
1 red onion
200 g baby string beans, topped and tailed
70 g bacon
butter for frying

Service with:
lettuce or baked potato

Procedure:
Trim any membranes away from the fillets. Cut off the small pieces at the ends and save them for another time, e.g. for a stew. Season the fillets. Brown them thoroughly all round in butter in a frying pan over a medium flame for 11–12 minutes. Reserve the pan juices for the sauce. Wrap the fillets in foil and keep them warm.

Now for the sauce. Sauté the onion in the butter from frying the fillets of pork, without letting it change colour. Lower the heat, stir in the cheese and let it melt. Pour on the wine, whisky and concentrated veal stock. Whisk together thoroughly and dilute with the cream. Simmer the sauce for a few minutes. Season to taste. Keep warm.

Blanch the string beans for about 3 minutes in lightly salted water. Drain them in a colander. Cut the bacon into strips, Peel the red onion and chop small. Sauté the bacon in pieces until it starts getting crisp, then put in the onion and continue sautéing for a minute or so. Finally add the string beans and carefully turn the whole mixture.

Remove the fillets of pork from their foil and cut them into wide pieces or "stubs". Pour the pan juices into the sauce and stir. Put out the "stubs" on warm plates and drizzle with the sauce. Serve with the string beans sautéed in red onion and bacon, a fresh salad and/or baked potato.

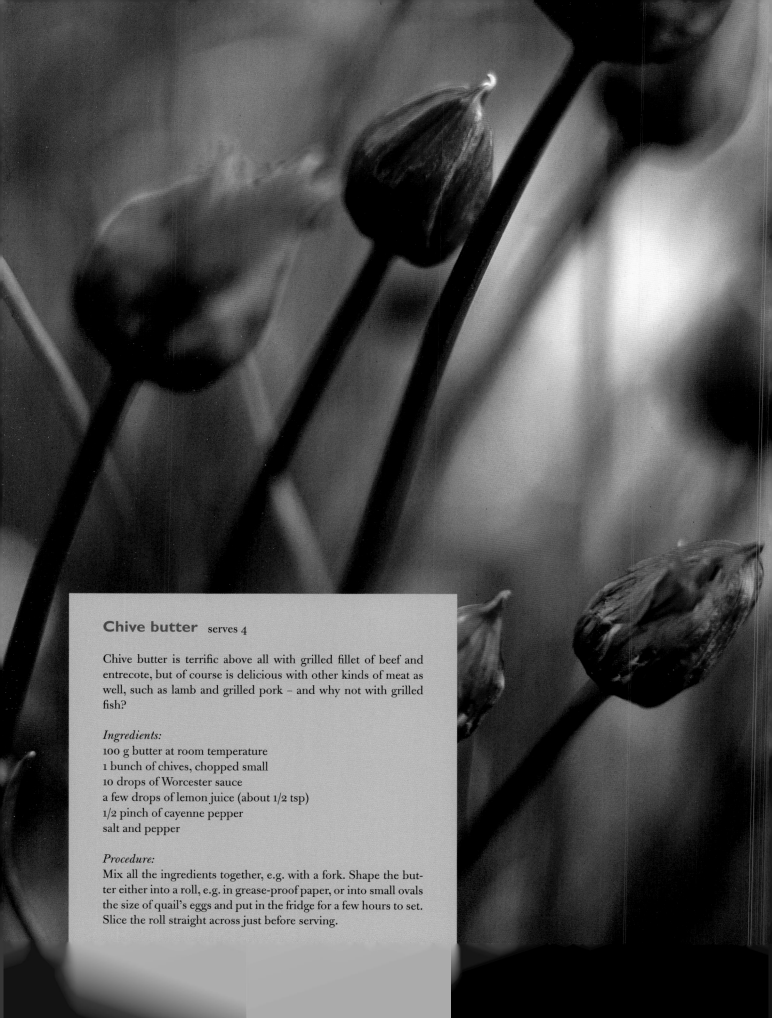

Chive butter serves 4

Chive butter is terrific above all with grilled fillet of beef and entrecote, but of course is delicious with other kinds of meat as well, such as lamb and grilled pork – and why not with grilled fish?

Ingredients:
100 g butter at room temperature
1 bunch of chives, chopped small
10 drops of Worcester sauce
a few drops of lemon juice (about 1/2 tsp)
1/2 pinch of cayenne pepper
salt and pepper

Procedure:
Mix all the ingredients together, e.g. with a fork. Shape the butter either into a roll, e.g. in grease-proof paper, or into small ovals the size of quail's eggs and put in the fridge for a few hours to set. Slice the roll straight across just before serving.

Kalmar casserole serves 4

Lamb chops with ham or bacon served with Skåne potatoes and pickled gherkin are usually collectively termed Kalmar casserole. The reason is anyone's guess, considering that Kalmar is in Småland, not Skåne, but never mind.

Either way, this is a real autumn recipe when there is fresh lamb and newly pickled gherkins to be had (unless you've pickled some yourself, of course). If you fancy making your own concentrated veal stock, there's a recipe for it on page 250.

Ingredients:
12 lamb chops
12 slices of smoked ham or bacon

Skåne potatoes:
1 large onion
1 kg potatoes
butter for frying
1 tsp white flour
4 dl cooking cream or milk
1/2 dl concentrated veal stock
2 tsp Kikkoman soy
salt and pepper

Serve with:
chive butter
salt gherkin or *ättika*-pickled gherkin

Procedure:
Make the butter and shape it into a roll. Put it in the fridge. Cut up the salt gherkin or pickled gherkin into long sticks or diagonal slices.

Peel the onion and chop it quite small. Peel the potatoes and cut them into centimetre cubes. Fry the potato in butter and add the onion. Fry until it just changes colour. Sprinkle with the flour, pour on the cream, concentrated veal stock and soy. Simmer over a low flame till the sauce thickens. Season to taste. Dilute with additional cream or milk if the sauce gets too thick.

Brown the ham or bacon and pat away the fat on kitchen tissue. Keep warm. Season the lamb chops and fry them for a couple of minutes on each side; the core of the meat must be pink.

Transfer the creamed potato, chops and ham or bacon to a serving dish. Serve immediately with the butter and the gherkin sticks.

207

Shepherd's pie serves 4

At a guess, this spicy, feisty pie originated in the northern regions of the British Isles, where great flocks of lambs roam the hillsides.

You don't need me to tell you that close links have existed between Sweden and the British Isles ever since the Viking era, and shepherd's pie could be "living" proof of the connection.

A fancy nozzle on the end of your piping bag will pattern the mashed potato attractively.

Ingredients:
600 g minced lamb
butter for frying
1 onion
1 carrot
2 tbsp tomato purée
2 tbsp concentrated veal stock (bottled or otherwise)
1 dl water
1 tsp newly crushed allspice
1 pinch of ground cloves
2 bay leaves
2 cloves of garlic
salt and pepper

Pommes duchesse with celeriac:
600 g potatoes
200 g celeriac
2 egg yolks
100 g butter
3 tbsp neutral oil
a few scrapes of nutmeg
salt and pepper

Serve with:
crisp green salad
farmhouse bread
matured cheese

Procedure:
Set the oven to 200°C. Start by making the pommes duchesse. Peel the potatoes and celeriac, cut them up fairly small and boil them in salted water till soft.

Meanwhile sauté the minced lamb in butter in a frying pan till it has disintegrated and is starting to change colour. Add salt and pepper. Peel and chop the onion and garlic. Peel and grate the carrot. Add the onion and garlic, the grated carrot, the tomato purée, the concentrated veal stock, the water and the spices to the contents of the frying pan and simmer till you have a fairly thick mixture.

While all this is going on, finish off the mashed potato. Pour off the cooking water and beat the potatoes and celeriac together with the other ingredients to form a smooth mash. Transfer this to a piping bag.

Retrieve the bay leaves from the mince and transfer it to a greased oven-proof dish. Spoon the mash over the mince, or else pipe it as pictured. Bake on the middle shelf of the oven until the mash is a nice colour. Serve with a crisp green salad, farmhouse bread and matured cheese.

Pork Chop Esterhazy serves 4

I'm uncertain as to the origin of this recipe, because the Hungarian Esterhazys are such an ancient aristocratic family and are spread out all over Europe. Perhaps it was a military man who wanted his pork chops done this way, or one of the patrons of the arts who took such musical titans as Schubert and Haydn under the shadow of their wing.

What I do know is that this way of doing pork chops has long been a popular classic in Swedish restaurants, introduced presumably by one of the talented German chefs working here in the old days.

This recipe also works with fresh veal cutlets or slices of lamb. And try drinking a Hungarian red wine with it.

Ingredients:
4 marbled pork chops (200 g each)
1 leek
1 carrot
1 parsnip
1 tbsp paprika powder
1 1/2 tbsp white flour
butter for frying
salt and pepper

Sauce:
1 tbsp tomato purée
2 dl beef or veal stock
2 dl cooking yoghurt
salt and pepper

Serve with:
boiled floury potatoes
sour cream (crème fraîche)
salt gherkin

Procedure:
Set the oven to 175°C. Peel the carrot and parsnip. Shred the vegetables into narrow strips. Sauté them in a little butter in a frying pan. Mix the sauce ingredients in a saucepan and bring to the boil. Season to taste.

Mix the flour and paprika powder. Season the chops and turn them in the flour mixture. Heat the butter in a sauté pan and brown the chops for 6–7 minutes on both side, until they are a beautiful golden brown. Drizzle over the sauce, distribute the vegetables over the chops and cover. Leave the chops to simmer and finish frying in the middle of the oven for 12–15 minutes.

Serve instantly with boiled floury potatoes (to soak up the wonderful sauce), sour cream and salt gherkin.

Calf Liver Anglais serves 4

The name notwithstanding, this is probably the commonest way of frying calf's liver in Sweden. It is a culinary triumph and one of the healthiest foods obtainable.

Fried bacon and capers are classic accompaniments, but I don't think either Brits or Swedes will object if I add browned apple wedges and browned red onion. Beer or mineral water goes best with this one.

Ingredients:
800 g calf's liver
140 g bacon
1 red onion
1 sharp apple
butter for frying
white flour for breading
2 tbsp capers
salt and pepper

Serve with:
boiled floury potatoes
gravy sauce (see page 121)

Procedure:
Fry the bacon to the right degree of crispiness, then drain it on kitchen tissue. Keep it warm. Peel the red onion and cut it into narrow strips, and do the same with the apple. Sauté both of them lightly in butter in a frying pan. Keep warm.

Trim the liver and cut it in centimetre-thick slices. Season them, dredge them in the flour and fry them quickly on both sides in a frying pan at fairly high temperature. The liver can very well be a little pink on the inside. Quickly sauté the capers in the same pan and add the onion and apple wedges. Serve the liver on warm plates with the sautéed vegetables, potatoes, bacon and gravy sauce.

Loin of pork larded with fruit   serves 4–5

Loin of pork larded with fruit is one of the most Swedish concoctions I can think of, a real classic, especially at Sunday dinner-time. I can still see my father standing there, carving juicy slices from a large, well-braised loin of pork. "That's the stuff to give the troops!" as the saying used to be.

Here I've tried using plums, apricots, dried apple and really large dried grapes instead of tiny raisins. To drink with this I recommend a few noggins of Norrlands Akvavit (if you can get it) and a round-flavoured beer.

Ingredients:
1 1/2 kg fresh loin of pork
2 onions
1 handful of tender, stoned prunes
1 handful of tender, dried apricots
1 handful of dried apple
1 handful of dried grapes
butter for frying
5 dl water
2 veal stock cubes
salt and pepper
cotton thread (optional)

Gravy sauce:
3–4 dl liquid from cooking the meat
a little corn starch flour (Idealmjöl), if needed
1 dl whipping cream (optional)

Serve with:
boiled or riced potatoes
pickles of your choice
jelly, e.g. red or black currant

Procedure:
Peel and quarter the onions. Trim away all surplus fat from the pork. Make some generous holes in it with a carving knife sharpener or a knife point. Lard it with as much dried fruit as there is room for, reserving the rest for cooking. If you truss the meat with cotton thread it will keep its shape better. Season generously.

Heat a large cast iron casserole and put in the butter. Brown the meat all round till it is a nice colour. Pour on the water, put in the stock cubes, the onion and surplus fruit. Bring to the boil, then lower the heat and cover. Let the meat simmer, still covered, for about 1 1/2 hours. Check the seasoning once or twice. Remove the meat and keep it warm.

Take 3–4 dl of the cooking liquid and reduce a little, perhaps thickening with a little corn starch flour and adding cream. Keep warm.

Carve the meat and arrange it neatly, garnishing with the fruit and onion in the stock.

Serve with boiled or riced potatoes, the sauce, some of your best pickles and jelly.

Onion soup serves 4

Swedish eating habits have been influenced by French cooking in many more ways than one, and onion soup on a chill autumn day is about as French as it gets. Heartily recommended! A glass of good ordinary red wine will suit the occasion excellently, or else a cool, full-bodied beer with a tang to it.

Ingredients:
3 large onions
2 cloves of garlic
1/2 dl olive oil
25 g butter
1 pinch of caster sugar
1 l chicken stock
2 dl dry white wine
a few sprigs of thyme
4 slices of white bread
200 g grated gruyere or matured Grevé cheese

Procedure:
Set the oven to 200°C. Peel the onion and garlic and slice them thinly.

Sauté everything golden brown in oil and butter. Sprinkle with a punch of sugar, then season. Cut the thyme up small. Pour on the stock, the wine and the thyme, cover and simmer slowly for about 30 minutes, till the onion is soft.

Toast the bread. Grate the cheese.

Put the soup into four oven-proof bowls. Put a slice of bread in each bowl and sprinkle generously with cheese. Bake in the oven on a high shelf until the cheese has turned a crispy golden brown. Serve immediately and don't forget to warn the guests about the plates being hot.

Shrimp soup serves 4

I've said it many times before and I'll say it again: never throw shellfish shells away! For they are the very essence of a delicious shellfish bouillon. Here you get the best of both worlds, enjoying the shrimps and the wonderful shrimp soup on one and the same occasion. A glass of cold white wine goes down well – a Muscadet, for example, or something of the kind.

Ingredients:
600 g fresh shrimps in their shells
1 onion
1/2 fennel bulb (about 50 g)
2 tbsp olive oil
1 tbsp tomato purée
6 dl fish stock
1 dl dry white wine
3 dl whipping cream
1 tbsp brandy
4 slices of white bread
1/2 bunch of dill

Procedure:
Peel the shrimps and reserve the shells. Peel the onion and chop small. Trim the fennel and cut it into small cubes.

Sauté the shrimp shells in the oil in a saucepan for a couple of minutes, stirring all the time. Add the onion, fennel and tomato purée. Sauté for another minute or so. Pour on the fish stock and wine. Simmer over a medium flame for 10–12 minutes. Strain.

Pour on the cream and simmer for about 10 minutes. Season to taste, with a dash of cognac to heighten the flavour still further.

Arrange the shrimps neatly and close together on the bread and garnish with dill sprigs. Serve the shrimp sandwiches with the soup. First, though, you may care to froth it up with a stick blender.

Fish balls with scallions stewed in caviar

serves 4

Whenever we're serving fish balls with scallions stewed in caviar as the day's special at Sjömagasinet, the rumour spreads like wildfire. And I can understand it, because, with all deference to our captains of industry, anything further removed from the tinned variety just can't be imagined.

Fish balls are as easy to make as ordinary meatballs, and they're just as cheap and good. Since its introduction many years ago, this dish has grown so popular that there are now quite a few Göteborg restaurants serving it.

Ingredients:
600 g fish mince
2 small onions
butter for frying
1 tbsp cold boiled potato
2 eggs
3 tbsp dried breadcrumbs
a pinch of sugar
salt and pepper

Creamed onion:
1 bunch of scallions
1 dl crème fraîche
1/2 dl whipping cream
1 tbsp bleak roe "caviar" (Slotts kaviar)
salt and pepper

Serve with:
boiled or riced potatoes

Procedure:
Peel the onion and chop it up fine. Fry it in butter till it is soft but has not changed colour. Mash the potato with a fork in a mixing bowl. Mix in the eggs and dried breadcrumbs and leave to swell for a moment. Mix in the fish mince and fried onion, adding sugar, salt and pepper. Blend to a smooth mixture. Preferably, fry a small sample to check the seasoning.

Shape the mince into round balls. The professional and fastest way of doing this is by putting the mixture into a piping bag and squeezing out suitably sized blobs. Fry them golden brown in butter.

Meanwhile, clean the scallions and cut them up small. Boil them for a few minutes in lightly salted water, then drain off. Warm the crème fraîche and cream in a saucepan. Mix in the "caviar", check the salinity and add pepper. Carefully fold in the onion.

Serve everything piping hot with boiled or riced potatoes. Boy, what a treat!

216

Sautéed chicken liver with button mushrooms, grapes and pork serves 4

Chicken liver recipes, perhaps not exactly a Swedish tradition but more of a French speciality. Never mind. Chicken liver, in my opinion, is an excellent but underrated raw material which is both tasty and very good for you.

It's had some difficulty catching the public eye, and I'd like to change that a little by tipping you off about this way of preparing it. A moderately bitter beer is the best drink to go with it.

Ingredients:
600 g chicken liver in pieces
200 g salt pork
30 button onions
2 cloves of garlic
150 g button mushrooms
butter and oil for frying
1 small bunch of grapes (about 100 g)
a handful of sugar snap peas (about 100 g)
1 sprig of fresh thyme or 1/2 tsp of the dried version
1 1/2 dl veal stock
2 tbsp brandy
1/2 bunch flat-leafed parsley, shredded fine
salt and pepper

Croutons:
day-old white bread
butter for frying

Serve with:
mashed potato (see page 103)

Procedure:
Cut the pork into "matchsticks". Peel the onions. Peel and crush the garlic. Fry the pork in a little butter and oil in a frying pan. Add the mushrooms and button onions. Flavour with garlic, thyme and marjoram. Fry slowly for about 10 minutes, or until the onions are soft, then put aside for the time being.

Make the mashed potato and keep it warm.

Divide the grapes, perhaps deseeding them. Top and tail the sugar snap peas and split them obliquely in half. Cut the bread into croutons and fry these in butter in a frying pan. Keep them warm.

Pat the liver dry in a little kitchen tissue and divide it in pieces. Add salt and pepper. Heat up the oil in a frying pan. Brown the liver quickly all round. Lower the heat, pour on the brandy and flambé (though not under the fan hood, of course). Pour on the stock. Heat up and then add the sautéed pork and the pan juices. Simmer for 2–3 minutes and add more seasoning if necessary. Put in the sugar snap peas, grapes and parsley at the last minute and bring everything to the boil. Garnish with the croutons and serve straight from the casserole together with the mashed potato.

Brisket of beef, mustard-grilled with a Swedish "anchovy" sauce serves 4

This is a classic, and the mustard-grilling and "anchovy" sauce give it that little extra pungency.

You're well advised to buy a fairly big piece of meat, because the spare can go into a rich meat soup, be cooked with horse-radish or turned into salt brisket.

In case you wonder what is the point of putting brisket under pressure after cooking it, the answer is that this way the meat retains its shape and will be easier to carve into neat slices. You can prepare the meat a day beforehand, then the job will be half-done already.

Ingredients:
1 netted, salted brisket of veal/beef (1 1/2–2 kg)
1 onion
1 leek (the white part)
2–3 carrots
2 bay leaves
about 10 parsley stalks
6–8 white peppercorns
salt if required

For breading:
Swedish mustard
2–3 tbsp white flour
1 egg
1 dl dried breadcrumbs
butter for frying

Sauce:
2 tbsp butter
1 tbsp white flour
1/2 l stock from cooking the meat
1 dl whipping cream
8 "anchovy" fillets
1–2 tbsp "anchovy" liquor
1/2 bunch of chives, chopped fine
juice of 1/2 lemon

Serve with:
boiled potatoes
boiled vegetable of your choice
lemon

Procedure:
Day 1. Peel and slice the onion. Clean the leek and cut into thick slices. Peel the carrots and cut them into thick slices. Bring the meat to the boil and cook for a minute or so. Remove it, rinse it under the tap, return it to the pot and pour on fresh water. Bring to the boil again, skim if necessary and put in the vegetables and herbs and spices. Cover and cook slowly for 2–2 1/2 hours. Test to see when it is getting tender. Leave it to cool in the cooking liquid, then remove it and store it under pressure for the night.

Day 2. Make the sauce. Melt the butter in a saucepan, Whisk in the flour. Dilute with the stock and cream. Reduce the sauce till it starts to thicken, then put in the "anchovy" fillets, a little of the liquor they came in and the chives. Add salt, pepper and lemon juice to taste. Keep warm.

Remove the meat and carve slices 1/2 cm thick. Double bread it by smearing mustard on both sides, dredging in white flour, dipping in egg and, finally, turning the slices in dried bread-crumbs. Fry the slices crisp in lots of butter in a frying pan.

Serve instantly with potatoes, vegetables and the hot sauce.

Beef roulades with cold-smoked pork

serves 4

Beef roulades too have their appointed, pivotal position in traditional Swedish home cooking. They used to be literally larded, with whole slices of the stuff, but that would make them unnecessarily fat now that we don't need so many calories to keep us going.

These roulades of mine are a modernised version with a filling of cold-smoked pork, apple slices and onion instead. A little different but just as good as the original, if not better.

Ingredients:
8 slices of beef silverside or rump (about 600 g)
4 slices of cold-smoked pork (70–80 g)
1 red onion
1 (yellow) onion
1 salt gherkin
1 apple
2–3 tbsp Dijon mustard
butter for frying
salt and pepper

Sauce:
1 l pan juices
1 beef stock cube or concentrated beef stock (optional)
1 onion
2 apples
2 carrots
1/2 "anchovy" liquor
salt and pepper

Serve with:
potatoes or mashed potato (see page 103)
"matchsticks" of salt gherkin (optional)

Procedure:
Cut the pork lengthwise into strips. Peel the onions and cut them into narrow strips. Cut the salt gherkin into sticks. De-core the apple and cut it into sticks. Spread out the slices of meat on a chopping board and flatten them out a little with your knuckles. Spread with Dijon mustard. Add salt and pepper. Distribute the pork, onion, salt gherkin and apple on the slices of meat and roll up tight. Put the roulades onto skewers, four roulades at a time. Brown them nicely in butter in a wide frying pan. Remove them and deglaze the pan with a little water. Top up with a litre of water and bring this to the boil. Season to taste, also adding stock (concentrated or otherwise) if you like.

Peel and slice the onion for the sauce. De-core the apples and cut them up nicely. Peel and cut up the carrots. Transfer the skewers to an iron pot. Cover and simmer for about 1 hour until the roulades are tender. Put in the vegetables at half time.

Serve straight from the pot with boiled floury potatoes or a good potato mash, and perhaps additional salt gherkin sticks.

223

Boiled chicken legs in tarragon sauce

serves 4–5

Boiled chicken legs in tarragon sauce are frequently in evidence in the Mannerström ménage. Mainly because this is a superb method of preparing a well-fed chicken or just chicken legs, but also because my son Sebastian always gets it. In my opinion he has absolute gastronomic pitch, as witness the perfection of the sauce.

Chicken done this way evokes powerful memories of family holidays in France. Myself I prefer a glass or two of Alsace wine or a well-made Riesling to drink, but you could do worse than a cold, flowery lager.

Ingredients:
1 1/2 kg fresh chicken legs
2 onions
2 carrots
2 dl dry white wine
1 bunch of fresh tarragon or 1/2 tbsp of dried
2 bay leaves
10 white peppercorns
salt

Vegetables:
2 carrots
2 parsnips
4 potatoes
2 scallions

Sauce:
2 dl whipping cream
1 tbsp Dijon mustard
3 dl crème fraîche
2 tbsp tarragon vinegar
1 bunch of fresh tarragon
salt and pepper

Serve with:
potatoes boiled with the vegetables, or else boiled rice

Procedure:
Rinse the chicken legs carefully and put them in a casserole. Pour on enough water to cover them. Bring to the boil and skim carefully. Peel the onions and cut them in wedges. Peel and cut up the carrots. Add the carrots, onion, wine and herbs and spices to the pot. Start with 1/2 tsp per litre of water and check the salinity later on, with the stock reduced. Cook slowly for 25–30 minutes until the legs are tender. Remove the chicken legs and keep them warm, e.g. by wrapping them in foil.

Prepare the vegetables. Peel the carrots and parsnips and cut them in sticks. Peel and slice the potatoes. Trim and divide the scallions. Boil them in the stock until they are just tender, then keep them warm.

Reduce the cooking liquid until you have 1/2 l strong, tasty bouillon. Strain this and pour it back into the pot. Add the cream, mustard and crème fraîche. Add tarragon vinegar to give the right degree of acidity – a matter between you and your taste buds. Check the seasoning too. Strain the sauce. Pour it back into a saucepan and keep it warm. Pluck the tarragon leaves from the stems. Chop the leaves up small and put them in the sauce. Transfer the chicken legs to a warm serving dish and drizzle the hot sauce over them. If you are serving rice with the chicken legs, the potatoes can be dispensed with.

Rädisa ✻ Radis
Reddik ✻ Retiisi
(Københavns Torve)

Hammenhögs   ② #1684

Raphanus sativus

Sausage stew serves 4

Sausage of every shape and kind comes top of the Swedish pops in whatever part of the country you may happen to be. Most food stores abound with sausage of good quality, and there is absolutely no reason for making do with second best.

A good sausage stew like this one is ideal for a dinner party, whether large or small, and especially if there are different age groups represented. And to drink with it? A battery of good export beers for the guests to choose from isn't a bad idea at all.

Ingredients:
6–8 sausages of different kinds, e.g. kabanoss, Frankfurter, Nuremberg, Bratwurst and Käsekrainer
1 large onion
1 parsnip
1 large parsley root
800 g potatoes
3 carrots
1 small wedge of cabbage (about 200 g)
1 bottle of light beer (33 cl)
1/2–1 l chicken stock
10–12 allspice corns
2 bay leaves
a few sprigs of thyme
1/2 bunch of flat-leafed parsley, chopped fine
salt and pepper

Serve with:
fresh-baked farmhouse bread
good strong mustard

Procedure:
Cut the sausages into big pieces. Peel the onion and cut into wedges. Peel the parsnip and cut into thick sticks. Peel the parsley root and shred it fine. Peel the potatoes and cut them up in wedges. Peel the carrots and cut them into thick sticks. Shred the cabbage.

Put all the ingredients in layers in a big casserole which can be put straight on the table afterwards. Season each layer. Tie the thyme and parsley into a bouquet garni and put this in the middle of the pot. Pour on the beer and chicken stock, enough to cover. Bring to the boil and then cook everything gently till the potatoes and vegetables are done, but not to death. Sprinkle with the parsley and serve with the suggested accessories or something else of your own choosing.

Hints:
Sausage stew is the perfect thing to chew on at a beer tasting, for example.

Stuffed onions serves 4

Here I go again with my beloved minced meat; I believe there are thousands and thousands of ways of ringing the changes on it!

One day when you have picked some fist-sized onions in your garden or bought a bunch of fresh biggies at the market, take the opportunity of making onion dolmades with a minced meat filling.

This particular variant has a touch that a lot of people may recall from holidays in Greece, which is exactly the intention.

Ingredients:
4 large onions
500 g mixed (pork and beef) mince
1 red paprika
2 cloves of garlic
100 g feta cheese
50 g kalamata olives
1 sprig of fresh thyme
1 sprig of fresh rosemary
1 egg
about 1 tsp paprika powder
1/2 dl olive oil
salt and pepper

Serve with:
boiled potatoes or rice
warm tomato sauce (see page 232) or gravy sauce (see page 121)
Greek farm bread or coarse white bread of some other kind

Procedure:
Set the oven to 225°C. Make the tomato sauce first if you are going to serve it. Keep it warm.

Peel the onions, keeping them intact; the secret is not to cut off any of the tip and not too much of the root. Bring them to the boil in lightly salted water and simmer them for about 10 minutes, until they are getting tender. Leave them to cool until you can handle them. Cut off quite wide "caps" and reserve them. Carefully squeeze out as much of the inside of the onions as possible, until 3–4 layers remain. Put the onions in a greased oven-proof dish.

Chop the "innards" of the onions up small. Peel and crush the garlic cloves. Divide the paprika and remove the core. Cut the paprika into small pieces. Divide the feta cheese into small cubes. Stone and chop the olives. Strip the leaves from the thyme and rosemary and chop them up. Mix all the ingredients together with the mince. Add salt and pepper.

Fill the onions generously and press the caps back on. Bake on the middle shelf of the oven for about 20 minutes, until the onion dolmades are a really nice colour. If the caps look like getting over-browned, you can remove them for the last few minutes. Serve the stuffed onions piping hot together with the accessories of your choosing.

Tomato sauce serves 4

This is a really delicious and useful tomato sauce to go with fried or roast pork and lamb, meatballs, onion dolmades and baked root vegetables. It's a good idea to make a big batch for the freezer. In the fridge it'll keep for six weeks at the outside, since it contains no preservatives.

Ingredients:
1 onion, chopped small
2 crushed cloves of garlic
1/2 dl olive oil
1 tin of crushed tomatoes
2 tbsp tomato purée
2 dl water
1 tsp caster sugar
1 tsp oregano
salt and pepper

Procedure:
Peel the onion and chop it up small. Peel and crush the garlic. Sauté both in the olive oil without letting them change colour. Add the tomatoes, the tomato purée and the water. Stir well. Add the sugar and oregano. Season to taste.

Simmer gently for 10–15 minutes until it starts looking thick and smooth. If you strain it through a coarse-meshed sieve this will make it extra smooth, but there's absolutely no need.

Hints:
The tomato sauce will be extra good if you slip in a slice of bacon already when sautéing the onion. Remove it when the sauce is done and its mission accomplished.

This sauce also has exactly the right flavour to go with home-made pizza, so try it some time and let your imagination rip.

Béarnaise sauce serves 4

Believe it or not, but the history of béarnaise sauce goes back something like 450 years, though not in Sweden but in France. For a long time now it has been a popular classic in Sweden too, mainly with grilled dark meat but also with fried fish.

The simplest way of making a béarnaise sauce is to make a batch of hollandaise sauce and flavour it with a béarnaise reduction.

Ingredients:
2 shallots
2 tbsp water
2 tbsp tarragon vinegar
5 white peppercorns
1 batch of hollandaise sauce (see page 33)
1/2 dl flat-leaved parsley, chopped small
1/2 dl tarragon, chopped small
salt and black pepper

Procedure:
Peel the shallots and chop them up small. Put them in a steel saucepan along with the water, vinegar and crushed peppercorns. Bring to the boil and reduce until 1/3 of the liquid remains.

Strain the shallots in a fine-meshed sieve and press out the last drops of concentrated, reduced liquid. Mix this into the hollandaise sauce and add the parsley and tarragon.

On no account must this sauce be allowed to boil, but it can be kept suitably warm over a bain-marie. Béarnaise must not be served hot but rather lukewarm. Before serving, add a little salt according to taste.

Hot dog with potato salad serves 4

Although I've often been privileged to sample the most delicate and exquisite of comestibles, I don't mind admitting that, like so many other Swedes, I also love sausage. But only if it's well made, well spiced and has a generous meat content.

I think we should be grateful for the salutary effect that immigration and other foreign influences have had on our sausage tradition, which they have both broadened and enriched.

If, in addition, I get a good, home-made potato salad, plus a wee drop of the creature and a feisty beer, that just about makes my day. I hanker for this kind of treat above all in summertime, when there are new potatoes to be had.

Ingredients:
1 kg sausage, e.g. Bratwurst, cheese sausage (Käsekrainer) or Nuremberg sausage

Potato salad:
600 g potatoes
1 red onion
1 (yellow) onion
2 tbsp capers
2 1/2 dl mayonnaise
1 1/2 dl cultured cream (*gräddfil*)
1 crushed clove of garlic
1 bunch of chives, chopped small
1 tbsp Dijon mustard
1/2 tbsp "anchovy" liquor
salt and pepper

Garnish:
1/2 red onion
large capers

Procedure:
Scrub the potatoes, then boil them tender in lightly salted water, taking care not to overdo them. Leave them to cool completely. Peel the onions and chop them up small. Rough-chop the capers. Mix the mayonnaise and gräddfil thoroughly. Add the rest of the ingredients, except the potatoes, stir together and season to taste. Slice the potato and fold it into the sauce. Peel the red onion and cut it into little "boats". Scatter it over the potato salad. Store cold for a couple of hours.

Grill the sausages nicely and evenly. Serve them at once, piping hot, with the cold potato salad and a cool drink.

Sailor's stew serves 6

Sailor's stew is a good old autumn and winter stew recipe, and just the thing when the sailing enthusiasts have already begun dreaming of the next summer season. And of course for ordinary landlubbers who feel the need for something warm and satisfying when icicles hang by the wall. The pork makes everything juicier and elevates both flavour and fragrance by a few points.

Vodka and beer go particularly well with sailor's stew – a drink to calm seas and prosperous voyages, and homage to the seductive aromas of the pot.

Ingredients:
800 g beef, e.g. silverside or sirloin
200 g salt, lean pork
1 kg potatoes
2 large onions
1 leek (the white part)
1 tsp allspice
1 tsp white pepper
2 cloves
butter for frying
1/2 tbsp flour
6 bay leaves
5 dl beef stock
1 bottle of beer (33 cl)
salt

Serve with:
pickled gherkin (see page 119)
fresh-baked bread or crisp bread

Procedure:
Set the oven to 175°C. Peel the potatoes and cut them into slices about 1 cm thick. Peel the onions and slice them thin, and cut the leek into thin rings. Carve thin slices of the beef and pork. Pound all the spices, except the bay leaves, thoroughly in a mortar.

Brown the meat, onion and slices of potato quickly and separately in butter, without letting them change colour.

Put alternate layers of potato slices, beef, pork and onion into a greased dish or cast iron casserole, beginning and ending with potato. Season between layers, sprinkle with a little flour and put in the bay leaves. Pour on the stock and beer.

Cover and cook gently for about 1/2 hour in the oven. Test with a skewer to make sure everything is tender and ready. Serve immediately with gherkins and fresh-baked bread or a crunchy crisp bread.

Minced meat sauce   serves 4

I don't think people in Sweden began eating minced meat sauce and spaghetti until some time in the 1950s, when a lot of Italian immigrants settled in our country and more Swedes started going abroad for their holidays.

That was all such a long time ago that minced meat sauce with different kinds of pasta has incontrovertibly become part and parcel of the Swedish culinary heritage.

Make your own sauce because, properly made, it's indescribably good! Try the simple recipe set out below, going on to evolve the family favourite through your own experimentation. Use preferably good-quality pasta which you are already acquainted with. Our picture shows a fairly thick one which we have mixed with the minced meat sauce and shredded basil leaves, with everything dished up together.

A light Italian red wine is of course the perfect accompaniment.

Ingredients:
800 g minced beef or pork and beef mince mixed
1 large onion
butter or oil for frying
2 crushed cloves of garlic
1 tin of crushed tomatoes
2 tbsp of tomato purée
1 dl white wine
2 tbsp concentrated veal stock (bottled)
2 tsp dried oregano
10–12 cherry tomatoes
salt and pepper

Serve with:
basilica leaves

Procedure:
Peel and chop the onion, or else cut into short, narrow strips. Halve the tomatoes. Heat a frying pan and put in the butter or oil. Add the mince and onion when the oil is hot or the butter has stopped sizzling. Brown on a high flame until the mince is a nice colour.

Add the other ingredients except the tomatoes and lower the heat. Season to taste. Simmer gently for about 20 minutes. Add the tomatoes at half time. Add water or stock if needed. Meanwhile boil the pasta.

239

Braised pork bones serves 4

Another filling recipe from my food-loving Aunt Astrid in Helsingborg, a divinely talented weekday cook who seemed almost to cast a spell over her raw materials. With luck you can also be treated to this delicacy in the home of my brother Kenneth, an adventure-loving police officer who also happens to be a home chef of professional calibre, in between foreign assignments.

One of the secrets of this lovely recipe is that the pork bones must be fresh and have plenty of meat on them, and another is to choose a good apple juice from the year's harvest. An earthy red wine or a cold pilsner is the best choice of drink.

Ingredients:
2 kg meaty pork bones
1 onion
1 parsnip
1 apple
butter for frying
2 dl fresh apple juice
5 dl water
2 beef stock cubes
2 bay leaves
1 sprig of fresh thyme
2 dl whipping cream
butter for frying
salt and pepper

Serve with:
boiled floury potatoes
pickled gherkin (see page 119)
pressed cucumber (see page 26)
pickled tomatoes
red or black currant jelly
red onion marmalade

Procedure:
Peel the onion and parsnip and cut them into chunks. De-core the apple and cut it into chunks. Season the meat well. Brown the pieces thoroughly all round in butter, in a casserole. Remove them and brown the vegetables. Return the meat to the pot, and pour on the apple juice and water. Crumble the stock cubes into the pot and put in the bay leaves and thyme. Cover and simmer gently for about 1 hour.

Remove the pork bones when the meat starts coming away from them. Put them in the oven to keep warm. Strain off the stock into a saucepan and reduce it by half. Pour in the cream and simmer until the sauce looks opaque and smooth. Check the seasoning.

Put the meat onto a warm serving dish. Pour on the sauce. Serve with boiled, floury potatoes and a number of bowls containing various preserves, jellies or freshly made compotes, e.g. red onion marmalade.

Red onion marmalade serves 4–5

Fresh red onion marmalade is a first-class accessory, together with various pickles from the larder, when there is meat on the table. The flavour needs to have a balance between sweet and sour, and this is something which, if you like, you can influence one way or the other by a process of trial and error.

Ingredients:
2 red onions
oil for frying
1 dl red wine
1 tbsp red wine vinegar
2 tbsp honey
1 bay leaf
1 pinch of ground cloves
salt and pepper

Procedure:
Peel the onions and cut them into nice leaves or "boats". Sauté these in the oil for a few minutes, without their colour turning. Add the rest of the ingredients and stir well. Simmer the marmalade over a low flame until it starts to thicken, seasoning every now and then. Remove the bay leaf before serving.

241

Wallenbergare with petits pois serves 4

A child of our time might be disposed to rename this recipe "Wallenburgers", which of course is quite out of the question. Both the name and the content of Wallenbergare are eminently deserving of preservation. This tasty classic is of course named after a member of the Wallenberg dynasty of Swedish financiers and industrialists. Many present-day food gurus have tried to take most of the cream out of Wallenbergare, which isn't at all a good idea, because then you end up with something quite different.

Serve with a well-flavoured and not over-firm potato mash seasoned with butter, salt, pepper and a few scrapes of nutmeg. A fresh lager or a soft, round Burgundy will do nicely if you're wondering what to drink.

Ingredients:
500 g fine-ground light veal mince
6 egg yolks
5 dl whipping cream
dried breadcrumbs for breading
butter for frying
salt and pepper

Petits pois (small green peas):
2 dl small green peas
2 shallots
4 slices of bacon or salt pancetta
2–3 leaves of iceberg lettuce
butter for frying

Serve with:
mashed potato (see page 103)
browned butter (optional)

Procedure:
Prepare the ingredients for the petits pois. Peel the onion and chop small, cut the pork into narrow strips. Shred the lettuce small. Put everything to one side for the moment.

The best way of mixing the farce is in a food processor. All the ingredients must be cold from the fridge. First run the mince for about 1 minute with the egg yolks and salt and pepper, then pour in all the cream at once and run for another minute or so. Scrape the sides carefully with a pot scraper so that nothing gets left out. Sift half the dried breadcrumbs onto a large chopping board. Shape four equal-sized patties about 2 cm thick on top of them. Flatten these out carefully with a frying spatula dipped in cold water. When you are satisfied with their shape, score a criss-cross pattern into them with the edge of the frying spatula, then sift the rest of the dried breadcrumbs over them.

Melt the butter in two frying pans. When it stops sizzling, transfer the patties very carefully – they're pretty loose at this stage – to the frying pans. Fry them for about 3 minutes on each side, until they are golden brown.

Brown the butter for the petits pois in a pan while the patties are frying. Sweat the onion a little, then put in the pork, followed a minute or so later by the peas. Season to taste. Finally fold in the lettuce. This only takes a few minutes.

Serve the Wallenbergare piping hot on a large, heated serving dish with the petits pois to one side, the mashed potato and (optional) browned butter.

Hints:
On the west coast of Sweden, Wallenbergare are quite commonly served with a cream sauce and uncooked, stirred lingonberry jam, which isn't at all a bad idea. Another coastal variant worth trying is fine-ground farce of cod, haddock or pike instead of minced veal. But then you would do well to serve the Wallenbergare with a white wine sauce or a shellfish sauce.

Macaroni casserole serves 4

I dedicate this macaroni casserole, as simple as it is tasty, to my good friend Baron Johan Ehrensvärd. His proud ancestry and blue blood notwithstanding, he's a sucker for *husmanskost*.

He usually makes a superb macaroni casserole when we meet, and here is my recipe as it has evolved since my childhood. With the Baron spending half of every year in Spain, nothing but Spanish red wine will do to drink, at least when we're having one of our macaroni casserole sessions.

Ingredients:
4 dl macaroni
2 dl water
6 dl milk
1 tsp caster sugar
a few scrapes of nutmeg
400 g heavily smoked pancetta
1 onion
1 bunch of scallions
oil for frying
3 dl grated matured Grevé or Manor House (herrgård) cheese
about 50 g butter

Scrambled egg:
4 eggs
2 dl milk
2 dl whipping cream
salt and pepper

Serve with:
a little browned butter (optional)

Procedure:
Bring the water and milk to the boil in a capacious saucepan. Boil the macaroni as per the instructions on the packet. Add salt and pepper, sugar and a few scrapes of nutmeg. Stir and set aside.

Set the oven to 200°C.

Cut the pork into oblong "cubes". Peel the onion and chop fine, Cut the chives up small. Brown the pork in oil for a few minutes, then add the onion and scallions and sauté for a minute or so longer. Season lightly. Grease a large oven-proof dish. Mix the macaroni thoroughly with the pork and onion, then fill the dish with alternate layers of this mixture and the cheese, ending with a layer of cheese on top. Put on a few knobs of butter.

Whisk the ingredients for the scrambled egg together and drizzle the mixture over the oven dish. Poke the mixture a little with a spoon, so the egg mixture runs down inside properly. Bake on the middle shelf of the oven for about 45 minutes or until the casserole is golden brown. You may care to cover it over with aluminium foil towards the end of the baking time. Probe it a little with a fork, to make sure it is firm and nice all the way to the bottom. Put the dish piping hot on the table, preferably accompanied by a little browned butter.

245

Fried salted brisket of beef with parsley-creamed carrots and potatoes serves 2

This is Swedish traditional home fare in all its glory, and I mean it. Erik Lallerstedt and I go way back as friends and colleagues, and once every year we have the same lunch together, a lunch that, strange as it may seem, often continues into the hours of evening.

It starts off with some marvellous canapés (see next spread), both of us having had the privilege of working together with brilliant cold buffet manageresses whose dexterity, sad to say, can only be reproduced pictorially. So in that respect the field is free for your creative imagination.

The canapés are followed by a little croustade with a filling of creamed veal sweetbreads and a topping of just a little crisp-fried bacon.

The main course is fried salted brisket of beef with parsley-creamed carrots and potatoes, which we are both childishly fond of, and to drink we always have a bumper glass of each his favourite beer and a freezer-misty dram of vodka.

Cook a really big piece of brisket and you'll have meat left over for several other recipes in this book.

After our taste buds have quietened down, we usually round off with home-made vanilla ice cream and warm chocolate sauce. If in Denmark, we always order in a Danish Olé – the cheese, you know – together with a bowl of fine-chopped onion and a small bottle of Solbaerrom, Danish black current liqueur.

Procedure:
Boil the brisket, e.g. as described in the recipe for fresh brisket of beef Flamande (see page 64). Store it cold and under pressure after it has cooled in the cooking liquid.

Boil the veal sweetbreads for about 20 minutes in lightly salted water and drain off the water. Peel the onion and chop it small. When the sweetbreads have cooled, pull away the membranes and pull the sweetbreads themselves apart. Sauté the onion and sweetbreads in the butter in a saucepan for a few minutes and then pour on the cream. Add chives, salt and pepper to taste and amalgamate for 5–6 minutes. Meanwhile crisp-fry the bacon, cut it in pieces and drain it on a little kitchen tissue. Fill the croustades with sweetbreads, top with bacon and serve immediately.

Peel the potatoes and carrots and cut them into thin slices. Melt the butter for creaming the vegetables in a saucepan and whisk in the flour. Dilute with the cream and milk to give a smooth sauce. Fold in the sliced potato and carrot, add salt and pepper and warm thoroughly. Mix in the parsley just before serving.

Heat a frying pan with some butter in. When the butter stops sizzling, fry the brisket quickly on both sides and serve instantly on warm places with the creamed vegetables. Food fit for a king!

247

Ingredients:
8–10 big slices of boiled salted brisket of beef
butter for frying

Creamed vegetables:
400 g boiled potatoes
2 carrots
1 tbsp butter
1 tbsp white flour
2 1/2 dl milk with the top on (2 dl milk, 1/2 dl cream)
1 bunch of flat-leafed parsley, chopped small
salt and pepper

Croustades:
100 g veal sweetbreads
1 shallot
1 dl whipping cream
1 dl chives chopped fine
butter for frying
4 slices of bacon
4 croustades
salt and pepper

The gems of the cold buffet

Shrimp canapé

Salmon canapé

Lobster canapé

Duck liver canapé

Concentrated stock recipes

Much can be replaced in this life of ours, but there is no substitute for proper concentrated stock. It is the foundation of really good sauces, and the whole of the classical cuisine is built on concentrated stocks of different kinds. All reputable restaurants therefore make their own, and so too, nowadays, do ambitious home cooks. I know weekday cooking often runs to a tight schedule, but why not go for concentrated stocks one rainy weekend? Believe me, the satisfaction of loading your freezer with small packages of concentrated stocks for ordinary weekdays to come takes a good deal of beating.

In particular, let me again remind you never to throw away shrimp, crayfish or lobster shells without first boiling them to extract and preserve the wonderful flavours they contain. A reduced concentrated crayfish or lobster stock is a superb taste amplifier in fish sauces, just like "anchovy" liquor and matjes herring pickling liquid, which should never be thrown away either.

Remember never to salt concentrated stocks. Leave that until they are being used and depending on what they are being used for. Concentrated crayfish stock, though, serves a natural salinity from the shells.

Fish stock, makes about 5 dl

A concentrated fish stock is best made with the bones of flat fish. Cod and other white fish will also do, but not salmon or mackerel.

Ingredients:
1 kg fish bones
1 onion
1 leek
2 bay leaves
3–4 white peppercorns
1 sprig of parsley
2 l water

Procedure:
Trim the fish frames and cut away the gills with a knife or scissors. Rinse carefully in cold water. Peel and chop the onion roughly, clean and cut up the leek.

Put the fish bones, onion and leek, the herbs, pepper and water into a capacious saucepan. Bring everything to the boil and skim carefully. Simmer over a low flame for about 20 minutes. Remove from the heat and leave to stand for about 15 minutes. Strain the broth.

Reduce the stock till 1/2 remains. Leave to cool, then pour into, say, plastic mugs with lids and store in the freezer.

Concentrated crayfish stock makes about 2–5 dl

Don't throw away the shells from your next crayfish party or shrimp orgy. Make concentrated stock with them instead and you will have the perfect foundation for an exquisite fish sauce or a creamy soup.

Ingredients:
1 kg shells of Norway lobsters, freshwater crayfish, lobster or shrimps
1 onion
1 carrot
1 small leek
1 1/2 dl rapeseed oil
1 1/2 tsp paprika powder
1 l fish stock or chicken stock
1 l water

Procedure:
Peel and rough-chop the onion. Peel and slice the carrot, clean the leek and divide it into 4–5 pieces.

Clean the shells. Cut off the tops of the heads with a pair of scissors so as to get rid of the stomach, otherwise your stock will be bitter. Crush the shells in a mortar or cut them up into small pieces.

Heat the oil in a saucepan and sauté the shells with the vegetables. Add the paprika powder before pouring on the stock and water. Bring to the boil and simmer for about 30 minutes. Strain the broth and reduce till 1/2 remains. Leave to cool, then pour into, say, plastic mugs with lids and store in the freezer.

Chicken stock makes 5–7 dl

Chicken stock goes well in sauces for poultry dishes but can also be mixed with concentrated fish stock in sauces or soups, e.g. white wine sauce or mussel soup. The chicken meat left over is used in salads or pasta dishes.

Ingredients:
2 kg chicken carcases or 2 broilers
1 large onion
1 clove of garlic
1 piece of celeriac
1 carrot
2–3 l water
1 sprig of thyme
3 bay leaves
a few white peppercorns

Procedure:
Put the chicken carcases or broilers into a capacious saucepan and pour on enough water to cover. Bring to the boil and keep boiling for a minute or so. Rinse the bones or birds in cold water to get rid of the protein substances which otherwise cloud the stock.

Peel and rough-chop the onion. Peel the garlic. Peel and cut up the celeriac and carrot. Give the bones a change of water, bring it to the boil, add the vegetables, herbs and peppercorns, cover and simmer for about 2 hours, adding more water if needed.

Remove from the heat and strain the broth (reserving any meat that has come away from the bones). Skim to remove a little of the fat if possible. Clean the saucepan and return the broth. Reduce till 1/2 remains. Leave to cool, then pour into, say, plastic mugs with lids and store in the freezer.

Concentrated veal stock makes about 7–5 dl

Concentrated veal stock, of course, is best used as a base for any number of sauces to go with meat recipes, but it can also be the foundation of dark sauces to accompany grilled sole or turbot.

Ingredients:
2 kg veal bones, chopped up fairly small
1 large onion
1 leek
1 carrot
1 piece of celeriac
2 tbsp tomato purée
3 bay leaves
a few white peppercorns
a few sprigs of thyme
3 l water
2 dl red wine

Procedure:
Set the oven to 200°C. Peel and rough-chop the onion, clean and cut up the leek. Peel the carrot and celeriac, slicing the carrot and cutting the celeriac into large cubes.

Put the veal bones into an oven-proof dish and brown them golden brown together with the vegetables on an upper shelf of the oven for about 2 hours. Now transfer them to a capacious saucepan. Add the tomato purée and the herbs and pepper and stir a little. Add the water and red wine and bring to the boil. Skim well, cover and cook gently for about 3 hours, adding more water if necessary. Remove from the heat and strain the liquid.

Clean the pot and pour the liquid back into it. Reduce to about 1/2. Leave to cool, then pour into, say, plastic mugs with lids and store in the freezer.

Butter rose à la Marita Olsson

Making a beautiful butter rose like the one pictured here isn't for the tyro. Like a number of other kitchen operations, it takes training.

Just as in the natural world, the butter rose is built up leaf by leaf, working from the inside outwards. Restaurants sometimes use a special sharp-edged wooden spoon for making the leaves, but you can try with a well-worn tablespoon.

The butter must be at room temperature, otherwise you won't be able to scrape out the leaves. Up-end them, working from the inside outwards, until you have built up a rose in bloom.

The one pictured here was made by Sjömagasinet's Marita Olsson, in my belief the best cold buffet manageress in the land.

Alphabetical index

254

© 2006, 2007 Leif Mannerström and Prisma
Original title: Husmanskonst

Project management and production: Lill Forsman, Anki Hedberg and Lisa Sjölin, Bokbolaget AB
Editor: Jesper Lindberg
Swedish text: Tord Melander
English translation: Roger Tanner
Recipes: Leif Mannerström and Ola Andersson
Recipe checking: Malin Landqvist
Accessories and styling: Sarah Bergh
Photography, food and still-lifes: Tomas Yeh
Photography, settings: Lisa Nestorson
Graphic design: Christer Strandberg
Origination: Karin Strandberg
Typefaces: Bulmer Monotype and (headings) Gill Bold
Repro and printing: Fälth & Hässler, Värnamo 2007
Paper: MultiArt matt 150 g from Papyrus Sverige AB

ISBN 978-91-518-5025-2

Bokförlaget Prisma
Personal callers: Tryckerigatan 4
Box 2052
SE-103 12 Stockholm, Sweden
prisma@prismabok.se
www.prismabok.se
Prisma is a member of Norstedts Förlagsgrupp AB, founded in 1823

FLY FISHING TAILWATERS

TACTICS AND PATTERNS FOR
YEAR-ROUND WATERS

FLY FISHING TAILWATERS

TACTICS AND PATTERNS FOR YEAR-ROUND WATERS

Pat Dorsey

STACKPOLE
BOOKS

Published by
STACKPOLE BOOKS
5067 Ritter Road
Mechanicsburg, PA 17055
www.stackpolebooks.com

Printed in China

10 9 8 7 6 5 4 3 2 1

First edition

Photography by Pat Dorsey unless otherwise noted
Illustrations by Dave Hall

Library of Congress Cataloging-in-Publication Data

Dorsey, Pat, 1963–
   Fly fishing tailwaters : tactics and patterns for year-round waters / Pat Dorsey. — 1st ed.
      p. cm.
   Includes bibliographical references.
   ISBN 978-0-8117-0512-7
   1. Fly fishing. 2. Fly tying. I. Title.
   SH456.D67 2009
   799.17'57—dc22

                                                            2008046861

CONTENTS

To the memory of John T. Dorsey, a great fisherman, friend, and grandfather. Our annual family pilgrimages to the fabled Gunnison Country taught me to love and respect our beautiful trout streams. Thanks for all the memories.

ACKNOWLEDGMENTS

First and foremost, I would like to thank my family for their endless support of my fly-fishing endeavors. Without your strength and guidance, making a living in the fly-fishing industry would not be possible. Your unselfishness is truly amazing to me. Thanks for your patience and understanding while I chase my fly-fishing dream.

I have been truly blessed with five wonderful children—Forrest, Zach, Hunter, Michael, and Nicole. Each one of you is very special to me and I love you dearly. I would especially like to thank my wife, Kim, who has literally changed her life to revolve around my passion. You are my favorite fishing partner, and I feel blessed to have you in my life.

It would be impossible to list all the authors, outdoor writers, fly fishers, professional guides, and streamside companions who have fueled my addiction to pursue selective trout with tiny flies. To all of you, I am very grateful.

It would be disrespectful, however, not to mention a few by name. I have been fortunate to fish and work with some of the best professionals in the fly-fishing industry. Each one of you has had a direct impact on my growth in this industry. I would like to thank Dan Wright, Matt Miles, Bob Saile, Charlie Meyers, Ed Dentry, Randy Smith, Paul Roos, John Smith, Clay Anselmo, Monroe Coleman, John Perizzolo, Steve Parrott, Roger Bittell, Jonathan Keisling, Jim Cannon, Eric Atha, J. Core, Bob Dye, Chris Wells, John Barr, Landon Mayer, Ross Purnell, John Randolph, Jim Pruett, Bruce Olson, Brian Schmidt, Mike Clough, Mark Bressler, Tom Evenson, Van Rollo, and Michael White. Words cannot express my deepest appreciation—I can only hope the relationship has never been lopsided.

Next, a big thank-you to regional experts Terry Gunn, Denny Breer, Dave Opie, Aaron Carithers, Trent Tatum, and Erik Aune for sharing their knowledge on each of their corresponding watersheds. They are the true authorities on their home waters.

I would also like to thank Billy Atkinson, Jeff Spohn, and George Schisler from the Colorado Division of Wildlife, who were always there to lend their expertise pertaining to electroshocking data, aquatic biology, research, and other related topics.

This book would not be possible without research from other printed materials on aquatic entomology, hatches, fishing strategies, hydrology, trout, and many other topics. While only one name appears on the dust jacket of this book, it is not at all true that I wrote it completely alone—nothing could be further from the truth. This book is a conglomeration of experiences from many top-notch professionals and numerous readings, for which I am grateful.

I would like to thank renowned authors such as Gary Borger, Mike Lawson, Rick Hafele, Gary LaFontaine, René Harrop, A. K. Best, Jack Dennis, Dana Rikimaru, Tom Rosenbauer, Denny Rickards, Fred Arbona, Marty Bartholomew, Roger Hill, Ed Dentry, Landon Mayer, and Ed Engle for sharing their experiences. Ed Engle has been especially helpful; we share a special affection for the South Platte watershed and fishing small flies to selective trout. Ed Engle's knowledge pertaining to tailwater fisheries is mind-boggling, to say the least.

I would also like to thank my dad, Jim Dorsey, for his help with proofreading this book to make it clear, concise, and understandable. He was always there to bounce ideas back and forth and offer encouragement. My father is a mentor and a true inspiration in my life.

I would like to thank Jay Nichols for his support, patience, and friendship, and for guiding this project. I would also like to thank Dave Hall for his excellent illustrations. Finally, I would like to thank Judith Schnell and Stackpole Books for publishing this work and having faith and confidence in me to write another book.

PREFACE

Throughout the western United States, dozens of world-class tailwaters—streams that flow from the bottoms of deep reservoirs—support a rich and diversified aquatic life and are loaded with huge populations of hard-fished trout. Each tailwater has its own character and nuances, for sure, but tailwaters also have many similarities: most are technically challenging and provide consistent, year-round fishing, and all can be unpredictable from time to time.

A few years ago, I wrote my first book *A Fly-Fishing Guide to the South Platte River,* sharing experiences and lessons learned on one of the greatest tailwaters in the western United States. The South Platte, and especially Cheesman Canyon, is my home water. Not only is it the best trout fishery within an hour's drive of any major metropolitan area in America, it is one of the most technically challenging tailwater fisheries in the West. You'd be hard-pressed to find a better place to learn the basic fundamentals of catching selective trout.

Though I've fished Colorado streams my entire life, a big phase in my education as a trout angler didn't begin until I started traveling outside the state to explore other noted tailwaters, such as the Bighorn, North Platte, San Juan, Colorado at Lees Ferry, Green, Shoshone, Wind, and Madison. I learned that many tricks of the trade that I applied on my home waters worked well on other tailwaters too, and I learned a lot of things from anglers on other rivers that I was able to take back home and put to good use.

It won't take you long to figure out that I place special emphasis on western tailwaters. It is important to note, however, these strategies and techniques apply to all hard-fished rivers with selective trout—whether you're fishing a western or eastern tailwater.

While I have fished eastern tailwaters, my experiences there have been limited compared to my time on the water throughout the Rocky Mountain region. I have spent thousands of hours on western trout streams pursuing some of the most hard-fished and selective trout in the country. While there are a few differences between western and eastern waters, you should be able to take a fly box stuffed with tiny midge and mayfly imitations and successfully master any number of tailwaters throughout the United States.

Traveling and fishing around the West reminds me how important it is to remain open-minded—because you can always learn a new trick by reading a book or magazine article or spending a day on the river with another angler. I have learned many valuable lessons from others—many of which I teach on a regular basis on guided trips and in schools and advanced nymphing clinics. Often the subtleties and simple refinements make the biggest breakthroughs in improving your skills.

I'm not an expert on every tailwater throughout the Rocky Mountain region. It takes someone who spends thousands of days on each watershed to become a true authority or expert on his or her drainage. That's why I have called on regional experts from northern New Mexico, Utah, Colorado, Wyoming, Idaho, and Montana when researching this book. What you'll find in these pages is an accumulation of many years of fishing with some of the best professionals in the world. The methodology and strategies you are about to read are time-tested and should help take your skills to the next level.

On all tailwaters—all trout rivers, for that matter—knowledge leads to success. In many ways, fly fishing is a problem-solving exercise. On a daily basis, the river does certain things, at certain times, for certain reasons. Your job as angler is to collect data, refine that information, and solve the "problem." After that, you'll be able to approach a trout stream with confidence and a clear-cut tactical approach. Having a plan and executing the plan are two important parts of fly fishing. The more you know about trout, the physical makeup of their underwater world, entomology, matching the hatch, and specific techniques required to catch them, the better an angler you'll eventually become.

My primary goal in this book is to teach you everything I know about tailwaters. To that end, I've included chapters about what makes tailwaters tick, how to understand dams and their releases, and an in-depth look at trout and their environment. I cover the challenges of each season, reading the river, and refining technique. I've included a thorough discussion on observation, both surface and subsurface strategies, and a detailed orientation into entomology and matching the hatch, including all the fly patterns that have been effective for me over the years. In addition, I discuss tailwater equipment in detail, in the event you need to purchase or upgrade your gear.

Fishing all of the West's great tailwaters is no easy task. It will take a serious commitment on your part. There are so many rivers, yet so little time. Think of your westward journey as a marathon, not a race. You'll need to stop and smell the roses along the way. Trout country is a very special place—trout don't live in ugly places. Along the way, you'll make friends and life-long memories—and I hope you'll learn a thing or two. If you do, my goal for this book will have been met.

Pat Dorsey
Parker, Colorado

CHAPTER 1

The Nature of Tailwaters

If it were not for concrete tucked between two towering canyon walls, angling meccas such as the Green, South Platte, Grey Reef, and Bighorn would not exist. Where humans have captured moving water in semiarid and arid climates, icy cold and nutrient-rich water flows forth from dams, providing some of the world's best trout fishing. In many cases, the birth of a tailwater buries miles of existing trout stream under the massive reservoir. But these often mediocre fisheries have become great because of the cold, nutrient-rich releases flowing from below the dams.

Now, with icy cold, clean water, trout thrive where they didn't live before. These transplants (mostly rainbows but also browns, cutthroats, and cuttbows) take to their new environment remarkably well. A 5- or 6-inch stocked fingerling rainbow will grow to 10–12 inches in its first year. A second-

year rainbow trout will measure 14–16 inches, and typically reach 18–20 inches by its third year. Fish over 20 inches are not uncommon, weighing 3 to 4 pounds. This is not a bad deal at all for a river that previously held only razorback suckers, carp, squawfish, and other warmwater species.

Bob Saile's explanation of tailwaters in his book *Trout Country* sums up their paradoxical nature best: "The San Juan is an aberration as far as trout rivers go. It flows blue-green, clear and cold out of the bottom of Navajo Reservoir and slides in a weaving pattern of channels, riffles and holes through what is essentially desert country. Red sandstone bluffs and ridges dotted with chaparral and juniper provide the backdrop, with willows and cottonwoods framing some of the flats. Where tepid, muddy water once flowed in unpredictable spurts and trickles, reservoir outflows ranging from 500 to

The San Juan River benefited greatly from the construction of Navajo Dam. Prior to the completion of the dam, only warmwater species inhabited the river.

1

Tailwater fisheries provide anglers with consistent, year-round fly fishing. Ron Kless ties on a tiny nymph as he prepares to fish the Taylor River below Taylor Park Dam.

Each tailwater has its own character and set of challenges. Some tailwaters are small and expeditious, while others are large and untamed. You can float larger tailwaters in a drift boat or raft, and on some, such as Lees Ferry of the Colorado, anglers travel from place to place in jet or power boats to fish large gravel bars and midchannel shelves that would be otherwise unreachable for the walk-and-wade angler.

5000 cubic feet per second are released from the dam. The water temperature is an almost constant and shocking icy forty-two to forty-four degrees, regardless of the time of year."

Tailwaters are managed by humans rather than by the forces of nature, and the day-to-day management of the dam has a profound impact on the stream below. Unfortunately,

these rivers were never intended to be "managed" strictly as trout fisheries, but despite all odds, their conditions are so ideal most of the time that trout populations can't help but prosper.

Unlike freestone streams, where the river and the fishing fluctuate according to Mother Nature's whims (see sidebar, page 10), tailwaters are more or less predictable. Instead of the smorgasbord of hatches in a typical freestone stream, small midges and mayflies make up the bulk of a trout's diet, and only a master of minutiae is consistently effective through the year, dead-drifting tiny nymphs and larvae with thin tippets in the clear currents. Though nymph fishing with small flies is generally the main game for most of the year, tailwaters present many great dry-fly-fishing opportunities, as well as the chance to catch large trout on streamers in the spring and fall.

Rather than considering it the tail end or outtake of a reservoir, I like to think of a tailwater as a new beginning. As the river exits the dam, it has a whole lot more going for it than it did before entering the reservoir.

ROLE OF THE RESERVOIR

The primary goal of any Western reservoir is to trap and hold running water. The water generally accrues from snowmelt and rainfall, which may travel hundreds of miles via feeder creeks and other tributaries before it enters the dammed main channel. The water is used for variety of purposes, including supplying major metropolitan areas with water for day-to-day living, urban expansion, building new highways, and watering lawns, gardens, parks, and golf courses. Other important uses include agricultural needs such as irrigating crops and pastureland, and watering cattle. Recreational activities such as boating, fishing, and other water sports also fill an important niche within the reservoir itself. In some cases, the stored water generates hydropower.

TAILWATER BENEFITS

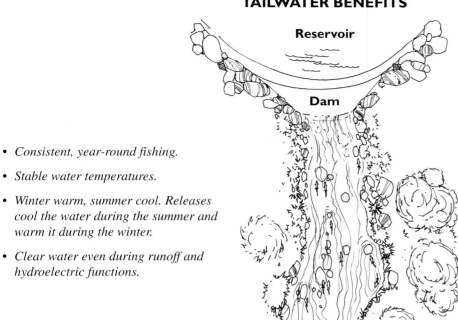

Reservoir

Dam

- *Consistent, year-round fishing.*
- *Stable water temperatures.*
- *Winter warm, summer cool. Releases cool the water during the summer and warm it during the winter.*
- *Clear water even during runoff and hydroelectric functions.*

- *Nutrient-rich water promotes a weed-rich substrate with algae-covered rocks.*
- *Large populations of trout.*
- *Stable banks because of consistent flows.*

SUMMER STAGNATION

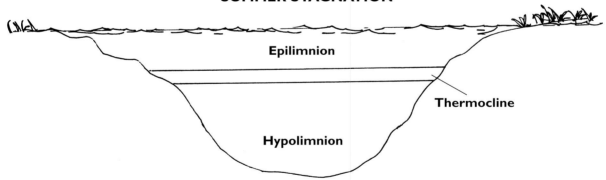

Epilimnion

Thermocline

Hypolimnion

WINTER STRATIFICATION

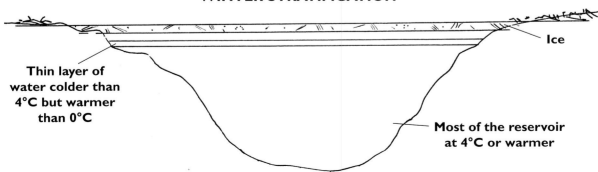

Ice

Thin layer of water colder than 4°C but warmer than 0°C

Most of the reservoir at 4°C or warmer

Large bodies of water undergo seasonal changes based on water temperatures. These processes are referred to as summer stagnation and winter stratification.

SPRING OVERTURN

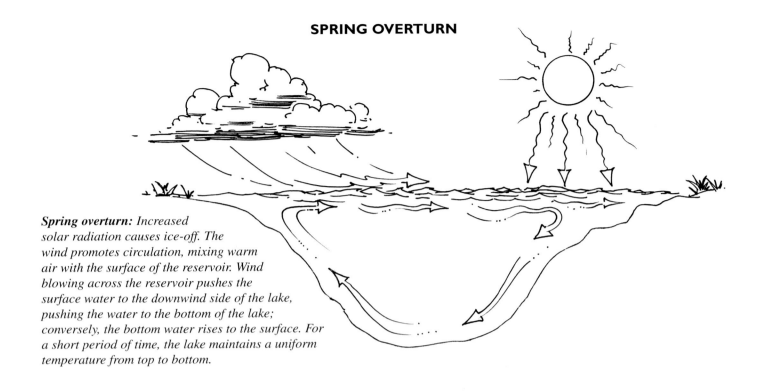

Spring overturn: Increased solar radiation causes ice-off. The wind promotes circulation, mixing warm air with the surface of the reservoir. Wind blowing across the reservoir pushes the surface water to the downwind side of the lake, pushing the water to the bottom of the lake; conversely, the bottom water rises to the surface. For a short period of time, the lake maintains a uniform temperature from top to bottom.

FALL OVERTURN

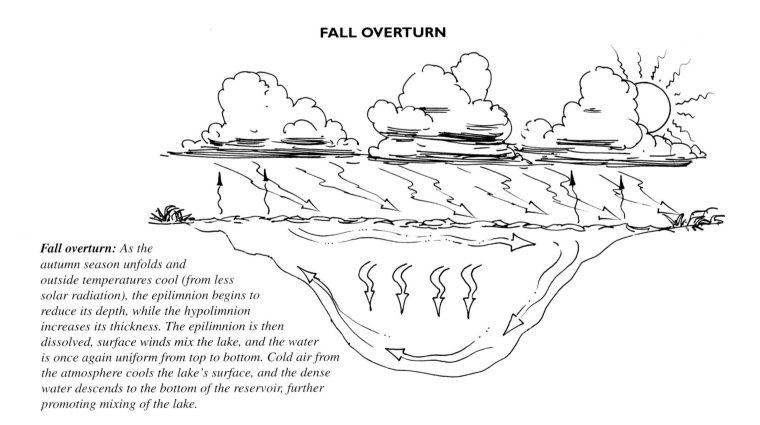

Fall overturn: As the autumn season unfolds and outside temperatures cool (from less solar radiation), the epilimnion begins to reduce its depth, while the hypolimnion increases its thickness. The epilimnion is then dissolved, surface winds mix the lake, and the water is once again uniform from top to bottom. Cold air from the atmosphere cools the lake's surface, and the dense water descends to the bottom of the reservoir, further promoting mixing of the lake.

Western reservoirs turn over twice a year—once in the spring and once in the fall.

In addition to water storage, the reservoir provides several key ingredients to the great trout fishing below, including ideal water temperatures year-round, stable flows, and clear, nutrient-rich waters.

Thermal Stratification

Deep lakes and reservoirs experience seasonal temperature fluctuations based on light penetration, wind, wave action, and air temperatures. During the summer, lakes and reservoirs stratify into three different layers according to their water temperature, a process called summer stagnation.

The upper layer of water is known as the epilimnion. The epilimnion is warmest layer; therefore, it is the lightest (least dense), so it stays toward the surface. Intense sunshine, coupled with warm winds, mixes with the surface currents, warming the upper layer quickly. The depth of the epilmnion increases between spring and summer. The thin middle layer, called the thermocline (metalimnion), is cooler (denser) than the epilimnion. This layer changes temperature quickly with depth. The bottom layer, the hypolimnion, is located in deepest part of the lake and is significantly cooler than the other two levels.

In autumn, air temperatures gradually get cooler and cooler. The southerly exposure of the sun is less intense, so the water gradually gets colder. The wind continues to mix the colder air with the epilimnion, causing it to equalize with the thermocline, and eventually with the hypolimnion. This results in what is referred to as fall turnover when, for a short period of time, the water temperature is uniform from top to bottom.

As air temperatures continue to drop, the upper layer continues to cool, becoming colder than the bottom layer of the lake. The water on top generally freezes or stays slightly above the freezing mark. The reservoir's water is densest at 40 degrees F and consequently the surface water (which is colder than 40 degrees) is less dense, so it stays on top of the lake. As this cooling process takes place, the water expands, becoming lighter (less dense), often forming ice. The reservoir stratifies again, with the densest water (40 degrees F) near the bottom of the reservoir. This is often referred as winter stratification.

After spring ice-out, the surface of the reservoir will be 32 degrees, and the bottom of the reservoir will be in the 40-degree range. As the warmer water rises, and the colder (more dense) water sinks to the bottom, it brings up nutrients and other debris (from decomposed organic matter) that have settled on the bottom of the reservoir. Also, the oxygen-depleted (anoxic zone) water rises from its winter stratification.

Next, the epilimnion cools to the temperature of the hypolimnion, dissolving the thermocline. Surface winds and other currents mix the lake, resulting in spring turnover. Once again, the lake or reservoir becomes uniform from top-to-bottom for a short duration. Then the whole process begins anew, with the top layer being warmed by solar energy and warm winds causing the water to stratify again.

How does this impact the fishing on a tailwater? The seasonal changes in temperate zone reservoirs and lakes with bottom-release mechanisms provide the trout with cooler water temperatures during the summer and warmer water temperatures in the winter for several miles below the dam, a phenomenon that Ed Engle refers to as "winter warm and summer cool." This makes the water temperatures more conducive to fish growth and feeding than in freestone rivers, providing a longer window of fly-fishing opportunities.

COLD WATER

Over the course of the year, the temperature variation in a tailwater is minimal compared to that in unregulated or freestone

Water temperatures on the lower Blue River are considerably warmer than those found below Dillon Dam. The flows below Dillon Dam are an icy 38 to 40 degrees most of the year. Farther downstream near Palmer Gulch (15 miles below the dam), the water temperatures average 55 to 60 degrees throughout the summer season, and growth rates are double or triple the growth rates of the fish near the dam.

A high level of nutrients promotes a weed-rich stream bottom supporting a dense aquatic life including scuds, sow bugs, and midge larvae.

Seasonal stratification produces a phenomenon referred to as "winter warm and summer cool." This allows anglers to fish throughout the winter months in tailwater fisheries such as the Frying Pan below Ruedi Reservoir. JERRY VIGIL

streams (see the Freestone Rivers sidebar later in this chapter) because of the constant source of cold water. The temperature of the water that flows from a dam is determined by the type of release and the depth of the reservoir, which I discuss in detail in chapter 2. On average, releases from deep bottom-release reservoirs can be as cold as 40 degrees, which provides cool water and prime trout conditions for many miles downstream. Closer to the dam, where the water is coldest, the food base is limited, but as the water warms farther from the dam, the aquatic life broadens. Because of this, it is common to have different trout growth rates between the dam and several miles downstream, based on water temperatures and diversification of aquatic life.

As the water flows downstream, tributaries can enter, creating irregular flows, changes in clarity, and temperature fluctuations that alter the fishing conditions and can make the stream more like a freestone stream in character.

Nutrient-Rich Water

Reservoirs produce nutrient-rich water, which promotes a dense aquatic life, a weed-rich substrate, larger populations of trout, and ideal growth rates below the reservoir as compared to a typical unregulated stream. Scuds, sow bugs, midge larvae, and other high-protein foods thrive under these conditions. Trout that feed on them tend to grow rapidly and have rich, vibrant colors.

The nutrients are the end result of the sun penetrating the large surface area of the reservoir, promoting increased plant and animal life (photosynthesis), combined with decaying matter and other organic debris within the reservoir itself. The water being discharged from the reservoir has a much higher nutrient level than the stream that enters the lake above. Think of the nutrients as fertilizer for the fishery below.

Because of the enormous biomass and conditions conducive to trout growth, many of our Western tailwaters are labeled as blue ribbon or gold medal trout streams, with more than 60 pounds of trout per acre, with 12 trout per acre larger than 14 inches. These quality waters are not stocked in routine management unless there is an extreme die-off. Both from an aquatic biology standpoint and a fly fisher's point of view, these fisheries are simply legendary. Special regulations—catch-and-release, flies and lures only, two fish over 16 inches, and barbless hooks—have been enforced to protect these areas.

CLEAR WATER

The crystal clear currents from the dam above allow sunlight to penetrate the shallow riffled areas, producing algae, moss-covered rocks, and a weed-rich environment for aquatic insect life to thrive. Photosynthesis gives our underwater world a boost by producing oxygen and other nutrients critical for all life forms. Larger leafed plants and wavy grass provide additional oxygen and hiding places for juvenile trout.

The reservoir acts as a sediment trap, collecting a wide range of debris and sediments that enters the river from tributaries and the main river channel. Spring runoff is often the main culprit when it comes sedimentation and off-colored water. To a lesser degree, heavy afternoon rain showers can discolor streams and cause problems with sediment. Heavily burned-out areas and sections of the river corridor that have been affected by beetle kill can cause huge problems with erosion and off-colored water. Both the Green and South Platte have had recent forest fires, and now have tremendous problems with sedimentation.

The amount of sediment can vary dramatically, however, depending on whether or not there is another dam above the reservoir. If there is another dam upstream from you, the fishery will be much more stable and less likely to be influenced by runoff, heavy sedimentation, and off-colored water. In any event, the sediment generally settles to the bottom of the reservoir before exiting the outflow gates. The clarity may vary depending on the size of the reservoir, and whether it is a top release or bottom release (see chapter 2 for more information on dam releases), but in most cases, high, roily water that enters the reservoir during spring runoff generally exits the reservoir gin clear.

TURNOVER

In many cases, the releases from the dam may be off-colored for up to three weeks during the lake turnover process, which changes the way you'll approach the river. Prior to the Hayman Fire, I never really noticed the impact of lake turnover on the South Platte in Cheesman Canyon. Maybe I wasn't savvy enough to notice, but I don't recall local experts talking about any significant changes during spring and fall turnover. Now, with a graveyard of sediment, decomposed granite, soot, and ash on the floor of Cheesman Reservoir (from the Hayman Fire) the lake now has a pronounced turnover. In recent years, the releases have been noticeably off-colored during the latter part of September and the first two weeks of October. The spring turnover begins toward the latter part of April and extends into the first part of May. It, too, changes the clarity substantially.

I've had varied results when the lake is turning over—some days I've caught a lot of fish and on others I could hardly get a strike. At this time, nymphing can be challenging, because you are continually cleaning moss and other debris from nymphing rigs. I fish dark streamers, leech patterns (rabbit fur and chamois leeches), and other brightly colored flies such as San Juan Worms, scuds, and egg patterns as attractor patterns, and trail a smaller midge or mayfly nymph behind them. The poor clarity makes sight-nymphing difficult.

Not all tailwaters will turn off-colored when the lake turns over, but if water temperatures shoot up from the 40s to the

Tailwater fisheries are known for their clear water. The dam and reservoir assist in settling out silt before the water exits the outflow gates. Rivers like the Bighorn are known for their exceptionally clear water.

Seasonal turnover may change the river's clarity for a two- to three-week period each spring and fall. This is a common occurrence on the San Juan River below Navajo Dam.

Electroshocking surveys conducted by fish and wildlife agencies verify that there are several thousand trout per mile in many of our Western tailwater fisheries.

mid- to high 50s, it is probably pretty safe to assume the lake is mixing. Because of these escalating water temperatures, I have observed caddis, Yellow Sallies, and stoneflies hatching late in the fall. In *Fly Fishing the Tailwaters* (Stackpole 1991), Ed Engle notes: "In many cases the season's highest water temperatures may be delayed well into the fall when the reservoir turns over."

The trout will still feed in both selective and opportunistic phases when the lake turns over. If anything, their metabolism is increased, and they'll really be on the feed. Despite the fact that the water is often off-colored, a trout's eyesight is truly amazing! I have "pumped" (using a stomach pump) a fish and found it was filled with size 24 *Baetis* nymphs during the afternoon in Cheesman Canyon when the water looked like a glacial stream. During the same day, we had fish rising to large dry flies (Amy's Ant) in riffled water. Don't let the dirty water fool you: fishing can still be very good.

When a reservoir turns over, you'll also notice an odor that smells like dead fish or rotten eggs from the hydrogen sulfide in the hypolimnion getting stirred up during the mixing process.

Stable Releases

In addition to the increased nutrients and kind temperatures, the stable releases are a critical factor in creating these abundant fisheries. On the South Platte River, there are five dams between the headwaters and where it enters the Denver metropolitan area. Below each reservoir is a tailwater fishery, which keeps the river stable throughout its entire journey.

I often ponder what the South Platte in Cheesman Canyon was like before the dam was built in 1905. As a freestone, it must have raged for several weeks during spring runoff, almost drying up in the late summer. Many anglers hike in and out of the "canyon" and never realize (or care) that a mighty freestone river once ripped through this scenic canyon. Evidence of erosion along the streambanks, and deep, swirling grooves in the Pike's Peak granite prove that large quantities of water once surged through this fabled canyon. I'm sure that back then it wasn't even remotely the fishery that it is today.

A traditional runoff is almost nonexistent in the South Platte watershed (with the exception of the Middle Fork of the South Platte River river that enters the first reservoir—Spinney Reservoir) because the dams store the water and moderate the flows. Because the flows are generally very stable, a strong network of rooted grasses, fern-type plants, trees, willows, and a wide range of other assorted ground foliage (poison ivy, weeds, wildflowers, etc.) provide bank stability and a place for adult aquatic insects to molt, mate, seek protection, and rest.

Scouring runoff flows tend to wash away part of the aquatic life. Aquatic insects such as midges, green drakes, and stoneflies, however, tend to cope moderately well under these higher fluctuating flows. The only problem is that huge populations of trout cannot survive if the aquatic life is only mediocre.

The hatches found on tailwaters are spectacular. Anglers will find trout rising to incredible hatches of midges, blue-winged olives, pale morning duns, Tricos, caddisflies, and Yellow Sally stoneflies throughout the course of the year. Because of this abundance of food coupled with prime water temperatures, many tailwaters have several thousand trout per mile, compared to substantially lower numbers found on unregulated trout streams.

While tailwater flows are generally closely managed, they still have a tendency to fluctuate during certain times of the year. The biggest fluctuations occur between May and September. River levels vary depending on incoming snowmelt, rainfall, downstream demand, or hydroelectric commitments. Even during higher flows, tailwaters are much more stable than a free-flowing or unregulated stream. While the flows may be high, they are generally clear and fishable. In fact, even when there is a flow increase on some tailwaters, scuds, aquatic worms, and midge larvae are frequently dislodged, providing for great fishing.

Tailwaters remain fishable even during high flow regimes. Anglers fish the Blue River below Dillon Dam with flows exceeding 900 cubic feet per second (cfs) near Silverthorne.

Managed flows help promote good bank stabilization with willows, trees, rooted grasses, ferns, and other assorted ground foliage. This provides places for adult aquatic insects to propagate, molt, seek protection, and rest.

FREESTONE RIVERS

Unlike tailwaters, which are regulated by humans, freestone rivers are free-flowing or uncontrolled rivers. In Colorado, well-known freestone streams include the Arkansas, Eagle, upper Gunnison, Clear Creek, Roaring Fork, Animas, and Rio Grande. Arkansas River guide Greg Felt of Salida, Colorado sums up a freestone river best. "Fishing freestones means meeting nature on her own terms . . . flows, water temperatures, water quality . . . The diversity of food sources coupled with an often steeper gradient and a prevalence of pocketwater means that fish are less focused in specific holes or runs and more apt to be distributed throughout the river corridor and feeding on a variety of bugs. The fish in a freestone are frequently less selective, but are also more impacted by the presence of humans, putting stealth, presentation, and drift at a higher priority than specific fly pattern."

Freestone rivers keep you on your toes at all times, because you are constantly reacting to unpredictable conditions. Some days you can do no wrong; other days, you'd swear there wasn't a fish in the entire river. While you can fish tailwaters year-round, freestone rivers have a much more limited window. Many freeze in the winter, and for several weeks during the ideal growth period for trout (May through August) the river is high and unfish-able because of spring runoff—Mother Nature's way of "spring cleaning" by flushing away insect-choking sediments and dislodging large clumps of aquatic weeds, moss beds, and other vegetation that may jam up the trout's living quarters. During these higher flows, the fish hunker down and hold tight to the edges of the stream, trying to battle the high, roily water. At this time, survival is a trout's main goal.

Snowpack has a tremendous impact on a freestone river's overall condition and flow throughout the entire year. In lean years, runoff will peak quickly (mid- to late May), leaving low flows that can be problematic during the latter part of July, August, and September. With the low water volume, the water temperatures rise quickly. Summer drought can severely impact river levels on a freestone river. Unlike a tailwater, there is no "backup source" to help assist with summer flows when the natural flows are low. And when Mother Nature blankets the Rockies with heavy snowfall, our freestone streams may run high and roily until the middle part of July.

Unregulated rivers do not have anywhere near the stable aquatic life that tailwaters have. Why? Because the flows constantly bounce up and down, wreaking havoc with the aquatic life and causing stress to the trout. During part of the ideal growing season (May through July),

Unregulated rivers, commonly called freestones, like the upper Gunnison River, are much less predictable than tailwaters. Water clarity and temperatures will vary dramatically compared to a classic tailwater.

The best fishing on a freestone river is early spring, late summer, or autumn. In Colorado, from May through Father's Day (June 15), most freestones are high and off-colored, making fishing conditions difficult at best. During spring runoff, anglers typically concentrate their efforts on fishing tailwater fisheries, which have stable flows.

flows are often high and roily from runoff. The trout are hunkered on the bottom, or tucked tight to the bank underneath willows, or in other soft-flowing spots, just trying to survive the high, muddy water. Temperatures are consistently inconsistent. As result of these fluctuations, the trout populations are not nearly as impressive as those found below a dam.

Unregulated streams often turn muddy during a substantial flow increase. Their streambanks are considerably less stable compared to those of a tailwater. Fluctuating flows stir up sediments and erode the soil along the river's edge. Flow increases can be a result of spring runoff, or a heavy afternoon rain shower, causing tributaries that enter the main river corridor to rise quickly. These scouring currents can turn a clear river muddy in minutes. In many cases, unregulated waters remain unfishable for several days to several weeks under these circumstances.

While the typical freestone still boasts fair to good populations of midges, blue-winged olives, pale morning duns, caddis, red quills, green drakes, and stoneflies, they are not as dense as insects commonly found on tailwater fisheries.

Sometimes the classifications are not so cut and dried. Many tailwaters, such as the Williams Fork and the lower Blue River, resemble classic freestone streams. But the last time I checked, their releases were from deep, ice-cold, bottom-release reservoirs.

The Williams Fork reminds me of a miniature version of the Gunnison River, which is a noted Western freestone river. The Williams Fork is lined with towering stands of cottonwoods, dense walls of willows, and the occasional blue spruce. Beavers have gnawed down trees and built dams. The gradient of the stream channel is severe, producing swift riffles, runs, and highly productive pocketwater. It looks and feels like a freestone. But the fact of the matter is this: you'll need to approach the Williams Fork like a classic tailwater fishery if you plan on being successful.

The Blue River, on the other hand, is a classic tailwater fishery, but the savvy angler will approach the lower Blue like a conventional freestone river. Dead-drifting large stonefly patterns, caddisfly larvae, crane flies, and Green Drake Nymphs will catch a lot of trout. This section is a pocketwater paradise! Pale morning duns, caddisflies, stoneflies, green drakes, and red quills offer explosive dry-fly fishing during the post-runoff period.

CHAPTER 2

Understanding Dams and Releases

To completely understand a tailwater fishery, it makes sense to start at the source—the dam. Dams come in all sizes and configurations, and their purposes vary, from water storage, day-to-day metropolitan demands, irrigation needs, flood control, environmental factors (such as increasing flows to flush away harmful sediments), making room for incoming snowmelt, and hydroelectricity.

In many cases, the dams and the river below are nothing more than a water storage system and a conduit to move water to urban areas. The South Platte is a prime example: along the river's entire length, the South Platte creates a series of major metropolitan water storage facilities for the Denver Water Board and the City of Aurora.

These government agencies are faced with an ongoing dilemma: trying to meet the demands of senior water-rights holders, outdoor enthusiasts, fly fishers, and the three-million-plus people who have trickled into the Denver metropolitan area demanding their fair share of "liquid gold" for day-to-day living. Aside from the trout taking the brunt of the punishment, and attorneys and politicians making lucrative careers out of litigating who gets water and when, things aren't all bad. Below each reservoir there is a tailwater fishery

Releases in our tailwater fisheries are dependent on many variables, including water storage, day-to-day metropolitan needs, irrigation, flood control, and hydroelectricity. The Green River's water level below Flaming Gorge is affected by downstream demand and hydroelectric commitments.

The Spinney Mountain Ranch section of the South Platte imitates a spring creek in almost every way, with the exception of fluctuating flows from the dam above.

that wasn't there before, and while conditions are not always ideal, the trout have adapted over time to adjust to these ever-changing conditions.

The management of the reservoir hinges on many factors. First and foremost, the primary purpose of the reservoir is to collect snowmelt to be used to supply arid and semiarid areas during the hot and dry summer months. As spring unfolds, the water board or the Bureau of Reclamation is faced with making an educated guess whether or not they'll need to hold water back to fill the reservoir, or release water to make room for the incoming snowpack. In most cases, the water managers will err on the conservative side to ensure a full reservoir. In their eyes, a full reservoir is a good reservoir, and water flowing over the spillway is a bonus. Improper management—resulting in low flows or high flows—caused by miscalculating incoming water and reservoir levels often produces unfavorable conditions and poor fishing below the dam. But in most cases, the storage and movement of water take precedence over the trout's living quarters.

A few Western reservoirs are operated predominantly to generate hydroelectricity. While these reservoirs are less common in the West than those tailwaters found in East (Arkansas, Missouri, Georgia, Virginia, North Carolina, Kentucky, and Tennessee), they do account for some excellent fishing in areas such as the Colorado River below Glen Canyon Dam (Lees Ferry).

Some Western reservoirs are multifaceted: they store water and provide electricity to the grid as an added bonus. Examples include the San Juan River below Navajo Dam, the

The day-to-day management of the dam has a major impact on the tailwater below. River levels may vary depending on incoming water, downstream demand, and hydroelectricity.

Bighorn below Yellowtail Dam, the North Platte at Grey Reef, and the Green River below Flaming Gorge Dam. These fisheries tend to fluctuate less compared to traditional reservoirs that operate solely for generating power. As a general rule, tailwater fisheries that fluctuate less have much more stable conditions. Tailwaters that fluctuate several feet on a daily basis are less likely to have stable streambanks, a weed-rich

Strontia Springs Reservoir is a bottom-release dam that produces a beautiful tailwater, which flows through Waterton Canyon just south of the Denver metropolitan area.

Bottom-release tailwaters allow trout fisheries in arid areas such as the Colorado River in Arizona and the San Juan River in northern New Mexico. What had previously been a warm, off-colored, slow-moving native squawfish stream now boasts large populations of rainbow trout thriving in the cold, clear water. After the construction of the dam, temperatures plummeted to the low to mid-40s. This cold water, coupled with the nutrients from the lake above, created the perfect environment for trout to thrive.

stream bottom, a diversified population of aquatic insects, and self-sustaining populations of trout.

If the dam is constructed on the base of a lush valley floor, anglers can expect to find classic meandering meadow stream conditions with riffles, runs, pools, oxbows, midchannel shelves, gravel bars, and undercut banks more reminiscent of Montana's renowned spring creeks. The weed-rich stream channel is a hotbed for aquatic insects to thrive, supporting excellent trout populations. Provided that there are no cattle grazing, bank stabilization and erosion improve over time because of the absence of fluctuating flows during spring runoff.

Because of the valley terrain, the reservoir is generally not as deep as one that might be placed in the heart of a majestic canyon. The level at which the water is released (see the section on releases later in this chapter) will dramatically impact the density of hatches, the overall activity of the fish, and their growth rates.

Dams that are nestled between two gigantic canyon walls typically create fisheries comprised of faster riffles, runs, pools, and highly productive pocketwater. For the most part, the stream channel is devoid of any large quantities of fine sediment and silt because the faster currents continually scour the streambed. The lack of extreme runoff in the canyon allows ponderosa pine, blue spruce, fir, cottonwood, aspen, and other trees, as well as grass, ferns, poison ivy, and other assorted ground foliage, to secure a good root system and for aquatic vegetation to take hold.

RELEASES AND THEIR IMPACTS

Western reservoirs incorporate a wide range of strategies for releasing water into the river system. These include releases that occur from the bottom of the reservoir, topwater releases, or a combination of both, in which mixing towers take water from different levels of the lake, integrating them before the water exits from the outflow gates. Let's take a closer look at each, exploring the trade-offs and compromises in fishing quality that are associated with the different types of release mechanisms.

Bottom-Release Dams

On a bottom-release dam, the outflow gates are near the base of the dam, and ice-cold water gushes from the deepest part of the reservoir. Generally, the first several hundred yards below a bottom-release reservoir is closed to fishing as a safety precaution because of life-threatening currents, undertows, and flow fluctuations. Since September 11, 2001, the reins have been tightened dramatically on the no-fishing zones. Many of the off-limits boundaries have been extended farther downstream in an effort to protect against any possible terrorist threat. For instance, the upper parking facility on the San Juan has been closed, which makes for difficult access in the upper reaches below the dam. There has been an increased alertness around Flaming Gorge Dam too—several law enforcement officials are continuously monitoring the area for any suspicious activity.

Temperatures vary greatly from one bottom-release tailwater to another. In theory, the deeper the lake, the colder the water. Deeper reservoirs (250-400 feet deep) like Navajo (on the San Juan River) or Dillon (on the Blue River) will release ice-cold water (typically in the low 40s) into the tailwater below. In the first mile below the dam, anglers rarely see water temperatures rising above the 42-degree mark, except for short periods when the lake turns over. The cold water affects the diversity of the aquatic life, the insect hatches, and the feeding behavior of the trout. As a result of these cold water temperatures, anglers will be required to fish with small (#20-24) midge and mayfly patterns the majority of the time. In most cases, this means nymph fishing to trout holding deep in the river.

Reservoirs less than 200 feet deep tend to have warmer releases, which promotes better hatches and makes it easier to find more feeding trout. Spinney Mountain Ranch (on the South Platte) is an excellent example. The reservoir is not as deep as Cheesman Reservoir. Water temperatures reach the mid- to high 50s (and many times the mid-60s) throughout the summer, creating excellent caddis and Yellow Sally hatches.

In most tailwaters, water temperatures are usually in the high 30s to low 40s throughout the winter and spring, and in the mid- to high 50s throughout the summer and autumn. It's rare to find a bottom-release tailwater with huge temperature extremes unless some of the water is coming over the spillway, during a seasonal turnover (see page 4), or in a severe drought that causes low lake levels.

Spilling Reservoirs

When the reservoir fills, and there is no downstream demand (because of excessive rain, above-average snowpack, flooding, or other reasons), the extra water flows over the spillway, which can be good or bad for fly fishing, depending on the time of the year.

Some of the best fishing of the year in Cheesman Canyon occurs when the reservoir is spilling. Warmer water temperatures, coupled with ice-cold water from the base of the dam, produce scouring flows that dislodge some of the larger food organisms such as stoneflies, aquatic worms, crane flies, and scuds. CHARLIE MEYERS

A spilling reservoir almost guarantees that there will be better than average flows for the remainder of the summer season, which produces ideal conditions for the trout to prosper. The aquatic bug life thrives because the river's substrate is completely immersed in water, dramatically increasing the surface area for insects to propagate. Mother Nature takes the reins, making the flow adjustments. The flow might rise slowly after a steady afternoon rain shower, causing tributaries and the main river corridor to swell above the lake. The flows below the dam rise accordingly. These adjustments are gradual (an extra inch or two coming over the spillway) as opposed to fluctuating several hundred cubic feet per second (cfs) in a 24-hour period when adjustments are made by dam managers opening the bottom-flow gates.

The reservoir may spill for a few days to a few months, depending on snowpack, runoff, and daily precipitation. When the warm surface water of the reservoir mixes and warms the several hundred feet of cool water from the bottom of the reservoir, water temperatures can climb into the mid-50s or 60s. The result is better hatches and overall better feeding opportunities for the fish on crane flies, stoneflies, aquatic worms, and scuds—until the flows drop and all the water is drawn from the bottom of the reservoir. When this occurs, the fish go into shock for a short period of time, and fishing can be tough until the trout get reacclimated to the colder waters.

But if little water is being released from the bottom of the lake, and only warm surface water is spilling over the top, water temperatures can quickly rise to the high 60s, having detrimental impacts on both the aquatic insect life and the trout. If these conditions do exist, please voluntarily refrain from fishing until the water temperatures drop back into the mid-60s. Catching fish when the water is too warm can stress them unduly and impair their chances of survival.

Flow Fluctuations on Water Storage Tailwaters

Water flow fluctuations can make or break your day of fishing. In most cases (with the exception of hydroelectric dams), a change in flow dramatically changes the fishing conditions, and generally for the worse.

At other times, small flow increases on tailwaters such as the Williams Fork or South Platte dislodge midge larvae and create a small feeding frenzy. During these phases, I usually fish a pale olive midge larva and have enjoyed tremendous success.

There is no doubt that fisheries with stable flows, such as the San Juan River, fish better on a day-to-day basis compared to rivers like the South Platte River that fluctuate daily. I have been in the middle of an incredible Trico hatch on the South Platte River when the flow was increased—and the river shut off like someone threw a switch. The city of Aurora could care less that you were stalking a 20-inch rising rainbow that was feeding relentlessly on spentwing mayflies.

Keeping an eye on water conditions is very important from a wading safety standpoint as well as the overall fishing conditions. While these changes are not as dramatic as those found below reservoirs that generate power, anglers must be aware of changing conditions. Flow increases can put the fish down for a short period because the clarity changes from all the free-floating debris kicked up due to the increase in volume. This is exactly the opposite of a hydroelectric fishery because the trout tend to go "on the feed" when the flow is increased. I learned a long time ago from a seasoned South Platte veteran—the late Dave Miller—to put a small rock along the streambank at the edge of the water to keep an eye on water levels.

It is very easy to keep an eye on water levels this way: If the rock is submerged, the flow has increased, and if there is exposed sand between the water line and the rock there has been a decreased flow. One trick that I use is to pay close attention to the streambank. Little bubbles will appear on the sand just as the river is beginning its initial rise, before you start to see floating debris such as moss, branches, and pine needles. Watch the edge of the stream closely as you move from hole to hole.

Flow increases generally shut the fish down for a while, and in some cases ruin fishing for the entire day. During a flow increase, your best bet is to fish imitations of larger food organisms such as crane flies and stoneflies, and San Juan Worms, or dead-drift dark-colored streamers.

To detect a decrease in flow, watch the rocks along the edge of the stream and look for a noticeable darkened line (not a normal wave or splash line) that indicates a dropping water level. If given the choice, I'll take a decrease in flow rather than an increase.

TOP-RELEASE DAMS

Many dams throughout the West release their water into the river below via a top-release spilling basin or spillway. Although they are less common than other dam types, they generally have good to excellent trout populations for several miles below the dam.

Colorado's Elevenmile Canyon (on the South Platte near the town of Lake George) is an excellent example of a Western top-release dam. The 2-mile stretch between the dam and Springer Gulch is a "model" Western tailwater, supporting a self-sustaining rainbow population of 3,500 fish per mile. Catch-and-release regulations help protect this fine fishery in its upper reaches. This stretch is an aquatic biologist's dream.

As a general rule, top-release dams have much less impact (with regard to being "controlled" fisheries) on the river below, and have considerably warmer water temperatures than bottom-release tailwaters. In theory, top-release reservoirs operate on a "full pool" premise. ("Full pool" refers to the lake always being full, as opposed to the typical reservoir that fills and then slowly loses its water as the runoff and rainfall decrease, and the demand increases.) The primary goal is to collect and store snowmelt and rainfall, allowing the excess to simply flow over the concrete raceway. The reservoir stays full, and the excess flows over the spillway. The water levels can vary greatly depending on runoff, rainfall, and drought. This means you could have several inches to several feet of water spilling over the spillway.

In 2002, Evergreen Lake, which has a top-release dam and is fed by Bear Creek, nearly dried up. As a result of the dry conditions, only a few cfs made it over the spillway, resulting in dangerously low water, high temperatures, and a large fish kill below Evergreen Lake.

As you might imagine, runoff will be much more substantial from a top-release dam than a bottom-release dam. Once runoff has subsided, Mother Nature manages the flows, and the flow increases and decreases are usually minimal compared with bottom-release dams. Flows from bottom-release dams can rise and fall several hundred cfs in a 24-hour period, whereas flow increases from top-release dams are gradual, unless heavy rains substantially raise flows.

Flows fluctuate greatly on tailwaters that store water for irrigation needs. Keep an eye on water levels at all times. Look at high-water lines and plan accordingly to prevent any unforeseen problems. On tailwaters with large fluctuations, consider wearing a small, inflatable personal floatation device (PFD) for emergencies.

Many dams throughout the Rocky Mountain West release water from the surface of the reservoir. Olympus Dam is a top-release dam below Lake Estes that forms the tailwater on the lower Big Thompson River.

Colorado's Elevenmile Canyon flows beneath a top-release dam. It is speculated that the absence of whirling disease is a result of the top-release configuration of the dam.

In the case of Elevenmile Dam, the Denver Water Board can release water from the bottom if the need arises. In 2002, when severe drought and the Hayman Fire taxed water levels in the South Platte drainage, a substantial amount of water was "moved" downstream to replenish Cheesman Reservoir. Unfortunately this meant that reservoir levels were below the spillway level; therefore, water was released from below. Water was then moved from Antero Reservoir, draining it, to refill Elevenmile Reservoir.

The absence of whirling disease in Elevenmile Canyon is surprising, and it's suspected that this horrible parasite does not live here because of the top-release design of the dam. Dave Leinweber, local guide and owner of Angler's Covey in Colorado Springs, says: "I believe the sole explanation that Elevenmile Reservoir escaped the curse of whirling disease is because it is a 100 percent top-release dam. This despite the fact that the reservoir contains extensive numbers of whirling disease spores." Through intensive research, the Colorado

Division of Wildlife has discovered that whirling disease spores are nonbuoyant, which suggests that these spores are concentrated on the bottom of Elevenmile Reservoir. The spores are unable to escape via the top outflow and enter the South Platte River.

During the early season, higher water temperatures from a top-release dam produce increased trout activity and better hatches from the warmer water. In addition, the oxygen content is much higher below a surface-release dam, and there are better growth rates from the warmer water and more diversified aquatic insect life.

The biggest disadvantage to top-release dams is higher water temperatures, which may approach the high 60s to low 70s between mid-June and the latter part of August. Please refrain from fishing if the water temperature exceeds 67 degrees. In addition, during drier times, or droughts, the fishery below dam often becomes a trickle, stressing the aquatic life and trout.

A diversion dam is another form of top-release dam, typically used to divert water for irrigation purposes, for filling ponds or lakes, or for other water needs such as metropolitan consumption. In theory, streams below diversion dams are not true tailwaters, but these dams do change the river system by warming the water, increasing oxygen levels, and creating some additional structure and river habitat.

There is a generally a run or pool below the diversion dam that houses several nice trout. The riffle-run configuration above the diversion dam is the least complex. Cover the water methodically, showing your flies to as many trout as possible. Both long-line and short-line nymphing tactics are effective in these areas.

Fishing below diversion dams presents great challenges because getting a good drift is difficult with the severe reverse currents and swirly undertows. Opportunistic trout will hug tight to the stream bottom, where the current is at a minimum, but will frequently rise to the surface to eat a dry fly swirling in a reverse current, or chase a large forage item. Heavily weighted streamers, large bushy attractors, and dry/dropper rigs perform best here. I'll typically keep all the fly line off the water and just allow the dry fly to float on the surface. Let it float around for a while—the chances are good you'll entice a large trout to rise from the bottom of the river. The key is to use something that makes it worth their while to expend the energy required for them to move several feet.

Diversion dams vary in size dramatically. Marston Diversion in Waterton Canyon (on the South Platte below Strontia Springs Reservoir) is quite large compared to many of the other small concrete or wooden barriers that cross the river to form irrigation head gates.

Marston Diversion creates a lake that is several hundred yards long. This water is funneled into an underground pipeline to Marston Lake, which is controlled by the Denver Water Board for metropolitan consumption. Anglers will find excellent fishing above the lake, and the quarter-mile stretch mile stretch below the diversion dam is some of the most productive water in the lower reaches of Waterton Canyon.

An angler works a nice run above Marston Diversion in Waterton Canyon. Flows are higher above the diversion before water is diverted to Marston Lake for the Denver metropolitan area.

DAMS WITH MIXING TOWERS

Some dams can mix water from various levels of the reservoir system, producing ideal water temperatures year-round. The Bureau of Reclamation (BOR) or other governing water agency can manipulate water temperatures—if they wish to do so—by drawing water from different levels of the lake, depending on the time of year, stratification, and reservoir temperatures.

At certain times of the year, especially during the winter, water temperatures aren't manipulated, or are influenced on a smaller scale. Regional experts such as Denny Breer, Terry Gunn, and Fred Arbona tell me that this is important because it helps some aquatic insects such as mayflies complete important life cycle stages. According to Fred Arbona: "Though growth to maturity takes place over hundreds of days, it does not take place uniformly during that time because it is a function of prevailing water temperatures, which undergo a very dramatic general cycle from one season to another. Actually, the growth of nymphs occurs when the water exceeds the 45-degree mark, and this will take place in a trout stream for only about seven months of the year. Full

maturity, then, must be accomplished in approximately 210 days out of 365." They all alluded to the same theory.

Many of the older dam systems are bottom-release, but some of the newer dams are retrofitted with modern mixing towers. Flaming Gorge Dam is a good example. It was built in 1962 and started out as a bottom-release dam, but by the winter of 1977–1978 a mixing device was integrated into the dam system. This project had a price tag of nearly $5 million.

"Prior to these changes the water temperatures in winter dipped to 35 to 37 degrees, and over the years the water saturation of nitrogen worsened and these high levels were a part of the releases," said veteran guide Denny Breer, owner of Trout Creek Flies in Dutch John, Utah. With those low water temperatures it was nearly impossible to find feeding trout during the winter months.

Breer explained that the key to a multigated dam is using the available surface temperatures within the upper 40- to 50 feet of the reservoir. In the springtime when water temperatures rise, the BOR will start mixing water. One gate can be opened at a certain level, and another at a different level to control the water temperatures effectively. Small changes can

Flaming Gorge Dam has mixing towers, which significantly impacts trout feeding behavior on the Green River below the reservoir.

happen in April, starting at 39 to 40 degrees, and slowly climb until early May, when temperatures will hit 50 degrees. In early June, water temperatures reach around 54 to 57 degrees, when the reservoir surface temperatures reach 70-plus degrees.

Biologists have seen more diversification in the aquatic life and increased trout growth rates when dam managers simply draw water from 40 feet below the surface of the lake and mix it with ice-cold water from the bottom. Where water temperatures were once in the high 30s to low 40s before mixing the water, they're now between the mid-40s and mid-50s most of the year.

Breer says: "The changes to the fishery were remarkable. Cold water temperatures had previously stunted the growth of insects, their diversity, and the fishes' growth rate. The high nitrogen levels didn't help much either. Growth rates climbed after installation of the mixing towers, and nitrogen levels were greatly reduced. Increased water temperatures increased fish metabolism and feeding—hence improved growth and catchability."

The trout populations changed after the dam was integrated with the mixing towers. Prior to the changes, the coldest water temperatures were near the dam, and the ideal water temperatures (from thermal warming) were closer to Browns Park, which is nearly 15 miles downstream. The rainbows that once inhabited the lower river migrated upstream to the cooler water, and brown trout began to dominate the lower river where large rainbows once thrived. Brown trout will tolerate much warmer water temperatures than rainbows. Throughout the West, it is rare to find heavy populations of

After the mixing towers were retrofitted into Flaming Gorge Dam, the rainbows that inhabited the lower river moved upstream toward the cooler water.

brown trout right below ice-cold, bottom-release reservoirs. They tend to populate the river a few miles downstream, where water temperatures are warmer. The aquatic insect life also became much more diversified on the lower river with the increased water temperatures.

Breer says: "One oddity is that our brown trout spawn is later, in mid-November through mid-January (compared to other tailwaters) because water temperatures stay warm for longer periods. It must delay the whole process. In addition, the dry-fly fishing with beetles and ants remains very effective clear into November because the water temps are high for that time of year."

As good as this might sound, mixing towers may not always be in the best interest of the trout if water temperatures are already in the ideal range. On average, the water temperatures at Lees Ferry are 48 degrees, which is conducive to excellent growth rates and year-round trout fishing.

The BOR is considering multilevel gates to try to warm up the river to benefit the humpback chub. However, the warmer water temperatures would allow predatory fish such as bass and stripers to invade the river, and have adverse effects on the trout populations.

HYDROELECTRIC DAMS

Many tailwater fisheries capture flowing water and turn it into hydropower or hydroelectricity. Hydroelectric dams require an elevation drop for the gravity-fed system to operate. The hydroelectric process is straightforward: the water from the reservoir enters an intake valve flowing through a penstock, which in turn passes through a turbine propeller connected to a generator that produces power, then the water flows through an outflow system back into the tailrace below. The electricity is upgraded and stored in a transformer to be delivered to nearby cities.

These tailraces are unpredictable and difficult to understand because of the extreme flow variations causing the river to rise, in some instances, from 2 to 4 feet. Guide Terry Gunn says that the fluctuating flows at Lees Ferry make guiding this section of river very complex and variable on a daily and monthly basis.

"It is essentially like fishing several different rivers on any given day. Areas that have good fishing in low water might be dead in high- or medium-high water, and vice-versa. Rising water is generally the best fishing, but dropping water might turn on an area that fishes poorly in higher water. I'm still trying to figure it out after 25 years and 5,000 days on this stretch of water," Gunn adds.

While these severe currents are sometimes intimidating, tailwater fisheries below hydroelectric dams can be terrific. In addition to generating power, hydroelectric dams buffer the river from scouring spring-runoff flows, control flooding, store water for arid and semiarid land, and produce cool water during the warmest months of the year, supporting large populations of trout that would otherwise be nonexistent. The reservoir system above still produces the much-needed nutrients to support the ecosystem in the tailwater below.

Flows can fluctuate several thousand feet per second below dams that generate hydroelectricity. The Colorado at Lees Ferry fluctuates on a regular basis.

As you might imagine, the greatest challenge to fishing below a hydroelectric dam is the day-to-day fluctuations of flows. Flows can rise as much as several thousand cfs in a matter of minutes. For example, when all eight generators at Glen Canyon Dam are operating at full capacity, nearly 15 million gallons of water can pass through the penstocks each minute. Similar flow fluctuations occur below Flaming Gorge Dam, where releases range from 800 to 5,000 cfs.

The quality of the fishery hinges on the severity of the spikes in flow and the composition of the river channel. If the tailrace is relatively narrow or constricted, the fishing is generally nonproductive because the increase in flow causes a raging torrent. If the river has islands, braided sections, protruding logs, bridge abutments, and sweeping bends to deflect and absorb the flow increase, the river can be highly productive, often giving up some very large trout. In Glen Canyon's prime—the early to mid-1980s—it wasn't uncommon for an angler to hook trout in the 10- to 12-pound range.

Dr. Eric Atha cradles a beautiful rainbow he fooled sight-casting with a tiny midge nymph on a gravel bar below Glen Canyon Dam. "Early spring fishing at Lees Ferry is some of the best fishing of the season. Our March midge fishing is often off the charts and mostly sight-casting," says Terry Gunn, owner of Lees Ferry Anglers.

The afterbay below Yellowtail Dam absorbs flow fluctuations resulting from the Yellowtail Dam power plant. If you didn't know better, you might never guess that the Yellowtail Dam generated power. KIM DORSEY

These irregular flows affect the density and variety of the aquatic insects. The aquatic life varies from one hydroelectric tailwater to another. Midges, crane flies, and scuds seem to be the dominant aquatic insects because they can tolerate flow fluctuations more readily than mayflies, stoneflies, and caddisflies.

Aquatic insect life is much more resilient than we might think, however. Freestone rivers prove this every season during spring runoff. The Colorado River (the upper Colorado) near the town of Parshall, Colorado, runs in excess of 3,000 cfs during spring runoff, yet somehow the river still produces very reliable midge, mayfly (blue-winged olives, pale morning duns, red quills, and Tricos), caddisfly, and stonefly hatches. During the remainder of the year, the flows are between 200 and 600 cfs.

Certain varieties of stoneflies and mayflies (green drakes and red quills), however, cope moderately well with the fluctuating torrents and swift water. Scores of rising trout feast on these adult mayflies during the late summer and autumn months, when flows become manageable for the walk-and-wade angler. The midges of course are the strongest, and seem to prevail even under the most extreme conditions. I routinely see heavy swarms of midges in the morning, even when the flows are raging outside the riverbanks.

The density of blue-winged olives, *Pseudocloeons,* pale morning duns, caddisflies, and stoneflies varies greatly from one hydroelectric tailwater to another. The Green River below Flaming Gorge, Grey Reef, and the Bighorn River below Yellowtail Dam have dense populations of blue-winged olives, but the Colorado River below Glen Canyon Dam is devoid of mayflies for all practical purposes. Terry Gunn believes that the apparent reason that the Colorado does not have the "normal tailwater hatches" is because the water temperatures do not fluctuate. He also believes that Glen Canyon is the beginning of the river system, so nothing can migrate downriver.

Don't let the absence of mayflies fool you. Gunn notes: "We have a multitude of midges, 40 or more different varieties, from size 32s to 16s. Midges are the river's most prolific aquatic biomass. In addition, we have what is arguably the best cicada hatch of any Western river. It usually starts in early July and can last three weeks to two months. We also have other terrestrials, including spiders, moths, caterpillars, and hoppers."

The Bighorn River is an interesting and unique hydroelectric tailwater because of the Yellowtail Afterbay, which is 2.2 miles below the dam. The afterbay has a capacity of 3,140 acre-feet, which acts as a buffer minimizing the peak demand flow fluctuations from the power plant by releasing a steady flow of water from the afterbay dam. If you didn't know better, you wouldn't realize that the Bighorn River is a hydroelectric tailwater. The afterbay reduces the normal bank erosion that is commonly found below hydroelectric dams. The North Platte at Gray Reef is very similar. It too has an afterbay below Alcova Dam to help absorb the flow fluctuations that are a result of generating power.

Some tailwaters use hydroelectricity on a smaller scale. Aaron Carithers says that there is a small power plant below

Navajo Reservoir, which generates enough power to operate the dam and return small amounts of electricity to the grid. "You do not see huge flow variations on the San Juan, like some tailwaters that generate power. In fact, they tend to be very consistent. The river flows are managed to satisfy the downstream demand of irrigators, including the Navajo tribe," Carithers adds.

As you might imagine, tailwater fisheries below dams that generate power have less stable banks than other rivers, because of the powerful surges of water. It is not uncommon for them to experience a 2- to 4-foot rise and drop on any given day, wreaking havoc with streamside foliage. Without adequate streamside vegetation, fluttering insects such as caddisflies and stoneflies have problems getting a strong foothold.

Terry Gunn notes that at Lees Ferry "release patterns are consistently inconsistent." Most months of the year, the day starts with lower water and there is an increase in the morning—sometimes early, and in some months, later in the morning. In some months, there is a drop at midday that may or may not be followed by another rise. When the water rises or drops at the dam, it takes a few hours for the water flow change to travel the entire 16-mile stretch of the river. The rate of change depends on the velocity. Higher water flows travel faster than lower flows. "This all comes into play in our strategies for fishing specific areas. We use power boats, and we often chase water in an effort to be at the right spot at the right time," Gunn adds.

Rising flows can kick scuds and midge larvae loose from the aquatic vegetation, creating a feeding frenzy. On tailwaters that fluctuate substantially, like Lees Ferry, the rise and fall of the water actually helps the fishing during the initial phases of the generation period. I was flabbergasted to see how productive the Colorado River at Lees Ferry can be during a flow increase. From my previous experiences, a flow increase was usually disastrous, especially on the South Platte River.

Fluctuating flows make water levels a primary concern, not only for the fishing, but for safety. If possible, call ahead or check online for updated information about the release schedule of the tailwater you plan to fish. But keep in mind that flows are generally subject to change. Flows usually run higher on weekdays, when the power demand is at its highest, and lower during weekends, when the need for power has diminished. When you are on the water, listen and watch for signs such as loud horns (some dams sound a horn to indicate the release of water, while others increase the flow without warning); a lot of free-floating debris followed by a blast of cold air from upstream; or a sudden increase in the feeding activity of birds. The increase in water volume may be unnoticeable initially, unless you are standing on a piece of dry land, or on the leading edge of a gravel bar or shoal. Since river levels can rise dramatically, allow enough time to get back to the river's edge before the water peaks. I recommend keeping a whistle in your vest or on your chest pack in case of an emergency, when you need to get someone's attention.

Keep an eye on water levels at all times by watching a streamside marker such as a rock, branch, or similar object. Most of your casting should take place in calf-deep water or less to avoid any risks of being swept away by powerful rising currents.

The clear currents are often misleading, and can be extremely strong. I remember my guide at Lees Ferry telling me not to wade out past knee-deep water because if I slipped, he would never get the jet boat started in time to save me. I paid attention to that comment! Also, gravel bars and mid-channel shelves drop off quickly into deep water. Although the smooth-flowing, clear water may appear to be moving slowly, think again. It moves with a purpose. It is extremely important to always respect the power of water. Unfortunately, as a result of the dangerous currents below hydropower dams, many fly fishers drown each season, in situations that could have been avoided had they simply been prepared.

CHAPTER 3

Seasons of a Tailwater

As previously mentioned, one of the biggest advantages to a tailwater fishery is the opportunity to catch trout year-round. While the typical freestone is jammed with ice, or completely frozen, tailwater enthusiasts have the opportunity fish, if they opt to do so, during the cold and blustery winter months.

There are certainly challenges to each season, but anglers can expect to find consistent fishing throughout the majority of the year. Understanding the nuances of each season will dramatically increase your odds of catching more trout. Choosing the appropriate apparel must also be taken into consideration—that is, if you want to be comfortable and enjoy the experience on a year-round basis. Let's take a closer look at each season so that you can plan accordingly.

WINTER (NOVEMBER–MARCH)

Tailwaters rarely freeze in the first 3- to 4 miles below the dam. Water temperatures are generally in the mid-30s to low 40s in the winter. This allows anglers to have the pleasure of fishing year-round if they opt to pass on other winter activities such as snowmobiling, snowboarding, ice skating, or cross-country and downhill skiing.

Winter fly fishing is the most challenging of the year. Diminished hatches, cold water, and low flows set the stage

The Bighorn River is a popular year-round destination. Doug McElveen persuades a Bighorn brown trout to the net on a beautiful winter morning.

24

The lowest flows of the year are between November and April when reservoirs are holding back water for the upcoming season. Releases are generally at "minimum flows" for a several-week period throughout the winter months. Jonathan Keisling sight-nymphs to a pod of Cheesman Canyon rainbows with releases from the dam above at 50 cfs.

for technical, yet rewarding, fishing. You'll earn every fish you catch during the winter. By the latter part of November, most of the major hatches (mayflies, caddisflies, and stoneflies) have run their course, leaving only midges as the mainstay of the trout's diet. For several months (November–March), anglers must think simple, sparse—and most important, small. This in itself makes fishing tough.

Winter anglers must adjust expectations, because a good day between November and March may mean only a handful of fish. Sometimes just getting outdoors is half the battle, and hooking a trout or two is a bonus.

Anglers should come prepared for any type of weather before they head into the Front Range or Rocky Mountain region. I strongly recommend dressing in layers to keep warm. This allows you to take off a layer, if you are too warm, and add a layer of clothing if you get cold. If you run out of layers and become chilled, the experience deteriorates quickly. Additionally, you should come prepared with a warm fleece hat, gloves, vest, and breathable rain jacket. It is not a bad idea to carry a spare change of clothes in the event you take an unexpected plunge into the river. A Thermos of hot coffee, cocoa, or soup is a good idea too, to help take the chill off.

At this time of year, the stretch of fishable water varies greatly from one tailwater fishery to another. The depth of the reservoir, location and altitude, winter releases, water temperatures, the gradient of the stream channel, and hydroelectric commitments can all affect the fishery and how you approach it.

While cold water is an extremely important component to a great fishery, it can be a double-edged sword. It's difficult to find many feeding fish when the water temperatures dip below the 40-degree mark. However, a small rise in water temperatures (2–4 degrees), can make a huge difference in the overall outcome of your day, especially during the winter.

Guide Aaron Carithers from Anasazi Anglers of Durango, Colorado, notes that the Navajo Dam was completed in 1963 and at that time was the largest earthen dam in the world. It releases water from near the bottom of the dam at a constant 42 degrees. "The only time the fishing gets truly hard on the Juan [the San Juan River] is when the water temperatures fall below 42 degrees," he adds.

Releases are generally at minimum flows, and it is not uncommon to see the San Juan River at 500 cfs (sometimes 250 cfs), the Green River at 800 cfs, the Blue River at 50 cfs, the Bighorn at 1,500 cfs, and the South Platte River at 40 cfs. The fish stack up in their traditional winter holes, weathering these lean times. Their metabolism comes to a screeching halt, and they may fill their bellies only once every third day or so when a good midge hatch occurs. This no doubt is the most challenging time of the year to consistently fool trout.

The volume of the water—measured in cubic feet per second (cfs)—being released from the reservoir determines whether the river will remain ice-free. Generally speaking, if there is at least 100 cfs, the average tailwater will remain ice-free for several miles below the dam. Freezing-up is not even

Tailwater angling can be surprisingly productive on tailwaters that generate power. The author displays a beautiful Lees Ferry rainbow. ERIC ATHA

a consideration on some of the larger Western tailwater fisheries such as the Bighorn, Green, Grey Reef, or Lees Ferry.

The gradient of the stream channel is another factor. Rivers that sweep slowly through lush valleys and pastureland have a tendency to freeze quicker than rivers that carve their way swiftly through majestic boulder-filled canyons. The faster the currents, and the greater the volume, the less likely the river will freeze during the winter.

Successful winter anglers will need to target the slow, deep pools. The feeding window is very narrow during the winter. The best fishing occurs at midday—generally between 11 A.M. and 3 P.M. Finding a feeding trout will be your greatest challenge. For every dozen trout you see, only a handful will actually be feeding. Look for suspended trout—this tells you that the fish are actually feeding. Your fly selection should consist of tiny midge patterns that are tied thin and sparse, ranging in sizes from 18–24. Anglers will find sporadically rising trout in the shaded areas and tailouts of many pools. You should also carry adult midge imitations in sizes 22–26 and plenty of 7X tippet.

SPRING (APRIL–MAY)

By mid-April, fishing conditions improve immensely with increased water temperatures and improved flows. Strong hatches of blue-winged olives help trigger increased feeding activity from the trout. Once the water temperatures rise above the 42-degree mark, the fish move from the slow, deep pools back into the shallow riffles once again.

Some very good nymph fishing occurs in the transitional areas—gravel bars and midchannel shelves—during these hatches. Aggressive trout will suspend themselves in the current, voraciously chasing emerging *Baetis* nymphs.

A long-sleeved shirt and fleece vest are standard apparel for this time of year. I keep my fleece hat and fingerless gloves readily available for cool, crisp mornings. Weather can change quickly during the spring months, and unsettled spring wind often brings in an unexpected rain shower or snow squall. Bring your breathable rain jacket—you may need it when you least expect it. It is always a good idea to keep a spare set of clothes in your truck, boat bag, or backpack in the event you need them.

Egg patterns become effective as the rainbows and cutthroats begin their annual spawning ritual. Concentrate your efforts in the faster slots and seams below the shallow-water spawning areas. Avoid fishing to spawning trout positioned on redds. These are easily identified: look for lighter areas on the bottom or scoured-out, bowl-like depressions. If you see rainbows grouped up in shallow water (12 to 18 inches deep), you can generally assume that they are spawning.

One of my favorite rigs in the spring is an egg or an orange scud pattern dropped with either a mayfly nymph, such as a size 20 Mercury Pheasant Tail or size 20 Sparkle Wing RS II, or a midge pupa like a Mercury Black Beauty. Such rigs imitate three of the food organisms most prevalent at this time of year—free-floating eggs, midge pupae, and *Baetis* nymphs.

As the snow melts, the flows begin to rise, but the primary purpose of the dam is still a positive intake in the reservoir above until the lake fills. If there is an unusually high snowpack, the water board may opt to move water downstream prematurely. This rarely happens, however, because this is risky business on the water board's part. Warm spring winds can evaporate snowpack quickly, reducing estimated water levels and leaving a substantial shortage later in the season.

By the latter part of April, flows begin to rise as a result of spring runoff. Tailwaters still experience a higher than normal flow regime during spring runoff, but for the most part the rivers remain clear and fishable. During the initial phases of runoff, the river discolors mildly, but the stream quickly clears and fishing is generally good once the trout adjust to the increased flow.

In fact, some of the best nymph fishing of the year occurs during these flow increases, because some of the larger food organisms such as crane flies, stoneflies, aquatic worms, and scuds are dislodged in huge numbers. This creates a feeding frenzy, and for a short time, fishing seems easy—because the

During the spring months, trout move into the shallow riffles looking for Baetis *nymphs. Bob Dye nymphs with a* Baetis *pattern in the shallow riffles during the early stages of a blue-winged olive emergence downstream from Alcova Dam.*

higher flows cause gluttony. The fish are easier to catch with more water flowing over their heads. They're less spooky and are less impacted by movement, poorly executed casts, sloppy presentations, and other mistakes. In lower flows, the fish become leader-shy and drift into the deeper currents after a cast or two.

On certain tailwaters—including the San Juan River and the North Platte River—the Bureau of Reclamation on a semi-annual or annual basis, ramps up the flows to simulate normal historic runoff flows to flush away sediment that has accrued over the year. The river will turn muddy for a day or two, but after the initial surge of water, fishing can be pretty good.

According to Aaron Carithers of Anasazi Anglers in Durango, Colorado, the overall reason for the ramped-up flow is to mimic the natural hydrograph in order to help the squaw-fish, as well as to scour the river and make room for future inflow into Navajo Reservoir. The fishing can be very good between 3,000 and 5,000 cfs—especially the first week at 5,000 cfs—as the fish are pushed into the little remaining "soft water" and gorge themselves on aquatic worms. The back channels also become floatable at 1,000 cfs and a large percentage of the trout population moves into these backwaters. "Once we get to about 3,000 cfs, the wading becomes pretty tricky. Therefore, I keep my clients in the boat. All things considered, fishing is pretty good," he says.

The Gray Reef section of the North Platte is one of the best tailwater fisheries in the West. Flushing flows help free the gravel of silt and other harmful sediments that have adverse effects on both spawning trout and aquatic insect life. Jim Cannon holds a beautiful rainbow he fooled with an egg pattern.

Tricos provide consistent dry-fly fishing for several weeks between late June and late October. Anglers will find technical, yet rewarding, dry-fly fishing. KIM DORSEY

Erik Aune of North Platte Lodge and The Reef Fly Shop in Alcova, Wyoming says that the flushing flows on the North Platte River at Grey Reef are a great trout spawning habitat program. The flushing flow is meant to purge critical spawning gravel of silt. It has been very successful for rainbow reproduction. The higher flushing flows typically last for five days, and the quantity of water will vary. Flows normally start at upwards of 4,000 cfs for the first couple of evenings. This is during winter flows of 500 cfs. From 500 cfs, dam managers open the gates to about 4,000 cfs and gradually return to 500 cfs over the course of ten hours or so. Over the next couple of days, they may release a maximum of only 2,500 cfs, depending on river conditions. The Bureau of Reclamation and the Wyoming Game and Fish Department cooperate in this effort.

"If we are lucky we get a fall flush. The fall flush does a good job of scouring the river of the summer's algae and other vegetation. There are many other tailwaters that would benefit from a flushing flow. The trick is to get the Bureau of Reclamation to understand that the rivers should be treated as wildlife habitat as well as irrigation ditches," Aune says.

All in all, flows may be erratic, but fishing is generally good for those willing to change their tactics to match the prevailing conditions. Anglers can expect hatches of blue-winged olives until late May, overlapped by caddis. Nymphing is generally the most productive method during the higher flows. During low-water years, the dry-fly fishing can be spectacular.

SUMMER (JUNE–AUGUST)

The high-water season generally peaks by mid-June. As spring runoff recedes, the flows begin to drop. Flows will vary for the remainder of the season based on irrigation, metropolitan consumption, and power demand. Rain and cooler temperatures can also affect the downriver demand.

Summer apparel is straightforward—wear a long-sleeved shirt to protect yourself from the excruciating sun and biting insects such as deerflies, horseflies, and mosquitoes. Wearing a bandanna is a good idea too; it protects your neck from the sun and annoying insects. I also carry a breathable raincoat, especially during the monsoon season, because an afternoon rain shower is always a possibility. Carry plenty of water to stay hydrated. Dehydration can cause unexpected leg cramps, which can have detrimental effects on the outcome of your day. A water filtration system is a good idea if you do a lot of fishing and hiking in remote areas such as Cheesman Canyon, Waterton Canyon, or on the Blue, Green, or Williams Fork rivers.

As the flows recede, anglers can expect hatches of stoneflies—both golden stones and Yellow Sallies. Imitations of these bugs provide excellent nymph fishing in the faster currents, and good dry-fly fishing in riffled currents that are 18–24 inches in depth. Dry/dropper rigs, such as a size 12–14 Yellow Stimulator, 12–14 Rubber-Legged Stimulator, or 12–14 Yellow Pearl Stimulator dropped with a small mayfly nymph or midge pattern work well. Stimulators fish well this

Some of the best fishing of the season occurs during the autumn months. Consistent flows and good hatches set the stage for some reliable fishing on the Williams Fork near Parshall, Colorado.

time of year because they imitate a wide range of fluttering adult insects, from caddisflies to stoneflies. Amy's Ant (the word "ant" is misleading) in sizes 8–12 is one of my favorite adult stonefly imitations. I have fooled selective trout all over the West with this pattern, using it both as an attractor, and for a dry/dropper rig, suspending a midge and mayfly dropper off it. One of my favorite droppers is a Mercer's Micro Mayfly with a tungsten bead. The stonefly hatches are followed by excellent pale morning duns, green drakes and Trico hatches starting in late June or early July. This can be some of the best dry-fly fishing of the year.

August brings the continuation of excellent Trico hatches and the beginning stages of the red quills and blue-winged olives. Terrestrials can be very effective too—especially on windy days. Anglers will find some very good midge hatches this time of year.

AUTUMN (SEPTEMBER–OCTOBER)
The autumn months bring excellent hatches of midges, red quills, and blue-winged olives. The Trico hatches begin to fizzle, but the hatch still provides some sporadic dry-fly action with both duns and spinners. Autumn apparel is similar to the suggested guidelines for the spring months. Mornings are cool, but midday temperatures are pleasant. It's not uncommon to get a cold snap in September, but an Indian summer usually prevails until mid-October. Never leave anything to chance, however—come prepared with the appropriate apparel.

One of the greatest advantages to autumn fishing is that the flow becomes more stable as the need for water becomes less important for agricultural users. You'll see the San Juan drop to 500 cfs, the Green drop to 800 cfs, and the Bighorn drop to 1,500 cfs and stay there for weeks. The Blue, Williams Fork, Frying Pan, and South Platte still fluctuate between 200 and 300 cfs, but not to the same degree as during the summer months. Consistent flows set the stage for very prolific blue-winged olive hatches. Anglers catch trout on both nymphs and dries during these hatches.

Streamers and egg patterns are very effective as the brown trout begin to spawn. Egg patterns dropped with a mayfly or midge nymph once again becomes the rig of choice. It's hard to go wrong with the "egg-midge" combo. Several tailwaters offer the opportunity to catch spawn-run Kokanee salmon with brightly colored flies. They will eat conventional tailwater nymphs and egg patterns too.

Fishing will remain productive until mid-November, when diminished hatches and falling water temperatures reduce the metabolism of the trout. When this occurs, you'll work hard for every fish you catch. Successful anglers will fish with tiny midge nymphs, using very precise dead-drifts in the slow transitions, tailouts of runs, and pools.

During autumn, the fish will once again move into the slow, deep pools, preparing for leaner times, until the whole process begins all over in the spring.

CHAPTER 4

The Fish

Trout are true masters of their environment, and in the end only the strongest survive the forces of nature such as drought, seasonal runoff, temperature fluctuations, fire, flood, fishing pressure, spawning, and most important, predators. Instinct and intuitive senses guide them through their precious journey in life—one small hiccup and the fish hits the frying pan or is gobbled up by a bird.

Locals often say: "Those Cheesman Canyon trout sure are smart. I have tried everything in my fly box, and they still won't eat anything that I have to offer." Trout are not smart; they are instinctive. They know that their food is a certain size, shape, and color, and most importantly, that it travels at the same speed as the current. Anglers who stray from that basic formula will have extreme difficulty consistently catching trout.

Trout do not have the ability to rationalize, or think—which is why they ignore a huge adult crane fly that's fluttering above the water, and focus instead on the hundreds of size 22 midge pupae drifting in the water—they simply react to certain situations based on imprinting and being in a survival mode. Their senses teach them from past experiences, associating certain behaviors, movement, bright colors, and other activities with danger. A trout that has been caught several times will become increasingly more difficult to fool in the future, and in that sense, may become "educated."

Trout are not smart—they survive by instinct. They react from past experience, associating certain conditions with danger. A trout that has been caught several times will become "educated" and more difficult to fool in the future.

IDENTIFYING FEEDING FISH AND UNDERSTANDING THEIR TENDENCIES

To survive over an extended period of time, trout must adapt to their environment: hiding, feeding, and instinctively defending a strategic position in their underwater world. They must be able to find locations that provide the greatest amount of food, while expending the least amount energy. When there is a shortage of hatching insects the energy required to intercept the sporadic emerging insect is often less than the energy obtained from the food supply. When this occurs, it is very difficult to find a feeding fish.

Watching a trout feed is one of the most valuable lessons you'll ever learn on a trout stream. Closely watch their tendencies and graceful movements in the water to understand a river's hydraulics and how a trout uses the flow and current-blocking structures for efficient feeding and protection. It won't take you very long to figure out that trout are incredibly instinctive and proficient feeders. In most cases, a trout will move only a few inches to obtain a small morsel of food, ensuring that they expend minimum amounts of energy.

Trout feed in one of two ways: opportunistically or selectively. When trout feed in an opportunistic fashion, they eat anything that is available and take advantage of anything that comes their way, at any given time. Nonselective feeding patterns occur when there is no hatch, and these are the toughest conditions for fooling trout with flies. There seems to be no rhyme or reason for the feeding preferences. Anglers must be willing to change flies frequently under these circumstances.

Selective feeding occurs when there is a tremendous number of one particular food organism, such as during a heavy hatch. Prime examples: trout keying on a 22 midge pupa

Trout are masters of their environment. Only the "best of the best" survive over an extended period of time. Mitch Knutson shows off a beautiful Arkansas River rainbow that was caught in standard regulation waters upstream from the Nature Center below Pueblo Dam.

when a midge hatch is in progress, or trout focusing on a size 20 *Baetis* nymph during a dense blue-winged olive hatch, or trout eating sunken Trico spinners toward the latter part of a Trico hatch.

During these selective phases, trout key on one particular food organism and ignore all the rest. This can be one of the most difficult fishing situations, because anglers must have

Trout that are suspended in the water column are actively feeding. Trout that are hugging the bottom are typically not feeding.

Identifying a feeding fish will increase your odds of catching more trout. Matt Miles spotted this feeding fish on the Taylor River before casting to it.

the right size, shape, and color, respectively, to fool a trout with an artificial.

SURVIVAL OF THE FITTEST

Once the fry emerge from the gravel (redds), they must immediately find protection from current and predators. Initially, their living quarters are in shallow water: along a grassy streambank, under a log, bush, or deadfall, hiding in dense aquatic foliage, or in other slow-moving sections of the stream.

Juvenile trout feed on zooplankton and other microscopic food organisms until they are large enough to intercept free-drifting aquatic insects, such as midge larvae and mayfly nymphs. As they mature, they seek new locations that provide better opportunities for food, growth, and protection.

During this process, there is a fine line between finding food and becoming food, and protection from predators is always at the top of the list of survival skills. Trout can never let their guard down, because birds such as blue herons, bald eagles, pelicans, kingfishers, water ouzels, and mergansers are all threats from above the water's surface.

I recently watched a bald eagle capture a trout on the South Platte River while I was guiding three guests above the small community of Deckers. Bald eagles show up in the Deckers/Cheesman area every winter, adding to the overall fly-fishing experience. It was about 10 A.M. on a cool and crisp winter morning. The sun had not peeked over the canyon's lip yet, so it was a bit on the chilly side. The releases from Cheesman Dam were characteristic of the winter months—50 to 70 cfs—and the fish were stacked in their traditional winter lies.

We were fishing the Rock Garden, a beautiful stretch of pocketwater interspersed and highlighted with boulders of all sizes. Overall fishing was good that morning—our group was hooking and landing fish in the middle of the winter on one of the most technically challenging rivers in the West. What else could you ask for?

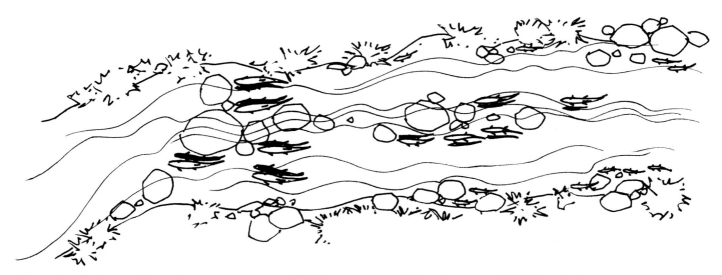

There is a distinct pecking order on a trout stream. The largest trout reside in the areas with the best feeding opportunities.

As I was reflecting on this beautiful morning, a bald eagle swept down into the purplish, riffled currents and grabbed a 13-inch rainbow trout. The bald eagle immediately went to the streambank, placed the wiggling trout on a fresh blanket of snow, killed its prey, and abruptly flew away to enjoy a fresh breakfast. It was like watching something from a National Geographic television show. The bald eagle had a clear plan of attack, and executed it flawlessly.

At that point, it became clear to me that only the trout with the best senses—vision, smell, hearing, and taste—will survive for an extended period of time. The weaker trout will be culled from the gene pool. There is an ongoing battle to master the elements: a competition based on their size, and the ability to find strategic feeding lies and the best spots for protection from currents and predators. There is no downtime; the process goes on 24 hours a day, seven days a week.

Whether in riffles, runs, pockets, or pools, there is a clear-cut pecking order based on size. The larger fish take the best lies. If the genetically superior trout is removed from its strategic holding position by a streamside predator or an angler, the next trout in line, based on the natural hierarchy, will quickly fill the void, and so on. You'll frequently observe this type of behavior on a smaller scale in a feeding lie where a trout quickly moves into the best feeding location after another trout has been spooked, or caught and released downriver.

To the casual observer, the surrounding currents all look the same, but the trout position themselves where they have the best opportunity to obtain food and protection. If the flow remains stable, you'll find fish in the same lie, over and over again. But if the flow changes even slightly, the trout will reposition themselves in other locations that best suit their needs.

Large trout generally reside in the best lies, which offer both food and protection. A trout that exceeds 18 inches has not grown so big by chance: it has mastered its environment.

This trout was fooled with a Baetis nymph imitation during the initial phases of a blue-winged olive hatch. During heightened periods of selectivity, anglers will need exact imitations to fool trout. This trout was fooled with a Stalcup Baetis. KIM DORSEY

Brown trout average 13–16 inches in most of our Western tailwaters. Keith Lang holds a beautiful Williams Fork brown that he fooled with a size 18 Buckskin.

Anglers will have the opportunity to target large prespawn trout above certain Western lakes like Elevenmile Reservoir. Josh Behr landed this 12½-pound prespawn cuttbow on a size 22 Mercury Pheasant Tail.

A trout's feeding pattern varies greatly depending on its size and species. Smaller rainbows put themselves at risk, feeding in shallow riffles in an attempt to get a strong foothold in their environment. Larger rainbows tend to sit in the transitional zones, areas where shallow riffles funnel into deeper pools. They can escape any threat of danger by slipping into the deeper currents.

However, a larger, crafty brown might move only a few inches from a protruding log or undercut bank to eat. In most cases, a big brown will feed at night on large forage items, and avoid the risks associated with feeding in well-lit conditions. If a large trout does move into a shallow riffle during a heavy hatch, you may get only one or two drifts to fool it. This is where a careful approach, a perfect cast with the correct flies, a flawless dead-drift, and setting the hook at any indication of a potential strike (a flash, a movement in the water column, a moving strike indicator, or an opening mouth) must all come together without a hitch.

WESTERN GAMEFISH

Rainbow and brown trout are the dominant species in most Western tailwaters, though populations vary depending on the drainage. Some rivers are known as rainbow fisheries, while other watersheds are known as brown fisheries (since the disappearance of rainbows from some waters because of whirling disease), and still others boast a mixed bag of both species.

Water temperatures, flows, and the availability of certain food organisms dramatically influence a trout's growth rate. Rainbow trout can grow exceptionally large (exceeding 15 pounds) in some tailraces where Mysis shrimp are plentiful (see chapter 12 for more information on Mysis shrimp). Otherwise, rainbows average between 14 and 18 inches in most Western tailwaters, with a few fish that surpass the 20-inch mark. If there is an abundant supply of larger food organisms like sculpins, crayfish, aquatic worms, crane flies, and scuds, the brown trout can get large, too (exceeding 24 inches). On average, brown trout range between 13 and 16 inches in most tailwaters throughout the West.

On occasion, you'll catch a cutthroat or brook trout, which adds some spice to the day. In certain drainages, including the Blue, Taylor, Williams Fork, Yampa, and Frying Pan Rivers, they'll migrate from neighboring tributaries and feeder creeks. In addition, cuttbows—rainbow-cutthroat hybrids—are commonly found in many Western tailwaters. A grand slam—catching rainbows, browns, cutthroats, and brookies on the same outing—is never out of the question.

Influxes of lake-run trout from reservoirs also produce some very large fish during the spawning season. Anglers who target the Spinney Mountain Ranch section of the South Platte have the opportunity to catch trout in the 20- to 26-inch range for a three- to four-week time frame each spring and fall. I have personally observed trout between 10 and 14 pounds landed in this section.

Many anglers develop a special affection for a certain species of trout. This preference is often based on the trout's unique behaviors such as feeding patterns, coloration, the way they fight, and overall challenge when it comes to fooling them. Rainbows are known for their selective feeding phases, while browns are recognized as crafty, stubborn, and difficult to find and fool. Cutthroats are often dubbed as being stupid and poor fighters, but their magnificent beauty tips the scale in their favor. Brook trout are known as some of the best opportunistic feeders—especially with surface offerings like Royal Wulffs, H & L (House and Lots) Variants, Limeades, and Renegades.

Rainbow Trout

Rainbow trout *(Oncorhynchus mykiss)* are among the most sought-after gamefish in the western Rocky Mountain region. Originally native to the Pacific Northwest, they now inhabit streams and lakes in nearly 50 countries and are found in every continent, with the exception of Antarctica.

Their quick, strong surges of power make them unlike any other member of the trout family, and for that reason, fly fishers have a special fondness for them. After the initial hookup, a rainbow typically jumps several times, attempting to dislodge the fly from its jaw. Even after being persuaded close to the net, it never gives up, frequently busting fine tippets with one last powerful run.

Rainbow trout are easily identified by the pinkish-red stripe that runs lengthwise from their crimson-colored gill covers to their slightly forked, spotted tails. Rainbows have dark green backs with irregular spots scattered above and below that brilliant red stripe. The underside is a gorgeous silvery-white, generally without any spots.

Rainbow trout that eat Mysis shrimp are magnificent. Bob Dye landed this 7-pound rainbow with a tiny midge nymph on the Taylor River.

Rainbow trout vary in color depending on their natural diet and surroundings. Rainbows that feed on a smorgasbord of Mysis shrimp or scuds have considerably brighter colors than those that feed exclusively on midges, caddisflies, stoneflies, and mayflies. Trout that reside in the Frying Pan, Taylor, and Blue Rivers (reservoirs with dense populations of Mysis shrimp) are excellent examples. These beautiful trout have brilliant candy-apple red stripes and gill covers, with dark olive backs that phase into a golden-yellow belly.

Rainbows are popular Western gamefish. They are identified by the red gill plates and the red stripe that runs lengthwise along their flanks. Rainbows have dark green backs with irregular spots sprinkled across the body.

In addition, their coloration may vary depending on the composition of the streambed. If the streambed is dark, sprinkled with moss-covered boulders and dense aquatic foliage, rainbows will have deep olive colors, with bright red stripes. If the stream bottom is comprised of light-colored sand or rose-colored granite, the trout will be lighter in color for camouflage purposes.

Some rainbows are more silvery, especially the Kamloops rainbow. Native to Kamloops Lake in British Columbia, they have become a favorite trout to be stocked by ranchers and private fishing clubs. They grow fast, fight like an ox, and survive under a wide range of conditions.

Kamloops rainbows can be easily identified by their steel-blue color. Because they are often escapees from private fishing clubs, they are typically large—18–26 inches in length. Kamloops readily take brightly colored flies like egg patterns, orange scuds, and San Juan Worms, and they provide an angler the opportunity of a lifetime to hook and land a trophy trout. They are also eager to eat large dry flies like Jack Dennis's Amy Ant. We routinely fool these large rainbows in Cheesman Canyon and the Deckers area with "Amy."

Stocked rainbows are also silver-colored from the pellet diet they eat in the hatchery. They are quickly identified by their ragged or tattered fins, which have literally been rubbed raw against the hatchery's concrete walls. These 8- to 10-inch "catchables" are planted near areas with intense angling pressure, with the hope of alleviating some of the stress on the wild trout.

To assist in the ongoing battle against whirling disease, fish and wildlife departments have initiated aggressive stocking programs in many tailwater fisheries. These agencies stock fingerling rainbows and cuttbows (5- to-6 inch trout, lacking most of the wear and tear on their fins) in many of the tailwaters that were once self-sustaining rainbow trout fisheries. In time, the fingerlings take on all the characteristics of wild trout, and the casual streamside observer would never know the difference between a planted trout and a wild trout.

Rainbows thrive in a wide range of conditions, from fast riffles to slow pools. Anglers commonly find rainbows in faster slots with midchannel structure, such as gravel bars, shelves, and other drop-offs. They also thrive in highly oxygenated pocketwater during the summer months.

Rainbow trout are most active when the water temperatures are between 42 and 62 degrees, with the crest of their activity being between 55 and 62 degrees. If the water temperature exceeds 62 degrees, please be careful, as the warmer water tends to have adverse effects on them. If the water is warm, and you know you have a rainbow hooked, play it quickly to the net, wet your hands before handling it, and cradle the fish carefully as you release it. Rainbows may take some special nurturing if you exhaust them from a long fight.

Rainbow trout make up the bulk of the catch throughout the winter because they seem to be less affected by the colder water temperatures. While not as active as during the summer months, they still feed when the water temperatures are between 38 and 42 degrees. If a good midge hatch is in progress, anglers will have the opportunity to catch a handful of rainbow trout each day. Brown trout seem to disappear (sitting on the bottoms of deep, dark pools) during the winter, because they become extremely lethargic from the cold water temperatures.

Rainbows tend to position themselves in angler-friendly lies all season long. It is not uncommon to see several rainbow trout in one riffle, feeding aggressively when a midge or mayfly hatch occurs. They are clearly visible most of the time—even when they are not feeding—stacked up in the slow, deep pools.

Rainbows will eat just about anything, from tiny midges to forage items, but on the whole they tend to be selective feeders, concentrating their efforts on tiny aquatic insects. I must admit that I am particularly fond of rainbows for that reason. They are true masters of minutiae, requiring nothing less than a perfect presentation with tiny flies and spider-web-thin tippets.

Anglers must be careful, however, with that assumption. Large rainbows (18 inches plus) can be territorial! They compete for prime feeding locations and will chase other rainbow trout of equal or smaller size from their territories. They become especially aggressive during the spawning season, and anglers can capitalize on this with large, heavily weighted streamers.

Most rainbow trout spawn from mid-March through May. I have observed rainbow trout spawning as early as mid-January, continuing through the second week of June. Rainbows are consistently found spawning in Cheesman Canyon until the second week of June. But a number of strains of rainbows spawn during the fall months, as a result the crossbreeding that has been conducted by fish and wildlife departments over the past few years. Each year, I have noticed an increasing number of rainbow trout starting to spawn in September, continuing through the middle part of December. A prime example is the large number of rainbow trout that spawn in the fall months on the San Juan River below Navajo Dam. Over the course of the past few seasons, I have observed spawning rainbows in Cheesman Canyon, and at Deckers and the Spinney Mountain Ranch during the fall months, some lasting as late as mid-November. For that reason, egg patterns can be effective year-round.

Spawning rainbows tend to find locations with a moderate flow, often in the tailout of a nice glassy pool, or just above a shallow, riffled area. Once the pair has identified a location suitable for their spawning needs, the female digs an oval-shaped cavity with her tail and body, pushing the rocks and fine gravel off to the side. This spawning area is referred to as a redd. It is not uncommon to see community redds, where several pairs use the same gravel. I have observed large community redds at Spinney Mountain Ranch, with several 5-pound-plus trout concentrated in these areas.

These spawning areas are generally lighter in color than the surrounding streambed. Please watch your step around spawning areas, and avoid fishing to a trout during the egg-laying process. This is unethical: it hurts the future of our sport. Don't let a guide catch you (especially on the Bighorn or Gray Reef) fishing to spawning trout—or you'll get an earful! It is acceptable to fish egg patterns in the faster slots and seams below the spawning area, and this, as you might imagine, can provide some explosive fishing during the spawning season.

Once the redd is complete, both the male and female slide into the redd with their vents in close proximity. As the female deposits her eggs, the male oozes a white cloud of milt around the eggs as they settle to the bottom of the bowl-like depression. The female immediately covers the eggs by pushing the gravel from both sides to protect them from predators. The male and female go their separate ways. The female is completely exhausted, but the male may mate with another female, until he is completely exhausted too.

The eggs hatch in 21 to 30 days, depending on the water temperatures. The baby fish (fry) remain in the gravel until their yolk sacs are completely absorbed. Then the baby trout must face life on their own, seeking protection from the current and predators. The average rainbow lives five to six years, with an old, wise rainbow making it to seven. Colorado River rainbows are the exception; they may live nine to ten years.

Brown Trout

Brown trout *(Salmo trutta)* are wary, crafty, and the most difficult of all trout species to fool. They are native to Europe and Asia, but through artificial stockings, they have established a strong foothold in North America, South America, New Zealand, and Australia.

Populations of wild brown trout have exploded in several Western tailwaters because of the rapid decline in rainbow populations due to whirling disease, and they're currently the bulk of the catch in many watersheds. The Williams Fork River near Parshall, Colorado, is a prime example: populations of 3,500 wild brown trout per mile make this one of the best self-sustaining brown trout fisheries in the West. Anglers can routinely catch fish of all sizes, from "young of the year"

HOFER RAINBOWS

Several Western tailwaters have been hit hard by whirling disease, resulting in a rapid decline of rainbow populations. There seems to be some light at the end of the tunnel, however. Lately, a few rainbow strains have been identified that show a strong resistance to whirling disease. One in particular is the Hofer rainbow, which has been imported from Germany. It is speculated that since whirling disease originated in Germany, some of the strains that have been reared there exhibit a strong resistance to the deadly parasite.

In years past, the Colorado DOW has stocked Colorado River rainbows (CRR) because of their longevity, superb color, energetic behavior, and ability to survive. Unfortunately, whirling disease has taken a toll on most of the wild rainbow populations, leaving brown trout to fill the void.

Recently, the DOW has begun experimenting with crossbreeding CRR with Hofer rainbows to see if the resistance can be inherited by their offspring. So far, the results look promising. According to George Schisler from the DOW: "The Hofer/CRR have demonstrated varying levels of resistance, with some as resistant as the Hofer themselves."

Hofer/CRR were planted in 2004 in certain sections of the lower Gunnison (Ute Trail and Smith Fork), and circumstantial evidence suggests that these fish are now reproducing on their own. Hofer/CRR have also been planted in the South Platte River above Elevenmile (between Spinney and Elevenmile), and in Antero and Spinney Reservoirs, as well as in the Rio Grande. Only time will tell, but things seem to be heading in the right direction.

The Colorado Division of Wildlife is now stocking Hofer rainbows in selected tailwaters. So far, the results look encouraging, with circumstantial evidence from electroshocking data suggesting that the Hofer rainbows are reproducing on their own. GEORGE SCHLISLER/ COLORADO DIVISION OF WILDLIFE

Brown trout are never far from subsurface structure such as rocks or submerged logs.

Brown trout are identified by their golden color and dark brown spots sprinkled along their flank. Interspersed among the darker spots are red dots outlined with silver-blue halos.

to five- and six-year-old trout. Cheesman Canyon was once predominantly a rainbow fishery, but now it has swung to nearly 70 percent brown trout, according to electroshocking surveys conducted by the Colorado DOW. The lower Frying Pan River near Basalt is another example of a great wild brown trout fishery.

Brown trout can be identified by their golden, olive-brown coloration, dark green backs that shade into a rich yellow, with dark brown spots sprinkled all over their flanks, from the eye areas to the base of the caudal fin. Interspersed among the dark spots are several red spots outlined with brilliant silver-blue halos. Unlike rainbow trout, they have very few, if any, spots on their squared-off tail. Lake-run browns (when not in spawning mode) are more silver-green in color, with prominent dark spots.

In the Spinney Mountain Ranch section of the South Platte, you can find thick-bodied brown trout called "humpback" browns. These lake-run browns (this influx has nothing to do with spawning) move upstream into the South Platte during the summer to capitalize on an increased availability of caddisflies, Yellow Sallies, pale morning duns, and Tricos.

Brown trout have big, broad tongues and a dozen large teeth, which allows them to be more aggressive than other trout and eat larger food organisms, and forage fish. Keep your fingers out of a brown's mouth, or you'll get torn up from its razor-sharp teeth.

Browns thrive in well-oxygenated, low-elevation rivers with submerged logs, rocks, undercut banks, and overhanging willows and other vegetation. They frequently hide along the edges of the stream in cracks and crevices, or any of the aforementioned habitat. Finding them is only half the battle—getting them to eat is a whole different scenario. For every dozen brown trout you spot, only a handful may be actually feeding.

The best time to fool brown trout is during a good blue-winged olive or pale morning dun hatch. They eagerly rise to mayfly duns, especially during overcast conditions. They are selective, but can be fooled during these hatches with a size 16–22 Mathews's Sparkle Dun.

If you want to catch brown trout consistently, you'll need to dredge heavily weighted nymphs around rocks, logs, and other hard-to-fish areas. You'll earn every one you catch and will frequently snag and lose your nymphing rig. The trade-off, however, is some very nice fish that rarely get caught.

Brown trout are now dominant in many Western tailwaters since the appearance of whirling disease. Populations of 3,500 wild brown trout per mile are common in certain tailwaters like the Williams Fork in Colorado.

Once hooked, browns run hard and deep. They frequently swim toward subsurface structure, bulldogging and pointing their noses toward the streambed, making repeated short spurts and trying to free themselves by rubbing up against sharp objects. Contrary to what many anglers believe, brown trout do jump—in fact, they may jump several times during the fight, especially in shallow riffles and runs when water temperatures exceed the mid-50s.

I had an eye-opening experience late one morning when I was guiding two anglers from the Houston, Texas, area. Both of these anglers were good sticks, and we had covered a beautiful piece of pocketwater thoroughly. We had caught a good number of trout in a 200-yard stretch, but the numbers were nothing to brag about. About the time we finished fishing this stretch, several Colorado DOW vehicles pulled into the parking lot adjacent to the river. It was clear that they were going to electroshock this section of river. My guests were interested in watching this, so we took a short break.

I knew it would take the DOW officials a few minutes to set up their generator and electrodes, so we took a break for lunch. After our streamside meal, we watched them shock the same piece of water that we had just fished. It was amazing! They pulled several hundred brown trout out of that 200-yard stretch of river. We watched with astonishment as the DOW people waved their electrodes around the submerged structure. Brown trout floated to the surface like logs, temporarily disoriented. They were scooped up and gently placed into a boxlike floating apparatus to be measured, weighed, and recorded.

Watching that electroshocking experience illuminated for me and my clients how difficult brown are to find and, more important, how difficult they can be to fool. That experience, on an otherwise routine day on the stream, changed my tactics and approach to targeting brown trout.

Brown trout are the most difficult of all species to fool. Finding them is only half the battle; getting them to eat is your biggest challenge.

Because brown trout are territorial, it is rare to find a group of them together. Typically there will be one brown in a pocket, in front of a rock, under a log or undercut bank, or next to the rock in a dark crevice. Each little nook and cranny can be a home for a brown trout. Covering the water methodically and thoroughly is of the utmost importance when fishing for brown trout.

Brown trout prefer water temperatures between the mid-40s and the upper 50s. They are most active when the water approaches the low 60s. When these conditions exist, anglers will no doubt have the best opportunity of the year to catch a bunch of brown trout. Usually this is during the summer

In order to fool a brown trout, you'll need to dredge your nymphs around submerged structure.

(May through August) when air temperatures warm the water. With warmer water, and an increased metabolism, the brown trout migrate into the shallow, highly oxygenated riffles looking for larger food organisms.

Anglers welcome warmer water temperatures because the brown trout move out of their traditional holding areas to capitalize on larger food organisms such as stoneflies, pale morning dun nymphs, scuds, aquatic worms, crane flies, and terrestrials. This is a prime opportunity to sight-nymph for brown trout in riffles that are 18–24 inches deep. These opportunities are rare, so you must take advantage of them while you can.

Fishing is almost easy at this point. The higher flows wash loose these larger food organisms, causing gluttony. The trout will eat anything that resembles an aquatic worm: in fact, it is not uncommon to see a brown trout with worms literally hanging out of its mouth. I have watched a brown trout move nearly 2 feet to eat a San Juan Worm in a shallow riffle when the water temperatures were in the low 60s. This fishing period is short-lived, as the brown trout become wise to worm imitations as the flow recedes and many of the naturals have been consumed.

On the other hand, when the water temperatures are below 45 degrees, browns seem to disappear into the depths. If you didn't know better, you would swear there were none in the stream. This is why rainbows make up the bulk of the catch throughout the winter. Brown trout are still there, but they are hiding in places where you don't see them—not to mention that their metabolism comes to a screeching halt, to the point where very little food is required to maintain their body weight, and their growth in winter is minimal. Starting in mid-April, brown trout begin to put weight back on as the midge and blue-winged olive hatches intensify. The average brown will easily bulk up a half a pound over the course of a three-month period.

Brown trout have longer lifespans than native North American trout species. While the average brown trout ranges between 13 and 16 inches, many get very large—researchers have observed brown trout living up to 13 years and exceeding 35 pounds. In May 1992, Howard "Rip" Collins caught a 40-pound, 4-ounce brown trout on the Little Red River in Arkansas, a noted Eastern tailwater.

Large browns are extremely wary and are nocturnal feeders. They eat aquatic insects, crustaceans, lizards, small rodents, and smaller fish. Big browns hold in dark, deep holes; underneath overhanging brush and streamside foliage, logjams, and protruding logs; and near undercut banks. They are also active during the early morning hours, and just before dark.

Brown trout put weight back on as spring midge hatches intensify and the blue-winged olive hatches become a daily occurrence.

Your best chance to hook a large brown is during the autumn spawning season, when they come out of their traditional deep holes and other hard-to-get-to holding areas. Cold water temperatures trigger their annual spawning urge. This typically occurs during the middle part of October and lasts until the first week of November.

Many browns move upriver from lakes and reservoirs to spawn. Some of the biggest brown trout in the West have been caught and released in the South Platte River above Elevenmile Reservoir. Fish exceeding 28 inches are caught here each season.

According to big-fish specialist Landon Mayer, the best time to catch trophy trout in any tailwater system is prespawn, when the fish are the largest in size and girth. Ethically, prespawn and postspawn are the safest times to pursue trophy trout in any tailwater situation—anglers should leave them alone when they are in spawning mode. This will ensure future populations of naturally reproduced wild trout. If you pursue trout while they are spawning, you run the risk of pulling the female off her spawning bed and preventing her from properly incubating her eggs and producing healthy trout populations in the future.

Timing is everything when you are targeting prespawn trout. Whether the trout are resident river fish or are migrating from a larger body of water, the key is to time your hunt one to two months prior to the time of the year when the fish spawn. A good example of this is in the fall, when browns begin to migrate within a river system or from a larger body of water. They can begin to move as soon as late July to early August.

Typically, males and females will concentrate in deep pools or runs where they can find cover and shelter while they rest and feed before the spawn. The male trout are the first to enter the shallow water, and they become territorial against other males when they find prime habitat. This is why, closer to actual spawning, it is common to find males in shallow, riffled water and females in deep pools or runs. You know that you are catching quality prespawn trout when there are no marks on the fish's fins, belly, or mouth. As the season progresses, the fish continue to move about in shallow water. They begin to spawn and fight with other trout, and battle wounds and scratches appear. If you see scratches and wounds on a trout you catch, you know it is past the prespawn stage and spawning has begun.

"The next time you are pursuing trophy trout in any tailwater system, time your hunt early and you will catch more and larger trout while knowing you are ensuring the safety of future generations of wild trout," Mayer explains.

Prespawn brown trout are absolutely magnificent. Their glowing, vibrant colors cap off the autumn season. LANDON MAYER

Large browns enter the Colorado River tributaries to spawn during the latter part of October. While the average spawner on the Williams Fork, for instance, is 13–15 inches, several fish exceeding 20 inches are caught each year.

These large trout would be nearly impossible to target under normal lake conditions, but their spawning migration into smaller streams provides anglers a chance to catch a lunker. Large streamers, egg patterns, and other brightly colored flies like size 18 Mercury Blood Midges, 18–22 Sparkle Wing RS2s, 16–18 red Copper Johns, and 14–16 San Juan Worms are great producers.

Brown trout in spawning colors are simply magnificent. The fish become extremely dark, and their bellies have a deep butterscotch golden glow. Their flanks shine with a peacock-colored hue, and their outlined silvery-blue and red spots are brighter than ever. Large males develop a hooked jaw, called a kype.

Similar to rainbows, brown trout look for shallow and gravelly areas to spawn. Brown trout spawn during low-light

Your best opportunity to target a large brown trout is during the autumn. Anglers who target prespawn brown trout will have the opportunity of a lifetime to catch a lunker. Dr. Paul Regan landed this prespawn brown trout near the "barns" at the Spinney Mountain Ranch section of the South Platte. LANDON MAYER

Cuttbows—rainbow-cutthroat hybrids—are popular throughout the West. They look similar to rainbows, but have finer spots and orange-red slashes underneath their jaws. This cuttbow was caught on the Blue River during a green drake hatch.

conditions such as dawn or dusk, or under a full moon. The female creates a redd by digging a bowl-like depression in the stream bottom, and the pair deposits eggs and milt into the redd. Then the female covers the egg with gravel. Please refrain from fishing to spawning brown trout on redds.

Cutthroat Trout

Cutthroat trout *(Oncorhynchus clarki)* are the jewels of our Western trout streams. Native to western North America, they were the first trout to be found in the Pacific Northwest. Many cutthroat species are threatened today because of the decline of natural habitat, heavy mining, logging, silt, road construction, and angler harvest.

There are several species of cutthroat in the West, including greenback cutthroat, Rio Grande cutthroat, Snake River cutthroat (also called fine-spotted cutthroat), and Colorado River cutthroat. They thrive in clean ecosystems with clear, highly oxygenated water.

The Snake River cutthroat, commonly referred to as a fine-spotted cutthroat, is native to the Snake River in southern Idaho and western Wyoming. Today it is probably the most abundant cutthroat throughout the Rocky Mountain region. While their populations are considerably smaller than those of rainbows or browns, it is not uncommon to hook a Snake River cutthroat or two in the course of a day's fishing.

Cutthroats are easily identified by the distinctive reddish orange slashes on the bottoms of their jaws. Brad Coors caught this nice prespawn Snake River cutthroat on the Spinney Mountain Ranch stretch of the South Platte.

Cutthroats vary greatly in color and size, depending on their subspecies. Their coloration varies from a grayish green to a golden-red. Anglers identify them in the stream by their brightly colored golden flanks. The average length of a cutthroat is 12 to 15 inches. Their average life expectancy is from five to seven years, which is similar to rainbows.

Cutthroats are similar to rainbows, and the two fish are frequently crossbred. In their natural surroundings, they are spring breeders and conduct the spawning process in the same manner as rainbows. Their hybrids, commonly called cutbows, form dense populations throughout the Rocky Mountain West.

One of the best areas to target cutthroat trout is the Spinney Mountain Ranch section of the South Platte. Large groups of prespawn fish travel upriver with the rainbows during the spring. The biggest surge of Snake River cutthroats is between late February and the first week of April. They will sit in the shallow riffled areas (2 to 4 feet deep) and eat egg patterns. Cutthroats as large as 5 to 8 pounds are caught during this annual spawning run. Anglers occasionally catch Snake River cutthroats during the summer season too, as they migrate back and forth from Elevenmile Reservoir.

Another popular stream for Snake River cutthroats is the Blue River near Silverthorne, Colorado, just 60 miles west of Denver. In Silverthorne, the Colorado DOW stocks Snake River cutthroats ranging from 13 to 16 inches. In the lower reaches of the Blue River (above Green Mountain Reservoir), many nice Snake River cutthroats migrate upriver from the reservoir, and swim upstream or downstream from many of the highly desirable private fishing clubs in the Summit

County region. In the fall of 2006, John Perizzolo, a guide buddy of mine, hooked and landed an 27^1/$_2$-inch, 12-pound Snake River cutthroat above Green Mountain Reservoir. The fish ate a mini Nuclear Egg in a deep run.

Cutthroats thrive in the same habitats as rainbows—fast riffles, pocketwater, and slow, deep pools. They are most active in water temperatures that range from the high 40s to the high 50s. Cutthroats rise eagerly in riffled currents for dry flies, with a slow, confident riseform. They will eat an assortment of attractor patterns, such as Renegades, Limeades, House and Lots, Royal Wulffs, and Humpies in sizes 12–16. They become very selective during a *Baetis,* pale morning dun, or Trico hatch, sipping tiny mayflies in a foam line tucked under a willow or other overhanging streamside foliage. Watch closely for surface feeders tight to the bank during these hatches. Their unusually bright colors will help identify what species of trout you are attempting to fool.

They'll eat everything from tiny midges to large stonefly nymphs, and they readily take egg patterns during the spring months. Dry/dropper rigs are especially productive, with a large bushy dry fly rigged with a tungsten bead dropper. Cutthroats will hit streamers in the spring, during the spawning season.

Brook Trout

One of my most memorable moments as a kid involved catching an 11-inch brook trout during the latter part of July with my father on a small tributary that enters the East River near Crested Butte. As part of our family vacation, Dad and I made annual pilgrimages to the Gunnison Valley every summer. Fishing small streams—the Slate, upper East, Brush Creek,

Brook trout enter our tailwaters from nearby feeder streams. They frequently rise to dry flies such as a Rubber-Legged Stimulator.

and Cement Creek—for brook trout was always part of the trip, and those experiences are etched in my memory forever.

Brook trout *(Salvelinus fontinalis)* are native to small creeks, streams, and beaver ponds in eastern North America, but have been introduced in the West. Although they are commonly called speckled trout, and considered to be members of the trout family, they are actually char, lumped into the same family with lake trout, bull trout, arctic char, and Dolly Varden.

Brook trout thrive in cool, crystal clear, pure habitats with highly oxygenated water. Brook trout are extremely sensitive to water pollution and can tolerate only moderate changes in pH. Unfortunately, brook trout have been eliminated from many watersheds by industrialization and land development, which have had detrimental effects on native populations, altering water temperatures and the natural courses of their waterways.

Brown trout now inhabit what was native brook trout water because browns can tolerate a wider range of conditions. In addition, creel limits have been very generous with brook trout (in Colorado, anglers can harvest ten brook trout under 10 inches), but anglers should consider practicing catch-and-release to ensure future populations of brook trout.

The average brook trout ranges from 7 to 10 inches, although tailwaters such as the Frying Pan hold brook trout that exceed 20 inches from feeding on the Mysis shrimp that flow from the bottom of the reservoir. Brook trout as large as 8 pounds have been caught and released in the Frying Pan section in the last decade. Brook trout live short lives, rarely surviving longer than four to five years.

Brook trout are few and far between in our Western tailwater fisheries; however, the occasional brook trout enters certain rivers via feeder creeks each season. As you might imagine, tailwaters without a large number of feeder streams will probably not have populations of brook trout, but I have caught them on tailwaters such as the Frying Pan, Yampa, Blue, Taylor, South Platte, and Williams Fork.

Brook trout can be identified by their brilliant colors—a dark green back, with a squiggly or marbled pattern referred to as vermiculations. These beautiful markings extend across the flanks to the dorsal fin, often encroaching into the tail area. Red dots are sprinkled along their silver-blue flanks, outlined with turquoise-blue halos. The lower fins—pectoral, ventral, and anal—are a deep reddish orange, outlined with a black and white strip on the leading edge. Their bellies are red, especially during the spawning season.

Brook trout are eager to rise to small dry flies and often reside in shallow riffles that dump into deeper pools. Their peak activity is at temperatures from 45 to 55 degrees. They are scrappy fighters, often jumping several times during the fight.

Brook trout are fall breeders, and generally spawn in tributaries, beaver ponds, and lakes in late summer or early autumn. The female digs the redd, and after the eggs are fertilized, she covers the eggs with fine gravel. The eggs hatch in 90 to 100 days. During the fall and winter, brookies will readily take egg patterns like the Nuclear Egg, especially in chartreuse.

Mountain Whitefish

Mountain whitefish *(Prosopium williamsoni)* or simply whitefish or "whities" are among the most widely distributed gamefish throughout the Rocky Mountain region. Unlike the

Whitefish are a common gamefish in many of our Western tailwaters. They eat a standard assortment of nymphs and occasionally rise to eat dry flies. A size 14 Prince Nymph is effective if you want to target whitefish.

previously mentioned species, anglers have mixed feelings when it comes to catching whitefish. You don't routinely hear anglers bragging about the number of whitefish they caught on a float, or see a picture of a 20-inch whitefish in a guy's office.

Many anglers consider whitefish to be a nuisance because they catch several of them for every trout. Contrary to what you might believe, some anglers specifically target whitefish because of their willingness to take an artificial fly. Whitefish have been known to "save the day" for a guide or two when fishing was extremely tough. Therefore, they are often welcomed by guides and outfitters because they keep the rods bent and their paying customers happy. Whitefish are completely absent from many tailwaters throughout the West.

The average whitefish is between 8 and 12 inches long, but specimens as large as 5 pounds have been caught in recent years. A whitefish has a cylindrical silver-green body with large, rough scales, a forked tail, and a small, pointed mouth about the size of your pinkie finger, which is overhung by its snout.

Whitefish thrive in cold, clear streams with deep pools. Biologists believe that whitefish represent very little competition for trout. Competition is minimal because they reside in different sections of the stream. Whitefish get most of their food from the bottom of the streambed, whereas trout concentrate their efforts on free-drifting food organisms in the water column. Their pointed mouths allow them to eat invertebrates from the substrate. Make no mistake about it, whitefish do eat everything from eggs to terrestrials. They frequently feed on suspended nymphs in the water column, and even rise to surface offerings, but the bulk of their feeding occurs near the bottom of the stream.

Mountain whitefish hold in slow, deep pools and congregate in large schools. Anglers who want to target whitefish should fish slower water. Whitefish eat a standard assortment of nymphs, and their willingness to take artificial flies will amaze you. A Prince Nymph is deadly if you want to specifically target whitefish. If you want to *avoid* catching whitefish, concentrate your efforts in the faster riffles, runs, and slots, and fish toward the head of the run. And don't forget to take off the Prince Nymph!

Kokanee Salmon

Kokanee salmon *(Oncorhynchus nerka)* are landlocked sockeye salmon that range in size from 1 to 3 pounds; some occasionally exceed the 4-pound mark. They provide a "poor man's Alaska" in a several of our Western tailwaters each autumn as they migrate aggressively upstream from large bodies of water such as the Blue Mesa, Granby, Gross, Green Mountain, and Elevenmile Reservoirs. While not as important as other gamefish, they play a unique role for a several-week

When Kokanee enter the river, they have silver flanks and green backs. After they've been in the river for two or three weeks, they quickly turn red and the males develop hooked jaws and razor-sharp teeth.

period in a handful of fisheries, including the Blue, Taylor, Colorado, and South Platte Rivers.

Prime areas to target are the tailwaters between Green Mountain Reservoir and Dillon Reservoir; the Taylor above the confluence of the Gunnison River; the Colorado between Granby and Shadow Mountain Reservoirs; and the South Platte above Elevenmile Reservoir. Anglers await the arrival of Kokanee salmon with anticipation each season, as they provide some of the more exciting nymph fishing during the autumn. The South Platte River above Elevenmile Reservoir boasts some of the biggest Kokanee salmon in the West, with some Kokanee occasionally exceeding the 22-inch mark.

Kokanee spend the majority of their lives in large lakes and reservoirs. They are among the West's best gamefish for stillwater anglers. In the lake environment, their diet is consists mostly of plankton, but they will occasionally eat midges and other aquatic insects. Once they move into streams and tributaries to spawn, they will take any brightly colored fly or streamer. Western Coachmans are also very productive when you're trying to fool Kokanee.

The majority of Kokanee salmon reach spawning maturity during the fourth year of life, then swim upstream into the river above the reservoir, or its tributaries, in search of areas to spawn. They spawn in large groups in shallow riffles with lots of smaller stones, gravel, and loose rubble. They dig redds just like their cousins in Alaska and British Columbia. Trout key on these eggs, and nymphing can be explosive for a several-week period. An orange Hot Tail Flash Egg in size 18 perfectly imitates a Kokanee egg.

Kokanee undergo an impressive transformation during the spawn. Normally, Kokanee have silvery green, smooth-skinned flanks and very delicate mouths. When spawning, they develop a brick-red, leather-textured skin and a dark green head. The males develop tweaked, hooked jaws and sharp teeth the size of a poodle's. Kokanee perish after spawning, providing a tremendous food source for a wide array of wild animals, including bald eagles, black bears, and raccoons.

Spawning success varies depending on the drainage. In Colorado, the water temperatures are too cold for self-sustaining reproduction; therefore, the Colorado DOW maintains several field locations where DOW personnel strip the eggs and artificially inseminate the roe. The DOW then stocks the resulting salmon into rivers and reservoirs, and the process repeats itself every four years.

As Kokanee salmon migrate upstream, they hold and rest in the slow, deep pools. Finding these locations is the greatest challenge. You may find a large group of salmon in one area, and not see another pod for several hundred yards, or even a mile or two. Anglers can hook these salmon with conventional nymphing rigs with egg patterns, pink San Juan Worms, red Mercury Pheasant Tails, Western Coachmans, and a variety of small bead-heads such as Copper Johns, Prince Nymphs, and Flashback Pheasant Tails.

Successful anglers fish riffled areas that funnel into deep water without any tricky, slow water sections. Stay away from

Kokanee salmon provide a "poor man's Alaska" in several of our Western tailwaters. They will eat brightly colored flies, egg patterns, small nymphs, and streamers on the dead-drift. John Higgs caught this large Kokanee salmon on an egg pattern above Elevenmile Reservoir.

Large brown trout follow Kokanee salmon up the river as the salmon prepare to spawn. They routinely position themselves downstream from pods of Kokanee salmon, capitalizing on the high-protein diet of free-drifting salmon eggs.

Anglers will find Kokanee salmon in riffled areas that funnel into deeper pools. Dr. Eugene Soechtig hooked this Kokanee salmon in a deep slot in the Shale Hole on the Blue River.

complicated drifts, i.e., swirly currents, undertows, reverse currents and so on—otherwise you'll foul-hook a lot of fish. Look for obvious seams, and fish evenly paced riffles and runs, as they tend to allow your flies to drift better in the current. The strikes are very soft; only a keen eye and sense of touch will detect the subtle takes. If the strike indicator abruptly sinks and darts upstream, the chances are good you have foul-hooked a fish. Look for a slight pause in the indicator, and set the hook promptly.

Kokanee begin migrating upstream as early as mid-August, but mid- to late September (sometimes October) is when most salmon enter the river. The run lasts for six to eight weeks. Kokanee congregate in large schools, often turning the stream bottom black. They are among the most powerful gamefish for their size you can fight on a fly rod. They will jump several times before you can play them to the net. Most anglers use a 9-foot, 5- or 6-weight fly rod with 4X tipped on their nymphing rigs.

Large brown trout often move upstream with the Kokanee salmon, eating loose eggs from the females, and preparing to spawn themselves. Over the years, my clients have hooked a number of 5-pound-plus brown trout that were sitting in a deep transitional zone among a pod of about 30 Kokanee salmon. We usually do not see the large brown trout nestled among the salmon—we simply dead-drift our egg patterns through the group of salmon. The browns will sit downstream of the salmon too, capitalizing on any eggs that drift down to them. This approach is the best way to target the big browns; avoid targeting these fish when they are on their redds.

CHAPTER 5

Reading the River

Anglers who are unfamiliar with a trout's environment often waste a tremendous amount of valuable time with a "casting their flies into the river and hoping for the best" philosophy. Their success—or lack thereof—is a result of poor preparation and research, lack of observation, or inability to pinpoint exactly where the trout are positioned. In their minds, they're simply not having any luck, or they have the wrong fly, or better yet, the fish are just not biting.

Even a blind squirrel finds a nut now and then, but those who hone their skills by carefully reading and approaching the water will catch considerably more trout than those who flog streams randomly. A careful approach includes hunting, stalking, and observing the fishes' behavior at all times. One

of your biggest angling breakthroughs will be learning how to read a trout stream successfully and closely analyzing a river for key, current-blocking structures before you start casting. When you can do this, you'll be able to approach any river with confidence.

I can remember, when I was a young boy, my dad pointing to specific locations in a trout stream and saying, "There ought to be a beauty right there." More times than not, he was right—within a few minutes, he was fighting and landing a nice trout. I sat there in amazement (of course, taking mental notes), as he hooked several fish precisely where he thought they should be. At the time, it seemed almost magical. How could he do that?

Anglers who consistently catch trout have a good understanding of how to read a river. Trout are not randomly spread out in a river, but rather position themselves in strategic places that break the current and provide a steady food source.

49

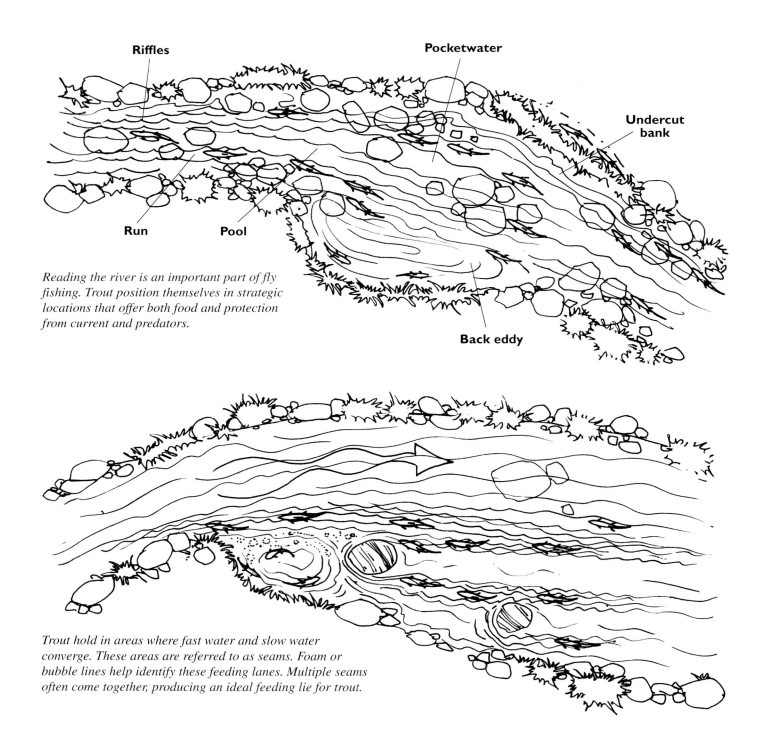

Riffles **Pocketwater**

Undercut bank

Run **Pool**

Reading the river is an important part of fly fishing. Trout position themselves in strategic locations that offer both food and protection from current and predators.

Back eddy

Trout hold in areas where fast water and slow water converge. These areas are referred to as seams. Foam or bubble lines help identify these feeding lanes. Multiple seams often come together, producing an ideal feeding lie for trout.

Through dad's teachings, I learned to be patient, observe carefully, and closely watch the river. "If you do these things, son, the fish will eventually come," dad continuously reminded me. And was he ever right! This was one of my biggest revelations as a young angler. I quickly learned that if a trout is going to survive over an extended period of time, it must find protection from predators and must reside in a location that provides a break from the current. In addition, this area must be a place where a trout can easily find food. In general, trout are lazy feeders. The common denominator of all good feeding lies is a steady source of food and the ability to avoid life-threatening situations.

In a river, current carries food to the fish in a concentrated feeding lane, which provides a steady flow of food that trout can capitalize on for an easy and effortless meal. A feeding lane can be thought of as Mother Nature's conveyer belt. Feeding lanes are often created by subsurface structure that is not always clearly defined. Watching foam or bubble lines can help identify them. If there is a large concentration of food, in almost all cases there will be an excellent population of trout. If food is absent, finding a lot of trout is highly unlikely.

A proficient angler can identify, understand, and strategize according to the river's hydrology, and how the river's variety of currents impact a trout's feeding behavior and positioning in the stream. Trout face into the current, unless they are cruising in a lakelike pool or flat looking for food. But a current is not necessarily always upstream, which throws a twist into things. A good example is a back eddy or reverse current. Anglers should pay special attention to which direction the foam (food) is traveling, because in some cases there may be back eddies or reverse currents (see the section on eddies later in this chapter) that concentrate large quantities of food, and that flow in a circular motion. Depending on which part of the reverse current the fish occupies, the direction in which the trout are facing may vary greatly, which affects your approach and presentation. If you approach an eddy incorrectly, you may spook several trout that are feeding on or near the surface. Everything must be carefully planned and executed if you plan on hooking trout consistently in these scenarios.

Where fast and slow water converge expect to find highly productive holding and feeding areas, commonly called seams. Seams between the confluence of the reverse current and the main channel are especially productive. Look for seams in other parts of the stream too. Prime examples are seams that are created by rocks, logs, and other protruding objects. Seams may converge, creating a V shape and a likely holding spot for several trout. Seams are key areas to present both dry flies and nymphs.

Observation is a powerful tool. Familiarize yourself with a river's habitat and understand its composition and hydrology, and you will see that trout are positioned in certain areas based on the river's physical makeup rather than arbitrarily spread out in the river. Study the river before fishing. Dr. Eric Atha carefully watches a pod of rising trout on the San Juan River below Navajo Dam.

Doug McElveen hooked this nice rainbow in a foam line on the Yampa River. Foam or bubble lines help anglers identify feeding lanes or seams.

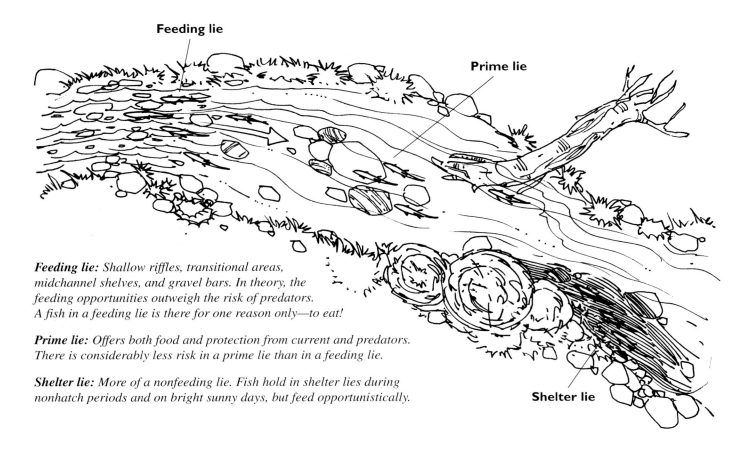

Feeding lie

Prime lie

Shelter lie

Feeding lie: Shallow riffles, transitional areas, midchannel shelves, and gravel bars. In theory, the feeding opportunities outweigh the risk of predators. A fish in a feeding lie is there for one reason only—to eat!

Prime lie: Offers both food and protection from current and predators. There is considerably less risk in a prime lie than in a feeding lie.

Shelter lie: More of a nonfeeding lie. Fish hold in shelter lies during nonhatch periods and on bright sunny days, but feed opportunistically.

PRIME LIES, FEEDING LIES, AND SHELTER LIES

In his book *Presentation* (Tomorrow River Press, 1995), Gary Borger identifies three specific lies that are important to all fly fishers: feeding lies, prime lies, and shelter lies.

Feeding lies offer a steady, concentrated food source without any protection from predators. These areas are typically in shallow water (18–24 inches deep) such as gravel bars, midchannel shelves, and shallow riffles toward the head of the run. Anglers will find trout in these areas during a good hatch when there is a high concentration of moving nymphs or larvae floating in the water column.

I like to think of this scenario as one in which the food source outweighs any potential risk from predators. A fish that moves into a shallow riffle is there for one reason only—to eat! Therefore, anglers can assume a riffle fish is a feeding fish.

I have watched fish eating *Baetis* nymphs—at the height of the hatch—so aggressively that it was nearly impossible to spook them. On the front end of the hatch, or toward the end of the hatch when the bug activity is considerably less, the trout are more sensitive to movement, sloppy presentations, and predators, so you'll need to be careful with your approach.

A prime lie is an ideal spot for trout because it offers both food and protection. Anglers should target areas with protruding logs where the substrate has been scoured, undercut banks, overhanging bushes and trees, weed beds with small openings, the hearts of runs, and heavy foam or scum lines.

Prime lies produce large numbers of fish because they provide three vital elements for survival: protection from predators, deflection of current, and a steady food source.

Places that offer protection from predators are called shelter lies. Shelter lies, for all practical purposes, are nonfeeding lies. Good examples of shelter lies include spots under or tight to a rock, underneath logs, and deep pools with lots of subsurface structure. After a trout has been hooked in a feeding or prime lie, it will run to its shelter lie trying to break you off or throw the hook.

My good fishing buddy Monroe Coleman often says: "You're in the trout's neighborhood now." In other words, the trout know exactly where the hidden obstacles are—the large rocks, the logs—and they make every effort to wrap you around the aforementioned structure or cut your tippet material on a sharp object.

Think ahead about landing the fish to avoid any disasters while you are fighting it. If the fish does runs toward structure, put a tremendous amount of side pressure on the fish, trying to persuade it away from the danger, because you're likely to lose the fish one way or another—too much pressure might pop the tippet, or the fish will cut you off on a log, branch, or other obstacle.

RIVER HYDROLOGY

The powerful force of water is mind-boggling. Rivers are constantly changing, as Mother Nature is always trying to find the path of least resistance. Erosion continually carves away parts of the stream bottom, creating new pools and depositing rocks and gravel in other areas, and producing flats, riffles, runs, gravel bars, and midchannel shelves. I have seen a river completely alter its course, leaving the old river channel dry and abandoned.

Beavers gnaw down trees, creating obstructions in the river, deflecting currents, and eroding the stream channel, producing deep slots in the substrate. Other forces of nature—strong winds and lightning—create natural habitat by knocking down trees. Streambanks erode from high spring runoff currents, creating new undercut banks, which produce excellent trout habitat for large, crafty brown trout.

Here are a few general rules to help you understand the hydrology of a trout stream. Water travels at different speeds in the stream channel based on friction created from the different underlying objects. For example, the bank and other shallow, rocky areas cause friction, which slows down the pace of the water. The middle of the river is generally the fastest because it is deeper, and has less friction. During higher flows, trout will migrate toward the edges of the stream to avoid these demanding currents.

The fastest current may be on the outside of the river, usually on rivers with sweeping bends, or rivers with meandering meadow sections winding their way through lush valleys. Heavy currents carve away the substrate, producing deep holes, often with undercut banks. Such an area may have a nice gravel bar, producing a feeding lie on the front end of the hole. Usually in conjunction with a gravel bar is a nice seam

Fish that move into shallow riffles are feeding fish. Clay Anselmo works a transitional area on the Green River, sight-casting to trout that are positioned in shallow riffles and are eating Baetis *nymphs during a blue-winged olive emergence.*

Understanding the different aspects of river hydrology will increase your success on a trout stream. Glenn Minarcik fishes a productive riffle-run-pool stretch in the fabled Cheesman Canyon.

The river may flow almost twice as fast on the surface as on the bottom. Trout often position themselves in faster currents, but they are lower in the water column, where the current is considerably slower.

Riffles are hot spots where you will find a lot of feeding fish. Gary Hort nymphs the Palmer Gulch section of the Blue River below the majestic backdrop of the Gore Range.

on the inside corner, producing prime conditions for nymph fishing.

The speed of the water varies throughout the water column. The surface current flows almost twice as fast as the water on the bottom of the stream. If you don't believe me, stand knee-deep in a swift run and wiggle your wading shoe, and you'll see exactly what I am talking about—the current is almost nonexistent near the bottom of the stream. You'll feel considerably more pressure near your knees compared to the amount of force you feel near the bottom. In some cases, the river is hardly moving on the bottom of the stream because of tricky reverse currents and submerged structure. I have observed cases where trout were positioned facing downstream, holding deep in the current, near the substrate, and the surface of river was flowing in the opposite direction.

Understanding this discrepancy in current speed is critical for nymph fishing. Trout will position themselves toward the bottom of the stream channel, where the current speed is considerably less. I have hooked fish in swift currents where I never thought it was possible. In order to catch these trout positioned along the stream bottom, you need to add enough weight to compensate for the quick-moving surface currents.

UNDERSTANDING THE ANATOMY OF A TROUT STREAM

Understanding the dynamics of a trout stream and its underlying habitat will help you pinpoint specific areas that attract and hold trout. There are many visual clues—some obvious, and many less apparent because they are hidden below the riffled surface currents.

Your ability to identify productive holding areas for trout is an important part of fly fishing. The most productive spots vary greatly depending on the time of the year, hatches, and water temperatures. Let's take a look at some of the places you're likely to find trout in tailwaters.

Riffles

Riffles are fast, shallow sections of a trout stream that are comprised of small- to-medium-size, smooth stones, jagged rubble, and fine gravel. Riffles have a choppy, nervous, or ruffled appearance as a result of the river flowing over a shallow, coarse substrate. Sunlight fully penetrates these areas, producing ideal conditions to harbor rooted aquatic foliage and algae, which support a dense population of aquatic insects, crustaceans, and other food organisms. The available surface area (from all the gravel, smaller stones and rocks) for the aquatic life to thrive is double or triple of that of other sections of the river. For that reason, riffles become a high-powered food factory and are important areas to target.

The broken, agitated water gives the angler a distinct advantage when fishing the head of a riffle-run configuration, because the riffled currents help mask your silhouette, casting motions, leader, tippet, and weight. Fish must decide quickly whether to eat your fly, so there is little time for inspection, and strikes are generally fairly aggressive.

Several feeding fish position themselves in the heart of the run because it offers both food and protection. Mary Barker works a beautiful run loaded with rainbows.

The riffled currents can make locating fish in choppy water difficult. Anglers need a keen eye, concentrating and staring into the water closely, searching for elongated shapes, bright colors, shadows, flashes or rising motions, and any movement. The riseform disappears quickly, as the moving water displaces any evidence of a fish feeding on the surface.

Fish tend to reside in riffles between mid-March and late October when water temperatures are conducive for good hatches and the trout are actively feeding mayfly nymphs, caddis larvae and pupae, stoneflies, and crane flies. The number of feeding fish in such riffled areas varies greatly depending on the aquatic insect activity. If a hatch is in progress, fish will move from nonfeeding lies to riffled areas to capitalize on the increased volume of emerging insects. Fish generally move into shallow riffles only to eat. After the hatch, they move back into protective lies to avoid predators, and they seek current-blocking structures to prevent any unnecessary weight and energy loss caused by fighting the current.

Runs

A run connects the riffle at the head of the pool with the tail-out. The current is steady and the water depth is consistent. In most rivers, runs are usually between 3 and 6 feet deep, but may range from 4 to 8 feet deep in larger rivers. Unlike a

John Higgs fishes a small pool with an Elk Hair Caddis on the South Platte near Deckers. He spotted two or three brown trout feeding sporadically on adult caddis.

riffle, a run has a wavy appearance, from the bowling ball-size rocks that are scattered along the stream bottom. The medium-size cobble and stones produce current-blocking structures that are important to trout because they help trout feed efficiently. Trout use the submerged rocks for protection against the current. A rock the size of a beach ball can produce ideal structure for an 18- to 20-inch rainbow.

During a heavy hatch, many of the trout positioned in a run (prime lie) will migrate toward the shallow, riffled areas (feeding lie) to capitalize on the availability of hatching insects. The savvy angler will pick up on this selective feeding phase, and take advantage of this opportunity to hook several feeding fish in the shallow riffles. After the hatch, the trout will slip back into the heart of the run or the tailout of the pool to conserve energy.

Runs can produce some of the best nymphing in a trout stream because they are typically jam-packed with an assortment of nymphs and larvae. Suspending artificial nymphs off a yarn strike indicator with lots of weight is extremely effective most of the year. During the winter, however, you'll find more fish toward the tailout of the run, rather than in the heart of the run.

Pools

Pools are the tailouts of runs, and vary considerably in their width, depth, and composition. Pools are the slowest and

widest parts of a trout stream, and typically hold some very large, discriminating trout. Trout that reside in pools are generally seeking protection from the current and predators. In most cases, fish that occupy pools are feeding opportunistically. You'll find a large concentration of fish in a pool during nonhatch periods. This is not to say that you will not find a few bank sippers, or fishing rising opportunistically near the tailout of the pool.

Sunlight cannot efficiently penetrate deeper pools, and therefore the aquatic insect life and plant life are not as dense as in shallow, riffled areas. Sand, silt, and fine debris collect in pools because the current is slow-moving; these sediments have an adverse effect on the aquatic insect life, the hatches, and the number of fish feeding in pools.

Large deep, pools that are loaded with fish are often major distractions to anglers in pursuit of trout. Many anglers get trapped into fishing these areas—simply because they see a large pod of fish—but fail to recognize whether they are actually feeding. Suspended fish (or groups of suspended fish) are feeding fish. Pass by trout that are hunkered down on the bottom. Trout hugging the bottom of a deep pool are the least aggressive feeders, though many anglers will spend hours trying to entice them.

Occasionally, you'll find trout feeding on midge pupae and adults or mayfly duns along the edges or at the tailout of the pool. Terrestrials fall off overhanging foliage or deadfalls,

Pocketwater offers some of the best fishing opportunities during the summer. Trout position themselves in front of boulders, behind boulders, in the fast or slow seams on either side of the boulder, or in the slots created by several boulders.

presenting an opportunity to fish a dry fly. Because the water is as still as the surface of a quiet lake, these areas require a perfect presentation with a long leader and a delicate touch. One poor cast and the game is over.

Pocketwater

Pocketwater occurs where partially or fully submerged rocks and protruding boulders are randomly scattered throughout a long riffle or run. These current-blocking structures divide the river into smaller slots and gushing currents. There are small breaks in the moving water behind each rock or boulder, commonly referred to as pockets.

Pocketwater stretches are highly oxygenated sections of a trout stream with some of the strongest and swiftest currents. I strongly recommend using a wading staff if you fish pocketwater on a regular basis (see the section on wading staffs in chapter 15). The trade off is that pocketwater offers explosive nymph fishing and superb dry/dropper fishing during certain periods of the year.

Pocketwater generally gets little pressure because it is difficult to fish and wade; therefore, many anglers simply avoid fishing it. With the lack of pressure, trout rise eagerly to dry flies in the calm pockets and readily take nymphs in the seams. Fishing a piece of pocketwater is no doubt hard work. If you fish it thoroughly and methodically, however, you'll generally catch good numbers of nice trout.

Think of a pocket as a miniature pool. You'll find trout positioned in a variety of places when you dissect a piece of pocketwater—in front of rocks, behind the boulders, in the glassy "pool" (the pocket), or in the two distinct seams on either side of the boulders. Trout position themselves on the slow side of the seam, and move into the current to obtain a food organism, then move back into the slower part of the

current. Trout position themselves toward the back end of the glassy pool section of the pocket, where you'll often find another fully submerged boulder that backs up the flow, creating the ideal holding area. This is the perfect place to drop a dry/dropper rig behind a rock and let it drift toward the back of the pocket.

Pocketwater provides some of the best nymphing of the whole summer. As the water temperatures escalate, oxygen levels plummet, and trout will move into the turbulent water for increased oxygen. Because the water is swift, the strikes are aggressive. Imitations of larger food organisms such as crane flies, stoneflies, aquatic worms, and scuds are effective patterns when fishing pockets.

Rapids

Rapids are quick-moving sections of river. Rapids are generally preceded by slow to moderate stretches that funnel from a wide, relatively deep stretch into a quick, surging force that gushes downriver, producing what is called a wave train. Rapids vary in size from small rolling chutes to large, raging currents that may be several hundred yards long. Rapids are common on most of our Western tailwater fisheries.

Rapids can be dangerous. If it's your first visit to the area, you might want to follow another drift boat down the river to avoid any surprises or unforeseen problems. Or talk with a local fly shop and ask the staff, "Are there any dangerous sections of river that I should be aware of before I float this section?" It is a good idea to communicate your rowing abilities with the fly shop personnel to make sure that you are qualified to float this section of river.

Get their recommendations (and a map if possible) on the safest way to approach and navigate these tough swift-water

Pocketwater stretches are highly oxygenated areas that hold large numbers of feeding trout. John Horodyski dissects a piece of pocketwater with a standard two-fly nymphing rig. One of my favorite pocketwaters is on the Blue River, approximately 3 miles above Green Mountain Reservoir, in the Blue River State Wildlife Area. Locals refer to this area as Palmer Gulch. A fast-flowing part of the river, it is interspersed with boulders of all sizes and shapes, producing ideal structure for many feeding trout.

Fishing the fast-slow seam of a rapid can be very productive. This beautiful rainbow was fooled with a nymph fished deep along the edge of the Bighorn Rapid. Anglers routinely hook some of the larger fish on the Bighorn River along this 200-yard, fast-slow seam. KIM DORSEY

sections. If you have any doubts, eddy-out (if you can) and walk along the river, taking mental notes on any obstructions. Some rapids are well marked with signs, like the one on the Green River (Caution: Mother-in-Law Rapid Ahead), giving the oarsman a heads-up that some technical rowing lies ahead. Some fly shops—like Denny Breer's Trout Creek Flies in Dutch John, Utah—have descriptions of the local rapids on their web sites. The Green River has mile markers, and the web site describes each rapid in detail, with an approximate river-mile location. If you have never floated the Green River, it would be a good idea to print this off before you go. The walk-and-wade angler must be careful in these areas too—the currents are quick and often misleading. As a safety precaution, don't wade more than calf-deep in rapids.

Because the currents are fast, the bottom is generally devoid of smaller stones, fine gravel, sand, silt, and other debris, leaving the bottom composed of jagged rocks, rubble, and large boulders. These areas are slick and they drop off fast. Some of these rocks may protrude, making some excellent pocketwater opportunities. Nymphing along the edges of a rapid—in the distinct fast-slow seams—can be excellent.

Depending on the stretch of water, it may be good idea to eddy-out into some of the calmer bank water and anchor your

Midchannel shelves and gravel bars are key feeding locations when a mayfly or midge hatch is in progress.

boat in a secure place, rather than fish the edges of a rapid from a drift boat. Standing up while floating through a rapid is dangerous. If an angler is standing and fishing from the bow, the oarsman has difficulty seeing the water and navigating the boat. Therefore, the angler is at risk of falling out if the oarsman makes a quick decision to turn the boat to avoid a "sleeper" or other obstruction. You should always sit down while the oarsman maneuvers through a rapid.

The Texas Hole on the San Juan River is a highly productive rapid. Unlike the Bighorn Rapid, anglers do not float through the Texas Hole, because the boat ramp (there is no float access between the dam and the Texas Hole) is situated below the rapid in a calmer section, allowing anglers the ease and convenience of dumping their boats into softer currents. The Texas Hole drains a large, wide section of braided currents and islands from the Upper Flats to the Kiddie Pool. Depending on the flows, this can be an extremely fast chute, especially during the latter part of May when the river approaches the 5,000 cfs mark.

Walk-and-wade anglers routinely fish this hole, although the best approach is to fish it from a drift boat. This allows you to methodically cover the wide array of cosmic currents in this fabled piece of trout water. Anglers and guides dissect this productive water in a continuous, clockwise rotation, fishing the distinct fast-slow seam, as well as the technical reverse currents and back eddies. Several drop-offs and transition areas fish very well.

Drift-boat guides spend hours, if not the entire day, fishing this one location. It is considered poor etiquette to anchor in the area of the clockwise rotation. Please be considerate of others. My preference is to fish this area for an hour or two, then move on to the lower section of the Texas Hole, above the next braided area that flows into the Lower Flats. The lower section of the Texas Hole is lake-like, bringing out the best in any serious nymph fisherman. (For more information,

see Slow-Water Nymphing in chapter 6 for tips and tactics on fishing slower water.)

Midchannel Shelves and Gravel Bars
Changes in depth occur frequently on trout streams. Look for depth changes on the leading edges of midchannel shelves or gravel bars. Anglers can easily identify these drop-offs or depth changes by looking for a noticeable color change in the river bottom. These are hot spots, especially during midge or mayfly hatches, and should be carefully inspected and fished methodically. The drops can be dangerous to wading anglers. Keep your wits about you at all times.

Midchannel shelves and gravel bars offer some of the best sight-nymphing in our tailwater systems. The fish position themselves on the drop-off and are usually suspended in the current, which is a sure sign they are feeding.

Several years ago when fishing the San Juan River, I began to understand the importance of nymphing midchannel shelves—from a trout's perspective as well as from an angler's standpoint. I was standing knee-deep in clear water in the upper part of a well-known stretch called the Lower Flats. My buddies and I call this section the "playground," because the fishing is exceptional. You can spend hours in this section, or if you opt, the whole day.

I was methodically working my way across a large midchannel shelf and I saw good numbers of fish lifting in the water column that were positioned below the drop-off. It was clear there was a *Baetis* hatch in progress and the fish were eating heavily.

Through experimentation, I learned that the most aggressive fish (those that are feeding heavily) sit closest to the drop-off. Therefore, to catch those trout you need to cast your flies far enough above the drop-off to get your flies down to the fish. There is a tradeoff, however. If you fish too much weight, you'll hang on the leading edge of the shelf—and if

Midchannel shelves and gravel bars are excellent areas to find feeding fish, especially during a strong hatch of midges or mayflies. Dave Stout works a midchannel shelf with a small Baetis *nymph imitation.*

you don't use enough weight, your flies will not get deep enough into the water column to catch the suspended fish. The right combination of weight, strike indicator depth, and placement of your flies is critical for success. For ease and adjustment, I use moldable tungsten putty. Guides on the San Juan use split-shot rather than putty. I use split-shot in the slower water, but I use putty weights in the faster riffles, where more adjusting is required.

The density of the hatch dictates the number of feeding fish that will be on the leading edge of the midchannel shelf. If there is a heavy *Baetis* hatch in progress, there will be a good number of fish positioned below the drop-off. If nothing is hatching, the fish will sit farther back from the drop-off, feeding in an opportunistic fashion. These fish will usually eat a larger food offering, such as a San Juan Worm.

On this same run nearly 20 years ago, I was working my way across the shelf, and a fish rose in the water column near my yarn strike indicator. I thought to myself, "That was a nice fish! He obviously just ate something near my flies." Then I thought about it for a minute, and realized that the fish probably ate one of my flies and I didn't even realize it.

The next time I saw a fish rise near my strike indicator, I set the hook. To my surprise, the leader tightened, and a beautiful fish rolled in the water, shaking his head back and forth, trying to throw my fly. The yarn strike indicator never moved

to indicate any sign of a potential strike. I thought to myself, "How many fish am I missing on any given day?" It became clear that even with a good strike indicator, you'll still miss a lot of strikes if you rely on the strike indicator alone. From that day on, if any fish rises up behind a gravel bar or midchannel shelf, and my flies are anywhere close to the feeding fish, I set the hook.

Gravel bars are formed in a similar fashion and are found on the downcurrent sides of islands. During higher flows, the river transports fine particles via the current in the back channel and deposits them below the island, and as the flow recedes the main current carves away part of the substrate, creating a nice drop-off.

Trout (usually rainbows) will station themselves on the submerged gravel bar, positioning themselves in the seam that is created from the two currents mixing together below the island. The trout will sit on the leading edge of the downward depression, seeking protection from the current, then rising up in the water column to eat food organisms that drift over their heads.

Islands and Back Channels

Islands and back channels are good places to find feeding trout. Many anglers overlook backwater areas and only fish the main channel, but during higher flows (for example, after spring runoff), islands with back channels can provide some consistent fishing to trout rising to caddis and Yellow Sally stoneflies. As the high currents subside, target these prime areas with dry flies, especially attractors such as Limeades, Royal Wulffs, Renegades, and H & L Variants. I especially like to run a Rubber-Legged Stimulator with an #18–20 Bead-head Pheasant Tail dropper. By the second week of July, you'll find ideal conditions in these backwater areas, with the water ranging anywhere from calf- to hip-deep. It is not uncommon to experience some good green drake fishing in these back channels, too. Approach these backwater areas as you would any small stream. Be careful—stealth is important.

Back channels hold a lot of smaller trout, but don't let that fool you—there are plenty of large trout in these areas too, because back channels rarely get fished. You'll find a wide array of structure behind these islands and back channels: logs that were washed in during higher flows, and an assortment of nice riffles, runs, pools, pockets, shelves, and undercut banks.

I typically start at the back end of the island and work my way toward the front. Normally I cross to the inside section of the island and move upstream, hugging the inner bank. The outside section of the back channel has the best structure and is the deepest part of the stream.

It may be difficult to cross to the bottom of the island (depending on flows) as there is usually a deep shelf right below the island that dumps into the main channel. From my past experience, the largest fish are situated toward the head of the run or island, depending on the composition of the water. Take advantage of these opportunities while you can. During lower flows, these back-channel areas may be unfishable or completely dry.

Avoid fishing back channels during the spawning season (in March and April, and in October and November) because you find a lot of redds in these areas. However,

Back channels are excellent areas to target less-pressured trout. Hunter Dorsey caught this 15-inch brown trout during a Yellow Sally hatch with size 12 yellow Stimulator.

fishing egg patterns below the islands (on the gravel bars) can be effective.

Undercut Banks

Trout often position themselves in areas where heavy currents have washed away or eroded part of the soil underneath the streambank. These undercut banks provide safety and security for trout of all sizes, as well as a steady food source. Terrestrials, mice, and other foods fall into the river, becoming hearty meals for trout residing in these areas. Undercut banks can be difficult to fish, with numerous roots from trees, bushes, and

Undercut banks provide excellent structure for large trout.

Undercut banks are excellent areas to target large trout. Dr. Mark Sheehan works an undercut bank at the Spinney Mountain Ranch section of the South Platte.

Eddies are great places to find rising trout. Keith Lang fishes a Mathews's Sparkle Dun to a pod of rising trout in the Orange Moss Rock Hole during a blue-winged olive hatch on the Williams Fork River near Parshall, Colorado.

SURFACE AND SUB-SURFACE FEEDING

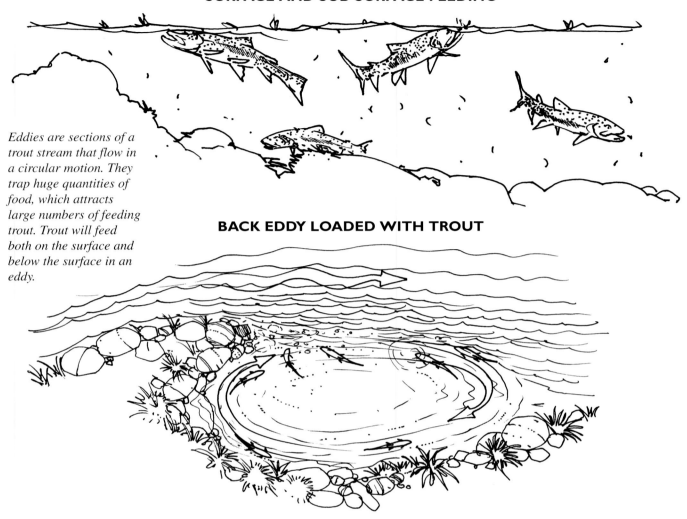

Eddies are sections of a trout stream that flow in a circular motion. They trap huge quantities of food, which attracts large numbers of feeding trout. Trout will feed both on the surface and below the surface in an eddy.

BACK EDDY LOADED WITH TROUT

other streamside vegetation, as well as other obstacles such as barbed wire or logs pinned underneath the bank. However, if you get your fly close to the edge, you'll get an aggressive strike. These areas are prime places to fish a heavily weighted streamer.

In spring and fall, large spawning trout hide beneath undercut banks for protection during the day and spawn during the night. If you see fresh redds, but no fish on the spawning beds, they are most likely hiding under the banks during the day. This is a good opportunity to fish a large streamer because spawning trout become very aggressive and will attack anything in their territory. A dead-drifted egg pattern is also effective.

Eddies

In many sections of a trout stream, extended portions of the streambank, large boulders, and protruding branches and logs cause the river to slow, and flow in a circular motion. These clockwise or counterclockwise currents are called eddies, and they are very important to anglers because they trap a tremendous amount of food. I have watched a piece of driftwood

float around the same hole for a considerable period of time, which suggests that aquatic insects and other food organisms do the same.

The prominent foam or bubble lines help you decipher which direction the food is traveling. Trout will feed on emerging midges and mayflies just under the surface, or take mayfly duns or midges from the surface. Eddies provide some of the best dry-fly fishing during these emergences. I spend an hour or two fishing the same eddy during a good blue-winged olive or Trico hatch.

Heavy blankets of foam provide a secure environment safe from predators. Look for surface disturbances in the foam—trout may be feeding on emergers or pupae just below the surface film. If I'm fishing dry flies, I'll use a Hi-Vis pattern of some sort (with a bright pink or orange wing) to help identify my fly in the foam.

Flats

Slow, wide sections of a trout stream that lack key structure on the river bottom are called flats. Flats are generally 3 to 6 feet deep, and provide very little protection from predators;

LOG ON THE SURFACE

LOG UNDER THE WATER

Protruding logs are excellent areas to find large trout.

therefore, trout on flats tend to cruise, feeding both opportunistically and selectively. You'll need a careful, stealthy approach when pursuing trout in these slow-water settings because they are extremely spooky. During a heavy hatch, flats can be excellent areas to target rising fish. You'll need long leaders (12–15 feet) and very precise, yet delicate, casting. Flats are also excellent areas to find trout feeding on emergers or pupae.

Protruding Logs

Some of the biggest trout I have ever caught on nymphs or streamers have been underneath a protruding log. Currents scour the substrate below the logs, producing a deep slot or groove in the streambed. In addition, logs provide overhead protection and cover for trout to hide from predators. You'll lose a lot of flies trying to get your nymphs tight to or underneath the log, but the rerigging is worth the effort.

Fishing dry flies near deadfalls and overhanging bushes is a great strategy during the summer months.

Sometimes logs run parallel to the stream channel; at other times they protrude partially into the stream, or extend completely cross the river. When many trees, logs, and large branches block the stream channel, this is referred to as a log-jam. Logjams are excellent areas to fish weighted streamers. They are also hot spots during hatches. Logjams back up the flows and concentrate duns so trout can easily feed on them. Protruding logs also produce some nice slack water and create eddies where fish feed on the surface.

Overhanging Bushes and Deadfalls
When it is bright and sunny, trout gravitate toward shady areas for protection from predators. If you can get your flies (nymphs or dry flies or dry/dropper rigs) to drift underneath the overhanging branches—without getting snagged—you'll generally hook a nice fish.

You'll find rising fish in these areas, especially during a blue-winged olive or pale morning dun hatch. The trout position themselves tight to the structure (deadfalls or leafed branches), capitalizing on a steady food source with little risk from overhead threats.

I frequently fish a dry/dropper rig around and underneath overhanging bushes. Fish dart out of the shaded area to grab my nymph. An Elk Hair Caddis or Rubber-Legged Stimulator with an #18–20 Tungsten Beadhead Pheasant Tail is the perfect rig.

When there is a breeze, this is a great place to fish terrestrials. I often use a drowned Black Ant around overhanging bushes. The contents from a stomach pump analysis will prove that trout eat a tremendous number of submerged ants between mid-July and September. For more information on dry/dropper rigs, see chapter 7.

Stream Improvements: Manmade Weirs and Boulder Gardens
In a perfect world, all our trout streams would have ideal structure suitable for thriving trout populations and aquatic insect life. Unfortunately, this is not the case—even Mother Nature needs a little help from time to time.

Stream improvement projects are designed to restore and stabilize streams that are in decline from a variety of factors. Heavy cattle grazing destabilizes banks, causing chunks

Stream improvement projects have enhanced many of our Western tailwater fisheries in recent years. Mitch Knutson fishes below a manmade weir on the Arkansas tailwater below Pueblo Reservoir.

of bank material, silt, and other insect-choking sediments to enter our streams and wreak havoc with trout populations and aquatic insect life. Flow fluctuations carve away bank sediments, making this an ongoing problem.

Troubles also arise from heavy afternoon rain showers that cause sediment and silt to enter the river system via tributaries. This is especially a problem in burned-out areas after forest fires, i.e., the Green River near Dutch John, Utah and the South Platte River in Cheesman Canyon. The large numbers of trees dying from beetle kill throughout the Rocky Mountain region has also increased erosion.

Drought is affecting the West, with average flows dipping well below their normal historic levels. In many cases, the river channel is simply too wide, resulting in poor structure and habitat in the shallow-water areas. With these low flows, silt and other debris collect in slow-moving areas, filling in the stream channel. These dark sediments are often problematic, as water temperatures escalate quickly in low-water areas.

In Colorado alone, Spinney Mountain Ranch, the South Platte below Elevenmile Reservoir (Elevenmile Canyon), the Blue, the Taylor, the South Platte in Waterton Canyon, the Arkansas below Pueblo Reservoir, and the Yampa—to name only a few—have had stream improvement projects in the past few years to improve their natural habitat. Weirs, inverted U-shaped barriers, or partial walls, boulder gardens, and bank stabilization with logs and roots are just some of the structure enhancements.

The primary goals of these stream improvements are many: to restructure the stream channel, to produce improved trout habitat to accommodate lower stream flows, to fabricate good holding water during higher flows, and to reinforce banks by planting streamside foliage such as willows to help reduce bank erosion and allow fluttering insects such as caddisflies to thrive.

Stream channel restructuring includes riffle and pool structures, midchannel work, deepening channels, creating gravel bars, and in certain cases, narrowing the river channel and placing boulders to create low-flow habitat. The currents scouring between rocks keep sediments from collecting on the bottom of the stream.

Many people complain about these stream improvements because the river structure looks phony or unnatural. In some cases, such as the "Dream Stream" (the stretch of the South Platte between Spinney and Elevenmile Reservoirs) many of the natural meadow stream characteristics are now gone, and anglers are left with a snag nightmare from the in-stream boulder and log placement. But the trout populations are up, and the holding water is greatly improved. You just have to drift your flies between the boulders and tight to the logs if you plan on hooking fish, and you'll probably lose plenty of flies if you are doing things right.

Irrigation Headgates

Irrigation headgates—walls built from huge boulders to divert water—create nice runs and pools that hold good numbers of trout. You'll have no problem locating an irrigation headgate.

Some very large trout are positioned in front of the rock wall that backs up the river before it flows into the irrigation ditches. In addition, trout position themselves between boulders. Therefore, you'll need to inspect these areas carefully and nymph around them methodically.

The lake-like tailouts (before the water enters the irrigation ditch) are great places to find rising fish. I have caught some of my biggest trout on the Williams Fork near the irrigation headgate where the ranchers diverts water to each side of the river to irrigate their hayfields. In some cases, a manmade island diverts water into a separate channel to feed the irrigation ditch. During higher flows, water spills off to the side of the island, producing an excellent holding area for trout. Such spots make for great dry-fly fishing.

WADING TIPS

Once you're in the river, savvy anglers use their feet to feel their way around the stream. Take your time and be patient—the trout aren't going anywhere. Keep one foot planted at all times, and avoid taking long strides, or taking the next step without secure footing.

Preplan your crossing, because the current can push you into a deeper part of the river, forcing you into areas that could be potentially dangerous or even life-threatening.

Ideal spots to cross a trout stream are in the wider sections—flats, shallow riffles, or toward the leading edges of gravel bars. Watch out for color changes, as these usually indicate a substantial depth change.

Other safe areas to cross are behind boulders. Look for piles of silt, sand, fine gravel or smaller stones, decomposed granite, or other fine debris, which ensures good footing and a major break from the current. Avoid walking across or hopping on the tops of boulders—these are usually slick, even if you're wearing studs on your wading shoes.

It's considerably easier to wade heavy water when your body is sideways to the current because there is less surface area or friction than if you face broadside. Wade down and across rather than fighting the current to go upstream. If you're in a heavy current, your hips and waist are the strongest parts of your body. Use them to your advantage.

Another word of caution: The first step off the bank is often deeper than it appears. Clear water can be misleading. If you're not careful, you could damage your knees, or twist or sprain an ankle.

Buddy wading—holding onto the arms of your fishing partner—is a safe way to get across a trout stream. Four or six legs are considerably stronger than two. With this synchronized approach, you can cross fast, moderately deep water safely. I use this technique on a regular basis when I'm guiding.

Buddy wading increases your stability. Four or six legs provide a strong foundation for crossing swift water.

CHAPTER 6

Nymphing Tactics

Somewhere around 80 to 90 percent of a trout's diet is comprised of subsurface food organisms, for the simple reason that aquatic insects spend the vast majority of their life cycles as nymphs. Trout eat a wide array of immature aquatic insects, including caddis and midge larvae and pupae—commonly referred to as nymphs—as well as other food organisms such as scuds, Mysis shrimp, aquatic worms, aquatic moth larvae, snails, and fish eggs.

Dead-drifting artificial nymphs made from natural fur, feathers, hair, and a wide assortment of synthetic materials to imitate trout food is the most effective method of fooling trout. Understanding the biology of each aquatic insect is imperative if you plan to master a tailwater fishery. Knowl-

edge of each phase, and fishing flies to imitate that specific stage, is as important as selecting the fly itself.

Read some of the resources in the back of this book, and take a class in aquatic entomology. Fly shops offer these classes in the winter, and they are a great way to learn more about aquatic insects and their habitat, which will help you select the correct fly in any given situation.

NYMPHING RIGS

Nymphing rigs vary depending on the river's conditions and the angler's choices. Most anglers prefer to use a 7$\frac{1}{2}$- to 9-foot leader terminating in a 4X, 5X, or 6X tippet. If you're fishing a slow, deep transition area, consider using a longer

About 80 to 90 percent of a trout's diet consists of subsurface organisms. Dead-drifting artificial nymphs is the most effective method of catching trout. A drowned Black Ant or sunken Trico Spinner can be equally deadly. Think outside the box from time to time, and never rule out experimentation.

In slow, deep transitional areas, plan to fish long leaders—10 to 15 feet. Fishing from a drift boat is the method of choice.

leader or adding some additional tippet to get your flies deeper in the current.

Fishing deep transitional zones—areas that funnel from shallow riffles into deep holes—is common on the San Juan, the Colorado River at Lees Ferry, and the Green, Madison, Gray Reef, and Bighorn Rivers, especially between late October and early March when the trout have taken residence in their traditional winter lies. It is not uncommon to fish 12- to 15-foot-long leaders under these circumstances.

From the terminating end of the leader, tie an additional piece of tippet—14 to 16 inches long—with either a blood knot or a surgeon's knot. Attach your upper fly with a clinch knot or improved clinch knot. When rigging two nymphs, some anglers use the eye-to-eye approach (a junction of tippet material between the hook eye of the upper fly and the hook eye of the lower fly) while others prefer dropping their second fly off the hook bend of the upper fly. Most anglers refer to the upper fly as the dropper, and the lower fly as the point fly. The distance between the two flies varies, but 14 to 16 inches is a good general rule of thumb.

My own preference is the eye-to-eye approach, because with this method your nymphing system is in-line, enabling a good hookup without any monofilament or fluorocarbon getting in the way of the hook point. The eye-to-eye setup keeps the dropper at a 90-degree angle to the point fly without any obstructions, keeping the hook free and clear to be impaled into the trout's jaw.

Tie on your second fly with another clinch knot or improved clinch knot. Many anglers fish with three flies in their nymphing rigs. But always check the local regulations

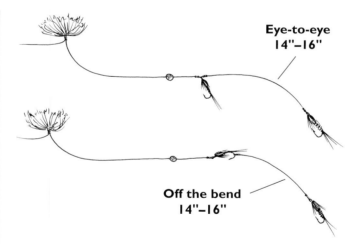

Eye-to-eye 14"–16"

Off the bend 14"–16"

There are two schools of thought with regard to the ideal two-fly nymphing rig. Some anglers favor tying their two nymphs with the "eye-to-eye" technique, while other anglers favor the point fly tied off the bend of the upper fly.

for each tailwater regarding the number of flies you can fish legally. Fishing with three flies increases the risk of tangles, and may not be worth the extra effort required to wrangle with knots.

Strike indicators vary in material, size, shape, and color. Your options include foam pinch-on strike indicators, cork and Styrofoam toothpick varieties, strike putty, balloons, a piece of Amnesia, or yarn strike indicators. The most popular seem to be yarn strike indicators because they are sensitive

BUILDING A STRIKE INDICATOR

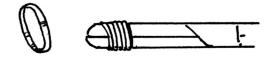

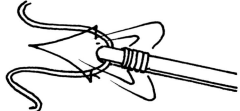

A. *Wrap rubber band around tips of hemostat.*

B. *Grab the leader with the hemostat.*

C. *Slip rubber band onto the leader.*

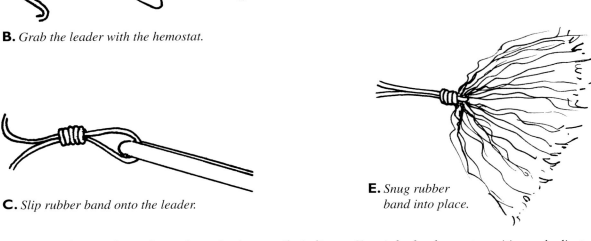

D. *Insert yarn into the loop.*

E. *Snug rubber band into place.*

There are many options to choose from when selecting a strike indicator. Yarn is by far the most sensitive and adjusts easily with an orthodontist's rubber band.

enough to detect subtle strikes, especially in slow, deep water. The latest revolution in strike indicators is the Thingamabobber. They are similar to balloon indicators, and they are especially helpful when casting in the wind and when you want an indicator that requires no floatant.

Most anglers keep their strike indicators $1\frac{1}{2}$ to 2 times the depth of the current away from their flies. The farther your strike indicator is from your flies, the longer it will take to detect the strike. Therefore, keep the distance as short as possible while still achieving a good drift. Don't get lazy. Expert anglers adjust weight and the position of the strike indicator frequently, reacting to the level of the feeding fish in the water column, the depth of the water, and the speed of the current.

Most premade yarn strike indicators have an O-ring for the ease of adjustment, allowing an angler to move the strike indicator up and down the leader. I build my own strike indicator with a 1- to 2-inch piece of tan craft cord, and incorporate an orthodontist's rubber band into the system to make frequent adjustments easy. Take a $5/16$-inch, 8-ounce orthodontist's rubber band and wrap it around the tip of a hemostat four to six times (A). If you are attaching the yarn indicator

toward the butt section of the leader (where the diameter is thicker), four wraps will hold the indicator in place. If the strike indicator will be positioned farther down the leader where it's thinner, wrap the rubber band six times to keep the strike indicator in place.

To place the yarn strike indicator on your leader, pinch the monofilament (or fluorocarbon) with your thumb and forefinger, producing a loop. Open the hemostat and pinch the leader on the circular part of the loop (B), slipping the rubber band onto the leader (C). Insert the yarn into the opening created by the loop (D), and snug the rubber band into place (E). Fluff the yarn with a piece of Velcro on a dowel, and apply dry-fly floatant to the strike indicator to keep it riding high on riffled currents. Refluff the yarn occasionally, and reapply dry-fly floatant whenever it begins to sink.

If you use a blood knot or surgeon's knot at the junction between the leader and tippet and leave the tag ends about $1/16$ inch long, you can place a split-shot above the knot to keep it from sliding down your leader. Lead and tin split-shot are available in several sizes, but anglers who use split-shot will not be able to make the finely tuned adjustments that are

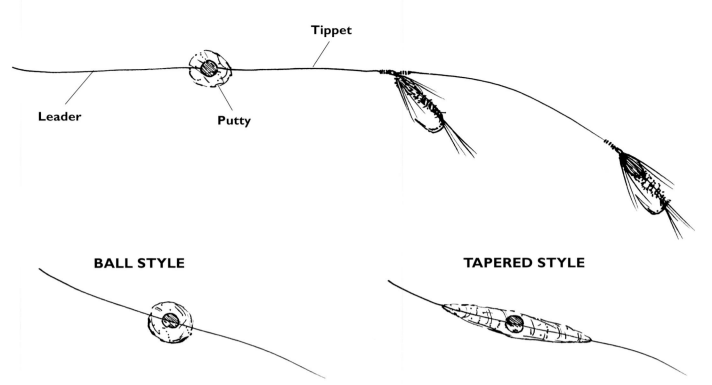

Moldable putties, such as John Perizzolo's Mojo Mud, allow anglers to adjust weight while they are nymphing. Placing the moldable putty over a split-shot keeps the weight from moving. Form your putty into a ball or a tapered-cigar shape.

possible with soft lead or moldable tungsten putty. Split-shot with wings or tabs on the sides allows for easier adjustment with a pair of forceps, but these are not available in smaller sizes, which are useful for small adjustments in depth or for slow-water nymphing. Tin is not as heavy as lead, so adjust your weight accordingly.

I use a combination of split-shot and moldable putty most of the time. I like to place a size 6 split-shot above the blood knot or surgeon's knot, then take a chunk of moldable tungsten putty and place it over the split shot. This keeps the moldable tungsten putty in place, alleviating any frustration from your weight moving down toward your flies, potentially leading to a snag and a lost rig.

Mojo Mud performs well in temperature extremes and caters to the anglers who make frequent adjustments to their nymphing rigs. Tungsten putty is considerably more expensive than lead, or nontoxic no-lead putties, but the sink rate is very impressive, and it's worth the extra money. Mojo Mud is available in gray, green, and brown.

You can attach the moldable putty to your leader in two ways. One is to use a cigar-tapered shape around the split-shot, and the other is to create a ball of putty. There are pros and cons to each: with the tapered method you'll encounter considerably fewer snags, but you'll get far more tangles in your nymphing rig because this rig tends to spin and twist in the water. The "ball option" hangs up more, but rarely tangles your leader. My preference is the ball style, because there is considerable less downtime in retying your nymphing rigs.

Keep a piece of moldable tungsten putty on the zipper pull of your vest, or attached to a clip on your lanyard. Use this to add to the existing piece, or for storing small pieces

that you remove. Start with more weight than you think you'll need, then back off until you occasionally hit the bottom. If you're not occasionally collecting some grass or moss, you may need additional weight.

Before adjusting your weight, check where the trout are positioned in the water column, and the speed of the current. It is not uncommon to need more weight in a fast, shallow riffle than in a slow, deep pool. In many fisheries, like the San Juan River, anglers routinely fish one or two split-shot (size 4) because the trout suspend themselves eating midge pupae much of the time. In many of Colorado's noted tailwater fisheries, we tend to dredge the bottom more often than not. Each fishery requires a slightly different approach based on the prevailing conditions.

SHORT-LINE NYMPHING

The primary goal of any nymph fisherman is to present the fly at the same speed as the current. While that seems fairly straightforward, executing the specific techniques required to achieve a drag-free presentation are not easy.

Sometimes imitating the behavior of the emerging insect is as important as getting a precise dead-drift. Watch a feeding trout's behavior closely; it will help you decipher what food organisms the trout is eating. Trout keying on swimming *Baetis* or emerging caddis pupae will move farther for food than trout that are eating free-floating midge larvae or pupae. If the trout are swimming downstream slowly and confidently, with gentle rising motions in the current, they're probably eating emerging mayflies. If the feeding behavior is violent and aggressive (often creating splashy subsurface disturbances), assume they're feeding on caddis. Swinging your flies under

Short-line or high-stick nymphing is a common strategy used on Western tailwaters. Bob Dye high-sticks a swift piece of pocket-water, keeping all the fly line off the water to achieve a precise dead-drift. In theory, the strike indicator is doing the fishing if you keep all the fly line above the strike indicator off the water.

these conditions can be an important strategy when trying to imitate an emerging *Baetis* or caddis. Swinging soft-hackles is another important strategy when trying to fool trout that are eating emerging insects. The time of year will help you identify which food organism the trout are feeding on.

You do not have to be a great caster to be a good nymph angler. The real game begins once your flies hit the water. A good presentation or drag-free float is by far the most important part of short-line (high-stick) nymphing. When I take out guests who have never fly-fished before, I can have them dead-drifting tiny nymphs and catching fish within 30 minutes with short-line nymphing strategies.

Now don't get me wrong. I'm not saying that casting is unimportant, because it is important. What I am saying, however, is that if you can roll-cast reasonably well, you can become proficient at nymph fishing. On the other hand, long-line nymphing, which we'll address shortly, is a whole different story. It requires some finesse and skill to master, especially if it is windy. Being a good caster will no doubt help your long-line nymphing.

Drag is your worst enemy on a trout stream, because it is often the deciding factor in whether or not you catch trout. So what exactly is drag? Drag is when an angler's fly travels too fast or too slow in relation to the surrounding currents. For a fly fisher, it's cut and dried: anglers who can dead-drift their

flies catch fish, and those who have difficulty presenting their flies at the same speed as the current will likely have a frustrating experience. That means catching a fish or two, or getting completely skunked.

Of course, there are exceptions to any rule. If a blue-winged olive hatch is in progress, you may get lucky and hook a fish on the swing when your fly is dragging across the current. A fish may actually strike your fly because he thinks your sweeping fly is an emerging *Baetis* nymph. But this happens only a small percentage of the time. Usually you'll need a precise dead-drift to catch trout.

In any fly-fishing situation, line control, or line management, is one of the key ingredients for success. The shorter the length of fly line you have to manage, the easier it will be to achieve a good dead-drift. Poor line control results in a sloppy presentation, and that most often occurs when anglers feel the need to lengthen their casts. However, when you long-line nymph, you lengthen your drift to cover larger areas of water. In certain situations, being restricted to short-line nymphing can limit your success.

From a distance, it's easy to identify well-seasoned nymph anglers—their posture paints a picture worth a million words. They are hunched over, focused, staring into the water, arm extended at a 90-degree angle to the body. The fly rod becomes an extension of the arm. Skilled nymph anglers make repeated casts, with only a short length of fly line. They are in the zone—one with the fish, no doubt—and fishing with a purpose. Their intuition guides them. They can be frequently observed with a fish on the end of the line—the telltale sign that their technique is sharp.

When short-line nymphing, the way you grip the handle and line is important. Place your thumb on top and wrap your fingers around the cork handle. Next, pull 4-6 feet of fly line off your reel—not including your tapered leader and tippet—and place the fly line under your casting index finger. This will allow you to proficiently manage your fly line, by stripping the fly line from behind your index finger. In this way, you can "clean up" any unnecessary slack that might result in drag. Don't hold the fly line in your noncasting hand. This bad habit may cost you valuable time on the hook-set, as well as cause problems with slack and poor line management.

Cast your nymphing rig upstream at a 45-degree angle, and immediately lift all the fly line and leader off the water. By executing this technique, the strike indicator will do the "fishing" as your flies float downriver. That's why a strike indicator is often referred to as a float. You do not have to be a Federation of Fly Fishers-certified caster to be an excellent nymph fisherman. You do, however, need to understand how to read a river, trout behavior, feeding patterns, hydraulics, and know how to dead-drift a nymph to catch fish.

By keeping all the fly line off the water, you'll alleviate most of the cross-current drag, increasing your odds of a strike. If you have any doubt where your flies are in relation to your strike indicator, watch for the splash when the weight and flies enter the water. If you're not happy with your cast, immediately pick up your flies and recast with as little surface disturbance as possible.

As your fly drifts naturally downriver, your arm should become an extension of the fly rod. Hold the rod perpendicular to the water's surface, rather than at a 45-degree angle. If you hold the rod tip high—to hold all the fly line off the water—you may run out of room to lift the rod tip vertically to set the hook. This is where line management is critical—strip the fly line with your noncasting index finger to keep the slack off the water, keeping the rod tip at about shoulder level. If you execute the technique properly, you'll feel as if you'd pitched seven innings of baseball at the day's end.

You can inadvertently cause drag either by pulling your flies, or lagging behind the strike indicator with the rod tip. To avoid this problem, point the rod tip at the strike indicator and follow the strike indicator from the 45-degree upstream angle to the 45-degree downstream position of your dead-drift. Once your flies have reached the 45-degree downstream angle, lower your rod tip to extend the drift. The lowering of the rod tip should be a slow and robotic motion, eliminating a pile of unmanaged line that may result in a poor hook-set. If you stop the rod tip high, the end result is a shorter drift, with a quicker swing. Don't shortchange yourself—allow your flies to drift as far as possible with each presentation.

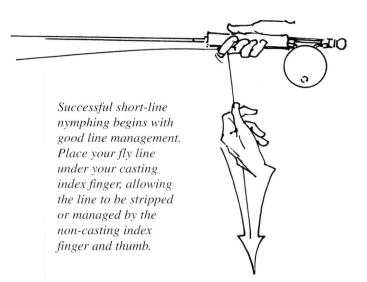

Successful short-line nymphing begins with good line management. Place your fly line under your casting index finger, allowing the line to be stripped or managed by the non-casting index finger and thumb.

Short-line nymphing can be broken down into two distinct categories: blind-fishing or sight-fishing. An angler who blind-fishes a particular piece of water assumes, based on prior experience and by carefully reading the water, that there may be a fish in a certain area. If you try this, begin your attack close to the bank. Methodically work your way to the opposing bank (providing you can do so) by breaking the river down into a grid, casting your flies in 12-inch lanes, and covering the water carefully and systematically. Rather than pull more fly line off the reel to reach farther across the current, use the same length of fly line and take one step out into the current, and fish the next section of the grid. Make four to six casts in each lane with a fixed amount of fly line, concentrating on a perfect dead-drift. The best chances of a hookup are on the first drift through that particular lane.

I firmly believe that your odds drop dramatically after each cast into the same general area. Cover the water thoroughly and quickly, covering as much water as you can. If you stay in the same area for extended periods of time, you're costing yourself fish in the long run. Many anglers tend to stay in one area too long. While I don't think you should leave feeding fish to find other fish, if you're not getting strikes, move on.

Sight-nymphing, as the name suggests, means that you are casting to a specific fish or group of fish. This is by far the most effective method of catching trout on a tailwater fishery. Many anglers opt to sight-fish most of the time, moving from one plainly visible trout to another. Be careful, however, because there are times when you may overlook fish that you cannot see. Therefore, a combination of sight-fishing and blind-fishing works the best.

SIGHT-NYMPHING

As you continue to polish and refine your skills as a nymph angler, you'll concentrate your efforts on spotting trout in the river before casting to them. This technique is referred to as sight-nymphing or visual nymphing, and will become an

Landon Mayer sight-fishes to a large rainbow in the Ice Box in Cheesman Canyon. Carefully watch the trout to see if it rises in the water column, makes any sideways movement, or flashes, or opens its mouth. If any of these occurs, set the hook immediately.

Sight-fishing, or casting your flies to a specific fish, will increase your odds of catching more trout. John Perizzolo targets a brown trout on the lower Blue River below Green Mountain Reservoir.

important tactic in your bag of tricks. Anglers with a keen eye catch more trout than those fly fishers who cast aimlessly into the riffled currents. Covering the water methodically, or casting to nonspecific fish is commonly referred as blind-fishing. It won't take you long to figure out which method is more effective.

Sight-nymphing is visually appealing, and draws many parallels with dry-fly fishing. The only difference is that the take occurs underneath the surface instead of on the surface of the river. Seeing a trout physically eat your nymph below the surface is a rewarding experience, especially when you detect the take without any movement from the strike indicator. Reaching this level of sophistication takes hard work and practice, however. Once you attain this level of expertise, the number of fish you hook and land will increase substantially.

Keeping your flies in front of feeding trout is the primary goal of sight-fishing. In one sense, you're controlling your own destiny rather than leaving your odds to luck or chance by blind-fishing. If your target is not feeding, hunkered on the bottom, and showing no evident signs of shifting in the water column, move on. Don't waste valuable time—concentrate all your efforts on actively feeding trout. For every dozen trout you find, only half may be actually feeding. The key is to cover the water, continuously looking for feeding trout.

Spotting a trout is no easy task, especially for the novice fly fisher. Fishing to trout you can see is an acquired skill that requires a lot of time, persistence, patience, and dedication to master. My guests often get frustrated when trying to spot a trout that I have identified in a shallow riffle. "I can't see it, but I believe you," they often say. Spend some time on the river without your fly rod, training your eyes to spot fish in different sections of your favorite trout stream.

Spotting trout is easier on some days than others. Variables such as overcast skies, higher flows, rain, wind, and water clarity affect your ability to spot trout. The greatest challenge will be spotting trout in riffled or nervous currents. Begin your efforts in slower water, then graduate to moderate-paced riffles. Then try to identify trout in faster currents and pocketwater.

Without good eyewear, spotting trout is extremely difficult (for a detailed discussion of polarized sunglasses, refer to chapter 15). You need to look in the right places to begin with. Identifying these key areas is often referred to as reading the water (see chapter 3).

Holding areas vary greatly depending on the time of year, water temperatures, water releases, seasonal hatches, and other external factors such as bright sunshine or overcast conditions. Having prior knowledge of the prevailing conditions will improve your chances of success.

Once you have identified a likely holding area, concentrate your efforts not on looking for a clear, clean-cut image of a trout, but on clues—specific colors, elongated shapes, and shadows. Rainbows have brilliant red stripes and gill plates, so it makes perfect sense to key on the color red when

you're searching for rainbows. Browns, on the other hand, are golden-olive. Cutthroats are a bright golden color, with distinct red fins, an orangish tail, and brilliant red gill plates. In time, you'll be able to detect each species quickly and simply based on the colors of their flanks and gill plates.

Other clues for spotting trout include fish rising in the water column, flashes, opening mouths, silhouettes, shadows, and any other movement. When a trout moves or shifts in the water column, its flank often produces a mirrorlike flash, enabling anglers to spot a trout they may have missed during the initial examination of the water.

When looking for fish, keep the sun at your back and cup your hands around the sides of your glasses to reduce glare. Stare into the river through smooth, flat spots in the current, called windows, and scan the stream bottom. The windows disappear quickly as the current moves past you. Stay focused on one area, looking for specific clues until you spot a trout. Wear drab-colored clothing, as brightly colored shirts, jackets, and hats can spook trout that are positioned in shallow riffles—specifically those that are feeding.

I prefer sunny conditions when trying to spot trout. If skies are overcast, the light is flat and the surface glare makes it almost impossible to see below the surface, let alone watch a trout eat your fly. In flat light, blind-fish the river carefully, covering the water methodically and meticulously. While this is not as productive as sight-nymphing, you'll still catch a few fish.

LONG-LINE NYMPHING

Short-line nymphing limits the amount of water you can meticulously cover—not to mention that fishing to some productive lies is impossible unless you cast your nymphing rig at least 30 to 40 feet. Long-line nymphing incorporates longer drifts, giving the angler a better opportunity to cover more water, and it is important on some of the larger Western tailwaters like the Bighorn, Madison, Gray Reef, San Juan, Green, and the Colorado at Lees Ferry.

Lees Ferry anglers and guides refer to their method of nymph fishing as the "Lees Ferry extended drift" or "full-line nymphing," a long-line approach that stacks mends (redistributing fly line to prevent drag), allowing the flies to drift for long distances drag-free. To achieve this extended drift, begin by making a long upstream cast, followed by an aggressive upstream mend, stacking line above the strike indicator as the two-fly rig floats downriver. Use a roll-cast mend to shoot fly line quickly upstream to eliminate drag.

Anglers fish the long gravel bars and transition areas below Glen Canyon Dam with 50-plus feet of fly line in an attempt to fool as many trout as possible with a single presentation. Many anglers use the entire fly line on a single drift; but the more fly line you have out on the water, the tougher it will be to manage—and setting the hook will be extremely challenging, if not completely impossible.

A combination of both short-line and long-line nymphing is the most effective method for most Western tailwater fish-

Long-line nymphing is an alternative to short-line nymphing. Long-lining allows anglers to cover more water, and is especially effective when fishing long runs, midchannel shelves, and gravel bars. Dr. Bob "Hawk Eye" Randall long-lines a beautiful run on the Yampa River.

eries. Large rivers are often intimidating because of their size, but breaking them down into smaller sections can be beneficial. Concentrate on fishing the banks hard, looking for subsurface structure, pocketwater, shelves, riffles, undercut banks, and protruding logs. Fish these bank areas as if you were fishing a smaller river and ignore the large and faster spots toward the center.

Use the strike indicator for more than just detecting strikes. To achieve a good drift, you'll need a steady or fixed point in your nymphing rig that allows you to control drag. Without a fixed point in your nymphing rig, it's nearly impossible to eliminate drag. I refer to this location in my nymphing rig as a "drift reference point."

If you allow any fly line or the butt of the leader to develop a "belly" below your strike indicator, you'll get a sweeping motion in which your flies are traveling across the current, rather than drifting naturally in the current. Micro-drag occurs when small sections of your fly line or leader lie on the water, creating the same effect. That's what makes short-line or high-stick nymphing so productive—drag is minimized by keeping all the fly line and the thick portion of the leader off the water.

If you opt to long-line nymph, you need to become a master at line management and mending. Each time a belly is

formed, you must control the drag by repositioning the fly line above or below the strike indicator (depending on the current), eliminating the sweeping or dragging motion. This process may be repeated several times during a drift. If you can short-line nymph, do so—and only long-line nymph when you absolutely have to.

SLOW-WATER NYMPHING

Slow-water nymphing is probably the greatest challenge when it comes to fooling trout under the surface. This is because the trout have a lot of time to inspect your flies. Faster riffles mask your leader and tippet, weight, and strike indicator, and force the trout to make a quick decision on whether to eat your artificial.

All the major Western tailwaters have a tremendous amount of slow, lakelike water between runs and holes. Anglers either row through or walk by this "frog water" in search of easier water to fish. But slow-water stretches of the river fish very well between November and mid-March.

Guides on the San Juan River spend hours nymphing the slow water with their guests, hooking fish after fish after fish. I watched Johnny Gomez, one of the best guides on the San Juan, put on a streamside clinic with his guests one afternoon. It was very impressive! He had more "doubles" than I care to

Slow-water nymphing is an excellent strategy from a drift boat. John Keefover fishes a slow, deep transitional area on the "Wedding of the Waters" float near Thermopolis, Wyoming.

talk about. And to made matters worse, my buddy Matt Miles and I were struggling.

Gomez was working several slow, deep midchannel shelves with a purpose. To the casual streamside observer, the water appeared to be hardly moving, and there seemed no rhyme or reason for the water he was fishing. After he had thoroughly fished a certain location, he would row back upstream and hit the water again.

Miles and I didn't fall off the truck last week. We knew Gomez was targeting these locations for a specific reason. It was early spring, the water was icy cold, and the hatches were lighter than normal. We had been on the river for two days and had found only a few fish in the riffles. Fishing was tough—we landed only eight or ten fish apiece each day. That might sound good, but those who fish the San Juan on a regular basis know that that is a slow day.

Everything was pointing toward classic winter conditions, even though it was mid-April. We changed our thinking and our tactics and began to hook some nice fish in the slower water. The trout had not moved into the riffled areas yet because of the cold water temperatures and lack of hatches. It took my buddies and me a while to figure out how to be productive in the slower parts of the Texas Hole, the lakelike section above the Lower Flats, Lunker Alley, Baetis Bend, ET Rock, and other slow-water areas. Once I learned how to fish

these areas, I was able to apply that knowledge to other rivers like the Green and Bighorn.

To be successful in slow water, you must have a good understanding of the river's structure and must be able to identify the areas that hold good concentrations of trout. By far the easiest way to fish the slower water is from a drift boat. From a boat you can see the fish and the river structure. What you are looking for is a midchannel shelf or drop off. You'll clearly see the edges of shelves, which can drop off dramatically.

To find these areas, I watch the guides to see what water they are working. The fish will be positioned downstream of the drop-off. If a heavy hatch is in progress, the fish will be suspended in the water column, the telltale sign that they are actively feeding. Under these circumstances you'll be able to sight-nymph, often watching the fish eat your fly well before detecting any strike indicator movement.

The oarsman can hold you in place, float slowly with the current, or drop anchor to nymph these areas. Fishing from the boat with a short length of line and an upstream mend is effective because you are drifting at the same speed as the current. It is best to row slowly back upstream and nymph the same slot several times. When the action subsides, I'll look for another drop-off.

To be successful, you'll need a 12- to 15-foot leader, and you will have to frequently adjust your strike indicator and weight. In the slower currents, I use one or two size 4 split-shot. Because the water is slow-moving, the fish will have a long time to inspect your flies, so I use fluorocarbon tippet. It's less visible than nylon monofilament.

I base my fly selection on the time of year and what insects are most prevalent. For example, if I'm fishing in the middle of the winter, I use two small midges. If I'm fishing in the spring or fall, I use one midge and one *Baetis* nymph imitation. If there is either a midge hatch or blue-winged olive hatch in progress, I fish two of the same fly because the trout are feeding selectively on one particular food organism. In the slower water, you may need an attractor such as a blood midge, annelid, egg pattern, or leech to draw attention to the dropper fly.

If you are wading, a stealthy and careful approach is critical for success. In slow-moving water, you need a delicate touch with both your cast and mending. Look for suspended fish, and cast slightly above the fish positioned on the drop-off. The strikes will be very soft. Once you hook a fish, get it out of the pool quickly so that you will not spook the other trout.

CZECH AND POLISH NYMPHING

An offshoot of short-line or high-stick nymphing, Czech and Polish nymphing (often called European nymphing) is quickly gaining popularity in the United States as an effective method of catching trout in moderate currents and riffled water. While Czech and Polish nymphing share many common goals and similarities with short-line or high-stick nymphing, they are significantly different in a number of ways. The main emphasis of Czech and Polish nymphing is to remove all forms of external weight (the flies are the weight) and strike indicators, while at the same time imitating "swimming bugs."

Czech nymphing incorporates scudlike, larvalike, and shellback nymphs with tungsten beads and lead-wrapped underbodies into a two- or three-fly nymphing rig. Czech nymphs are tied slim and as heavy as possible, which helps the flies sink quickly in fast-moving water. Flies with bushy hackle, legs, and other appendages such as rubber legs will not sink as fast.

Polish nymphs are similar, but they incorporate woven bodies imitating cased caddis, free-living caddis, crane flies, stoneflies, and scuds. Polish nymphs incorporate lead-wrapped shanks, Tungsten Fly Humps, and tungsten beads for rapid sink rates.

Most anglers who nymph in the Czech or Polish style build their own leaders, using a stiff butt section and three segments of thin tippet material. The goal is to reduce resistance and friction, allowing the multiple-fly rig to sink to the

Czech nymphing is different from short-line nymphing in that it calls for removing all external forms of weight such as split shot, moldable putties, and twist-ons. Steve Parrott incorporates weighted flies into his nymphing system as he fishes the South Platte River below the hamlet of Deckers, Colorado.

Jonathan Keisling landed this beautiful Blue River rainbow trout on a Czech nymph. Czech nymphing is quickly gaining popularity on Western tailwaters.

Czech and Polish rigs incorporate weighted flies that sink quickly to the bottom. Steve Parrott's patterns have enticed selective trout throughout the West. Czech and Polish nymphing rigs are made of two or three flies. Always check local fishing regulations for any restrictions that might exist on fishing multiple flies.

bottom quicker than a conventional tapered leader. Many construct butt sections from red or chartreuse Amnesia or use a nymph fly line to assist in the detection of strikes.

For leaders: keep the leader diameter as thin as possible and no longer than your rod. The typical setup is 3 to 4 feet of 10- to 15-pound monofilament, joined with three 20-inch sections of 3X, 4X, and 5X tippet (in that order), connected with double or triple surgeon's knots. If you're fishing smaller flies, it is a good idea to use 4X, 5X, and 6X tippets instead when building your leader. With this approach, you have a leader that will allow you to fish two droppers and one point fly. If you use only two flies, you'll have a dropper and a point fly.

If you hold the leader vertically after you complete your surgeon's knots, you'll notice that one of the tag ends will point up and other will point down. Clip off the tag end that points up and leave the other to be used for the dropper. The tag ends should be between 5 and 7 inches long. If you leave longer tag ends, there is a much higher risk of tangles.

This system allows anglers to change flies more quickly than the eye-to-eye or tying-off-the-bend approach in a conventional nymphing rig with a strike indicator. You're tying only one clinch knot rather than the two clinch knots with other methods.

In a Czech nymphing rig, the main line is used to construct the dropper tag. In Polish nymphing, the dropper tag is constructed of a separate piece of material with a loop at the end (either a double perfection loop or a twisted double overhand loop) and attached between two blood knots so the tag will slide up and down the line between those two knots.

Your approach will vary slightly depending on whether you are fishing two or three flies. If you are fishing three flies, the heaviest nymph should be in the middle. This assists in getting the flies to the bottom quickly. If you are fishing with two flies, the heavier nymph should be in the point fly position, except in shallow riffles, where you want to place the heavier fly in the top position and the lighter fly in the point position. This allows the flies to roll or bounce along the bottom, because you are holding the heavier fly slightly upward in the water column with the rod tip.

The heavy fly's primary purpose is to get everything down in the current quickly. Choose a heavily weighted fly that imitates the naturals abundant in the area, such as a large stonefly or crane fly imitation. The other two nymphs should imitate

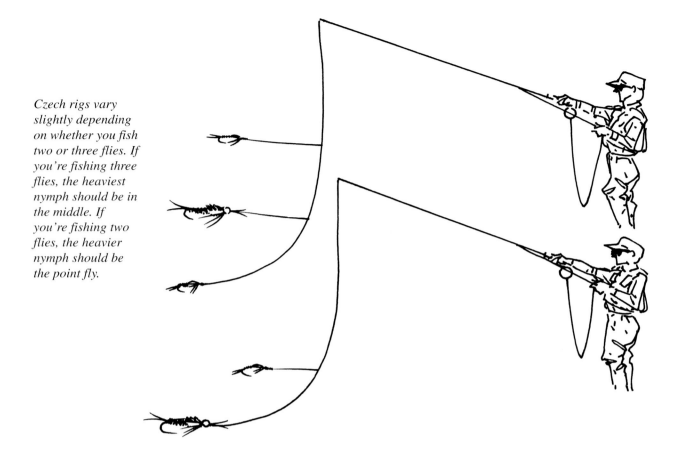

Czech rigs vary slightly depending on whether you fish two or three flies. If you're fishing three flies, the heaviest nymph should be in the middle. If you're fishing two flies, the heavier nymph should be the point fly.

bugs such as scuds, cased caddis, free-living caddis, and smaller stoneflies, depending on specific hatches and the density of each on the stream.

As with short-line or high-stick nymphing, you'll need to have a good understanding of why and where trout position themselves based on seasonal conditions (for more information on feeding lies, see chapter 5). Czech or Polish nymphing works best in faster riffles and slots that are 2–4 feet deep. The approach is similar to short-line nymphing because you only need 2–4 feet of fly line past the tip of your rod to catch fish. The ideal rod is 9 1/2 to 10 feet long with a soft tip.

Cast the flies upstream at a 45-degree angle, allow the flies to sink, then immediately lift all the fly line off the water. As in short-line nymphing, the rod is an extension of your arm, with the rod tip parallel to the surface current. The biggest difference between short-line nymphing and the Czech or Polish approach is that you are pulling the fly line slightly faster than the current rather than dead-drifting. Move the rod tip fast enough to keep a tight line while letting the flies roll or bounce along the stream bottom. If you are constantly snagging the flies on the bottom, your nymphs are too heavy and you need to switch to flies with less weight. Don't allow your flies to swing, or you'll lose touch with your flies from the slack that occurs with the swinging motion. Pick up your flies and recast before they drift below you. It is a good idea to do a position set just prior to recasting your flies.

This pulling, dragging motion goes completely against what I have learned, preached, and taught for the past 15 years as a professional guide. Many anglers believe, however, that the nymphs traveling faster than the surrounding current is what entices a trout to take the fly.

Positive tension, or a tight line, is created as you pull the flies downstream, which is why the technique is referred as tight-line nymphing. It allows the angler to feel the strike versus reading it with a strike indicator or watching where the leader enters the river for any type of hesitation. The hook-set is similar to short-line nymphing, too—it should be a quick and firm set, but a short range of motion. If you set the hook too hard, you risk breaking off a lot of flies, especially with the thinner-diameter tippet materials used in Czech and Polish nymphing.

There is a fine line between getting your flies to the bottom and getting snagged. For this reason, Czech and Polish nymph fishers tie a wide range of weighted nymphs to allow for weight changes by simply switching flies. For example, an angler can tie the same fly with different diameter (.025, .030, etc.) lead underbodies and tungsten beads for different sink rates. It is entirely possible to have the same fly pattern with four different weights based on the aforementioned variables. Anglers can also pull the flies slightly faster to avoid snags, fine-tuning the speed at which the nymphs are traveling. You'll need to do a lot of experimenting until you get the feel of it.

Not all strikes are detected with a strike indicator. Savvy anglers look for flashes, fish rising in the water column, and opening mouths to detect strikes prior to any strike indicator movement.

DETECTING STRIKES WITH A STRIKE INDICATOR

Getting a good drift is only part of becoming a proficient nymph fisherman. The other part of the equation is reading the strike indicator and watching what goes on around the strike indicator for any signs of a potential strike. Even with a well-adjusted, sensitive yarn strike indicator, you'll still miss up to a third of your strikes if you rely on the strike indicator alone. It is amazing how long it takes for the indicator to move after a trout has eaten your fly. I see it all the time when I'm guiding clients. I watch the trout eat the fly—but there is a delayed response from the indicator. If you don't see this subtle strike, the chances are good the trout will spit the fly, and you may never realize the strike occurred.

In order to "read" the highest percentage of strikes with your strike indicator, you need to continually adjust it from one and a half times to twice the depth of the water. If you get lazy, you'll miss strikes. The farther your strike indicator is away from your flies, the longer it takes for the slack between your flies and your indicator to tighten, which eventually twitches the yarn.

For that reason, you'll need to adjust the strike indicator when nymphing the back of the run, then readjust it when you fish the heart of the run, and make yet another adjustment when you fish the head of the run with shallow riffles. This is an ongoing process, but at the day's end, it makes a huge difference in the total number of fish you put into the net.

To detect strikes, concentrate on your yarn strike indicator and trust your instincts. Strikes vary from the slightest twitch to aggressive hits that pull the yarn strike indicator completely underwater. Eventually you'll begin to set the hook when the yarn slows down, rather than waiting for the yarn to submerge below the riffled surface currents.

It is important to react and set the hook at any movement from your strike indicator. If you wait and analyze whether the movement was a rock or a fish, it's too late—you've probably missed the trout. Set the hook at every little twitch. And it is important to keep an eye on what's going on around your strike indicator, watching for any visual clues indicating that a fish may have eaten your fly.

If you are suspending your nymphs with the strike indicator, pay close attention for flashes, opening mouths, or rising motions upstream of your strike indicator during the first part of your drift. Then direct your attention to below (downstream) your strike indicator during the second part of the drift. If you see any of these visual clues, set the hook immediately.

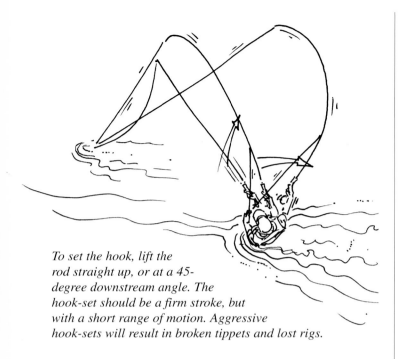

To set the hook, lift the rod straight up, or at a 45-degree downstream angle. The hook-set should be a firm stroke, but with a short range of motion. Aggressive hook-sets will result in broken tippets and lost rigs.

With a traditional nymphing setup, there is a tremendous amount of slack, which postpones any type of movement of the strike indicator. Before you can feel the strike—before it moves or goes under the surface—the slack between the flies and strike indicator must be taut. This rarely happens, because fish often move only a few inches to obtain a food organism, and by the time the leader straightens, the trout has rejected your fly.

Strikes are much harder to detect in slow-moving water than in faster riffles. Trout positioned in riffles hit the fly more aggressively, because they must make up their minds quicker. In addition, the faster currents tighten the slack between the strike indicator and the flies quicker, allowing an angler to detect the strike earlier.

In slow-moving water, the strike indicator rarely moves because there is a tremendous amount of slack and a long leader, and the relaxed leader rarely tightens with the slow currents. You must have a keen eye in slow water, continually looking for any of the previously mentioned clues to a strike.

Have you ever hooked a trout when you were getting ready to recast your nymphing rig? If you fish for any length of time, you quickly discover that a fair number of your strikes occur on the last 25 percent of the drift, when your flies are swinging or lifting in the current. The fly rising in the water column resembles the natural behavior of emerging caddis, or a swimming *Baetis* nymph prior to emerging.

Don't shortchange yourself on the latter part of the drift—keep focused—because you'll get a lot of takes from this realistic, uplifting action, especially if either caddis or *Baetis* are emerging. Once the flies have completed their swinging or rising motion, many anglers set the hook to see if a fish has taken the fly on the rise. This technique is often referred as a position set. I can't tell you how many fish I have hooked with a position set—it's mind-boggling.

The Leisenring Lift is another effective method to fool trout. Named for James Leisenring, this tactic entices a trout into taking your fly, especially trout that are feeding on caddis pupae in shallow riffles (18–24 inches deep). This is how to do it: Deliver your two-fly rig upstream, allow your flies to sink and drift downstream, stop the rod tip abruptly, and allow the flies to swing in front of a feeding fish. If you see a fish rise or flash, set the hook. You may also feel the strike when the line swings and becomes taut. Many anglers simply lift their flies in front of the feeding fish to achieve the same goal. This technique is also effective when you're trying to imitate a swimming or emerging *Baetis* nymph in a slow, glassy pool or tailout. The uplifting action triggers a feeding response because of the flies' behavior.

SETTING THE HOOK

There are two schools of thought with regard to the proper hook-set. One is to lift the rod tip straight up, and the other is to set the hook back into the trout's jaw. Many anglers set the hook in the wrong direction, pulling the flies out of the trout's jaw (upstream and away from the trout), resulting in a poor hook-set that may slip during the fight.

For that reason, lifting the rod tip straight up is the simpler method. If you lift the rod tip straight up, your technique is always correct, and it does not matter what side of the river you are fishing in relation to your arm movement and hook-set. If you prefer to set the hook back into the trout's jaw, your setting motion should always be downstream. Don't get trapped into always setting the hook to the "right," because this is effective only if the river is flowing from left to right. As you enter the river, remind yourself which direction the current is flowing, and keep in mind that the trout are always facing into the current.

If you're the type who sets the hook aggressively, you risk breaking fish off. The hook-set should be firm, but with a short range of motion. I set the hook hard, but my arm moves only 18 inches. If you set the hook hard with a wide range of motion, you'll be replacing a lot of two-fly rigs. If you have a lot of break-offs, you might consider a rod with a softer action to absorb some of the power on your aggressive hook-sets.

FIGHTING AND LANDING A TROUT

After the thrill and excitement of detecting the strike, you have to fight and land your trout. Like many other aspects of fishing, landing a trout requires a tremendous amount finesse and skill. This is largely due to the spider-web-thin tippets and small flies (#18–22) that tailwater enthusiasts use on a regular basis. The real challenge, of course, comes from the weight of the fish, which often surpasses the strength of the tippet material. There is a fine line between too much pressure and not enough tension to keep the fly in the trout's mouth.

If you hook a trout on a #10 golden stonefly nymph with 4X tippet, you have a greater chance of landing that fish than if it were hooked on a #20 RS2 on 6X tippet. To make matters worse, your odds drop dramatically when you use smaller hooks (#22–26) because there is less holding power. In my experience, even a good angler will land only two out of every three fish hooked. Average anglers will land about half their fish. Some days are better than others.

After you hook a fish the goal is to lift and apply pressure with the rod tip to raise the fish's head toward the surface. Before that, however, you may need to apply some bankside pressure to move the fish out of the faster currents. Once the fish is out of the heavy water, apply upward pressure again. After the trout's head is up, you have beaten it—at least in theory—because it loses the ability to make powerful surges that can potentially lead to any number of problems. Many anglers make the mistake of letting the fish's head slip back under the water's surface, allowing the fish to gain the advantage again. The longer the fish stays on the line, the greater the chance you'll have of losing it. I like to get the fish to the net quickly for that reason.

Once the trout's head is up, its flank and head rest sideways on the surface, allowing you to net the fish with ease by sliding the trout across the water, guiding the fish into a landing net. I like a long-handled net because the extra reach makes the whole process easier.

Generally speaking, anglers lose their fish in the first few seconds because they hold the fly line or reel handle with a death grip while the fish wants to take line. Trust your instincts: if it feels like you are getting heavy-handed, keep your tip high and let the fish run, pulling line off the reel smoothly. There are no set guidelines for applying power—it's a matter of feel, patience, finesse, and skill. I can tell you this: there is more give than take in the initial phases of fighting a fish.

After the initial hook-set, the fish generally makes a series of powerful runs, shaking its head, jumping, twisting, and turning, trying to throw the fly. Each run is shorter than the previous run. Keep even and steady pressure on the fish—not too much pressure, but enough to keep the barbless hook buried in the fish's jaw.

First, get the rod tip up. It becomes a shock absorber, flexing and bending to protect the flimsy tippet material. Second, get the fish on the reel. Always fight your fish by playing them on the reel. I don't care if they're 10 inches or 28 inches—getting them on the reel is always a good rule.

You must be willing to move downstream after the fish is hooked. I recommend staying parallel with your fish as it moves downriver. It is much easier to move a trout across the current than back upstream. In addition, the heaviest force is in the upper third of the water column; therefore, you risk break-offs from the extra force when the trout swings below you. When you stay parallel with the fish, the fish stays deeper in the current, alleviating some of the pressure on the tippet.

Fighting a trout with small flies and light tippet requires a lot of finesse and skill. There is a fine line between too much pressure and not enough. You will find that there is more give than take when fighting a trout.

CHAPTER 7

Dry-Fly Tactics

Some of the most rewarding fly-fishing experiences involve anglers fooling trout with surface offerings that imitate the emerging adult (emerger), adult stage, or spentwing stage of an aquatic insect's life. Anglers can also imitate terrestrials (ants, beetles, cicadas, crickets, grasshoppers, and others) that reside on nearby streambanks, trees, and bushes. If given the choice, most anglers would choose to fish with dry flies rather than chucking weighted flies into the depths of a trout's complicated world. I'm a diehard nymph fisherman, especially when it comes to visual or sight-nymphing, but I must admit that catching trout on the surface with dry flies is by far my favorite method of hunting, stalking, and fooling a selective trout.

Dry-fly fishing is exciting because the take occurs on, or near, the surface of the water. One of the most exciting aspects of dry-fly fishing is that there is no doubt when a trout has eaten your fly. One of two things will happen: you'll either hook the trout or miss it, but you'll know for sure you had a strike. In a few cases, you'll get a second chance, if the fish is feeding aggressively.

But in nymph fishing, the so-called strike may have been a rock, branch, or other snag that resulted in your indicator abruptly sinking. The only true indication of a take with a nymphing rig is seeing a flash, head shake, or roll after you have set the hook. You'll rarely get a second chance with a nymph if you miss the first time. Most often, the trout will develop lockjaw and slide into the deeper currents to seek protection.

While dry-fly fishing accounts for only a small percentage of your overall fishing time, it pays to be prepared with good

Dry/dropper rigs allow anglers to fish with both a dry fly and a nymph at the same time. Mark Krehbiel fishes a piece of pocketwater with a Rubber-Legged Stimulator, dropped with a size 18 Gold Beadhead Flashback Pheasant Tail Nymph.

technique in the event of a good hatch. Practice your casting at home or at a nearby park. There is no need to cast the entire fly line. Most of your Western tailwater dry-fly deliveries will be between 15 and 25 feet. Concentrate on turning over your leader (put a piece of Glo-Bug yarn on the end of the leader to represent a fly). Work on your accuracy. Use a dinner plate or a Hula Hoop for a target.

Some Western tailwaters (such as the South Platte River in Elevenmile Canyon, and the South Platte River below Spinney Reservoir) offer year-round fishing with dry flies. The midge hatches in these two locations are fantastic—even in the dead of winter. The tailwaters of the Green and Bighorn also offer reliable midge fishing throughout the winter. The tailwater below Pueblo Reservoir (the Arkansas River) is another renowned stretch to fish dry flies throughout the winter. December and January are two of the best months to find risers in the 8-mile section below Pueblo Dam. Consistent water temperatures from the dam above keep the trout active and looking up all winter, and hatches are much more reliable in this section of the Arkansas, compared to other tailwaters during winter. Anglers find both blue-winged olives—yes, blue-winged olives—and midges hatching during the winter.

The San Juan has fantastic midge fishing year-round. Dry-fly fishers should concentrate their efforts on some of the slow-moving bank water or the slow, deep glides in Texas Hole, Lunker Alley, Lower Flats, and the section between Baetis Bend and ET Rock. Anglers will find classic, yet very technical, midge fishing in these sections. I have had winter days on the San Juan when I have fished dry flies all day long. On those days, nymphing was not even a consideration because the dry-fly fishing was so good.

This list highlights only a few stretches that offer year-round dry-fly fishing, but the fact of the matter is this: you'll find at least a handful of rising trout on most Western tailwaters year-round if you really look for them. Carefully inspect the shaded areas; look in the slow back eddies and scum lines, along the banks, and in the tailouts of the slow, glassy pools.

DRY-FLY RIGS

Most anglers use 9- to 12-foot leaders for most of their dry-fly fishing. A 9-foot, 5X leader is the most versatile because you can add additional tippet to extend its length and prolong its life. This makes sense, because when changing flies you are cutting into tippet material rather than your leader, which would affect the original taper. I use a standard knotless tapered leader rather than building my own or using a pre-made knotted leader. Knotted leaders do turn over more efficiently, but they are often more trouble than they are worth. Knotted leaders tend to collect moss and other debris, which can become a maintenance nightmare.

If the river is low and clear, you'll probably want to fish a longer leader to reduce any chance of spooking trout. Under these circumstances, the trout are wary, spooky, and sensitive to movement above the water's surface. This would be

The tailwater below Pueblo Reservoir offers reliable dry-fly fishing throughout the winter. Matt Scandiff caught this nice brown on the Arkansas tailwater on a mild January day.
JOHN KEEFOVER

the perfect situation to fish a 9- to 12-foot leader with an additional 18–24 inches of tippet. But you should try to fish the shortest leader you can without jeopardizing a delicate presentation. Though long leaders are sometimes necessary, it is much harder to turn over your fly with a 12- to 15-foot leader.

If you're fishing faster, riffled currents, you can fish a shorter leader because the trout are not as spooky with the agitated surface. Under these conditions, you can fish a 9-foot leader with an additional 18–24 inches of tippet. If the water is high or slightly off-colored, you can generally fish a $7^1/2$- to 9-foot leader without any negative effects.

Keeping your dry fly properly dressed is an important part of fooling trout with surface tactics. In addition to floating your fly, they serve other purposes. Paste floatants help certain sections of your leader float when you're fishing emergers. Dry-fly crystals will make your small drys highly visible because the powdery crystals lightens the color of your fly.

For dry flies tied without cul-de-canard (CDC) and for yarn strike indicators, I use a paste or gel floatant in an inverted floatant holder, which hangs off a D-ring on my vest or attaches to my lanyard. Squirt a small quantity on your index finger and thumb and gently massage the floatant into the fibers. For patterns tied with CDC, I use dry-fly crystals such as Shimazaki Dry-Shake or Frog's Fanny; otherwise, you'll mat down the puffy CDC fibers, causing the fly to sink.

Dry/dropper rigs are effective when flows get low and clear and trout become suspicious of standard two-fly nymphing rigs.

Frog's Fanny has a handy applicator brush with which to apply the powdery crystals to the wing.

For flies tied without CDC, I typically put a gel or paste floatant on first, then apply dry-fly crystals to the fly to remove fish slime and water, which may cause the fly to sink or become waterlogged. By simply dropping your fly into the Shimazaki Dry-Shake bottle and shaking it a few times, you can restore floatation quickly. It may be necessary to reapply the gel or paste floatant after you have hooked a few trout.

Dry/Dropper Rigs

Fishing a dry fly and a nymph together is extremely effective in a wide range of conditions. In effect, the dry fly—whether it's a bushy Rubber-Legged Stimulator, a caddisfly imitation, or a Parachute Adams—becomes the strike indicator, enabling you to suspend one or two nymphs below it to imitate subsurface foods. For many anglers, this is the preferred method of attack when rivers get low and clear and trout get suspicious of a standard two-fly nymphing rig with a strike indicator.

Select your dry fly based on flows and any evident hatches. If it is mid-June, you might consider using a size 12 yellow Crystal Stimulator to imitate the Yellow Sallies that are hatching. If its late July, you might choose a size 10 Hen Wing Green Drake, and in August and September you might use a size 8 Dave's Hopper to imitate mature hoppers. Based on prior experiences with these food organisms, and imprinting, trout will feed opportunistically on them any part of the day or evening.

Drop a nymph (with 18–24 inches of tippet) off the bend of your dry fly, based on the current insect activity. For example, if you're fishing between 8 and 10 A.M. when the midges are hatching, you might use a Zebra Midge. If you're fishing between 11 A.M. and 1 P.M. when the pale morning duns are hatching, you might use a Beadhead Barr's Emerger (PMD). If there is no apparent hatch, it is hard to go wrong with a #18 Gold Bead (Tungsten Gold Bead) Flashback Pheasant Tail

Nymph. This is by far my favorite dropper fly for fishing with the high-low technique.

Dry/dropper rigs can be fished in riffles, runs, pools, back eddies, flats, and pocketwater, and may be fished upstream, downstream, or up and across the stream. Methodically cover the water, showing your flies to as many trout as possible. One of two things will indicate a potential strike: the dry fly abruptly sinks, or you'll see a flash below your dry fly. If either occurs, gently lift the rod tip to set the hook.

THE APPROACH: TRADEOFFS AND COMPROMISES

The primary goal when fishing dry flies is to get as close to your target as possible, positioning yourself in a place where you can make accurate casts—without spooking any trout. This often means crawling on your hands and knees, keeping a low profile, sneaking up on a rising trout, until you get into the desired casting location. All dry-fly anglers must carefully consider how they will approach a rising trout. Will you cast your flies upstream? Up and across? Downstream? Or down and across? Which side of the river should you position yourself on, based on surface glare and the visibility of your fly? How do you maximize your accuracy and line control? Will you need any type of specialty or slack-line casts to offset drag and swirly currents? Is there adequate casting room for your backcast? Which direction will you set the hook? And finally, where will you land the trout after you hook it?

You should have answers to these questions before you enter the stream. The approach can be a double-edged sword because there is often some risk involved. If you get too close to the rising trout, you may spoil your chances before you even get a chance to make a cast. I err on the conservative side when approaching rising trout.

The closer you get to your target, however, the greater chance you have of executing an accurate cast, managing your fly line, and getting a good hook-set. If you make a mistake, learn from it and move on. Some of my best lessons on

The ultimate goal when fishing dry flies is to get as close to the rising fish as possible without spooking it. There are several tradeoffs and compromises associated with dry-fly fishing.

a trout stream have come about from *not* catching a specific fish. It forces you to keep refining your processes and analyzing your approach. In the long run, you'll become a better dry-fly angler by learning from your mistakes.

Upstream Delivery

This approach involves standing broadside to the current, positioning yourself in a safe and strategic spot to make a delicate upstream presentation. You may be methodically covering the water with attractors, fishing dry/dropper rigs, or stalking a specific rising fish that may be sipping spentwing mayflies.

Because the fish are facing into the current, this method greatly reduces the chances of spooking fish because you're positioned and presenting your flies from the trout's blind spot. It is entirely possible, however, that your upstream delivery may not be upriver. A back eddy (see chapter 5) is an excellent example: fish may be holding in several locations depending on the direction of the oncoming current. Technically, an upstream presentation involves delivering your flies to a fish that is facing into the current.

Another benefit to fishing upstream is that it is much easier to control drag because your fly line and leader run parallel with the current. If you change your angle of attack, crosscurrent drag becomes a problem. For that reason anglers often use a curve cast, or an S or wiggle cast, to buy a little more time and help ensure a drag-free float.

With repeated false casting or a poorly executed (hard and splashy) delivery, you run the risk of spooking a trout. If your cast hits the water with a lot of surface disturbance, you'll more than likely put the fish down. The ideal upstream cast presents your fly 24–30 inches above your target. If you cast too far upstream, you'll lose accuracy as well as potentially

spook the trout with the thicker part of the leader, butt section, or fly line drifting over the trout's cone of vision.

If you put the fish down, you may need to rest the hole for a while, allowing the fish to regain confidence that it is safe to expose themselves and feed on the surface once again. There is a strong correlation between the density of the hatch and how quickly trout return to actively feeding on the surface. If a heavy hatch is in progress, they will return quickly. If there is a sporadic hatch, you may have ruined your chances.

To alleviate this problem, keep your false casting (see the section on false casting later in this chapter) to a minimum and to the side of your target. This allows you to judge your accuracy, without creating any unnecessary movement or activity above the fish's head. Another common strategy is to cast at a slight angle (rather than straight upstream) so that the fish will see your tippet and fly only when your delivery hits the water, and you won't line the fish.

After the fly has gently landed on the water, immediately place the fly line under your casting index finger. This will allow you to manage your fly line as your fly floats downriver. There is a fine line between good line management and drag. Be careful not to strip the fly line too fast, otherwise your presentation will be traveling faster than the surrounding currents. Flies traveling too fast will have a V behind them from the dragging motion, indicating an unnatural float. But if you allow too much slack to develop you'll have a difficult time setting the hook.

If you're in a heavy hatch (blue-winged olives, pale morning duns, or Tricos), pick out one rising fish and concentrate your efforts on that particular trout. Casting aimlessly, also called "flock shooting," will not produce the same results. It is important to focus on one rising trout at a time. Your delivery must be precise—a foot to the right or left is simply not accu-

Dave Laabo fishes a dry fly straight upstream. An upstream delivery helps reduce the chances of spooking trout because you're casting from the trout's blind spot.

A downstream cast is very effective in some situations, especially in front of logjams where anglers will find trout rising to both pale morning duns and blue wing olives.

rate enough. When a trout is feeding heavily on mayfly duns or spinners, it is typically suspended just below the surface of the water. Because the feeding window is only a few inches in diameter, you must be accurate to catch your fish of choice.

If there are no apparent risers, start fishing in the back of a run and work your way methodically toward the head of the run. If you're fishing attractors or dry/dropper rigs, cover the water thoroughly and meticulously. Break the river down into a grid, covering the water in 12-inch lanes. In theory, you want to show your flies to as many fish as possible. Once your fly has drifted through a given lane, immediately pick up your flies and recast.

One of the greatest advantages to an upstream delivery is the direction of the hook-set. With this approach, you are setting the hook back into the trout's jaw, which more often than not guarantees a good hookup. One of the biggest problems that dry-fly anglers encounter is setting the hook prematurely. Let the trout come up and eat your fly and drop below the surface of the water, then gently lift the rod tip.

Downstream Delivery

A downstream delivery may be anything from a down-and-across to a straight downstream approach. Many anglers incorporate specialty or slack-line casts—the reach cast, S or wiggle cast, and parachute cast—to help offset the drag that is encountered with down-and-across deliveries. In almost all cases, slack is your friend when fishing dry flies in these demanding currents.

Common trout stream conditions will prevent you from effectively making a conventional straight upstream delivery. High, fast water, transition areas that funnel into deep pools, algae-covered rocks that make for treacherous wading, heavy streamside foliage, boulders, logjams, and other protruding obstructions make casting difficult at best. This presents the perfect opportunity for a downstream presentation, allowing you to cast your surface offerings to areas that would be otherwise unreachable with a dry fly.

With this presentation, the first thing the trout sees is the fly, rather than the tippet, leader, or fly line. Be careful with the approach, however, because the trout are facing upcurrent and are easily spooked with a sloppy approach and wading. Wear drab-colored clothing, watch your silhouette closely, and move quietly and carefully.

One of the biggest challenges with a downstream approach is getting a good hook-set. Unlike the upstream delivery, you're pulling the fly away from the trout's jaw rather than back into its mouth. Be patient: allow the trout to sip your fly and drop below the surface before you set the hook. Use a sidearm or sweeping motion to set the hook, trying to gently impale the fly into the side of the trout's jaw, rather than pulling straight upstream.

Up-and-Across Delivery

One of the advantages to an up-and-across presentation is that you can cover twice the amount of water as compared to the two previously mentioned methods, but it requires more fly line and impeccable line management. Anglers will have to mend—redistribute the fly line to offset conflicting currents—because the additional fly line will be lying across a wide range of current speeds. The current may either speed up or slow down the drift, resulting in drag. By mending the fly line upstream or downstream, you can achieve a drag-free float.

In theory, the up-and-across delivery is a mixture of the two previously mentioned techniques. This method incorporates an upstream delivery during the first part of the drift, and a downstream delivery during the second part of the drift. Many anglers skate or skitter a caddis imitation, Yellow Sally, or hopper pattern during the latter part of the drift. By skittering the fly, you may entice an explosive strike.

SPECIALTY AND SLACK-LINE CASTS

Slack can be either good or bad depending on the situation. Unmanaged slack leads to problems, but slack that is pre-

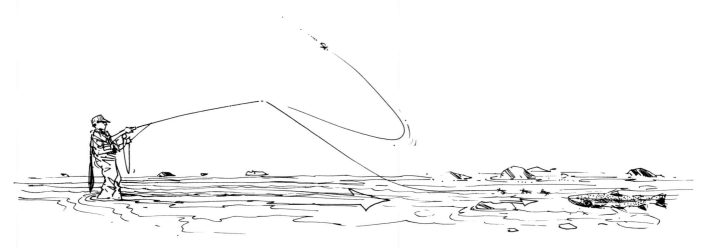

With a downstream presentation, the first thing the trout sees is the fly. This greatly reduces your chances of spooking a rising trout.

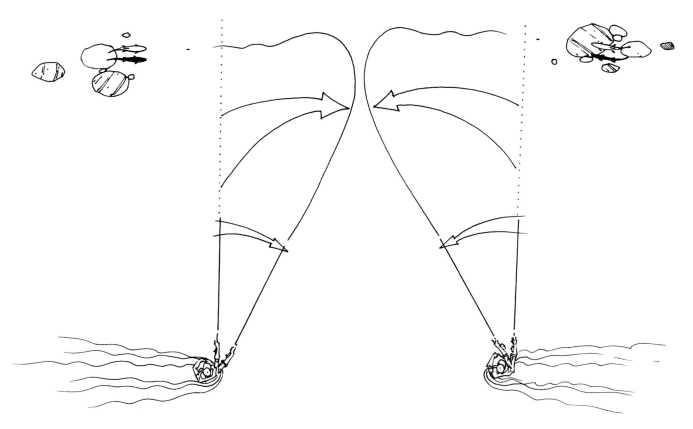

A reach cast will help eliminate crosscurrent drag. If the river is flowing from left to right, you'll need to reach the rod tip to the left by extending your arm upstream and across your body, placing the fly line parallel and upstream of the fly. To the contrary, if the river is flowing from right to left, you'll need to reach the rod tip to the right for the same effect.

planned and controlled to help reduce drag is an important part of fly fishing.

Reach Cast

If you cast your dry fly across a faster current with conventional tactics, you'll get drag immediately—and to make matters worse, you cannot mend quickly enough to offset the conflicting currents. With conventional mending in fast currents, you're constantly interrupting the fly's natural movement by attempting to redistribute the fly line from the belly created by the sweeping current, and the surface disturbance will spook the trout as a result of repeated and sloppy mending.

A reach cast, which is nothing more than an upstream mend in the air before the fly line hits the water, allows you get a 10- to 15-foot drag-free presentation that would be impossible with standard, on-the-water mending techniques. The first thing the trout sees with this approach is the fly—not the leader or fly line—and drag is almost nonexistent because the fly line is floating parallel with the current and, more important, above the fly. Reach mends are especially effective when fishing fast/slow seams, where the water on the opposing bank is slow-moving and glasslike. These stretches of

water near the streambank are excellent areas to find rising trout during midge and mayfly hatches.

The casting stroke is a bit different depending on which side of the river you are positioned, but in both cases, the reach cast is an upstream mend in the air with the primary goal of buying some additional time as you move the rod tip downstream, matching the current speed as your fly floats helpless in the current. If the current is moving from left to right, you'll need to reach or stab the rod tip to the left by extending your arm upstream and across your body, placing the fly line beyond and parallel with the faster moving currents. The ultimate goal is to get the fly to land where you want it, while placing the fly line and leader upstream of your target.

If the current is flowing from right to left, you'll need to reach with your rod tip to the right, accomplishing the same goal.

S or Wiggle Cast

An S or wiggle cast is another slack-line technique that will help offset drag in across, up-and-across, and down-and-across deliveries. S casts are effective when trying to buy some extra time in pocketwater, or on a straight upstream or downstream delivery.

ACROSS-STREAM "S" CAST

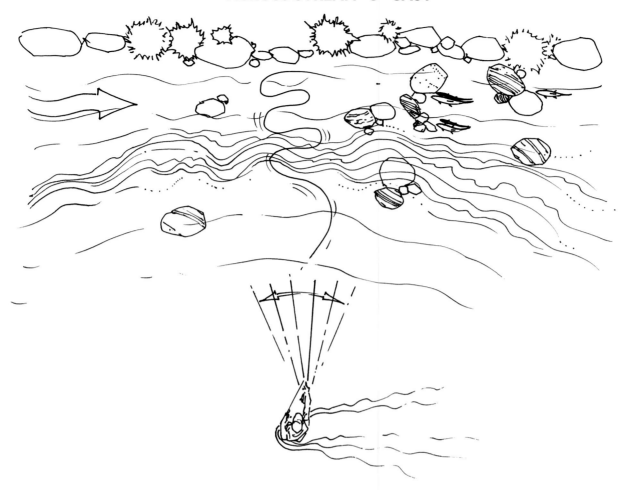

DOWNSTREAM "S" CAST

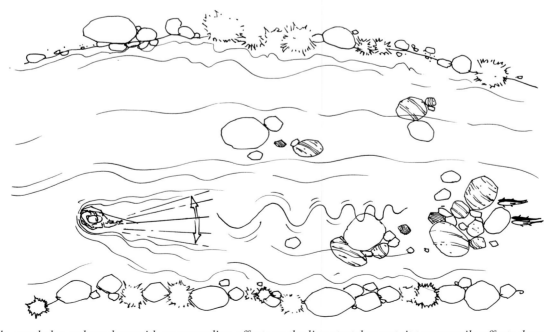

An S or wiggle cast helps reduce drag with an accordion-effect: as the line stretches out, it temporarily offsets drag.

To accomplish a successful S or wiggle cast, wiggle the tip of your fly rod back and forth, parallel to the river's surface, upon completion of your forward casting stroke. The back-and-forth motion should occur as your loop straightens, and just before the fly line hits the water, producing a series of S shapes or snakelike curves that unfold like an accordion. Drag will not become an issue until the line fully stretches out. The slack created will help with a long, drag-free presentation in a wide range of conditions. It is important to manage the fly line under your casting index finger to ensure the proper line control and a good hook-set.

False Casting

False casting is a series of back-and-forth motions in which you keep your fly line in the air, not letting it hit the water prior to the final delivery. A properly executed false cast is nothing more than a pick-up, lay-down cast, with one additional forward and backward stroke that remains in the air. Therefore, the false cast should be comprised of four strokes—two backcasts, a forward cast, and the final delivery.

False casting—if used correctly—is important for several reasons. First and foremost, the back-and-forth motion of false casting drys your fly. Because flies are tied with natural furs and feathers, they naturally absorb water and are affected by fish slime, dirt, and other grime, causing them to sink. If your dry fly sinks, your chances of hooking fish drop dramatically. Occasionally a fish will eat your fly underwater, but it is rare. Dry-fly floatants help immensely, but they are not the only answer to keeping your fly dry. A quick, crisp false cast will dry your fly in seconds by shaking off the water.

Another reason to false-cast is to increase your line speed. Increased line speed helps you make a precise and accurate delivery, and allows you to lengthen your cast by shooting line. False casting also allows you to judge accuracy when pinpointing a specific rising trout. Rather than flogging the water and casting your flies over the trout's head, you can judge accuracy to the side of your target before the final delivery. Trout are wary of moving objects above their heads due to predators, especially birds. The back-and-forth motion above their heads may ruin your chances quickly by putting the fish down. The final reason to use a false cast is that it allows you to change your casting direction. You can change your casting stroke in small increments in the air, adjusting the angle by as much as 180 degrees. This is especially effective if you are fishing to multiple targets.

CHAPTER 8

Streamer Tactics

Streamer fishing is exciting, and in most cases the fish you catch will be bigger than average. But because of all the casting and stripping involved, you earn every fish you catch. Because it is such hard work and catch rates are low, for most anglers streamer fishing accounts for about 10 percent of their overall fishing. But if you are a trophy hunter, streamers become a way of life.

Big fish are opportunistic feeders, and are more willing to hit a streamer than fish under 14 inches. Large trout have to eat a lot of food to maintain their body mass. Large trout are efficient with their feeding: they have figured out that it takes hundreds of midges to equal one minnow or baby trout. Once a trout reaches the 16- to 18-inch range, aquatic insects, crustaceans, aquatic worms, and terrestrials are no longer sufficient to sustain it. Big trout need big food that contains higher levels of protein. Big fish will seldom pass up an opportunity for a sizable meal.

Trout over 24 inches will eat a larger food organism such as a 4- to 6-inch trout, a mouse, or a crayfish and call it good for a day or two. Streamers imitating these foods work best during low-light conditions such as dawn or dusk, on overcast days, or during inclement weather when baitfish leave their protective lies and look for food, and when the large trout (especially browns) feel safe from predators themselves.

This brown trout took a Barr's Slumpbuster. For most of my streamer needs, I use short, 3- or 4-foot leaders of 0X to 3X because the trout are not leader-shy.

Large trout are opportunistic feeders. They'll frequently eat forage items such as minnows, sculpins, leeches, and crayfish.

Some of the best streamer fishing occurs just before dark or at night.

Fish may chase or attack a forage item out of curiosity, or strike at it because they are angry or territorial. Large rainbows and cutthroats in the spring, and browns in the fall, become very territorial for several weeks during the spawn. They will chase and attack anything in their general spawning vicinity, and streamers can be effective at this time.

Some of the best streamer fishing that I have ever encountered on is on the Williams Fork during the latter part of September and October. Fishing is almost easy for a while, as the Williams Fork brown trout are unusually aggressive during this three- to four-week period. The Williams Fork is a small tributary of the Colorado River with nearly 3,500 brown trout per mile. Toss in migrating brown trout from the Colorado, and you have a river crammed with aggressive fish. I've netted 25-plus fish in a single afternoon with black and olive Conehead Woolly Buggers.

I like to fish my streamers with a stiff rod, preferably a 9-foot, 6-weight. The Sage TCR is by far the finest streamer rod on the market. It is a fast-action, stiff rod that delivers the fly with great accuracy and minimal effort. The Orvis Helios in a

9-foot, 5- or 6-weight is another good choice. Stay away from soft-action rods when you're fishing streamers. Your rod needs some good backbone!

If you're floating in a drift boat, carry an extra 6-weight in the event you want to fish with streamers. Walk-and-wade anglers might want to carry a 6-weight as a backup rod. If you carry only one rod, make it a 9-foot, 5 weight. A 5-weight rod will perform moderately well as a streamer rod, but you may have some difficulty loading a heavily weighted, two-fly streamer rig. Under these circumstances, you might opt to fish a single streamer on your 5-weight rod.

Streamer fishing is not always the best way to fool trout. There are some days when you cannot buy a fish on a streamer. Streamer fishing is especially tough during the winter, when the water temperatures dip below 40 degrees. In their lethargic state, trout will not chase streamers, and it is a losing proposition to even consider fishing forage imitations. If there is not a tremendous number of larger forage items in the river you're fishing, then streamer fishing will be tough.

Trout can become selective with their feeding preferences, even with large forage items. When this is the case, observation is important. Look around the shallow areas for signs of forage fish. What size are they? Are they trout fry, minnows, or sculpins? Are there good numbers of crayfish? This information can be beneficial with choosing the correct streamer imitation. When the fish are aggressive or hungry, any kind of heavily weighted or bushy streamer will entice fish, regardless of the retrieve, size, shape, or color. Your success, or lack thereof, will come through trial and error and experimentation.

The most common method of fishing streamers is imparting action into the fly, producing a lifelike movement that represents the natural food organism you are trying to imitate. Streamers are typically tied with bushy materials such as marabou, rabbit fur, pine squirrel hair, and saddle hackles, as well as puffy synthetics, which "breathe" in the water when they are stripped. In many cases, these movements trigger a strike.

At times, however, dead-drifting streamers is effective, especially when the water is off-colored. I have enjoyed amazing results with dead-drifting dark streamers in stained water. Dead-drifting black woolly buggers is especially productive in waters where there is a high concentration of dark stoneflies. According to Steve Parrot, shop manager at the Blue Quill Angler in Evergreen, Colorado: "Dead-drifting streamers under a yarn strike indicator in high water is an extremely effective method of catching trout during runoff. Under these conditions, the fish are usually tucked tight to the bank where the water is a little slower. Dead-drifting Woolly Buggers in these areas gives you a longer presentation and will allow the fly to cover more water and get the fly deeper than conventional stripping tactics."

There are many options to consider when choosing the ideal streamer setup. Many anglers simply use a conventional weight-forward floating fly line and cast tungsten or brass cone-head or bead-head streamers. An additional large split-shot (or more than one, depending on water depth or speed) may be placed on the leader just above the eye of the hook to produce a quicker sink rate. If you're not getting strikes, add more weight to make sure you are down in the trout's feeding zone. Use loop-to-loop sinking-tip line system or an intermediate or sinking-tip line in deeper water where a quicker sink rate is necessary.

Use one or two streamers in your setup. If you use two heavy streamers, I recommend tying them eye-to-eye rather than tying one off the bend of the other. This will give a natural, lifelike movement. Also, I prefer to have the hook point free and clear of any monofilament that may get in the way of a good, clean hookup. With this approach, the action is irregular (twists and turns), rather than a straight, in-line jerky action. The distance between streamers can vary, but 14–16 inches is a good rule of thumb.

Save your old nymphing and dry-fly leaders to be used as streamer leaders down the road. Rather than pulling a brand new leader out of the package and cutting it back to the desired thickness, save your damaged leaders in your leader wallet and label them "streamer leaders." This is a very cost-effective approach to rigging streamers.

My favorite method of fishing streamers is from a drift boat because you can cover literally miles of river. It is important to have a good oarsman who can get you into the desired casting position. Cast your streamer tight to the bank, and immediately lower your rod tip parallel to the water. Place the fly line under your casting index finger to assist with good line management on the retrieve. Strip the line in 4- to 6-inch or 6- to 12-inch increments. The retrieve will vary depending on the food organisms you are trying to imitate. Leeches swim slowly; therefore, your retrieve should be a 6-inch, slow strip. On the other hand, if you are imitating a wounded minnow, the stripping action should be a 12-inch strip with a faster retrieve, to imitate the darting action of the natural bait-fish. Experiment with retrieves and find what works best under the prevailing conditions. If you're not getting many hits, change to a streamer of a different size and color.

Other productive areas to fish streamers are around protruding logs and submerged boulders. Carefully and methodically work your streamer around the structure. You will frequently see large brown trout shoot out of these areas to attack your streamer. You'll quickly learn the importance of accurate casting. If you miss your target or get snagged, you may not get a second chance.

Streamer fishing is considerably more productive in faster, riffled water than in slower sections of the stream. In slow water, the fish have way too much time to inspect your fly. For that reason, you'll get few strikes.

Walk-and-wade anglers can fish streamers upstream, downstream, and up and across. My favorite method is to cast the flies tight to the bank, and allow the streamer to swing in the current. You'll most often get strikes within the first few strips. Vary your retrieve to find what works best. I recommend taking one downstream step with each presentation, which ensures that you cover the water methodically, showing your streamers to as many fish as possible. Repeated casting in one specific location brings diminishing returns. Keep focused, cover the water quickly and thoroughly.

If you're fishing straight upstream, you need to be in the stream and you need a good, long, accurate upstream cast. Immediately place your fly line under your casting index finger, and strip the fly line with the appropriate retrieve. Because the current is moving toward you, you need to get aggressive with your retrieve. Carefully cover the water near the banks, deeper holes, transitional zones, and seams where fast water meets slow water. After a handful of casts in each area, continue working upstream. On smaller tailwaters, fishing from the middle of the stream works because it allows you to fish straight upstream and cover both streambanks.

If you're fishing straight downstream, cover the water in a similar fashion. Because the current is moving away from you, your flies will be riding higher in the water column than with a straight upstream or up-and-across delivery. Because the fastest water is at the surface, you may need to add an additional split-shot or two to get the flies deeper in the water column. After a few casts in each location, take a step downstream, using a searching pattern to cover the water.

One of the most exciting aspects of fishing streamers is the moment leading up to the take. Generally the fish you catch on streamers are big. In the back of your mind there's always the distinct possibility that you may hook and land the trout of a lifetime. I have observed fish as large as 26 inches eating streamers. Unlike nymphing (with the exception of Czech nymphing) and dry-fly fishing, anglers fishing streamers will generally feel an aggressive strike. There will be no doubt that a fish has grabbed your fly. In fact, it is not uncommon to lose your fly on a very aggressive strike.

There are always exceptions to the rule, however. Frequently a trout will hit the streamer between strips when the fly is on the fall and dropping in the water column. The trout is attacking the fly because he thinks it is an injured minnow or other food organism. If this occurs, you may not feel an aggressive strike, as you would if the leader were taut. Therefore, anglers who fish streamers should focus on the end of their fly line, looking for any change in direction or movement. If either occurs, set the hook immediately by lifting the rod tip straight up.

FLY RECIPES

CONEHEAD WOOLLY BUGGER

Hook: #6–10 Tiemco 5263
Thread: 6/0 black UNI-Thread
Tail: Black, olive, and purple marabou
Underbody: Lead wire or substitute (.020) wrapped around shank
Body: Black, olive, or purple chenille (Krystal Flash optional)
Hackle: Black, olive, or purple saddle hackle
Cone-head: Brass

BEADHEAD WOOLLY BUGGER

Hook: #6–10 Tiemco 5263
Thread: 6/0 black UNI-Thread
Tail: Black, olive, and purple marabou
Underbody: Lead wire or substitute (.020) wrapped around shank
Body: Black, olive, or purple chenille (Krystal Flash optional)
Hackle: Black, olive, or purple saddle hackle
Cone-head: Brass

BARR'S SLUMPBUSTER

Hook: #6–10 Tiemco 5263
Thread: 6/0 UNI-Thread, color to match pine squirrel
Tail: Pine squirrel (olive, rust, black, or gray)
Body: Sparkle Braid
Rib: Ultra Wire (Brassie)
Wing: Pine squirrel (olive, rust, black, or gray)
Cone-head: Brass or tungsten

HENG'S AUTUMN SPLENDOR

Hook: #6–10 Tiemco 5263
Thread: 6/0 UNI-Thread, brown
Tail: Brown marabou, with copper Krystal Flash
Underbody: Lead wire or substitute (.030) wrapped around shank
Body: Brown chenille
Rib: Ultra Wire, copper (small)
Legs: Yellow rubber legs (medium)
Cone-head: Brass

CHAPTER 9

Midges and Their Imitations

There are more than 3,500 aquatic species of Diptera in North America, outnumbering all species of mayflies, caddisflies, and stoneflies combined. Midges are part of the large insect order known as true flies, or Diptera, which literally means "flying insects with two wings" (di: two, and ptera: wings). In many tailwaters, aquatic midge larvae and pupae are the most important food for trout, especially in those fisheries located directly below deep, bottom-release reservoirs. Adult Diptera flutter around the stream banks of our rivers and streams, and when conditions are right, they are found—in singles and clusters—on the surface of glassy pools.

In *An Angler's Guide to Aquatic Insects and Their Imitations* (Spring Creek Press, 1995) Rick Hafele and Scott Roederer note: "There is probably no group of aquatic insects that has been able to exploit more habitats than Diptera. Larvae are found in every imaginable type of habitat and are fre-

quently the only aquatic insect present in extreme habitats, such as hot springs to Arctic streams."

That's good news, because without a heavy population of midges, both trout sizes and their total biomass would be severely impacted in our Western tailwater fisheries. In some tailwater fisheries, midges make up as much as 50-60 percent of a trout's diet.

Out of thousands of species of aquatic Diptera that are important to fly fishers, there only three families you should be concerned with: Chironomidae (midges), Tipulidae (crane flies), and Simuliidae (blackflies). In *Nymph-Fishing Rivers & Streams* (Stackpole Books, 2006) Rick Hafele concludes that there are several factors that increase the importance of aquatic Diptera. Aquatic Diptera produce several generations a year, which substantially increases their overall availability to trout. On a daily basis, larvae drift continuously in inconceivable numbers, and pupae twist and turn their way to the

Midges are one of the most important foods organisms for trout. In some tailraces, they make up 50–60 percent of a trout's diet.
DAVE HUGHES

MIDGE LIFE CYCLE

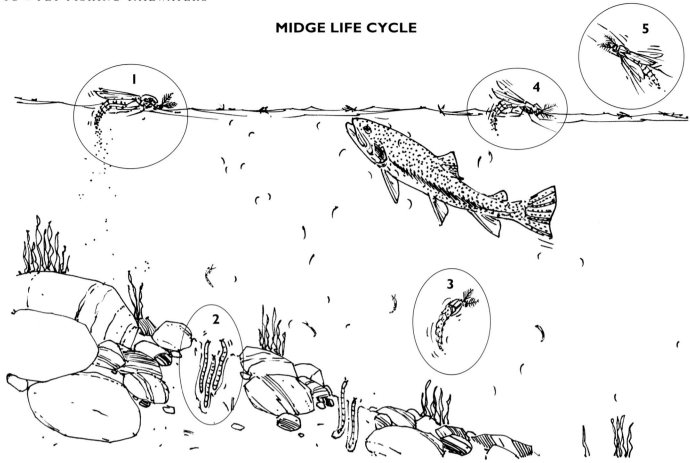

1. *Female adults lay their eggs; the eggs sink into cracks and crevices of the substrate.*

2. *Midges have three to five broods a year. The larvae look like worms and mature in a few weeks.*

3. *Midges go through a complete metamorphosis, and the larvae change into pupae before becoming adults. The larva is inactive for several days, then its bulbous head fills with gases, helping it float to the surface.*

4. *Pupae often drift for long distances before the adults break through the pupal skin.*

5. *The adult flies away to streamside foliage to mate.*

surface, slowly emerging into adults. This provides a steady food source 365 days a year. Many species of aquatic Diptera thrive in slow, sandy, silty areas where other aquatic insects such as mayflies, caddisflies, and stoneflies cannot survive. This in itself, increases their overall numbers and availability to trout.

MIDGES

Sooner or later, if you fish tailwaters on a regular basis, small flies will become a way of life if you want to consistently catch trout. There is a certain appeal to catching large, selective, trout with small flies. The playing field is level, if not slightly tilted in the trout's favor, because there is no room for error when pursuing trout with tiny flies and spider-web-thin tippets.

Twenty-five years ago, on a routine day of fly fishing on the South Platte River below the small community of Deckers, Colorado, I began to appreciate the importance of midges. The South Platte River is a classic tailwater fishery,

supporting a mixed bag of butterball-fat rainbow and brown trout, which make their living eating tiny midges and mayflies. Fishing was excellent that January day—in fact, it was uncharacteristic for the time of year.

It was unseasonably warm (in the mid-60s) and the fish were feeding aggressively in shallow riffles. A strong midge hatch was taking place, and several trout were positioned at the top end of a prime run, intercepting tiny midge pupae as they drifted off a midchannel shelf. My partner Bob Saile made it look easy for a while, as he hooked and landed 14- to 16-inch rainbows with tiny midge nymphs.

We hooked numerous fish in that particular run, so we decided to try another section of river a quarter mile downstream before we took a lunch break. While Saile and I were moving downstream to sample the water just above the fabled Swayback Ranch, I noticed 3-inch-wide bands of black midge shucks on both sides of the river, as far as I could see. I was flabbergasted at the enormous numbers of midges. I reached down, cupped my hand, and scooped up a handful of black debris (midge shucks). I sprinkled a few drops of water into my hand and spread the shucks out for a closer inspection.

After that eye-opening experience, that evening I sat down at my fly-tying vise and tied up a bunch of midge patterns for my next trip to the Deckers area. One pattern that was hot off the vise incorporated a black 8/0 UNI-thread abdomen, a copper wire rib to imitate a midge's segmentation, and a clump of black dubbing to imitate the bulbous thorax area. I named this fly the Black Beauty, and it became a mainstay for me on the South Platte watershed.

It quickly became apparent that midges fill an important void when other aquatic insects are inactive—especially from mid-November through mid-March. Much of this is due to their year-round availability and the dense populations that are found below deep, bottom-release tailwaters. Midges hatch daily in huge numbers and trout feed on them nonstop. As a result of the daily emergence, anglers find trout rising to adult midges 365 days a year, adding to the thrill and excitement of a day's fishing.

Entomologists point out that midges thrive in a wide range of habitats, from warm-water environments unsuitable for thriving trout populations, to trout-friendly ice-cold, bottom-release tailwaters. Midges are found in rivers with an abundance of sediment, including mud, silt, fine gravel, decomposed granite, and sandy bottoms. Large populations of midges are found in weed-rich streams with slow to moderate currents, which are common in many of our Western tailwater fisheries.

Midges are among the few groups of aquatic insects that can complete an entire life cycle throughout the ice-cold winter months. There have been times when I have questioned my sanity while fishing in January, especially at the Spinney Mountain Ranch, where air temperatures often dip well below the freezing mark. I have fished this area during blizzardlike conditions, traveling to the river by four-wheel drive, to arrive at the river and not find another soul. The midges could not have cared less that it was 2 degrees below zero; they just kept on hatching and carrying on with their business as usual.

Anglers can observe rising trout in this world-class section of the South Platte when the outside temperatures are just barely above the zero-degree mark. I have stood there shivering in my frozen waders with hands so cold after releasing a trout that I thought my fingers were going to break off. It was hard to ignore the fact the trout were rising, however; somehow this gave my partner and me the inner drive to battle the elements and persuade a few more trout to eat our size 26 Parachute Adams. My partner Dan Wright summed it up best that day: "It's so cold out here, even the midges have fleece vests on."

There are thousands of species of midges, which makes their identification difficult at best, but for the purposes of choosing an imitation, a midge is a midge. In most cases if you fish something small and black, you'll do just fine. The most prolific group of midges found on Western tailwaters fisheries and spring creeks are from the family Chironomidae. Most anglers simply refer to these midges as Chironomids.

If you fish tailwaters on a regular basis, you'll become a midge fanatic. Rick Danger selects a tiny midge nymph for the Arkansas tailwater below Pueblo Dam.

Imitations for midges range from sizes 14 to 28, with the latter being the most widespread. Not all midges are small. In fact, some species along the South Platte watershed are nearly an inch long. They hatch at the Spinney Mountain Ranch in May and June, and offer predictable midge fishing with pupae imitations. On the whole, however, midges common to Western tailwaters and spring creeks are small.

Many fly fishers underestimate the importance of midges because of their size. A large percentage of midges are so tiny they're nearly impossible to imitate, let alone hook and land a trout on an imitation, so many anglers avoid fishing with them. Successful anglers must adapt their skills to accommodate this important food source. This often means magnification aids and extreme patience. Sometimes it's a major accomplishment just to get an imitation tied on the end of your tippet. As your eyes age, you'll feel the same way—trust me.

In many Western tailwaters, midges make up 50 to 60 percent of a trout's diet. Kim Dorsey caught this beautiful rainbow on a size 22 Mercury Midge in Cheesman Canyon.
CLAY ANSELMO

I learned a valuable tip one day sitting in the Sportsman's Inn in Navajo Dam, New Mexico. I was drinking a cold beer with my buddy Matt Miles after a long, hard day of fishing on the renowned San Juan River. Across the bar were a group of guides who were discussing their day on the river. I must admit, I have been involved in similar discussions.

One guide in particular had a tough day because his client kept losing fish on the size 26 midge pupae. You could see the frustration on his face: it was like he left money on the table. One of his colleagues suggested that he should tie a 26 midge on a size 22 hook (keeping the proportions correct), and that should alleviate the problem. I didn't mean to listen in on their conversation, but I'm always interested in learning some new tricks of the trade. Why didn't I think of that? Of course, that makes total sense—fish a small midge imitation, but

potentially get a better hookup with a larger hook. Since that day, I have tied a lot of tiny midge imitations (size 24 and smaller) on a size 22 TMC 101 hook.

The life cycle of a midge consists of a complete metamorphosis, which is similar to that of caddisflies. The life cycle includes an egg, a larva, a pupa, and an adult. The interval between each phase varies depending on the species and water temperatures. Midges have anywhere from three to five broods during a calendar year. The latter occurs in warm-water environments. If conditions are right, mosquitoes can complete a generation in a week to ten days.

The entire life cycle of a midge is short-lived—only a few weeks between the egg and the emergence of the adult. The average duration for an egg is three to four days; for a larva four to six months; for a pupa five to ten days; and for an adult five to ten days. The warmer the water, the more rapidly each stage develops. During each stage of development, the midge becomes one full hook size smaller. For example, if the larvae were a size 18, the pupae would transform into a size 20, and so on.

In *Spring Creeks* (Stackpole Books, 2003) Mike Lawson writes: "There is perhaps no other aquatic insect that can strike as much fear into the heart of angler as a hatch of tiny midges. I have had this same experience myself, but I have learned from experience that midges aren't all bad." While fishing midges has its challenges, it also has its rewards. Once you learn some tricks and refine your techniques, you'll become more comfortable fishing midges, which are a significant food source for trout in all stages of their lives—larva, pupa, and adult.

Larvae

Midge larvae are found in a wide range of colors—red, pale olive, gray, cream, brown, and black—and are tubelike throughout their uniform, segmented bodies. Larvae do not have jointed legs, which gives their body a wormlike appearance. Some species have unjointed legs, called prolegs, which are short, squishy appendages commonly found in the thorax area or near the rear end of the abdomen. Larvae found in low-oxygen areas are commonly called blood worms because they contain hemoglobin. As their name implies, they are blood-red in color.

The development of larvae varies greatly, but it typically takes several months for larvae to mature. Most midge larvae molt three or more times throughout their development. Larvae feed primarily by being predators, scavengers, and plant eaters. The vast majority of midge larvae are poor swimmers; therefore, they are found at the bottom of the river or under rocks. In tailwaters, larvae sizes range from $^1/_8$ to $^1/_2$ inch in length.

I have had my best success with pale olive and red larvae (blood midge) imitations. To imitate the pale olive larvae, I simply use 8/0 UNI-Thread in Light Cahill color, wrapped around a size 18 TMC 2487 hook, and reverse-rib it with gold wire. Larvae have a wiggling or twisting action that is very difficult for the angler/fly tier to imitate. A curved hook helps

This trout took a midge larva pattern. Midge larva imitations are often effective during a flow increase. LANDON MAYER

recreate this life-like movement that is commonly associated with midge larvae.

Most larva patterns are easy to tie and effective when trying to fool super-selective trout. Red larva imitations can be tied incorporating red thread or red midge tubing with a red thread head. White is a great option when tying larva patterns. One of the best midge larva patterns ever invented is the Miracle Nymph, invented by Ed Marsh—it's a South Platte standby that fools trout throughout the entire South Platte drainage. A simplified version of the Miracle Nymph is the String Thing, another deadly larva imitation.

Larva patterns are not as important as pupa or adult imitations, but they certainly have a time and place. Almost any stomach sample contains a few midge larvae, which proves their importance to trout. Trout will root and dig into heavily weeded areas. I have sat at the Texas Hole, watching with amazement as a trout grabbed a clump of aquatic foliage and shook its head to jiggle free several midge larvae. Other trout quickly joined in on the festivities, eager to eat the wiggling larvae. Biologists stress the importance of midge larvae for young fish, because they depend heavily on midges to get a strong foothold in the wild. Larger fish key on larvae too,

because larvae drift in the currents, especially during any type of flow increase.

In *Fly Fishing the Tailwaters* (Stackpole Books, 1991) Ed Engle notes: "I consider any kind of disturbance in water flows a good reason to put on a larva imitation. A change in water discharge rates from the reservoir will sometimes knock midges into the drift, and since populations of midge larvae can be astronomical in some tailwaters, this can mean a real feeding orgy will occur." Because larvae are weak swimmers, they are highly vulnerable to predation.

I have noticed this in Cheesman Canyon, especially when Cheesman Reservoir is full and spilling. With heavy afternoon rain showers, river levels can rise slowly 50 to 100 cfs (as opposed to opening the gates, which creates an abrupt change). Tributaries above the lake swell, influencing the reservoir level, and increasing the volume that flows over the spillway. The slow increase in water volume kicks loose larvae from the weeds and vegetation, increasing their availability to the fish. Trust me—the trout are constantly looking for free-floating midge larvae in the water.

In *Presentation* (Tomorrow River Press, 1995) Gary Borger points out, "Because there are so many midge larvae,

Trout eat considerably more midge pupae than larvae and adults.

J. Core nymphs with a size Mercury 22 Black Beauty on the San Juan River. Pupae drift for long distances, giving trout an ample opportunity for a good meal.

they form a constant drift. In large rivers like Utah's Green, drift numbers can reach nearly a million per day passing any point in the stream."

Under normal circumstances, I dredge my larva imitations near the bottom, where most midge larvae are found. I have my best success with larva patterns during the first few hours of each day and toward early evening. When I see adults flying around the river, I usually switch to a pupa imitation.

Pupae

The next important phase—to both the trout and angler—is when midge larvae mature and pupate. Pupae have a swollen or bulbous head area, containing the wings and legs of the adult. During the developmental phase, they are protected in a cocoon called a puparium.

Prior to the emergence, the pupae become fidgety, moving up and down in the water column. The pupa wiggles, twists, and turns as it rises toward the surface; a highly reflective area of trapped air near the thorax aids in the ascent. This fidgety action may repeat several times before the final emerging process takes place. This restless behavior will attract the attention of several trout. As the midge emergence intensifies, so does the number of trout that move from nonfeeding lies to feeding lies, suspending themselves in the water column to capitalize on the increased food.

Pupae suspend themselves just below the surface film, giving trout the opportunity to take advantage of an easy meal. The emerging process is slow, so pupae drift for long distances before emerging into adults, presenting some of the best fishing opportunities for the angler.

Most pupa imitations are easy to tie. Simply use a thread body—usually brown or black 8/0 UNI-Thread—and reverse-rib it with gold or copper wire. For the thorax, use some Fine and Dry Dubbing in black or brown. To imitate the increased luster of the thorax area, add a Spirit River Quick Silver Bead (#260). One of the best patterns of all time is the Mercury Black Beauty. Ralph and Lisa Cutter's DVD, *Bugs of the Underworld,* points out the amazing similarity between the

Quick Silver (mercury) Bead and the gas bubble on the pupa as it ascends toward the surface of the water before emergence. J. R. Harris, in *An Angler's Entomology* (1956) wrote, "The tail end of the hatching nymph . . . assumes a much increased luster, and in fact, it strongly resembles a section of glass tube which has been filled with mercury. The effect is even more noticeable in the pupae of those long-legged midges, the chironomids . . ."

When the actual emerging process occurs, the adult pulls itself from the thorax area, then it uses its legs to help push itself through the surface film. The surface tension is tough to negotiate, and the pupa works extremely hard to break through this tough barrier. During this phase, the emerging midge may look bigger than its actual size because of the attached trailing shuck. Many midges do not complete the emerging process and get hung up in the pupal sheath. For that reason, many anglers have found success fishing with cripples or trailing shuck patterns.

Adults

The final stage in the midge's life cycle is the adult. Adults have only two veined wings, which lie straight back over the abdomen when they are at rest. My favorite pattern to imitate resting midges is John Betts's Z-Lon Midge. The fly incorporates a thin thread body, legs made of black or brown Z-Lon, and a wing (which lies straight back over the abdomen) made of Zing Wing. This fly fishes well, especially on slow-moving currents (pools, tailouts, and flats) where the trout have a long time to inspect your artificial offering.

Antennae are another prominent feature of midges. They are typically shorter than the body, but highly visible. Antennae are positioned along the midge's head, and look like a small piece of fuzz. Fly tier Greg Garcia uses frizzed-out Oral-B Ultra Floss to imitate the antennae for his Rojo Midge (pupa imitation). Other tiers like Eric Pettine use poly or Z-Lon to imitate the antennae on adult midges.

Once the adult has emerged, it sits on the water only long enough for its wings to dry. But during this time it becomes an available food source for trout. After its wings have dried, its primary purpose is to mate. A second opportunity for fish to capitalize on midges is during the egg-laying phase, when large mating swarms hover above the water.

Midges fly around the banks of the stream. They mate on streamside foliage, or in a mating swarm. Depending on the species, some midges lay their eggs in the stems of aquatic plants, while others lay them on the water's surface. The egg-laying phase is often the best opportunity for anglers to imitate the adult stage of midges. Small (size 24–26) Parachute Adams, size 24 Cannon's Snowshoe Midge, and size 22–26 Griffith's Gnats are the perfect imposters to fool trout feeding on adult midges.

It is not uncommon to see large clumps of mating midges on the surface of the water. On the Bighorn River (below Yellowtail Dam) I have seen clusters as large as dinner plates. They cling to the sides of your drift boat in huge numbers. Larger Griffith's Gnats (size 14–18) work well for imitating

Anglers can expect excellent midge hatches with inclement weather. This rainbow took a Matt's Midge on the Bighorn during a heavy spring snowstorm. DR. BOB RANDALL

clumps of midges. Although the Griffith's Gnat was originally designed to imitate the stage between the pupa and adult, it fishes well for just about any part of the adult stage. Jim Cannon's Snowshoe Cluster in sizes 20–22 is another excellent choice. Cannon has been intrigued with the properties of snowshoe rabbit fur for nearly 20 years. Cannon has studied the fibers of snowshoe rabbit carefully under a microscope. He noticed that there are 4 to 12 kinks per fiber. "These kinks trap air incredibly well and make the perfect wing for small dry flies and midge clusters," said Cannon.

FISHING STRATEGIES

Most successful anglers fish a two-fly nymph rig and imitate the various stages of the midge life cycle. If the fish are positioned deep and no midge hatch is evident, my recommendation is to fish with one larva and one pupa pattern. If you see suspended trout, or a midge hatch is in progress, fish with two pupa patterns.

As the emergence intensifies, so do the numbers of feeding fish that suspend themselves in the water column and move toward the heads of the gravel bars and midchannel shelves. Successful anglers must keep their strike indicators and weight adjusted according to the depth of the suspended trout. Typically only one size 4 or 6 split-shot is needed when the trout are actively feeding on pupa. Many anglers make the mistake of fishing too much weight, resulting in their pupa imitations drifting below the feeding fish. The importance of keeping your flies in the right feeding zone cannot be overemphasized. Too much weight can be as problematic as not enough.

It has been my experience that a trout feeding on midges will eat ten times more pupae than adults. Many anglers are fooled when they see adults buzzing around the surface and immediately start thinking about fishing with adult midge imitations. Novice anglers conclude that trout are eating adults, when in fact the trout are actually eating pupae just below the surface film.

An effective method is to fish a pupa off a dry fly. Simply attach 14–16 inches of tippet off the bend of a highly visible dry fly such as a Hi-Vis Matt's Midge or Hi-Vis Griffith's Gnat. One of two things happens to indicate that a trout has taken your pupa: a flash appears under your dry fly, or your fly abruptly sinks. If either occurs, gently lift the rod tip to set the hook.

I have recently started fishing a midge pupa under Jack Dennis's Amy's Ant. The fish will sometimes eat the ant as an attractor in an opportunistic phase, but most of the time the large dry performs very well as a strike indicator. In moderate to fast riffles, Amy's Ant will sink abruptly when a fish eats your pupa. The trout seem to be less suspicious of a dry fly than a strike indicator.

There is nothing more exciting—or challenging—than fishing with adult midge patterns. Midges have an aversion to bright sunlight; therefore, they hatch in greater numbers first thing in the morning and again later in the evening during low light conditions. Some of the best midge hatches occur when the sun dips behind the canyon walls and most anglers have gone home for the day.

Trout feeding on midges are generally suspended below the surface, so the feeding window is only a few inches in diameter. Only accurate casts will fool these rising fish. A few inches to the left or right is not good enough. Throw in cruising trout, and the experience becomes extremely challenging. In all cases, cast to individual fish, rather than flock shooting (casting and hoping for the best). If you're casting to nonspecific fish, your odds go down dramatically.

When I fish with adult midges, I use 12- to 15-foot leaders terminating in 7X tippet. My fly selection varies, depending on the situation. If a scum line is present, I recommend a Hi-Vis pattern. We routinely dump our boat in the Texas Hole (the put-in on the San Juan River) just before dark and fish to rising trout eating midges. Noses poke up, go down, poke up, and go down again. The Texas Hole often looks like Sea World because there are so many rising trout.

One of the greatest challenges to evening midge fishing is seeing your fly. If you use a fly with a bright orange indicator, such as a Hi-Vis Matt's Midge or Hi-Vis Griffith's Gnat, you'll have no problem. Another helpful strategy is to slide your fly across the water's surface to locate it. As you slide your fly, the dragging motion produces a "V" on the surface, allowing you to pinpoint it on the water. Once you locate your fly, allow it to drift naturally in the current once again. I typically drop another midge pattern, like a size 26 Parachute Adams, off the bend of the upper fly to increase my odds.

I keep my dry flies coated with Frog's Fanny to keep them riding high and visible. The Frog's Fanny lightens the top side of the midge, making it highly visible on the water's surface. It is important to look for a midging fish. Once you spot a regular surface feeder, cast repeatedly until you hook it or put it down. Sometimes resting the hole for a minute or two will get the fish rising again. If the trout doesn't begin feeding after you've rested the hole for a couple of minutes move on to the next fish.

It is a good idea to have a headlamp or flashlight to help you tie on your flies in the late evening; otherwise, if you break off your rig you may be finished for the night. Plan ahead, and this can make for some of the best dry-fly fishing of the day. Also, having a flashlight helps when trying to wade out of the stream when it is dark. Test your batteries before you enter the river to make sure everything is operating correctly.

CRANE FLIES

Crane fly larvae are easily recognized by the grublike body, which is 1 to 2 inches long with a distinct head that can be retracted into the insect's first body segment. They are medium to dark olive and are often referred to as rockworms. Not all crane flies are aquatic, however. In fact, most species are terrestrial with larvae that thrive in rich soils, such as your lawn.

Nevertheless, aquatic crane fly larvae are diverse and extremely importantly to our running water environments. There are more than 1,000 species, residing near the bottom of our streams, hiding in the sediment and under jagged rubble, logs, and rocks. It's rare to flip over a rock and not see a crane fly larva or two float downriver.

They become an important food source during a flow increase, as the scouring currents knock loose crane fly larvae from the bottom. A weighted, fuzzy dubbed version will fool a lot of trout during a flow increase. The fish are completely aware of their presence, and crane flies work well as attractors during higher stable flows throughout the summer months. I have watched with amazement as large rainbows moved great distances (2 or 3 feet) to eat a free-drifting crane fly larva.

The adults look like gigantic mosquitoes, and their legs are extraordinarily long in relationship to their bodies. They remain close to the water during their adult lives. Females crawl around the rocks and streamside foliage to lay their eggs, and often fall into the river. Their emergence is most prevalent on warm summer afternoons.

FISHING STRATEGIES

Large, spiderlike dry flies skated across the surface can create explosive fishing. When a trout eats a crane fly adult, there is a huge surface disturbance, which eliminates most other food organisms. I must admit that my success with adults has been limited, however. I'll pick up a handful of fish each season with adult crane fly patterns. It's hard to find a good adult crane fly pattern; therefore, I generally come up with my own concoction. Start with a standard dry-fly hook such as a TMC 100 in sizes 12–14. Dub in an abdomen, slightly tapered, with cream-colored Super Fine Dubbing. Use brown hackle tips, spent, for the wings. For hackle, use two turns of light grizzly and one turn of brown rooster hackle. Tom Rosenbauer, Marketing Director for Orvis Rod and Tackle, turned me on to fishing a Dun Variant (Flick style) to imitate adult crane flies. Rosenbauer has had his best success fishing this pattern slightly downstream and skating it to imitate the naturally fluttering behavior of a adult crane fly.

I have had tremendous success fishing with crane fly larva imitations, however. Crane fly larva patterns fish best during higher flows, such as the initial phases of spring runoff. It is hard to go wrong with John Barr's Crane Fly Larva. I'll use it as an attractor and drop a small bead-head, i.e., a Beadhead Pheasant Tail, Breadcrust, or RS2, or Barr's Emerger. It fishes best in faster, shallow riffles and pocketwater.

BLACKFLIES

The chances are pretty good you've seen blackfly larvae and never realized what you were looking at. Blackfly larvae are commonly found in moderate to fast-paced currents, and are present in most of our Western tailwater systems. They attach themselves to rocks, branches, wood, and broad-leaved aquatic foliage. When firmly secured to these structures, they can withstand heavy currents and fluctuating flows.

Blackfly larvae are commonly found in large groups. If the proper conditions exist, you will see thousands of larvae clumped together along the stream bottom. Several hundred are often on a single branch. Look for pupae in the water nearby, living right beside the larvae.

Adult crane flies look like giant mosquitoes. Fluttering adults attract opportunistic trout as they lay their eggs on warm summer afternoons. DAVE HUGHES

Crane fly larvae are important to tailwater anglers. This trout took a Barr's Crane Fly Larva. LANDON MAYER

Blackfly larvae are small—$\frac{1}{8}$ to $\frac{1}{4}$ inch long—and are identified by the swollen or bulbous areas on each end of the abdomen. Rick Hafele notes in *Nymph Fishing Rivers and Streams*: "Larvae are shaped like tiny bowling pins." For the fly tier, blackfly larvae are easy to imitate. Simply tie the abdomen of tan, olive, or black thread, and dub (with dubbing to match the thread) a bulbous, football-shaped hump on each end of the fly. One end of the abdomen should have a noticeably larger bulbous area. You can use Hareline Dubbin Micro Tubing and build a slightly tapered underbody out of thread on each end of the hook.

Larvae do drift from time to time, and when they do, they are an important food source for trout. I found this tidbit of information to be very surprising. Rick Hafele wrote, "Blackflies are second only to blue-winged olives in availability to trout." I have carried blackfly larvae in my fly box for years, but rarely fish them. It's clear that I'm missing the boat. I fish a Black Beauty, however, which has a crossover application for imitating blackfly larvae.

Hafele continues, "The pupae look like little tan slippers topped with a crown of slender gill filaments." During the emerging process, the adults rocket out of their pupal cocoons, floating to the surface trapped in tiny bubbles of air. The adults are known to cause a smutting rise, just below the surface; therefore, they are commonly called reed smuts. In certain drainages, blackflies complete up to six generations in a calendar year, which increases their overall availability to trout. As with other midges, their sheer density makes them a very integral part of a trout's diet. Fishing strategies are similar to those for other midges.

FLY RECIPES

DORSEY'S MERCURY MIDGE

Hook:	#18–22 Dai-Riki 135 or Tiemco 2487
Thread:	White 6/0 Flymaster Plus
Abdomen:	White 6/0 Flymaster Plus thread
Rib:	Fine copper wire, reverse-ribbed
Bead:	Silver-lined glass bead, extra small

DORSEY'S MERCURY BLACK BEAUTY

Hook:	#18–24 Dai-Riki 310 or Tiemco 101
Thread:	8/0 black UNI-Thread
Abdomen:	8/0 Black UNI-Thread
Rib:	Fine copper wire, reverse-ribbed
Thorax:	Superfine dubbing, black

DORSEY'S MERCURY BLOOD MIDGE

Hook:	#18–24 Dai-Riki 270 or Tiemco 200 R
Thread:	8/0 red UNI-Thread
Abdomen:	8/0 red UNI-Thread
Rib:	Fine gold wire, reverse-ribbed
Thorax:	Peacock herl
Head:	8/0 red UNI-Thread, colored with a black Sharpie pen
Bead:	Silver-lined glass bead, extra small

DORSEY'S TOP SECRET MIDGE

Hook:	#18–26 Dai-Riki 125 or Tiemco 2488
Thread:	Brown 8/0 UNI-Thread
Abdomen:	8/0 brown UNI-Thread ribbed with 6/0 white Danville Flymaster Plus thread
Wing:	Poly or Umpqua Fluoro Fibre, white
Thorax:	Superfine dubbing, rust brown

GARCIA'S ROJO MIDGE

Hook:	#18–22 Dai-Riki 270 or Tiemco 200 R
Thread:	8/0 black, red, or light olive UNI-Thread
Body:	8/0 black, red, or light olive UNI-Thread
Ribbing:	Copper wire, small
Thorax:	Peacock herl
Bead:	Silver-lined, ruby
Filaments:	Oral-B Ultra Floss

CRAVEN'S JUJUBEE MIDGE

Hook:	#18–24 Dai-Riki or Tiemco 2488
Thread:	8/0 white UNI-Thread
Abdomen:	Two strands of olive or chartreuse Super Hair, plus one strand of black Super Hair wrapped around the shank
Wing case:	Umpqua Fluoro Fibre, white
Legs:	Umpqua Fluoro Fibre, white
Thorax:	8/0 white UNI-Thread colored with a black Sharpie pen after the abdomen has been wrapped
Head:	8/0 white UNI-Thread (colored with the Sharpie pen), then whip-finished

GRIFFITH'S GNAT

Hook:	#18–26 Dai-Riki 310 or Tiemco 101
Thread:	8/0 black UNI-Thread
Body:	Peacock herl
Hackle:	Grizzly rooster, palmered

PARACHUTE ADAMS

Hook:	#20–26 Dai-Riki 310 or Tiemco 101
Thread:	8/0 gray UNI-Thread
Tail:	Brown and grizzly hackle, mixed
Body:	Superfine dubbing, Adams gray
Wing:	Calf tail
Thorax:	Superfine dubbing, Adams gray
Hackle:	Brown and grizzly, mixed
Note:	The Parachute Adams has a crossover application for blue-winged olive mayflies in sizes 16–22.

CANNON'S SNOWSHOE SUSPENDER MIDGE

Hook: #18–24 Dai-Riki 125 or Tiemco 2488
Thread: 8/0 brown or black UNI-Thread
Abdomen: Brown goose biot or natural Canada goose biot
Thorax: Brown or black beaver (or brown or black Superfine dubbing)
Wing: Snowshoe rabbit's foot hair, mixture of white and black-dyed

CANNON'S SNOWSHOE CLUSTER MIDGE

Hook: #16–26 Dai-Riki 125 or Tiemco 2488
Thread: 8/0 black UNI-Thread
Body: Snowshoe rabbit, black and white, mixed 50-50 with Sparkle Ice Dub, pearl
Wing: Grizzly hackle tied around upright, cluster parachute style, two turns

MATT'S MIDGE

Hook: #18–24 Dai-Riki 310 or Tiemco 101
Thread: 8/0 black UNI-Thread
Abdomen: 8/0 black UNI-Thread (brown or olive thread may be substituted)
Wing: Z-Lon, white, down-wing style
Hackle: Grizzly rooster

BARR'S CRANE FLY LARVA

Hook: #6–8 Tiemco 200 R
Thread: Olive Ultra Thread, 70-Denier
Tail: Pale olive-gray marabou
Rib: 3X tippet material
Shellback: Tan Thin Skin
Body: Gray-olive or tan Arizona Synthetic Dubbing

CHAPTER 10

Mayflies and Their Imitations

When you really stop and think about it, a large percentage of the flies we fish on a regular basis (i.e., Hare's Ears, Adams, Pheasant Tails, RS2s, and Barr's Emergers, to name only a few) were designed to imitate some phase of a mayfly's life. North America boasts more than 600 species of mayflies. Second only to Diptera, mayflies are the most important aquatic insects available to trout.

On tailwaters, the most common mayflies are blue-winged olives, pale morning duns, green drakes, red quills, and Tricos, all of which fill important roles between mid-March and November. A dense population of mayflies is a good indicator

MAYFLY LIFE CYCLE

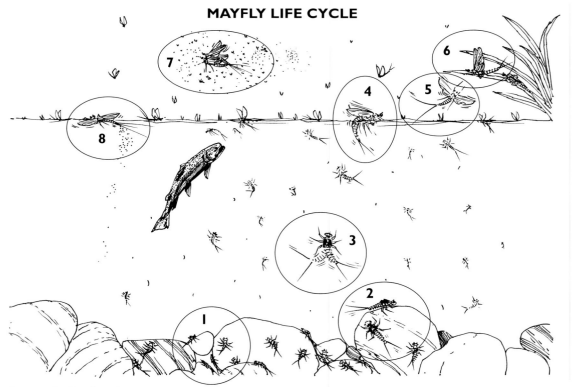

1. Most mayfly nymphs live for about one year.

2. Before emergence, nymphs become active and their wing pads darken.

3. Nymphs twist, turn, wiggle, or swim toward the surface.

4. Nymphs float helpless in the surface film as they transform from emergers into adults.

5. Newly hatched duns fly away to streamside vegetation to hide and to molt into spinners.

6. Spinners have clear, glasslike wings.

7. Males and females form a mating swarm that resembles a cloud of smoke.

8. Female spinners lay their eggs on or below the water's surface.

Clay Anselmo nymphs a transition area with a Baetis *nymph. Transition areas hold huge numbers of feeding trout during blue-winged olive emergences.*

that the water quality is excellent, because they are extremely sensitive to all types of pollution and other contaminants.

Mayflies vary in size from ⅛ inch to nearly 1 inch in length. Adult mayflies have two or three long tails (depending on the species), a thin, curved body, six delicate legs, a small pair of hind wings, which is missing in some species, and a pair of upright wings that make them resemble a sailboat.

Mayflies belong to the Ephemeroptera insect order, which means "short-lived, winged insect." The name is appropriate because adult mayflies rarely live longer than 24–48 hours. Unlike some other forms of aquatic insects, they do not take in fluids; therefore, they dehydrate and perish quickly. The best hatches generally occur during inclement weather, or when conditions are cloudy and overcast.

Mayflies pass through an incomplete metamorphosis. Their life cycle consists of an egg, nymph, and two adult stages known as the subimago (dun) and the imago (spinner). The dun is a winged version that hatches from the nymph. It can be identified by its opaque wings. Adults cannot mate in the winged form; therefore they undergo a second transformation.

One to two hours after the dun emerges, it molts by escaping from its exoskeleton, and it changes into a spinner. The spinner has clear, glasslike wings. Spinners form a mating swarm, and the females deposit their eggs into the stream. Some spentwing mayflies crawl under the surface of the water and lay their eggs on the bottom of the stream. Females deposit anywhere from several hundred to several thousand eggs.

A "spinner fall" is when the female spinners hit the surface of the water and die. This can produce selective feeding, and generally occurs during the morning or late evening. Anglers must fish spentwing patterns if they want to be successful—standard upright-wing patterns will not produce the same results.

NYMPHS

Some of the most aggressive feeding that I have personally witnessed on a trout stream involved trout eating mayfly nymphs. A trout positioned in a prime feeding location can easily eat 15 to 25 mayfly nymphs per minute with very little effort.

Under these circumstances, a trout feeds selectively, focusing on a certain size, silhouette, and color. The selectivity may vary from the beginning to the end of the hatch. Generally the most selective phase is during the peak of the hatch. In such cases, I strongly recommend fishing with two mayfly nymphs in your nymphing rig.

Mayfly nymphs have two or three tails, a segmented abdomen with platelike gills, a single tarsal claw at the end of each leg, and wing pads. Most mayflies have a one-year life cycle. The average duration of the egg phase is one to three months, the nymphal period is eight to eleven months, and the adult phase lasts one to two days. Throughout their development, nymphs molt 20 to 30 times before reaching maturity. The stage between each consecutive molt is referred to as the instar.

Seasonal variations in water temperatures cause different growth rates. The optimum growth occurs when the water temperatures climb above the 45-degree mark. This rise in water temperature only lasts for seven months, leaving only

Trout positioned in shallow riffles can eat 15 to 25 mayflies per minute during a good hatch. Under these circumstances, anglers should focus on choosing a fly of the right size, shape, and color. This trout took a Stalcup's Baetis Nymph during a mayfly emergence.

210 days for a mayfly nymph to reach full maturity. When a mayfly reaches maturity, its wing pads darkenen prior to emergence and its overall activity increases.

For identification purposes, mayflies have been classified into four groups based on their behavior. These include burrowers, clingers, swimmers, and crawlers. Burrowers excavate U-shaped cavities into soft, sandy, and muddy areas; clingers thrive in fast-water environments, and their flattened bodies allow them to cling to the stream bottom; swimmers swim freely around aquatic plants and other structures; and crawlers crawl along the stream bottom clinging to rocks, plants, and other substrate.

SEASONAL EMERGENCE

Western tailwater fanatics can predict mayfly hatches. The first mayfly activity of the year begins with blue-winged olives, most frequently called *Baetis*. These hatches may start as early as mid-March, depending on water temperatures. Temperature variations affect the timing and density of hatches, depending on the drainage you fish.

Anglers often find sporadic to good blue-winged olive hatches between late November and January on the tailwater below Pueblo Reservoir. While the rest of the upper Arkansas watershed is frozen, anglers are fooling trout with blue-winged olive imitations in the 8-mile stretch below the dam. This is uncommon in most drainages—that's why it is wise to check with a local fly shop for up-to-date information, current hatches, and suggested fly patterns before you visit your favorite fishing destination.

John Barr's Emerger is one of America's favorite mayfly nymphs. This version imitates an emerging Baetis *nymph, which is important in Western waters in both spring and fall.*

The next mayfly hatches are pale morning duns, green drakes, red quills, and Tricos. The observant angler notices that the timing of these hatches is very reliable, but a slight deviation in weather can alter the hatches by a few days to a few weeks. The majority of mayfly hatches occur during an eight month period: March through November.

If you're serious about learning more about mayflies, read Fred L. Arbona, Jr.'s *Mayflies, the Angler, and the Trout* (Lyons & Burford, 1989). It was one of my first purchases when I began my book collection many years ago, and I have gained a wealth of knowledge from it.

Arbona's discussion on how a mayfly adapts to its physical environment as the season progresses is interesting. He notes that these changes are brought about by warmer temperatures and drier summer conditions. Mayflies adapt to the environmental conditions by hatching both early and late, to preserve body moisture. In order for a mayfly to molt and shed its skin, it must have the correct moisture content.

In addition, Arbona notes that mayflies get smaller and lighter in color as the season progresses to regulate heat intake during these drier weather patterns. It's amazing how Mother Nature works: the darker mayflies hatch in the spring and fall when outside temperatures are cool, reducing heat intake, and the lighter mayflies hatch during the summer when outside temperatures are noticeably warmer.

EMERGERS

When the mayfly dun extracts itself from the nymphal shuck it is called an emerger. The emerging process—nymph to dun—occurs most frequently in the surface film or on the surface of the water. Some mayflies, however, emerge underwater or on land.

It is important to note that the emerger is neither a nymph nor a dun, but rather is a helpless in-between stage, trapped in the surface film trying to escape the nymphal shuck. This is a key phase for the angler, because trout have the opportunity to take advantage of an easy meal with little effort.

Soft-hackles are good fly choices when trying to imitate emerging mayflies. The hen hackle or partridge simulates the legs and wings of the emerging mayfly. Charlie Craven's Soft Hackle Emerger is perfect for these types of situations. Floating nymphs also work well.

Many mayfly duns never complete the emerging process and get stuck in their nymphal skins. Cool, humid, and overcast conditions are optimum for mayflies to survive the emerging process. Emerging duns drift for long distances before they raise their folded, clumped wings into the upright position. During moist, muggy, and humid weather, the dry-fly fishing is usually nothing less than spectacular. Shane Stalcup's Emerging Dun pattern is a good fly choice during these phases.

Harsh environmental conditions such as intense sunshine, low humidity, and wind dehydrate the mayflies, leaving them to perish quickly. Stillborns or cripple patterns effectively imitate a mayfly trapped in its shuck. As you might imagine, mayflies are extremely vulnerable to the trout during these most inopportune times.

Cripple patterns, such as Bob Quigley's Cripple, are effective when pursuing trout keying on cripples or stillborns. Cripple patterns imitate the part of the mayfly below the surface film (the hook bend is cockeyed or tilted downward, and the emerging wing is protruding above the surface), simulating a mayfly dun trying to escape its nymphal shuck. As mayfly emergers struggle to push their way through the surface tension, they drift long distances and often become hearty meals.

DUNS

When you are fishing, there is nothing more exciting than seeing several fish rising to mayfly duns. The dun is easily identified by its upright, smoky-colored, opaque wings. It remains on the water until its wings have completely dried,

Doug McElveen fooled this San Juan rainbow with a size 20 Mathews's Sparkle Dun. The San Juan River is known for its excellent blue-winged olive hatches.

preparing for flight. If it is overcast, the process is delayed; if it is bright and sunny, development is accelerated.

During inclement weather, mayfly duns can blanket the water. Too many or not enough mayflies can present a few problems. The fishing becomes more challenging as the mayfly hatch intensifies. In a heavy hatch, your fly gets lost in the shuffle: the trout have many to naturals choose from—so naturally your odds drop dramatically. Not enough mayflies can be problematic too. The perfect scenario is a trout that is eating a mayfly dun every three to five seconds. Fish that let a dozen naturals pass by are extremely difficult to fool. Toss in cruising trout, and things get really tough.

The most productive patterns for fooling trout rising to mayfly duns are "no-hackles" such as Mike Lawson's No-Hackle Dun, Craig Mathews's Sparkle Dun, or Jim Cannon's Snowshoe Dun. Conventional patterns like Blue-Winged Olives, Blue Duns, Adams, Parachute Adams, and Parachute Blue-Winged Olives all catch fish too, but not to the same extent as no-hackles, especially on smooth currents and glasslike pools.

Many anglers scoff at duck quill no-hackles because duck quills are not as durable as synthetics and deer hair. Anglers who fish duck quill no-hackles love them, because they simply get the job done. Mike Lawson swears that duck quill fibers are stronger than deer or elk fibers, and that they float and repel water better. Lawson further believes that they double for emergers when they have been fished for some time.

Mayfly duns cannot mate until a second metamorphosis occurs. After emergence—assuming they survive and escape the trout and hungry birds—they fly to streamside flora in search of shelter. Within a few minutes to several days (most mayflies mate the next day), the dun molts, transforming into a sexually active spinner. Moisture content is critical for the transformation to occur because the mayfly's body must remain pliable to break loose from the exoskeleton.

The spinner is identified by its clear, glasslike wings and glossy body. In addition, spinners usually have longer tails and thinner abdomen than duns. Mating flights generally occur during the morning or evening. Male and female spinners are different colors. For instance, the male Trico is solid black, whereas the female has an olive thorax and a black abdomen.

OTHER COMMENTS ON MAYFLIES

Although the various stages of the mayfly's life cycle— nymph, dun, and spinner—are important, fishing with nymphs is the single most productive method of fooling trout between mid-March and late November. Savvy tailwater anglers always include at least one mayfly nymph or emerger in their bag of tricks when assembling their two-fly nymphing rigs. It is important to note that the density of mayflies varies from one Western tailwater to another, and certain tailwaters—like Lees Ferry—are not known for their mayfly hatches.

If feeding trout are keying exclusively on mayfly nymphs, anglers should consider fishing with two mayfly patterns: one nymph, and possibly one emerger. Productive mayfly patterns include: Sparkle Wing RS2s, Mercury Pheasant Tails, Mercury Baetis, Pale Morning Dun Nymphs, Barr's Emergers (both Pale Morning Dun and Blue-Winged Olive), WD-40s,

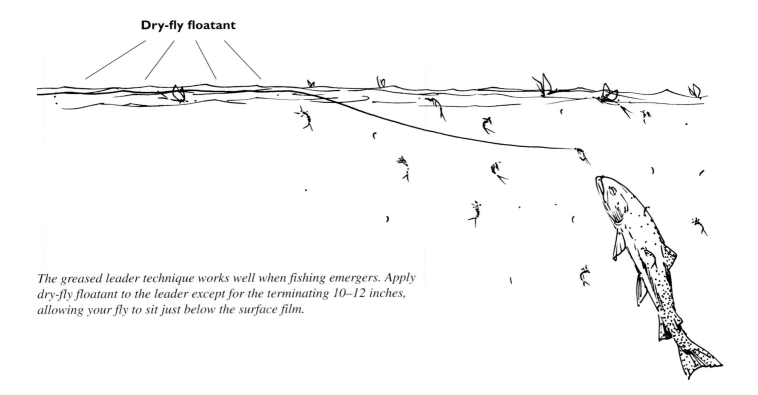

Dry-fly floatant

The greased leader technique works well when fishing emergers. Apply dry-fly floatant to the leader except for the terminating 10–12 inches, allowing your fly to sit just below the surface film.

Blue-winged olives, commonly called Baetis, *produce reliable hatches both spring and fall.* DAVE HUGHES

BLMs, Mighty Mite Baetis, Micro Mayfly Nymph, Jujubaetis, and small Hare's Ears in sizes 18–24.

As the hatch intensifies, look for the trout to move toward the heads of runs, midchannel shelves, and gravel bars. The trout will be suspended in the water column, feeding voraciously in a sweeping manner, eating several mayfly nymphs within a period of several minutes.

As far as emergers are concerned, use emerging patterns that incorporate wings tied of flashy materials like Pearl Braid, or use marabou or cul-de-canard (CDC) for the emerging wing. The riseform (see the section on riseforms in chapter 14 for more specifics) helps clarify whether the trout are eating emergers or duns. The telltale tip that a trout is eating emergers is seeing the trout's back roll above the surface rather than seeing its mouth poke through the surface film. If you see a nose poke through the surface, most likely they are taking mayfly duns. One of the most challenging aspects of trout fly fishing is trying to fool trout that are feeding on emergers. Your best bet is to get as close to your target as feasible, crawling on your hands and knees to your final casting position. Trout have a cone of vision behind them that—in theory—is a blind spot, and sneaking in from behind gives you the best chance of catching a specific trout. If you move quietly and carefully, your target will never even know you're there.

Keep your false casting to a minimum and to the side of your target, as casting repeatedly over the rising trout may put them down or spook them. If you observe a rise in the general area of your fly, gently tip the rod tip to set the hook. Too aggressive a hook-set may spook the entire pool.

Another accepted method is the greased leader technique. Apply dry-fly floatant to the entire leader, with the exception of the last 10–12 inches. This strategy works best when you cast upstream, allowing the emerger to sit just below the surface film. Again, the greatest challenge is determining whether or not you have a take.

If you see trout rise and eat five or six mayflies at a time, it's fairly safe to assume they are eating spentwing mayflies. Tailwaters like the Missouri in Montana; the South Platte River (Spinney Mountain Ranch, Elevenmile Canyon, Deckers, and Cheesman) in Colorado; and the Bighorn River in Montana are known for their great Trico hatches. Large pods of fish sip spinners in wolf packs, creating the perfect scenario for the dry-fly angler.

BLUE-WINGED OLIVES

Blue-winged olives, commonly called *Baetis*, are the first mayflies to hatch in the spring, and the last to emerge in the fall. These sleek, olive-bodied mayflies are multi-brooded, producing two or more broods annually. The emergence of blue-winged olives sets the stage for some of the best dry-fly fishing of the season. Hatches of blue-winged olives start as early mid-March if temperatures are unseasonably warm. The spring hatches generally last until mid-May, often overlapping caddis hatches.

Hatches of blue-winged olives are inconsistent, and sporadic at best. Occasionally, anglers see some blue-winged olives on overcast days, but it is rare. *Baetis* nymphs are a good choice throughout the summer, however, regardless of the hatches and flows.

Baetis nymphs have slender, tapered brown or dark olive abdomens with prominent darkened wing pads. They are abundant in weed-rich tailwater fisheries and spring creeks. *Baetis* are excellent swimmers, especially prior to emergence. Their enormous numbers and energetic behavior make them a key food source for tailwater trout.

Trout may move as far as 18 inches to feed on a swimming *Baetis*, especially in slow, glassy pools, or transitional zones that funnel into a deeper run or pool. Trout often key on the "behavior" of the emerging insects and ignore a dead-drifted mayfly nymph. When this occurs, you can use special lifting techniques, such as the Leisenring Lift, or allow your flies to swing prematurely in the current to entice a selective trout that is chasing emerging *Baetis* nymphs. With standard nymphing tactics, you'll get a lot of strikes on the swing. Don't shortchange yourself: allow your flies to swing in the current, then do a position set, prior to recasting upstream.

My occasional stomach samplings reveal that trout eat considerably more nymphs than duns during the emerging process. I have been on tailwaters like the Madison where mayflies have blanketed the river, and to my surprise, there wasn't a single rising trout. I have heard similar stories about the Missouri in Montana, where there were lots of blue-winged olive duns, but no rising fish. The fish do capitalize on this hatch, but they feed heavily on emergers below the surface instead of on mayfly duns.

This occurs frequently on the North Platte River below Gray Reef. According to Erik Aune, "The fish don't seem comfortable taking blue-winged olive duns . . . especially on

During a blue-winged olive emergence, swinging or lifting up a Baetis *nymph is very effective when trying to imitate the swimming behavior of the nymph prior to emergence.*

the upper reaches of Gray Reef. As you travel downstream, dry-fly fishing is much more predictable, but the water conditions aren't. At Gray Reef, the trout love to eat the emergers. They will stack up in the tight riffles, and a fly will be taken at any depth. They will spook off of brightly colored indicators and large tippet. We like small white or black polypro yarn indicators for this situation. The takes are crushing, and if you get excited and set the hook you will surely break 4X or 5X fluorocarbon tippet. You have to set the hook much like a dry-fly set and simply lift the rod."

This proves that there are times when the nymphs and emergers are so abundant that the trout don't rise to eat the duns on the surface, even when skies are overcast. Under these conditions, a skilled nymph angler will catch the majority of the fish during a blue-winged olive hatch. Having some prior knowledge of when the hatch begins is beneficial, and can be a determining factor for success. About an hour before the emergence, anglers should begin fishing with a mayfly nymph. It's hard to argue with Frank Sawyer's legendary Pheasant Tail Nymph. This pattern should be thin and sparse—bulky flies aren't nearly as effective.

Toward the front end of the hatch, the trout will not be as selective as during the middle of the hatch, and the selectivity tapers off toward the end of the hatch too. Once the hatch is in

progress, you'll see flashes and rising motions in the water. At this point, you may want to consider fishing with two mayfly patterns.

Getting your flies in the right feeding zone is important. Carefully adjust the strike indicator and weight during a blue-winged olive hatch. During the initial phases of the hatch, more weight is required, but as the feeding intensifies, less weight is necessary, and the trout will move farther to eat a swimming *Baetis* nymph. Once you solve this problem, you should be well on your way to catching several trout.

Consistent hatches reappear in September, and they continue through the latter part of October. Sporadic hatches last into mid-November on many drainages. The biggest difference between spring and fall hatches is the size of the blue-winged olives. They are much smaller, as much as one hook size, during the autumn. It's not uncommon to see blue-winged olives from size 24 to 26 late in the season. Stomach samplings reveal that autumn trout key heavily on tiny *Baetis* nymphs, especially at midday. *Baetis* nymphs are good fly choices prior to, during, and after the autumn hatches. My favorite fall *Baetis* nymph is a size 24 Mercury Baetis.

Some of the best blue-winged olive hatches occur during inclement weather—when snow is piling up on the bill of your hat, or you're getting drenched during a nice, steady rain shower. There are a few species of *Baetis* that can complete a full life cycle in ice-cold, nasty weather, when other mayflies have trouble surviving. This is good news for cold-weather anglers suffering from the winter doldrums.

Bar none, the best blue-winged olive hatches I have personally experienced have been on a drizzly day on the San Juan River. Other anglers have shared similar experiences on the Green River in Utah, or the Missouri in Montana, or the Bighorn at Fort Smith, Montana, where pods of trout feed voraciously for several hours on mayfly duns. It's not uncommon to hook and land two dozen trout in a two- to three-hour period under these circumstances. There have been times when I have questioned my common sense, but the dry-fly fishing was so good that the tradeoff was well worth it. I have stood in the stream, shivering—so cold and drenched I could hardly tie on another fly—yet somehow, I kept on casting to rising trout.

Under these conditions, the hatches start early, usually by noon, and may last up to three to four hours. Blankets of blue-winged olives cover the water, and hundreds of fish capitalize on an effortless meal. If you have never experienced a dense mayfly hatch, you owe it to yourself to fish the San Juan River below Navajo Dam. My fishing partners and I have seen times when there were 25 mayfly duns in a square foot of water, and fish were rising everywhere. It was one of the most amazing sights I have ever observed.

If crowded conditions bother you, the Texas Hole (the put-in for the upper float) might not be the best place for you. I have counted more than 30 boats in this hole. This hole is organized chaos: drift boats circle clockwise through a deep run, sprinkled with back eddies, scum lines, and numerous shelves, midchannel shelves, and depressions. It is an unwritten rule not to anchor in the Texas Hole, as this is considered poor etiquette. I must admit that I see a few visiting anglers drop anchor each time I visit, and this disrupts the normal flow in this hole.

If these types of scenarios give you the heebie-jeebies, investigate the Lower Flats, or Baetis Bend, where the crowds are a little more manageable. The Lower Flats is ideal, because you can float and cast to risers, or wade and walk and cover the water methodically. Matt Miles and I fish this section regularly. We trade off at the oars every other fish. Baetis Bend works well from a drift boat too, because you can access water that the walk-and-wade angler has trouble getting to because of the deep currents. It works well to have one angler fishing to rising trout, and the partner manning the oars, because the trout have a tendency to cruise in Baetis Bend.

Blue-Winged Olive Fishing Strategies

It's rare to find an angler fishing without a mayfly nymph in a two-fly nymphing rig. Day in and day out, mayfly nymphs are a good fly choice on the majority of tailwater fisheries. Anglers should use a slightly larger imitation during the spring and summer, and fish with sizes 22 to 24 during the autumn. (See the section on seasonal emergence earlier in this chapter.)

Prior to the hatch, fish with one mayfly and/or one midge pattern. Some anglers use an attractor such as a scud, blood midge, aquatic worm, or crane fly larva. While this strategy can be very effective, fishing two small flies seems to be the best option. As the hatch intensifies, the savvy angler will switch strategies and fish two mayfly nymphs, as the trout switch to feeding exclusively on mayfly nymphs. During this heightened selectivity, anglers will need exact imitations to be successful.

It is always a good idea to carry a few soft-hackles, integrating them into your bag of tricks. I recommend Mercer's Swing Mayfly and Swing Nymph. While soft-hackles are not as popular as dead-drifted tiny mayfly nymphs, they have their time and place. Cast a soft-hackle downstream at a 45-degree angle and allow it to swing in the current. The strikes occur on the last 25 percent of the drift or the swing, as the flies are rising in the water column. The strikes will be noticeable—the leader will tighten quickly and you'll feel the strike.

For dry flies, my all time favorite is Mathews's Sparkle Dun. Trout take it readily, and most important. with confidence. If it's presented on the dead-drift, you'll get very few refusals. In fact, you can sometimes get away with one hook size larger than the naturals, because the no-hackle dry fly sits flush in the film like the actual blue-winged olives. Other popular patterns are Lawson's No-Hackle, Parachute Adams, Hi-Vis Baetis, Cannon's Snowshoe Dun, and Barr's Vis-A-Dun.

Blue-winged olive duns take roughly 24 hours to transform into spinners. Once they molt into spinners, they return to the river to mate, with the females ovipositing their fertilized eggs. I have had limited success when it comes to fooling trout with blue-winged olive spinners. According to Jim McLennan, in his article "Western BWOs" in *Fly Fisherman* (May 2008), "The nymph, emerger, and dun stages are the most important to fly fishers. Spinners are the least important, probably because the females of many species crawl down into the water from a rock or the bank to lay their eggs." I rarely see trout feeding on blue-winged olive spinners, and for that reason, I rarely fish them.

PALE MORNING DUNS

Commonly called PMDs, pale morning duns (*Ephemerella infrequens* and *Ephemerella inermis* are important mayflies on Western tailwaters and spring creeks. Pale morning duns are the equivalent of the "sulphurs" found in Eastern waters. Pale morning duns hatch in midsummer, and the hatches last a few weeks to several months, depending on the drainage and water conditions. The pale morning dun is a medium-size mayfly, about the size of a dime. As the season progresses, pale morning duns become increasingly smaller, as much as one hook size smaller.

One of the determining factors for a good pale morning dun hatch is spring runoff—high water conditions produce poor dry-fly fishing. During extreme seasonal fluctuations, such as drought or other causes of lower-than-normal water, the dry-fly fishing is often excellent. However, nymphs are always an integral part of the trout's diet, regardless of the

Pale morning dun nymphs are important to summer anglers. Dennis Brand plays a thick-bodied rainbow at Spinney Mountain Ranch that he fooled on a size 18 Pale Morning Dun Barr's Emerger.

flow, even during high flow regimes. Don't let the high water fool you—the trout will still eat pale morning dun nymphs.

It's rare to find a good Western trout stream without a heavy population of pale morning duns. Pale morning dun nymphs are crawlers and thrive in stream bottoms that are comprised of smaller rocks, gravel, and thick vegetation. They prefer streams that are slow to moderately paced, and generally hatch in the slower riffles, flats, and pools.

The nymphs vary in color from light brown to dirty yellow. Their undersides are a shade lighter than the tops. One of the key identifying factors of the pale morning dun nymph is that they are much more robust than *Baetis* nymphs. These thick-bodied nymphs are poor swimmers; therefore, they spend most of their time crawling along the stream bottom, feeding on decomposed plant matter and algae.

Pale morning duns become an important food source by mid-June. Depending on the drainage, they may hatch through September. Cheesman Canyon is a prime hot spot for late summer pale morning dun hatches. Since the Hayman Fire, the pale morning duns hatches last clear into the latter part of September.

Emergence times vary from one tailwater to the next. I have observed pale morning duns hatching in the morning on certain drainages (10 A.M. to 1 P.M.), while on other drainages they hatch in the afternoon (1 P.M. to 3 P.M.). Much of this depends

Pale morning duns emerge midsummer. Hatches last a few weeks to several months, depending on water conditions.
DAVE HUGHES

on daytime temperatures, as pale morning dun mayflies try to preserve body moisture prior to emerging. According to Fred Arbona, Jr., *Mayflies, the Angler, and the Trout* (Lyons & Burford, 1989), "Not only do the species move to earlier and later times of the day for the preservation of moisture, they will also get smaller in size and lighter in color. Both of these physical body changes will ensure lower heat absorption which will help the mayflies remain internally cooler during the summer months." On the whole, however, pale morning duns hatch in the morning, as their name suggests.

During the hot summer months, the hatch may begin as early as 9 A.M. and last for an hour or so. Fishing emergers and stillborns can be important, too, as many pale morning duns dehydrate and perish before the emerging process is complete. You'll frequently see small bulges (see the section on riseforms in chapter 14 for more information), which are the telltale signs that the trout are eating emergers. If it is overcast, expect a full-blown hatch, bringing forth huge numbers of mayfly duns. It is not uncommon to see a sporadic hatch of pale morning duns throughout the afternoon. Fish often feed on Yellow Sallies and caddis during the same time frame. Watch the riseforms: caddis and Yellow Sallies tend to produce splashy rises.

On most Western tailwaters, the females are a pale or light yellow with an olive sheen, while the males are more of a rusty yellow color. Colors vary from river to river. On the Frying Pan River, local guides and anglers use pale morning dun imitations that are a rusty orange or pinkish color, whereas on the South Platte pale yellow imitations are more popular. Check with your local fly shop for up-to-date hatch information and effective patterns.

Pale Morning Dun Fishing Strategies
Pale morning dun nymphs begin to move around one hour prior to the hatch, feebly making their way to the surface to break loose from their nymphal shucks. Increased midday activity from the trout is the telltale sign that the fish are beginning to eat pale morning dun nymphs. During this emergence, an assortment of mayfly nymphs in sizes 16–18 will fool trout. The most common patterns are size 16–18 Barr's Emerger, red Mercury Pheasant Tails, Sparkle Wing RS2s, and Mercury Pale Morning Dun Nymphs. My favorite is a Beadhead Flashback Barr's Emerger in size 18. I use a silver-lined gold plastic bead.

Mayfly nymphs fished with a standard two-fly nymphing rig are effective in transitional zones such as midchannel shelves and gravel bars. As the hatch intensifies, so will the number of fish that enter the shallow riffles.

Dry-fly recommendations include Cannon's Snowshoe Dun, Mathews's Sparkle Dun, Stalcup's CDC Biot Comparadun, and Barr's Vis-A-Dun in sizes 16–20. If the fish are keying on emergers, you'll need a Quigley Cripple in a size 16 or 18. Concentrate your efforts in the slower riffles, flats, and pools.

Spinner falls vary from one Western tailwater to another. The spinners are a rusty color and can be identified by their vertical flight pattern. I would carry a few pale morning dun spinners in the event you need them. Typically the spinners show up the next day between 10 A.M. and noon.

GREEN DRAKES
Green drakes (*Ephemerella grandis*) are among the largest mayflies to emerge on Western waters, providing exceptional dry-fly fishing between mid-July and the third week of August. On certain watersheds, the green drake activity may last sporadically into the first part of September, overlapping with caddis, red quills, and blue-winged olives.

I have many fond memories of fishing green drake hatches on the Taylor River above Almont. Almont is a tiny resort community, a fly-fishing hub, and more important, the headwaters of the mighty Gunnison River. The Taylor and East Rivers form the Gunnison at their confluence. The Taylor River is, and always will remain, on the top of my list of favorite Rocky Mountain tailwaters.

Many of my favorite recollections involve my dad and our summer vacations fly fishing the fabled Gunnison Valley. Very few anglers know the Taylor River as well as my father does; in fact, he knows the water better than some of the local guides. We spent hundreds of hours exploring the gems of the Taylor Canyon with large, beefy dry flies—the green drake hatch was the centerpiece of our summer excursions.

Another memory is worth mentioning. One afternoon, my good friend Bob Saile and I were fishing a run called Smitty's Pool (named after Fred Smith, a local angler and buddy of my dad's), a glasslike riffle/run/pool a mile or so above the Almont post office. We arrived at our desired fishing location 30 minutes early, in anticipation of a good green drake hatch. We sat on the tailgate of Saile's faded gray Blazer, sipping an ice-cold beer and simply enjoying the magnificent beauty of the scenic Taylor Canyon.

It was a cool, overcast afternoon, extremely comfortable for that time of year. It started to drizzle at about 12:45 P.M., and the hatch began a few minutes early. Trout aggressively took the mayfly duns off the water as we sat and watched the beginning phases of a green drake hatch unfold. That meant one thing: the beer drinking was over—at least for the time being—because we had trout to catch! As the rain intensified, all hell broke loose, and the harder it rained, the more green drakes hatched, and the surface exploded with rising fish. There were at least two dozen rising trout in the pool, eating green drakes like they were going out of style.

Saile and I were perched on two submerged rocks toward the back end of the pool, like two drowned rats, just hammering fish after fish on size 10 Hen Wing Green Drakes and size 12 Mathews's Sparkle Duns. Once the hatch was over, cocktail hour began again, and we called it a day. What more could you ask for? A long time ago, a good friend of mine summed up a good day of fishing with this comment, "Pigs get fat, hogs get slaughtered." I think you get the point. We relaxed and treasured the great hatch for the rest of the day.

One of the distinct advantages to a green drake hatch is the size of the naturals—even an angler with poor vision will have little difficulty seeing a green drake mayfly or its imitation. Although they look like large sailboats floating downstream, the term "battleship" might be more appropriate when alluding to their size. The green drake hatch is one of the more important summer hatches—both the fish and the anglers look forward to this bonanza.

Green drakes thrive in swift tailwaters, faster spring creeks, and large, quick-moving freestone streams such as the Gunnison, Roaring Fork, North Fork of the South Platte, and the Colorado River. The common denominator for a good green drake population is quick currents, cobble bottoms, logs, and other woody debris, with an abundance of highly oxygenated pocketwater, riffles, and runs. The green drake population varies greatly from one stream to another, so check with local authorities or a hatch chart to see if there is a green drake hatch on the tailwater you are fishing. You'll experience excellent green drake hatches on noted tailwaters such as the Taylor, Frying Pan, and Blue Rivers.

Green drake nymphs are easily identified by the large, robust abdomen, squared-off head, and highly visible dark eyes. Other distinguishing features include long, platelike gills and three distinct tails fringed with hair follicles. The nymphs are crawlers and spend most of their time roaming freely, feeding on decomposed plants and algae.

Their rugged, flat bodies are adapted to fast currents. Rick Hafele notes that the nymphs' dense hairs that cover the underside of the abdomen "function like one side of a Velcro strip, providing a tenacious grip to the bottom rocks." Green drakes hide under bowling ball-size cobble, and rarely get knocked loose from the stream's substrate unless there is a substantial flow increase. When they do get dislodged, they provide a huge meal that no self-respecting trout would fail to capitalize on. For that reason, opportunistic trout are always completely aware of their presence. A two-fly nymphing rig

Green drakes hatch from mid-July to late August, producing some of the best fly fishing of the summer. DAVE HUGHES

with a green drake nymph as an attractor can be very productive during July and August. Effective droppers include a Pheasant Tail Nymphs and RS2s in sizes 18 or 20.

Prior to emergence, the nymphs migrate to slower seams near riffled areas. Most green drakes emerge under the surface of the water or in the surface film. They emerge in mid- to late afternoon, generally between 1 and 3 P.M. In many cases, you could set your watch by the beginning of the hatch.

Green drakes provide excellent dry-fly fishing on the Blue River between the Blue River Campground and Green Mountain Reservoir.

Zach Dorsey caught this beautiful rainbow on a size 12 Mathews's Sparkle Dun during a green drake hatch. Strong hatches of green drakes are often the highlight of the summer season.

As with other mayfly hatches, if the weather is cool and overcast, the green drake hatch may start early, and anglers should expect a very dense hatch. Many anglers use soft-hackles and other wet flies to imitate the emerging duns. Their emergence is slow compared to other Western mayflies. Nymphing with emerging green drake imitations can be effective before and during the hatch.

The hatch is in full swing by July 20. It is not uncommon to see some sporadic green drakes hatching shortly after the 4th of July, but not in enough numbers to get the trout rising with any consistency. During the initial phases of the hatch, the trout feed on the green drakes in an opportunistic fashion, but toward the latter part of July, the trout will feed selectively each afternoon for a two-hour period. Some of the most reliable green drake hatches are in the central Rocky Mountains in the Taylor River, the Frying Pan River, and the Blue River drainages.

The best dry-fly fishing occurs in the moderately deep runs where there are distinct fast/slow seams, in long pools and glides, and in the pocketwater. The strikes are explosive and splashy compared to the normal sipping action that is commonly associated with a mayfly rise. Early in a green drake hatch, you might be fooled into believing the fish are eating caddis because of the splashy rises. Careful observation of the water's surface will reveal the beginning of a green drake emergence. All of a sudden, there will be splashy rises all over the place, and many large green drakes will be visible on the water. It is not uncommon to see trout eating green drakes in pocketwater too. Once again, the strikes are violent, which helps remove some of the guesswork.

The green drake hatch progresses slowly upstream daily; therefore, pinpointing the heaviest part of the hatch is one of the key elements for success. The spinners fall at dark, and in my experience has not proven to be important. The females oviposit in the middle nighttime hours; therefore, I don't even carry green drake spinner imitations.

Green Drake Fishing Strategies

Prior to the hatch, a wide array of nymphs and emergers are effective in fooling trout. This is one of the larger food organisms available to trout, and they eagerly consume their fair share of these large, beefy mayfly nymphs. My favorite patterns include large (10–12) Olive Hare's Ears, size 12 Prince Nymphs, size 12 Twenty Inchers, size 12 Olive Pheasant Tails, and size 10 Stalcup's Beadhead Green Drake Nymphs. I typically drop a smaller mayfly or caddis nymph off my green drake nymph. Effective flies include size 18 Soft-Hackle Pheasant Tails, size 18 Beadhead Pheasant Tails, size 20 RS2s, size 16 Beadhead Breadcrusts, and size 18 Mercury Caddis. Swinging wet flies, or dead-drifting soft-hackles, can emulate the underwater emerging green drake mayfly.

For the dry-fly angler, a size 10–12 Mathews's Sparkle Dun, Cannon's Snowshoe Dun, or a Colorado Hen Wing Green Drake pattern is effective. No-hackles produce best, as the trout take them slowly and confidently. The feeding patterns are irregular, but very noticeable—trust me! The rise-forms are much more aggressive than those associated with blue-winged olives, pale morning duns, red quills, and Tricos.

TRICOS

Tricorythodes—commonly nicknamed Tricos or "Trikes"—often produce a feeding frenzy unequaled by any other mayfly emergence of the year. As this spine-tingling hatch unfolds each season, anglers' emotions flow like a gushing river—they often feel a sense of helplessness and deep despair when attempting to entice the super-selective surface feeders that sip the minuscule mayfly known as the white-winged black. Failure—in this case, not fooling your target—is never taken lightly; in fact, I have watched anglers try to persuade a selective trout in a cat-and-mouse ecstasy for nearly an hour.

Tricos are widespread across America and thrive in tailwaters and weed-rich spring creeks. In many drainages, Tricos are the premier hatches, producing dazzling numbers of mayflies, which take flight in mating swarms that resemble a cloud of smoke or blanket of mist. The hatch is so prolific at times that it brings inconceivable numbers of rising trout to the surface—even the most canny and wary trout will join in on the festivities.

Trico nymphs are crawlers—similar to pale morning duns—and they are inept swimmers. And they are robust; in fact, a good imitation is slightly chunky because of their enlarged triangular gills and short abdomens. Color varies from light olive to dark brown, depending on the watershed.

Unlike blue-winged olives and pale morning duns, there is no single effective mayfly nymph that routinely fools trout prior to the hatch. A few anglers have found that an olive or brown Pheasant Tail Nymph with a full thorax (utilizing peacock eyes, rather than strung peacock herl) produces moderately well prior to the emergence of Trico duns. This strategy shouldn't come as any surprise; Frank Sawyer's legendary pattern is routinely plucked from a trout jaws because it imitates several different mayfly nymphs in a wide range of sizes and colors.

In many watersheds, the Trico hatch begins as early as late June. However, the biggest concentration is between mid-July and the latter part of September. On occasion, I have observed sporadic Trico hatches lasting as late as the first week of November on certain sections South Platte River (Spinney Mountain Ranch and Elevenmile Canyon). Conditions vary depending on the rivers you fish; therefore, I recommend checking with local fly shops for up-to-date information.

The Trico hatch starts out sporadically; in fact, an angler may be fooled into thinking the trout are keying on pale morning dun emergers rather than Trico spinners. Even the riseform is misleading in the initial stages of the hatch because there are so few spinners on the water. Within three weeks the hatch will intensify, producing staggering numbers of fish rising to the surface. In my experience, this mayfly hatch is as regular as a cuckoo clock, and seems to be less affected by bright and sunny conditions, which typically influence other mayfly hatches. Flow fluctuations (an increase or decrease) can change the entire complexion of this hatch. If the flow changes, the hatch typically does not "come off" the way it would on a routine summer day; however, things usually return to normal in a day or two if the flows remain stable. Flow increases are often problematic, as the dislodged grass and other free-floating debris disrupts an angler's normal dry-fly routine.

A Trico hatch in progress is indisputably a thing of beauty; in fact, it may be one of the most valuable learning experiences an angler can ever encounter on a trout stream. It is a golden opportunity for anglers to observe the entire life cycle of a mayfly in a very short time frame. The real challenge, of course, happens when the spinners begin to hit the water at midmorning.

During the summer, the females (with olive abdomens and black thoraxes) start to emerge a couple of hours after dawn (around 7 A.M.). Anglers will have the opportunity to fool a few fish during the initial phases of the hatch, but unlike blue-winged olives and pale morning duns, the Trico spinner fall is the most productive part of the hatch. The males (solid black in color) hatch the evening before, typically between 6 P.M. and dark. This part of the hatch can also

Trico hatches produce feeding frenzies unequaled by any other mayfly hatches of the summer. DAVE HUGHES

be productive, yet many anglers overlook this stage, focusing primarily on the spinner fall the next morning.

Observation is a very powerful tool, but unfortunately, many anglers overlook this subtle aspect of fly fishing. When you first arrive at the river in the morning, millions of Tricos will be sitting on the streamside foliage. Both males and females need a strategic place to rest before they molt and transform into spinners. I have been known to crawl on my hands and knees looking for Trico mayflies, attempting to further understand the subtleties of this phenomenal hatch.

Both the duns and the spinners are on the riverbanks. Duns are named for the distinctive color of their slate gray, opaque wings; spinners are easily recognized by their clear, glasslike wings. The dun-to-spinner phase takes place several minutes after hatching; however, cool morning air can delay the process for up to two hours. Both sexes usually molt by 9 A.M., and that's when the fun begins.

Many anglers believe that Tricos molt in the air. A Trico may take flight with the exoskeleton still attached to the abdomen. When the glistening exoskeleton disengages in the air, many anglers are led to believe that the molting process is actually taking place in flight. Fred Arbona Jr.'s book

Trico mating swarms resemble a blanket of smoke or dense fog.

Mayflies, the Angler, and the Trout (Lyons & Burford, 1989) offers insight into this misconception. Arbona suggests that it is physically impossible for Tricos to molt in flight because of the process by which a dun changes into a spinner. During the molting process, a Trico mayfly's wings are pulled back over the abdomen as the insect exits the exoskeleton, enabling it to fly.

As the mating swarm intensifies, there will still be a few duns hatching; nevertheless, they become less important to the angler as the hatch progresses. Many anglers will continue to fish with dun patterns (with upright wings) with little or no success rather than switching to a small spentwing pattern.

The transition from duns to spinners is usually subtle. The savvy angler will notice a distinct difference in the trout's feeding behavior. Typically a trout consuming Trico spinners will be suspended just below the surface, feeding in a sweeping motion, eating five or six spentwing mayflies at a time before going back under the current. The Trico riseform is unmistakable. Nevertheless, it may go unnoticed if an angler doesn't carefully watch for rising trout in scum lines, transition areas above gravel bars and shelves, and overhanging streamside flora. Many fly fishers carry both male and female spinners. I personally have never observed a Trico feeder that would not be tempted by a solid black spinner fished with a good drift on 7X tippet.

Later in the season (October through November), the nighttime temperatures get cooler, resulting in a new twist to the Trico hatch when the males no longer hatch at night, but rather emerge during the morning. Mornings are cool as the autumn season unfolds; therefore, the hatch is delayed, with duns starting to hatch around 10 A.M. The two hatches evolve into one, lasting for nearly three hours. The males hatch first, followed by the females. Many anglers are fooled into believing that the "second hatch" is the beginning of a nice blue-winged olive hatch. More than any other time of the year, trout key on the duns as a result of their abundance and availability, setting the stage for some very productive autumn dry-fly fishing.

Trico Fishing Strategies

The single most important component to achieving success during a full-blown Trico hatch is to keep your casting position close to your target. The other key ingredients are a long leader (12 to 15 feet), precise accuracy, and a delicate touch.

It's not uncommon to see large pods of trout (20 to 30 fish, and sometimes more) feeding voraciously on Trico spinners. Since the trout are suspended just below the water's surface with a feeding window only a few inches in diameter, your casting must be razor sharp—only a few inches above the rising trout.

Nymphing with a drowned Trico pattern is a strategy that many anglers overlook. I have observed many cases where trout eat three times the number of drowned spinners compared to spentwing mayflies on the water's surface.

Pick out one riser, and cast to it. Flock shooting generally leads to frustration and defeat. If a fish eats a natural just before or after your fly has drifted by, immediately pick up your fly line and recast until the fish takes. Sometimes it's just a matter of figuring out the trout's feeding rhythm. After the fish eats your fly, allow its head go underwater, and then gently lift the rod tip. Many anglers get excited, and break their spider-web-thin 7X tippet with an overly aggressive hook-set.

As the hatch dwindles, you may notice many fish suspended in the water column (in 12 to 24 inches of water), voraciously feeding, sweeping back and forth several inches, capitalizing on a huge meal. This feeding pattern may last up to an hour after the hatch, and unfortunately, many anglers have already called it quits for the day. In my mind, this is one of the most overlooked parts of the Trico hatch. Numerous spinners worn out from the mating process get sucked underwater by the turbulent currents, and a drowned spinner imitation can be very effective.

For years, fishing a drowned spinner has been a guide's secret. I often see more trout feeding on drowned spinners than feeding on the surface. I hate to admit it, but there are times when I fish nymphs during the hatch (especially when I'm guiding clients) because it can be much more productive than flogging the water with dry flies.

During the initial phases of the hatch when the fish are keyed on mayfly duns, any conventional blue-winged olive pattern will fool trout. My favorite flies are size 24 Parachute Adams, size 24 White Poly-Wing Parachute Blue-Winged Olive, size 22 Mathews's Sparkle Dun, and size 24 Hi-Vis Baetis. Keep in mind that this is the easiest part of the hatch to entice a fish to eat your dry fly, simply because of the sheer density of mayflies available to the trout.

As the hatch intensifies, the fishing becomes more difficult. It's not uncommon to observe trout feeding opportunistically during this time frame—eating both adult midges and Trico duns. A size 24 Griffith's Gnat works well when the trout are eating midges during the initial phases of the hatch. As the hatch intensifies, the trout will key on the Trico duns.

My preferences for spinner patterns are a size 24 Poor Witch (named after the late Jim Poor), a size 24 standard Z-Lon Spinner, or a size 24 Stalcup's CDC Spinner. All these patterns can be difficult to see; therefore, I fish with a Compara-dun pattern of some sort. I have caught an amazing number of fish on a size 24 Stalcup's CDC Trico Compara-dun during the spinner fall. Selective trout will take this fly slowly and confidently, regardless of the fly being a "dun imitation."

The fanned "Compara-dun-style wing" also looks like a spinner from underneath. Stalcup's CDC Compara-dun caters to anglers who have difficulty seeing the tiny dry fly, because

Red quill hatches on the Williams Fork are spectacular. Brown trout rise eagerly to red quills on late August afternoons, often into September, overlapping the blue-winged olive hatches.

it rides high in the water, even in a size 26. Another distinct advantage is that it imitates a "sucked-under" spentwing mayfly when you nymph with it.

To fish this fly effectively as a drown spinner, I typically use a standard 9-foot leader, small yarn strike indicator, size 6 split-shot, and two drowned spinners of some sort (CDC Spinner, CDC Compara-dun, or Z-Lon Spinner). If you see a flash—or a fish rising in the water near your strike indicator—set the hook, because most likely a fish has just taken your fly. Watch a 3-foot circumference around your strike indicator, looking for any movement, opening mouths, or flashes from the fish, and set the hook accordingly. This explosive nymph fishing will last for up to an hour after the hatch.

SMALL WESTERN RED QUILLS

Western red quills *(Rhithrogena undulate)* are found in a wide range of conditions from soft, smooth flowing tailwaters to large, untamed freestones. Red quills show up in early August (sometimes late July) and last through September, filling an important gap as the pale morning dun and green drake hatches wind down. Hatches of blue-winged olives overlap the initial phases of the red quill emergence, further compli-

cating things as far as fly selection is concerned. In most cases, the red quills are the larger of the two mayfly duns.

Anglers will find excellent hatches of red quills on the Blue, Frying Pan, and Williams Fork. On the Williams Fork, the red quill hatch is one of the best hatches of the late summer and fall. Each afternoon, you'll find many fish rising along the grassy banks and shaded areas underneath the willows. It is not uncommon to hook a dozen or more trout between 4:30 and 6:30 P.M. with red quills.

August is one of the better months to fish dry flies, as river conditions—flows, water temperatures, and favorable weather—shape up nicely, affording anglers the luxury of getting to all the hard-to-reach places that were impossible to fish during high-water. A wading staff (see chapter 15 for more information on wading staffs) makes the wading process much easier—especially if you are negotiating some swift pieces of pocketwater and other heavy currents where red quill mayflies are found.

One of the best indications that there will be a red quill hatch is identifying the red quill spinners in the late afternoon or evening. If you see reasonable numbers of red quill spinners, assume that the duns are hatching in midafternoon; you might want to investigate this hatch a little more closely.

Many anglers call it quits in mid- to late afternoon, heading home before the hatch actually begins. This is a mistake, however—especially for the dry-fly enthusiast. Red quill hatches can be spectacular; I have observed several instances where anglers have hooked 15 to 20 fish on dry flies during the evening hours.

In certain tailwaters like the Williams Fork River, the red quill hatch is one of the highlights of the summer. Anglers will find consistent hatches every afternoon and evening between 3 P.M. and 5 P.M. Other noted red quill hatches are on the Blue River downstream from Silverthorne, and on the legendary Frying Pan River as well as the Big Hole, Beaverhead, the Henry's Fork, Madison, and Shoshone Rivers.

Red quill nymphs are clingers. They are found in just about any moving water, but seem to favor moderate to fast-paced riffles. The nymphs are tan in color, and have three tails, flat abdomens, six sturdy legs, a robust thorax, and a rounded-off head with prominent eyes. Upon closer inspection, you'll notice that they are well suited for quicker currents.

One hour prior to the hatch, the nymphs begin moving around the stream bottom, becoming increasingly active. As they emerge, they swim halfheartedly to the surface film, where the duns break loose from their nymphal shucks. Depending on the air temperatures (hot and dry summer afternoons versus humid conditions), the duns may leave the water quickly. Wet flies on the swing are productive if the duns are leaving the water too fast to give the angler an opportunity to fool them with dry-fly tactics. A Soft-Hackle Pheasant Tail in a size 16 fished down and across the stream in a searching pattern is a good tactic under these circumstances.

If conditions are overcast, the duns take considerably longer to emerge, drifting for extended distances before their wings dry. This leaves the duns extremely vulnerable; therefore, emerging dun imitations or standard upright-wing (dun) patterns are most effective with a conventional dry-fly approach. I'll frequently drop a Beadhead Soft-Hackle Pheasant Tail off a conventional hackled red quill to imitate the emerging duns (see the section on dry/dropper rigs in chapter 7 for more specifics).

The spinner fall (of red quills from the previous day) begins around 6 P.M., and rusty-colored spinner patterns are effective during the last two hours before dark while the females are ovipositing. The mating flight takes place 10 feet above the streamside foliage, and observant anglers will notice the mayflies moving elegantly up and down in 3- to 4-foot vertical motions. This is tricky fishing, however, because the evening glare can make it hard to detect the spinner fall. If you see trout rising, but cannot discern what they are eating, there is a good chance they are taking red quill spinners.

I have witnessed both splashy and sipping rises during the spinner fall. I am positive in both cases that the trout were eating spentwing Western red quill mayflies. My guess is that the trout are eating them during the descent in their up-and-down flight pattern, when the insects are hovering just above the water's surface. Once the spinners are on the water, the rise-

Kim Dorsey fooled this rainbow on the Williams Fork with a local favorite—A. K.'s Red Quill.

form resembles more of a sipping action, which is similar to the riseform of a Trico feeder. The only difference is that a trout that is keying on red quills eats one or two at a time, versus a Trico feeder that eats five or six spinners at a time.

Red Quill Fishing Strategies

Nymphing prior to the red quill hatch with a size 16–18 Pheasant Tail (or a Beadhead Soft-Hackle Pheasant Tail) is effective, especially in the faster slots and seams. I have mixed results with imitating this mayfly nymph and often find myself fishing the red quill hatch in the dun phase. I am fully aware that the nymphs are moving around an hour prior to the hatch, but I routinely find myself trying to fool rising trout that are eating blue-winged olives. As previously mentioned, the two hatches frequently overlap one another.

This of course presents a few problems, and you must carefully watch which mayfly the trout are eating. Observation can make or break your success. I have found that the larger duns are ignored during the initial phases of the hatch, but as the hatch intensifies and the blue-winged olives diminish, the trout start to key on the larger adult mayflies. In the early phases, I'll frequently fish two different flies: A. K.'s Red Quill dropped with a Mathews's Sparkle Dun (BWO), to cover my bases.

If a dense hatch is in progress, pick out one target and concentrate your efforts on fooling that rising fish. Start in the back of the pool, and methodically work your way upstream. If you're getting refusals with a standard Red Quill imitation, switch to a Compara-dun like Mathews's Sparkle Dun (Red Quill), or try a parachute pattern such as A. K.'s Red Quill. Local anglers and guides prefer the latter. During the peak of the hatch, I switch to two Red Quill patterns, incorporating one of each. I have also fooled trout on Green Drake patterns during a red quill hatch. Don't ask me why, but a Hen Wing Green Drake will often fool trout that are looking up during the red quill hatch.

The spinners fall between 6 P.M. and dark. If Red Quill spinner imitations fail to produce results, there's a good chance the trout have switched to feeding on midges. If this occurs, switch to a #24–26 Parachute Adams or Griffith's Gnat.

FLY RECIPES

CHURCHILL'S SPARKLE WING RS2

Hook:	#18–24 Dai-Riki 310 or Tiemco 101
Thread:	8/0 gray UNI-Thread
Tail:	Elk hair or gray saddle hackle
Abdomen:	Superfine Dubbing, Adams gray
Wing:	Pearl Braid
Thorax:	Superfine Dubbing, Adams gray

DORSEY'S MERCURY RS2

Hook:	#18–24 Dai-Riki 310 or Tiemco 101
Thread:	8/0 gray UNI-Thread
Tail:	Gray hackle fibers, two-thirds shank length
Abdomen:	Superfine Dubbing, Adams gray
Wing:	Z-Lon, white
Thorax:	Superfine Dubbing, Adams gray
Bead:	Silver-lined glass bead, extra small

DORSEY'S MERCURY FLASHBACK PHEASANT TAIL

Hook:	#18–24 Dai-Riki 310 or Tiemco 101
Thread:	8/0 black UNI-Thread
Tail:	Pheasant tail fibers
Rib:	Fine gold wire, reverse-ribbed
Abdomen:	Pheasant tail fibers, tied thin and sparse
Thorax:	Peacock herl
Legs:	Pheasant tail fibers
Bead:	Silver-lined glass bead, extra small

STALCUP'S BAETIS

Hook:	#18–22 Dai-Riki 270 or Tiemco 200R
Thread:	8/0 olive UNI-Thread
Tail:	Partridge
Abdomen:	Olive brown D rib
Thorax:	Superfine Dubbing, olive
Legs:	Partridge
Wing case:	Medallion Sheeting, brown

STOUT'S WD-50

Hook:	#16–22 Tiemco 2488
Thread:	8/0 UNI-Thread, olive, gray, or wine
Tail:	Mallard flank
Abdomen:	8/0 UNI-Thread, olive, gray, or wine
Emerging wing:	Mallard flank, clipped
Wing case:	Mylar tinsel, pearl
Thorax:	Superfine Dubbing, olive, gray, or rust brown

EGAN'S RAINBOW WARRIOR

Hook:	#18–22 Dai-Riki 135 or Tiemco 2487
Thread:	8/0 red UNI-Thread
Tail:	Pheasant tail fibers
Underbody:	8/0 red UNI-Thread
Abdomen:	Krystal Flash, pearl
Thorax:	Metz Sow Scud Dubbing, rainbow
Wing case:	Mylar tinsel, pearl (small)
Bead:	Silver-lined glass bead, extra small

BARR'S EMERGER (BWO)

Hook:	#16–22 Dai-Riki 135 or Tiemco 2487
Thread:	8/0 red UNI-Thread
Tail:	Brown hackle, clipped
Abdomen:	Superfine Dubbing, BWO
Thorax:	Superfine Dubbing, Adams gray
Wing case:	Gray hackle fibers
Legs:	Gray hackle fibers

BARR'S EMERGER (PMD)

Hook: #16–22 Dai-Riki 135 or Tiemco 2487
Thread: 8/0 UNI-Thread, Light Cahill color
Tail: Brown hackle, clipped
Abdomen: Superfine Dubbing, golden brown
Thorax: Superfine Dubbing, PMD
Wing case: Cream hackle fibers
Legs: Cream hackle fibers

DORSEY'S MERCURY BAETIS

Hook: #18–22 Dai-Riki 270 or Tiemco 200 R
Thread: 8/0 UNI-Thread, Light Cahill color
Tail: Black saddle hackle fibers, two-thirds shank length
Abdomen: Superfine Dubbing, BWO
Wing case: Z-Lon, black
Thorax: Superfine Dubbing, BWO
Legs: Z-Lon, black
Head: 8/0 UNI-Thread, Light Cahill color, colored with a black Sharpie pen
Bead: Silver-lined glass bead, extra small

DORSEY'S MERCURY PMD

Hook: #16–18 Dai-Riki 270 or Tiemco 200 R
Thread: 8/0 UNI-Thread, Light Cahill color
Tail: Brown saddle hackle fibers, two-thirds shank length
Abdomen: Superfine Dubbing, PMD
Wing case: Z-Lon, brown
Thorax: Superfine Dubbing, PMD
Legs: Z-Lon, brown
Head: 8/0 UNI-Thread, Light Cahill color, colored with a brown Sharpie pen
Bead: Silver-lined glass bead, extra small

CRAVEN'S JUJU BAETIS

Hook: #16–22 Dai-Riki 125 or Tiemco 2488
Thread: 10/0 White Gudebrod for abdomen
Tail: Brown Hungarian partridge body feathers
Abdomen: Two strands brown Super Hair and one strand black Super Hair
Thorax: 14/0 black thread
Flashback: Wapsi Mirage tinsel (medium), opal
Wing case: Umpqua Fluoro Fibre, gray
Legs: Umpqua Fluoro Fibre, gray
Body coating: Loon Outdoors UV Knot Sense

HI-VIS BAETIS

Hook:	#18–22 Dai-Riki 310 or Tiemco 101
Thread:	8/0 UNI-Thread, Light Cahill color
Tail:	Hackle fibers, medium dun, one shank length long
Body:	Superfine Dubbing, BWO
Wing:	Poly or calf hair, fluorescent pink (chartreuse or orange may be substituted)
Thorax:	Superfine Dubbing, BWO
Hackle:	Medium dun, tied parachute style

MATHEWS'S SPARKLE DUN (BWO)

Hook:	#18–22 Dai-Riki 305 or Tiemco 100
Thread:	6/0 Danville, #60 olive
Tail:	Z-Lon, light olive
Abdomen:	Superfine Dubbing, BWO
Wing:	Deer hair, Compara-dun style
Thorax:	Superfine Dubbing, BWO

MATHEWS'S SPARKLE DUN (PMD)

Hook:	#16–18 Dai-Riki 305 or Tiemco 100
Thread:	8/0 UNI-Thread, Light Cahill color
Tail:	Z-Lon, brown
Abdomen:	Superfine Dubbing, PMD
Wing:	Deer hair, Compara-dun style
Thorax:	Superfine Dubbing, PMD

MATHEWS'S SPARKLE DUN (GREEN DRAKE)

Hook:	#10–12 Dai-Riki 305 or Tiemco 100
Thread:	8/0 UNI-Thread, olive
Tail:	Z-Lon, olive-brown
Abdomen:	Superfine Dubbing, olive
Rib:	Thread, olive
Wing:	Deer hair, Compara-dun style
Thorax:	Superfine Dubbing, olive

A. K.'S RED QUILL

Hook:	#14–18 Dai-Riki 305 or Tiemco 100
Thread:	Danville's 6/0, #60 olive
Tail:	Medium dun spade hackle fibers, one shank length long
Body:	Stripped, light brown dyed rooster neck hackles
Wing:	White turkey, flat
Hackle:	Medium dun hackle, tied parachute style

STALCUP'S CDC TRICO COMPARA-DUN

Hook:	#20–24 Dai-Riki 305 or Tiemco 100
Thread:	8/0 UNI-Thread, black
Tail:	Betts Tailing Material, white
Abdomen:	Black goose biot, or black UNI-Thread
Wing:	CDC, white
Thorax:	Superfine Dubbing, black

CANNON'S SNOWSHOE DUN (BWO)

Hook:	#18–22 Dai-Riki 310 or Tiemco 101
Thread:	8/0 UNI-Thread, olive dun
Tail:	Betts Tailing Fibers, dun, two on each side
Abdomen:	8/0 UNI-Thread, olive dun
Wing:	Snowshoe rabbit hair, dyed dun
Thorax:	Mad River Beaver Dubbing, olive, or Fine and Dry dubbing, olive

CANNON'S SNOWSHOE DUN (PMD)

Hook:	#16–20 Dai-Riki 310 or Tiemco 101
Thread:	8/0 UNI-Thread, Light Cahill color
Tail:	Betts Tailing Fibers, ginger, two on each side
Abdomen:	Goose biot, Sulphur yellow, or just thread
Wing:	Snowshoe rabbit hair, dyed PMD
Thorax:	Mad River Beaver Dubbing, Sulphur yellow, or Fine and Dry dubbing, PMD

CHAPTER 11

Caddisflies and Stoneflies and Their Imitations

CADDISFLIES

While caddis hatches are not as prolific as other hatches found on Western tailwater fisheries, caddisflies are an important food source nonetheless. Depending on the drainage, caddis hatches may be sporadic or heavy, especially during the first two weeks of May. If conditions are right—flows and water temperatures—caddis hatches can last up to the end of June. Caddisflies continue to be significant food organisms throughout the summer, hatching intermittently until the latter part of August.

In the spring, the water farthest from the river's source—whether it's a large freestone originating from a chain of snow-

CADDISFLY LIFE CYCLE

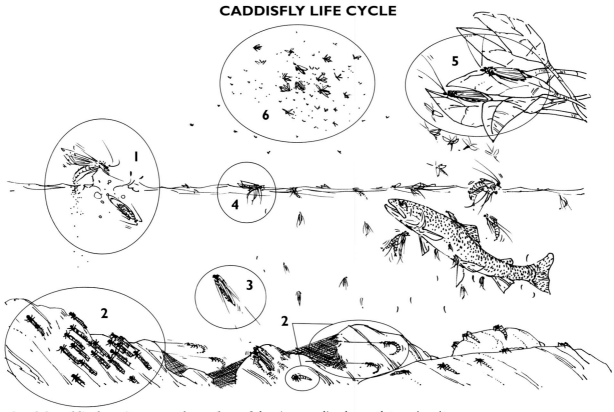

1. *Female adult caddis deposit eggs on the surface of the river or dive beneath to oviposit.*
2. *There are three varieties of caddis larvae—case builders, net builders, and free-living. The larvae mature in about one year.*
3. *The larvae change into pupae. The pupal area fills with gases, helping the caddis ascend to the surface.*
4. *The pupae may drift for long distances before the adults break through the pupal skin.*
5. *Adult caddis live for several days to two weeks prior to mating.*
6. *Mating flights occur most often in the evening.*

Caddisflies are important trout food on many tailwater fisheries. The adults have tent-shaped wings, which are covered with fine, silky hairs. JAY NICHOLS

capped peaks or a crystal-clear, bottom-release tailwater—begins to warm first. As the air temperatures rise, the warming pattern gradually moves upriver. When the river temperature escalates to 54 degrees, caddisflies emerge in huge numbers, blanketing the sky. If a cold snap occurs, the hatch stalls until the water warms once again. Strong blue-winged olive hatches may occur during these inclement weather patterns, so it's entirely possible to have good dry-fly fishing with mayfly duns during the absence of caddis.

Caddis are so well camouflaged that their importance is sometimes underestimated. Gary LaFontaine notes in *Caddisflies* (Winchester Publishing, 1981) that for many species, 40 to 70 percent of the fish predation for the entire caddis life cycle occurs just prior to, or during, the hatch. A trout benefits greatly from caddis hatches because as much as 50 percent of its yearly growth can occur during April and May when the caddis are hatching.

Certain stretches of the South Platte River—Spinney Mountain Ranch and Elevenmile Canyon—have good caddis hatches. Since the Hayman Fire, the caddis hatches have been spectacular on the South Platte drainage near Deckers. Prior to the fire, the caddis hatches were sporadic and unpredictable. For the past two seasons, millions of caddis

blanketed the water, creating a feeding frenzy for both dry-fly and nymph anglers. Scores of rising fish eat size 16–18 Elk Hair, Hemingway, Goddard, and Puterbaugh Caddis for several weeks. The caddis hatches start around the first week of June and last for three weeks. Then the caddis hatch sporadically for the remainder of the summer.

The Shoshone River near Cody, Wyoming is another noted tailwater that has tremendous caddis populations. The caddis hatch, which occurs right in town, is mind-boggling. Anglers find fish rising consistently by mid-April. The Blue River also has reliable caddis hatches, especially in the section above Green Mountain Reservoir near the lower Blue River State Wildlife Area. If the flows are right—200 to 300 cfs—the stretch below Green Mountain Reservoir has a reliable caddis hatch.

On some tailwaters like the Bighorn, the caddis fishing at the end of the summer and early fall is extraordinary. According to veteran guide Dave Opie, "Black caddis has recently been one of the most exciting and prolific hatches on the Bighorn. The hatch generally begins around August 1st and lasts through the end of September. The most effective patterns are size 16 to 20 Black CDC Caddis, Black Elk Hair Caddis, Slow Water Caddis, and dark Hemingway Caddis.

During the black caddis hatch, various patterns of a black caddis pupae are successful nymph patterns."

The biology of caddisflies is similar to that of midges in that both experience a complete metamorphosis. Their life cycle includes egg, larva, pupa, and adult stages. Caddisflies are from the order Trichoptera, which means "hair wing." They share many similarities with the moth family, but keep in mind that they spend the vast majority of their lives in the larval stage.

Throughout a caddisfly's one-year development, the aquatic larva passes through five instars—the stages between successive molts. There are a few species that produce two broods a year, and some case makers actually remain in the river longer than a year. Barr's Uncased Caddis and Oliver Edwards's Hydropsyche in sizes 12–16 are excellent fly choices when trying to imitate the free-living larvae. During the pupal stage the larva is protected in a sealed case or cocoon prior to the development of the winged adult. During emergence, the pupae rip through the cocoons and swim rapidly to the surface. Barr's Graphic Caddis in sizes 14 and 16 is a good choice for pupa imitations. The winged adult remains protected by the pupal cuticles until it breaks the surface tension (meniscus) and becomes airborne.

LARVAE

All tailwater anglers should familiarize themselves with three varieties of caddis larvae: free-living, net makers, and case makers. Free-living caddis roam freely, crawling in the cracks and crevices of the stream substrate looking for food. They prey on other aquatic insects. I have watched this aggressive behavior with amazement in the aquarium in my fly-tying room. Free-living caddis species are readily eaten by trout because they do not build shelters for protection.

Net builders fabricate their homes from fine debris and silk, and collect their food through a filtration process with their silk nets. Case makers, on the other hand, use silt, fine sand, twigs, and other debris to make their houses. Look for cased caddis camouflaged on logs, branches, and rocks where they find protection from predators. Although cased caddis appear to live in a sheltered environment, think again: hungry trout will eat them, case and all. As cased caddis grow, they build larger shelters suitable for their needs. This is done in one of two ways: they build a new shelter, or they add onto or remodel the existing home. Anglers frequently find cased caddis impaled by one of the hooks on their nymphing rigs. If you press on the branchlike case, you'll notice green, wormlike larvae inside the protective case. The larvae have six legs, and generally the head area is much darker than the abdomen.

Trout feed on caddis larvae in a couple of different ways: by catching them drifting in the current or by picking them off logs, branches, and rocks. Their bright green heads protruding from the case draws the attention of hungry trout. Some species of cased caddis look like clumps of small pieces of sand glued together. They attach themselves to rocks, sticks, and logs. The trout's digestive system quickly

The Shoshone River near Cody, Wyoming has an excellent caddis hatch. Matt Miles fooled this Shoshone rainbow with an Elk Hair Caddis during the second week of April.

absorbs the case, silk, and larva, excreting the remains. For that reason, cased caddis are a very important food source in tailwaters and spring creeks. I find myself fishing cased caddis more and more.

My favorite pattern is the Mercury Cased Caddis. It has proven itself time in and time out from the South Platte to the Henry's Fork. The silver-lined mercury bead and bright chartreuse dubbing fool even the most selective trout. You can see these tying materials flash as the fly floats downriver, twisting and turning in the water column. It drives fish nuts! A Beadhead Breadcrust is another great fly to imitate the cased caddis on hard-fished waters. My favorite sizes are 14–18.

In his book, *Presentation* (Tomorrow River Press, 1995), Gary Borger refers to insects that get randomly washed away from their footholds in the stream as constant drift. This may occur day or night, and these food organisms generally occur

Lance Humphries caught this Kamloops rainbow on a Barr's Graphic Caddis during the second week of June on the South Platte near Deckers, Colorado.

in small numbers, but they offer a fairly continual supply of aquatic insects that fill a void when other insects are inactive.

Sometimes aquatic insects drift in great numbers during a 24-hour period based on the behavior of the natural insects. For example, scuds are more active in subdued light—not pitch black, but during low-light conditions such as dawn or dusk. If these organisms move about more, the odds go up that they will get knocked loose and drift in large numbers. The same holds true with caddis: they too avoid bright sunlight, and become more active at dawn and dusk. This phenomenon is called behavioral drift. As you might imagine, the trout feed heavily during these phases.

PUPAE

As the larval phase comes to an end, caddisflies attach themselves to rocks, branches, or logs. A few species dig into the fine sand, gravel, or other organic debris and muck. Caddis that are not case makers build rough homes out of fine sand, gravel, and debris prior to pupating, or they fabricate shelters called "retreats" beside their silken nets.

The true master of caddisflies, the late Gary LaFontaine, wrote in *Caddisflies*, "Using the word pupae to describe the entire period between the larva and adult is actually inaccurate. The metamorphosis of the insect, lasting two to three weeks, consists of three stages: pre-pupa, pupa, and the pharate adult." LaFontaine explained that the pre-pupal phase begins with the closure of the case, when the caddisfly's activity ceases, and it rests for four to six days. During this metamorphosis, and only during this time, the caddis is called

a pupa. They are unavailable to feeding fish until the emerging process begins.

The next transformation occurs when the caddis pulls away from the cuticle; however, the insect still keeps its pupal shape. The caddis begins its final ascent to the water's surface by expelling gas bubbles from beneath its exoskeleton. This helps it float to the surface. The legs assist in the process, pumping like little pistons, as it rockets toward the surface. They may drift for long distances—anywhere from 4 to more than 25 feet—and that is when they are most vulnerable to hungry trout. The metamorphosis continues, and in the next stage they are dubbed "pharate adults" (derived from the Greek word *pharos,* meaning "garment").

Now the caddis is no longer a pupa, but rather an adult covered in a thin, transparent covering. Now they are extremely vulnerable to trout. Once the adult swims to the surface, the pupal skin splits open, and the caddis flies away quickly. Most caddis do not ride on the surface of the river, but there are a few species, called traveling sedges, that skate across the surface of the river until they reach the bank.

ADULTS

The next important stage in the life cycle of the caddis is the adult. Because caddis are sensitive to light, their greatest activity—whether emerging or laying eggs—occurs during low-light conditions such as dawn, dusk, or overcast afternoons. Large swarms of caddis form during the cool evening hours, fluttering several feet above the water's surface. This often triggers a major trout feeding pattern. Some of the best caddis fishing occurs between 6 P.M. and dark.

Adult caddisflies are characterized by their V- or tent-shaped wings, which range in color from tan or beige to dark brown or black. Their wings are one and a half times the length of the body, and are covered with fine, silky hairs. Their long, slender antennae are equal to the length of the body.

Adult caddisflies may live for several weeks because they take in fluids such as water and nectar from flowers to prevent dehydration. Most caddis adults fly away quickly after emergence. Traveling sedges run across the water to reach the streambank instead of flying. When caddisflies are not near the water, they hide in dark, moist places until they are ready to mate.

The mating stage is one of the most important stages for the angler. Caddisflies mate along the river's edge, flying in swarms upstream. The rarely fall into the river during this process, but hover between 5 to 15 feet above the surface. In *Caddisflies,* Gary LaFontaine noted that caddis eggs are deposited in one of four ways: near the river; or below, on, or above the surface of the river.

After mating, many caddis fly back to the water and deposit eggs. They touch their abdomens to the water to release the eggs, while others sit on the water momentarily to accomplish the same goal. Some caddisflies lay their eggs on streamside objects, while others stick masses of eggs under protruding logs, branches, or bridge abutments. Of course, if

An Elk Hair Caddis is an excellent choice when trying to imitate an adult caddis. Gary Hort fishes a dry/dropper rig consisting of an Elk Hair Caddis dropped with a Mercer's Micro Mayfly. If you opt to fish with a dry/dropper, carefully watch your adult caddis pattern for any type of movement or a flash under your dry fly that indicates the trout has eaten your nymph.

this occurs, they are not readily available to trout as a food source. When the larvae hatch they fall into the stream, where they will mature over a one-year period.

Many females dive under the surface of the river and deposit their eggs on rocks, presenting the perfect situation to fish with wet flies. Shane Stalcup's Beadhead Diving Caddis—in both tan and olive—is a good option for imitating this phase.

Caddisfly Fishing Strategies

I have tremendous success with caddis larva and pupa imitations on Western tailwater fisheries. Effective patterns include size 14–18 Beadhead Breadcrust, size 16 Mercury Cased Caddis, size 14–16 LaFontaine's Sparkle Pupa, and size 18 Buckskin and Barr's Graphic Caddis. I catch more trout by far on a size 16–18 Buckskin than any other caddis pattern. A bead-head version works equally well.

I learned the importance of the Buckskin from Bob Saile, who at the time was the outdoor editor of *The Denver Post*. We fished together frequently on the South Platte near Deckers, Colorado. Saile called his variation the Chamois Skin, and was his go-to nymph. His version had a beard tied

from brown hen hackles that swept back from the thorax area to simulate the legs of a caddis.

Before the hatch, a pupa pattern such as Mercer's Swing Caddis fishes very well suspended off a dry fly. Don't be afraid to let the flies swing—you'll get a lot of explosive strikes during the latter part of your drift.

It is a good strategy to just fish a wet fly by itself. According to Mercer: "I designed my Swing Nymph series of wet flies with tungsten beads behind the hackle, as I have been frustrated with patterns that are too light, or too bulky, and plane to the surface on the swing." His presentation with these wets is almost always across and down, and the key is to achieve a balance between a simple, tight-line, arcing swing and a gently "dropping" effect. If fish are going nuts on pupating caddis, you can get away with the former, but if they are more discerning, it won't be as effective. In those situations, Mercer casts across and slightly upstream of the leader and fly. At this point, the rod tip will still be high, as will the rod hand—imagine an outstretched arm using the rod to point to the tops of tall trees on the far bank of the river. Then, as the fly begins its slow swing (slow because of the initial mend that was made), Mercer will both follow that drift with the rod—tracking the swing of the fly with the rod tip—and slowly drop the rod tip, though not so quickly as to introduce strike-disguising slack into the system.

His aim is to create an alternately free-drifting and upwardly rising fly presentation, which is pretty much what the trout are used to seeing from the naturals. Mercer tries to split the difference between simply swinging the fly across the river currents and dead-drifting it like a nymph. As the fly reaches the end of its swing, the rod tip will have finished its descent to a point mere inches above the surface of the water. "The strikes will be completely obvious because you'll feel them. After you feel the strike, lift the rod tip to set the hook," he adds.

I have had tremendous success fishing with a Barr's Graphic Caddis during a caddis emergence. I use this pattern with a standard two-fly nymphing rig. Most of the strikes typically occur on the swing, however. When the trout key heavily on caddis pupae, I fish two of them at a time.

One afternoon I was guiding Steve and Scott Woolley several hundred yards above the Deckers Bridge. Caddisflies filled the sky—they were fluttering above the water's surface, creating a blanket hatch. Caddis were all over our waders, shirts, in our glasses, crawling up our shirt sleeves—one could almost say they were a nuisance. We had double hookups that afternoon—it was one to remember!

There was an occasional splashy surface rise, but for the most part the fish were feeding voraciously—sweeping back and forth 18 to 24 inches to intercept emerging caddis pupae. There were so many emerging pupae that the trout didn't need to rise to the surface and eat the adults. It was a sight to see! We sat up on the road and watched 50-plus fish in one run feeding heavily on caddis pupae. Barr's Graphic Caddis was the right fly that day. In fact, it worked so well that we fished two of them in tandem for several hours. That will be a day that the Woolleys will never forget.

As for dry flies, it's hard to argue with a 16–18 tan Elk Hair Caddis, invented by master fly tier Al Troth. My runner-up choice is a Goddard Caddis, but I sometimes opt not to use them because spinning deer hair is a much more complicated tying process than using dubbing, hackle, and a standard elk-hair wing. Both patterns float well on choppy water, and both perform well when you incorporate a dry/dropper scheme into your bag of tricks. If you're fishing a slow or smooth-flowing river or spring creek, you may want to fish with a Slow-Water Caddis.

Skating or skittering a caddis dry fly can be very effective too. This imitates the hopping, skipping, and fluttering motion of the adult. It's hard to botch a caddis drift, because you can dead-drift, skate, or swing them, and in all cases, trout will eat them. Some of my most explosive strikes with a dry fly have been when I have imparted action to the fly. When the trout won't eat my drifting Elk Hair Caddis, I skate or skitter it—and they hammer it. Experimentation pays huge dividends at the day's end.

Stoneflies are some of the easiest aquatic insects to imitate. Trout eat them in only two stages of their lifecycle—the nymphs and the adult. Adults are clumsy fliers; they often fall into the water, becoming hearty meals for trout. DAVE HUGHES

STONEFLY LIFE CYCLE

1. *Eggs develop into nymphs. Some stoneflies live up to four years so there are always several different sizes of nymphs in the stream.*
2. *Nymphs migrate to the water's edge and crawl out of the water onto a rock, log, or tree. They shed their exoskeletons and become adults.*
3. *Stoneflies mate while at rest on streamside vegetation or on the ground.*
4. *Clumsy adults fall in the water from nearby bushes or while in flight.*
5. *Females oviposit on the surface of the water.*

STONEFLIES (PLECOPTERA)

Though they are an important food source for trout, stoneflies are often overlooked because the nymphs hide in the cracks and crevices of the stream, and the adults prefer staying on streamside vegetation. It's rare to flip over a rock or large piece of sunken wood or log and not find a stonefly or two. A good fast-water seine sample shows their incredible abundance in cobbled areas.

Stoneflies are among the easiest aquatic insects to imitate, because they are available to trout in only two phases: the pre-historic-looking nymph, and the fluttering, egg-laying adult. Similar to clinger mayflies, stoneflies prefer fast currents, and the nymphs crawl freely along the stream bottom. They are poor swimmers and often get dislodged in the current, drifting freely until they get another foothold. This especially holds true during a flow increase, or during the winter months when ice chunks and/or anchor ice disrupt the stream bottom, knocking loose good numbers of stonefly nymphs.

Stoneflies have primitive gill structures, restricting them to highly oxygenated trout streams with a tremendous amount of rubble, debris, and bowling ball-size rocks. For that reason, anglers need to target faster runs, slots, and seams when fishing with stonefly imitations, and stay away from slow areas and deep pools. A dense population of stoneflies indicates excellent water quality.

Stoneflies are members of the order Plecoptera, which means "folded wings." Adult stoneflies can be identified by their two pairs of wings—two hind wings, and two forewings—with the former being one-third longer than the forewings and extending past the abdomen. Adults look similar to the nymphs, with the exception of the clear, folded wings that lie straight back over the segmented abdomen. They become a predominant food source when they come back to the water after mating to lay their eggs.

Stonefly nymphs look primitive—in fact, they are close relatives to the cockroach. Stoneflies have two tails; a

Stoneflies thrive in fast, highly oxygenated water. Contrary to what many anglers believe, tailwaters like the South Platte in Cheesman Canyon have good populations of golden stoneflies.

Dale Anderson fishes a stonefly nymph in fast, oxygenated water. Oliver Edwards's Yellow Sally is a good choice during the summer months.

segmented abdomen; thick, branched gills; three pairs of sturdy, double-clawed legs; two wing pads; a pro-thorax; a rounded head with two noticeable, widely spread eyes; and two slender antennae.

Like mayflies, stoneflies go through an incomplete metamorphosis—in other words, they do not have a pupal stage during their life cycle. The time between the phases—egg, nymph, and adult—depends on the species and water temperatures. The smaller species, such as the early winter stonefly and the Yellow Sally stonefly, have a one-year life cycle, while the larger stoneflies like golden stones and *Pteronarcys* stoneflies (large brown varieties) typically live between three and four years.

The average duration between the laying and the hatching of the egg is two to four weeks; the nymphal stage is seven months to four years; and the fluttering adults may live one to three weeks. Most of the stonefly's life is spent in the nymphal stage; therefore, trout most frequently eat the nymphs. There are several year-classes in the stream at one time, so even after the adults emerge, stoneflies are important trout food.

During the emergence, the nymphs migrate toward the river's edge, and crawl from the river onto land. They crawl up onto a rock, log, or other debris before they hatch. Evidence of stonefly cases on top of rocks and logs will help you determine if a population of stoneflies exists in your favorite tailwater. Trout are very aware of this migration—in fact, they follow the stoneflies to the edges of the stream, capitalizing on this great opportunity.

Similar to caddisflies, stoneflies live between one and three weeks because they are able take in fluids as food. Adult stoneflies rarely fly from the nearby bushes and other streamside flora, unless they are depositing their eggs. Stoneflies do not mate in a mating swarm, but rather breed on land. Most stoneflies release their eggs when the females dip their abdomens into the water. However, there are species that crawl under the surface of the water and deposit their eggs. There are also some stoneflies that lay their eggs above the surface of the water.

Stoneflies range in size from a quarter inch to nearly 2 inches long. Their importance varies from season to season. The early winter stonefly *(Allocapina granulate)* is a small black stonefly (6–8 mm) that is important to anglers in both late winter and early spring. A size 16 black Pheasant Tail imitates this stonefly to a T. You'll see early winter stoneflies crawling around on the snow along the streambanks in February and March, and during this migration period, nymphing with black Pheasant Tails can be excellent.

During the latter part of May and the first part of June, both *Pteronarcys californica,* the giant salmonfly (38–43 mm) and *Acroneuria evoluta,* the golden stonefly (17–23 mm), are important both in the nymphal and the adult stages. This hatch is often on the leading edge of spring runoff; therefore, the dry-fly fishing hinges on the flows. It is not uncommon to catch fish on stonefly nymphs along the river edges, even when the water is off-colored from the higher flows, but dry-fly fishing may not produce the results you are looking for.

This trout took a Barr's Tungstone. John Barr's Tungstone imitates the golden stoneflies that are found in many Western tailwaters. LANDON MAYER

Probably the most important stonefly on tailwaters is *Sweltsa coloradensis,* commonly called the Yellow Sally. For several weeks in early to midsummer these stoneflies emerge on the surface of the water, fluttering and skittering in an attempt to dry their wings while preparing for flight. The riseform is very splashy for that reason. It is not uncommon to see both caddis and pale morning duns hatching at the same time. Try to decipher which food organisms the trout are keying on by their riseforms.

Anglers must fish both Yellow Sally nymph patterns and yellow Stimulators for the adults if they want to be successful. Savvy tailwater anglers will fish Yellow Sally nymphs for a large part of the summer because they are so effective in the faster currents. My favorite Yellow Sally nymph imitations is Oliver Edwards's Yellow Sally. They are especially productive as an attractor in a two-fly nymphing rig.

Stonefly Fishing Strategies
Due to their year-round availability, stoneflies are effective trout producers for much of the year. They are especially productive during the first two weeks of June as they migrate to the edges of the stream to hatch into adults. During this time frame, nymphing can be explosive in a 3- to 4-foot area adjacent to the streambank.

In higher summertime flows, the most effective approach is a straight upstream delivery, managing the fly line under your index finger. Carefully strip the fly line as it floats back downstream to eliminate any drag. This tactic also helps reduce the possibility of spooking trout that are in the shallow riffles. The edges of the stream are the first areas to clear up during spring runoff, so the trout get a little on the edgy side. Cover the water slowly and methodically, then take a few steps forward and repeat the process.

In midsummer, a Yellow Sally nymph imitation such as Oliver Edwards's Yellow Sally Stonefly is the perfect attractor in a two-fly rig. Off the Yellow Sally, drop a small mayfly nymph like a size 18–20 Sparkle Wing RS2 or a Mercury Pheasant Tail.

Sofa Pillows, Fluttering Stones, Stimulators, and Foamulators all imitate golden stonefly and *Pteronarcys* adults. Cast your flies straight upstream, making sure they make a splat when they hit the water. Twitch them occasionally to entice a strike. For Yellow Sally adults, I like size 12–16 Yellow Stimulators fished in shallow riffles that are 18–24 inches deep. I often attach 18–24 inches of tippet off the bend of the Yellow Stimulator and tie on a size 18 Gold Bead Pheasant Tail nymph.

Cast to any splashy rises you see. You will generally not notice any type of regular feeding pattern with the sporadic hatches of stoneflies, so it pays to blind-fish the water methodically.

FLY RECIPES: CADDIS

BARR'S GRAPHIC CADDIS

Hook:	#14–18 TMC 2499
Thread:	6/0 Ultra Thread, olive or tan to match the fly
Body:	Round rubber tubing, green or tan
Butt:	Silver holographic Flashabou
Collar:	Dark natural ostrich
Legs:	Natural Hungarian partridge

BEADHEAD BREADCRUST

Hook:	#12–18 Dai-Riki 730 or Tiemco 5262
Thread:	6/0 or 8/0, brown UNI-Thread
Abdomen:	Red phase ruffed grouse quill
Underbody:	Yarn, black tapered
Hackle:	Grizzly hen, collar style
Bead:	Solid brass, $^1/_8$ or $^3/_{32}$

BUCKSKIN

Hook:	#16–22 Dai-Riki 305 or Tiemco 100
Thread:	8/0 UNI-Thread, black
Tail:	Brown hen hackle, two-thirds shank length
Body:	$^1/_{16}$ thin chamois strip

DORSEY'S MERCURY CASED CADDIS

Hook:	#16–18 Dai-Riki 270 or Tiemco 200 R
Thread:	8/0 UNI-Thread, tan
Abdomen:	Hare's mask and chartreuse Ice Dub
Thorax:	Hare's mask, black
Bead:	Silver-lined glass bead, extra small

PUTERBAUGH'S CADDIS

Hook:	#14–16 Dai-Riki 305 or Tiemco 100
Thread:	8/0 UNI-Thread, black
Abdomen:	2mm foam strip
Wing:	Natural elk
Hackle:	Brown rooster

LAFONTAINE'S SPARKLE PUPA

Hook:	#14–18 Tiemco 900BL
Thread:	8/0 UNI-Thread, brown
Tail:	Antron, tan, one shank length long
Shroud:	Antron, tan, ballooned over underbody
Abdomen:	Antron, green
Wing:	Deer hair
Head:	Dark brown dubbing

ELK HAIR CADDIS

Hook:	#14–18 Dai-Riki 305 or Tiemco 100
Thread:	8/0 UNI-Thread, tan, gray, brown, black, or olive
Abdomen:	Hare's mask, tan, gray, brown, black, or olive
Wing:	Elk hair
Thorax:	Hare's mask, tan, gray, brown, black, or olive
Hackle:	Brown, olive, or gray

FLY RECIPES: STONEFLIES

DORSEY'S PAPER TIGER

Hook:	#4–10 Tiemco 300
Thread:	6/0 UNI-thread, brown
Tail:	Goose biots, black
Weight:	.030 lead wire or substitute along shank
Underbody:	Brown yarn
Abdomen:	Tyvek strip
Legs:	Pheasant tail fibers, three pairs
Thorax:	Brown yarn
Wing cases:	Tyvek strip, cut into a V
Antennae:	Goose biots, black

BARR'S TUNGSTONE

Hook:	#6–14 Tiemco 5263
Thread:	Ultra Thread, golden
Tail:	Goose biots, ginger
Weight:	.020 lead wire or substitute along shank
Abdomen:	Sow-Scud Dubbing, light tan
Rib:	Monofilament tippet material.
Back:	Mottled Oak Thin Skin, golden stone
Thorax:	Sow-Scud Dubbing, light tan
Wing cases:	Thin Skin Mottled Oak, golden stone
Legs:	Grizzly hen saddle fibers, golden
Bead:	Tungsten

OLIVER EDWARDS'S YELLOW SALLY

Hook:	#12–16 Dai-Riki 730 or Tiemco 5262
Tail:	Microfibetts, yellow
Thread:	8/0, Light Cahill color
Abdomen:	Superfine Dubbing, PMD color
Thorax:	Superfine Dubbing, PMD color
Rib:	Monofilament
Legs:	Wood duck or mallard, lemon-dyed
Back and wing case:	Thin Skin, clear, colored with brown Pantone marker

YELLOW STIMULATOR

Hook:	#10–16 Dai-Riki 270 or Tiemco 200 R
Thread:	6/0 UNI-Thread, orange
Tail:	Elk
Abdomen:	Yellow or orange dubbing
Wing:	Elk
Hackle:	Brown and grizzly
Thorax:	Olive dubbing

CHAPTER 12

Crustaceans and Their Imitations

SCUDS, SOW BUGS, AND MYSIS SHRIMP

There are more than 1,100 species of freshwater crustaceans in North America, but only a few are important to tailwater anglers: scuds, sow bugs, and Mysis shrimp. Aquatic crustaceans are commonly identified by their two pairs of antennae, jointed legs, and highly visible segments along the abdomen. Unlike aquatic insects (midges, caddisflies, mayflies, and stoneflies) aquatic crustaceans do not go through an adult phase. As they grow and molt they all look the same, with the exception of their size, until they reach maturity. Because they remain in an aquatic state throughout their entire life cycle, there are no hatches associated with aquatic crustaceans.

Freshwater shrimplike crustaceans, commonly called scuds, are a significant food source in tailwaters and spring creeks. Scuds prefer stable shallow-water environments with steady flows and temperatures, alkaline water, slow to moderate currents, and a lot of aquatic vegetation. There are approximately 90 species of scuds in North America, but the most important group in tailwaters is from the family Gammaridae. One of the most important genera is *Gammarus lacustris*, the freshwater olive scud.

Scuds have a flattened, segmented body, fourteen pairs of legs, antennae, and a tail. They are powerful swimmers, darting around the bottom of the stream. They use their legs and tail to travel along the substrate, twisting and turning as they swim through dense aquatic vegetation. They curl up into a ball for protection when danger arises.

Some of the best scud fishing occurs during higher flows, or periods of extreme variation. For instance, in the South

Scuds are a significant food source on both spring creeks and tailwaters. They thrive in shallow, weed-rich environments with stable flows. DAVE HUGHES

Many tailwaters have heavy concentrations of sow bugs, especially the Bighorn in southern Montana. DAVE HUGHES

Scuds are an important part of a trout's diet on many Western tailwaters. Fish scud patterns when the naturals become active during low-light periods—dawn and dusk— and drift in large numbers. Scud imitations are also effective during higher flows or flow fluctuations, when the naturals get knocked loose.

Platte's Cheesman Canyon, the rising water during the initial phases of spring runoff flushes many of the larger food organisms—scuds, aquatic worms, crane flies, and stoneflies— loose. When fish key on scuds during that time, it can be some of the best nymph fishing of the year.

Tailwater anglers should carry a variety of colors in their scud collections. The most common colors are gray-olive, tan, and orange. When I take seine samples, 99 percent of the scuds are a gray-olive, with the occasional tan scud. To date, I have never collected an orange scud in a seine sample. Stomach pumps reveal a different scenario: frequently you get a mixed bag of orange and olive scuds. It's not clear whether the trout ate the dead scud, which turns orange, or if the scud turned orange in the trout's belly.

Olive scud patterns—especially in larger sizes—imitate larger food organisms such as caddis larvae and crane fly larvae, and are effective in larger sizes (8–10) during the spring, when the flows rise dramatically and many of the larger food organisms become available to the trout in huge numbers.

On certain tailwaters, imitations of tan scuds, *Crangonyx gracilus*, are effective. Back when I first began fishing the Green River in Utah, the 19$^1/_2$ Scud was the ticket (a 50-50 mix of Ligas Dubbing #19 and #20) to catching large trout below the dam. Scuds turn a tannish color when they molt, when the scud sheds its old shell and replaces it with a new, shinier shellback. Trout key on scuds when they are molting because they are soft and easy to eat. Other anglers, including Roger Hill, fish tan scud patterns to imitate trout eggs during the spawning periods. He has had tremendous success fishing tan scuds at the Spinney Mountain Ranch during February and June when the trout move up out of Elevenmile Reservoir to spawn.

Orange scuds are important too. Tailwaters with substantial flow variations due to hydroelectric power generation leave scuds stranded along the streambed when the river drops quickly. The scuds turn orange quickly after they die, and then get knocked loose when the flow rises again, creating a feeding frenzy. This occurs on most Western tailwaters where flow fluctuations occur. Trout also take orange scud patterns as egg imitations, and during the spawning periods, anglers frequently fish a scud as an attractor and drop a mayfly or midge behind it. Concentrate your efforts in the faster slots and seams behind the spawning areas where eggs are drifting downstream.

While not as prevalent as scuds, sow bugs, sometimes referred to as cress bugs, are important in a few Western tailwater fisheries. As the name implies, you'll find populations of sow bugs (cress bugs) in cooler spring creeks and tailwaters where watercress abounds. It's not uncommon to see trout trying to dislodge sow bugs from the rooted vegetation, and capitalizing on this helpless food organism as it floats downstream.

Sow bugs are extremely important on the Bighorn River in Montana below Yellowtail Dam. Sow bugs are typically gray, and have a flat, segmented body and seven pairs of legs that protrude sideways in relation to the abdomen. They are poor swimmers, and often drift long distances without movement if they get dislodged from the aquatic vegetation.

Mysis relicta, commonly called opossum shrimp or simply Mysis, are a major food source for trout, steelhead, salmon, smelt, alewives, sculpins, and many other fish. They naturally inhabit many lakes in British Columbia, and are a critical part of the ecosystem. In 1949, biologists began stocking Mysis shrimp in other lakes and reservoirs. The Colorado Division of Wildlife introduced Mysis shrimp into Dillon, Taylor Park, and Ruedi Reservoirs in the early 1970s to feed the Kokanee salmon residing in the shallow coves and bays. At the time, the Colorado DOW had no idea how these shrimp would impact the trout below these dams.

In one sense, the stocking of Mysis shrimp backfired (as far as a lake food source is concerned), because they feed on zooplankton, which is also a key food organism for small Kokanee and juvenile trout. Unfortunately, Mysis shrimp are light-sensitive and prefer water temperatures of 57 degrees or colder. They migrate daily, residing in the dark, deep areas during the day and swimming into shallow water at night. As it turns out, the Kokanee salmon's behavior is exactly the opposite, eliminating the opportunity for them to partake in the Mysis shrimp feeding frenzy. On a positive note, fishing below the tailwaters where Mysis shrimp were introduced has never been the same, because a shrimp diet makes trout grow big! The section below Taylor Park Reservoir is now called the Hog Trough because of the enormous trout that feast on the high-protein shrimp.

Living Mysis shrimp are transparent, but they die shortly after they hit moving water. You'll frequently see dead Mysis on weed-rich stream bottoms, but stomach samplings show that the fish key on the transparent version. One of the key identifying features is the dark, prominent pair of eyes. During certain times of the year (i.e., the lake turning over, and higher flows during spring runoff), massive numbers of Mysis

Trout that key on Mysis shrimp grow fast and have brilliant colors. John Keefover landed this Taylor River rainbow on a size 18 Mysis shrimp pattern below Taylor Park Dam.
DONNA KEEFOVER

shrimp flow from the base of the dam, causing tremendous trout growth rates, and often gluttony.

Mysis-fed trout are extraordinary colorful—rainbows have brilliant stripes and gill plates, and browns have reddish-orange tails with dazzling red spots. Trout that key on Mysis shrimp can double their weight in one year, and often reach weights of 10 to 15 pounds or better. When large numbers of Mysis are released from the dam, nymphing is explosive. In fact, there are many times when you can fish two Mysis patterns at once. Because they are such a familiar food source throughout most of the year, a Mysis shrimp imitation is a great attractor in your two-fly nymphing rig. When there is a shortfall of Mysis shrimp spurting from the dam above, the large trout often key on tiny midges and mayflies to fill the void.

Crustacean Fishing Strategies

Fishing with these crustacean patterns requires no special tactics, because most of the time you'll be bouncing them along the stream bottom. Scuds, sow bugs, and Mysis are most often fished as attractors in a two-fly nymphing rig. Many anglers do well fishing scud and sow bug imitations around thick weed beds, where fish are accustomed to feeding on them. Off the scud, most anglers will drop a small mayfly or midge pupa.

On occasion, you can fish a floating orange scud in certain rivers like the Colorado at Lees Ferry. Terry Gunn developed

Anglers at Lees Ferry routinely fish scud patterns dropped with a midge pattern such as a Zebra Midge. Dr. Eric Atha plays a thick-bodied Lees Ferry rainbow that he fooled with a scud pattern on a gravel bar below Glen Canyon Dam.

a pattern he calls the Unbelievable. According to Gunn: "The Unbelievable was developed to imitate a dead floating scud. When the scuds desiccate, they turn orange and float. It is a rare occurrence and takes specific water flow regimes to produce this 'hatch.' First we need sustained high water flows, which allow the scud populations to develop along the littoral areas of the river, followed by a short low-water episode, which dries up these areas and desiccates the scuds . . . the best time frame for this low water is two or three days. Then another episode of higher water arrives, which washes the dead scuds into the river. When this occurs the fish key in on the floating scuds and the fishing is wide open. I have seen one-hundred-plus-fish-per-rod days in this situation. It is rare, unpredictable, and crazy-good when it happens."

To fool trout rooting for sow bugs, remove your strike indicator (to help prevent spooking the trout) and time your casting with its feeding pattern as the trout drops back to feed on the sow bugs that are floating downstream. Get into a position where you can see the trout feeding; but maintain stealth, and make a series of quick, accurate casts. Set the hook when the trout is eating, shifting, rising, or flashing—all signs that it may have taken your fly.

FLY RECIPES

DORSEY'S UV SCUD

Hook:	#10–18 Dai-Riki 135 or Tiemco 2457
Thread:	6/0 UNI-Thread, orange, olive, or tan
Tail:	Orange, olive, or tan poly or Z-Lon
Body:	UV Hareline Dubbin, orange, green, or tan
Shellback:	Scud back or plastic bag strip (Ziploc bag)
Antennae:	Orange, olive, or tan poly or Z-Lon

SOW BUG

Hook: #16–18 Dai-Riki 135 or Tiemco 2487
Thread: 8/0 UNI-Thread, gray
Tail: Goose biots, gray
Abdomen: Gray dubbing
Shellback: Ziploc bag
Rib: Monofilament

SAND'S MYSIS

Hook: #16–20 Tiemco 200RBL (barbless)
Body: 5-minute Z-Poxy
Eyes: Burnt 16- to 20-pound fluorocarbon, color ends with a black Sharpie
Antennae: White CDC cut short with wood duck flank extending over top
Feelers: White Z-Lon tied directly under eyes
Thread: UNI-Mono, beige or white

LANEY'S MYSIS SHRIMP

Hook: #16–20 Dai-Riki 270 or Tiemco 200 R
Antennae: Antron yarn, white
Head: Antron yarn, white, and two strands orange Super Hair, pulled over two medium black round rubber legs, clipped and coated with 5-minute epoxy
Abdomen: UNI-Mono, overlaid with pearl Flashabou palmered toward the head and coated with 5-minute epoxy
Thread: UNI-Mono, size 4m or UTC Monofil, size 004

CHAPTER 13

Other Trout Foods and Their Imitations

AQUATIC WORMS

Aquatic worms, frequently referred as to annelids, are an important food source on almost all tailwater fisheries. Most aquatic worms look like their cousin, the common earthworm. Aquatic worms prefer environments with silty substrate and fine gravel. They are especially effective during high flows, when large numbers of aquatic worms get knocked loose by scouring runoff flows. I have observed cases where natural worms were literally hanging out of a trout's mouth.

Aquatic worms vary from an orangish-brown to a reddish-brown color. They range in size from 1 to 2 inches and can be easily imitated by lashing a piece of Ultra Chenille (earthworm brown color) to a hook. Taper the ends by burning them with a cigarette lighter, and you're ready to go.

Additional colors work well from time to time too. Pink and red are popular colors, especially in off-colored water. A pink San Juan Worm has often saved the day during runoff or another major flow increase below the dam.

Many anglers refuse to fish with worm patterns, because they associate them with—horror of all horrors—dunking bait! If you want to be successful you must match the "hatch," and dead-drift the correct food organism that attract the trout—

Egg patterns are effective in both spring and fall when the trout are spawning. An assortment of egg patterns in sizes 14–20 tied with McFly Foam and standard Glo-Bug yarn are effective in orange, pink, yellow, chartreuse, and apricot. Chartreuse is especially effective in off-colored water during spring runoff.

aquatic worms included. Some days that might mean imitating a size 22 *Baetis* nymph, or a size 20 midge pupa. During the spawning season, eggs might be abundant. In other situations, like fluctuating flows or spring runoff, it may be aquatic worms. There is a misconception that fishing with aquatic worm imitations is easy, but as with every other kind of fishing, success requires good presentation.

EGGS

Egg patterns are especially effective in the spring and fall. Rainbows and cutthroats spawn in the spring (March through late May), and brown and brook trout spawn in autumn (late September through mid-November). In certain drainages, it is not uncommon anymore to find fall-spawning rainbows, and egg patterns will be effective during the spawn.

One of the most effective egg patterns is the Nuclear Egg. Tied in a wide range of colors, this is my all-time favorite egg pattern. The fly consists of a nucleus tied from McFly Foam (pink, burnt orange, yellow, chartreuse, or apricot) and a halo of candy cane or white Glo-Bug yarn, which sweeps back over the nucleus. Keep in mind that orange scud patterns are also effective for imitating eggs in the spring and fall.

Aquatic Worm Fishing Strategies

The time of year and water flows generally dictate whether you'll use an aquatic worm or egg pattern. They both work well as an attractor in a two-fly nymphing rig, drawing attention to the small "bread and butter" fly, especially during high, roily conditions such as spring runoff. I use an egg pattern in the spring or fall when the trout are spawning and keying on eggs. Aquatic worm patterns are good choices during higher flows because the naturals get knocked loose in huge numbers, and the fish get accustomed to feeding on them. Opportunistic trout are always looking for a big bite—especially as they expend more energy fighting the heavy currents.

There is no need to use very fine leaders and tippet when fishing with aquatic worms and egg patterns. I usually use 4X fluorocarbon tippet, and drop an additional mayfly or midge nymph with 14–16 inches of 5X tippet. The advantage to fluorocarbon is that you can fish one size larger than with nylon monofilament, i.e., 4X instead of 5X, without any serious ramifications. The larger-diameter tippet allows you to put more pressure on the trout when fighting them in strong currents.

San Juan Worms and egg patterns fish best in fast riffles where the trout have to make up their minds quickly. You'll also find trout feeding more aggressively in the riffles. Trout that have moved into shallow riffles are looking to capitalize on a good meal. I have little success with worms or eggs in slower water. In slow stretches, such as pools or flats, the trout have a long time to inspect your fly so I avoid fishing with San Juan Worms in such areas. If I see a large group of trout that are actively feeding I'll switch to smaller flies to match the hatches.

Tim Karl fooled this big Missouri River brown below Holter Dam with a San Juan Worm.

FLY RECIPES

NUCLEAR EGG

Hook:	#14–16 Dai-Riki 135 or Tiemco 2457
Thread:	6/0 Danville thread, orange
Nucleus:	McFly Foam, dark orange
Halo:	Glo-Bug yarn, candy cane, egg, or white

FLASHTAIL MINI EGG

Hook:	#14–18 Tiemco 2487
Thread:	Orange UTC GSP 50
Embryo:	Glo-Bug yarn or McFly Foam, red
Tail:	Flashabou
Body:	Glo Bug yarn or McFly Foam

SAN JUAN WORM

Hook:	#14–18 Dai-Riki 730 or Tiemco 5262
Thread:	6/0 UNI-Thread, camel or dark brown
Abdomen:	2-inch piece of Ultra Chenille, color to match thread

TERRESTRIALS

While terrestrials are not found in the same numbers as aquatic insects (midges, mayflies, caddisflies, and stoneflies), they still play an important role in the trout's diet. "If I had to pick only one single dry fly to fish on spring creek waters, without hesitation I would choose a black beetle," writes Mike Lawson in *Spring Creeks* (Stackpole Books, 2003).

Unlike an emergence of aquatic insects, where the trout key on the progression of the hatch from bottom to top (i.e., larva, pupa, and adult), terrestrials become available to trout when they fly or fall from trees, bushes, logs, or grassy streambanks. Even though their availability to fish is somewhat random, there is still a rhyme and reason to fishing them. Windy conditions blow terrestrials into the water, setting the stage for some reliable dry-fly fishing. Pay attention

to clues that become available throughout the course of the day. Look at bushes and along the banks for terrestrials. Is the wind blowing? Which direction? I often find myself fishing terrestrials during nonhatch periods, when fishing is a little on the slow side. While their availability is sporadic, trout are conditioned to look for them. If a large beetle splats onto the water's surface, trust me, they eat it.

Terrestrials can be fished from one streambank to the other. Many anglers make the mistake of fishing beetles only under bushes and tight to the bank. Beetles have wings, so they're as likely to fall into the middle of the river as near the river's edge. Beetles can be used as attractors or as searching patterns. Cover the water methodically, presenting your fly to as many fish as possible.

Terrestrials catch trout from spring to fall, but the post-runoff period—as flows subside and become more manageable—seems to produce the best beetle, hopper, and ant fishing. Hopper fishing is fantastic on meadow streams like the South Platte at Spinney Mountain Ranch, the Williams Fork near Parshall, the Blue above Green Mountain Reservoir, or the Yampa River near Steamboat Springs, Colorado. Trout will eat a hopper imitation on just about any trout stream if you really fish it with confidence. Having faith in your fly ensures you'll fish it hard.

In the Deckers area and Cheesman Canyon, some of the best dry-fly fishing of the season occurs with a pattern called Amy's Ant. We typically pound fish up by sight-casting to rainbows suspended in the water column, which—as previously mentioned—is generally a telltale sign that the trout are feeding. More often than not, these suspended trout will rise slowly and confidently to eat a huge dry fly. One of the distinct advantages to this pattern is the size of the hook: you'll typically land your fish on a size 10 or 12. The Amy's Ant is especially effective when golden stoneflies are hatching, or later in the season when hoppers mature and become important foods.

Windy days almost always guarantees some good terrestrial fishing. The breeze knocks beetles, hoppers, spiders, crickets, caterpillars, inchworms, and ants into the water. Opportunistic trout will capitalize on this huge food offering. It takes a lot of midge larvae and pupae, and mayfly nymphs to equal a single grasshopper or large beetle. Trout are less sensitive to leaders, tippets, and false-casting in the wind-riffled water.

Rivers such as the Williams Fork, where lush hayfields parallel the river for several miles, are hotbeds for hoppers. Fishing is especially good when the ranch hands hay the fields, because the hoppers are on the move during the cutting and baling process.

I have heard that a beetle works great during a midge hatch. I'm not sure if the trout are feeding on the beetles because they have been conditioned to eat them, or if the trout are taking them as midge clusters. Instead of the hard-to-see Griffith's Gnat, a beetle with a bright orange or yellow foam indicator is easy to see, even with lots of glare on the water.

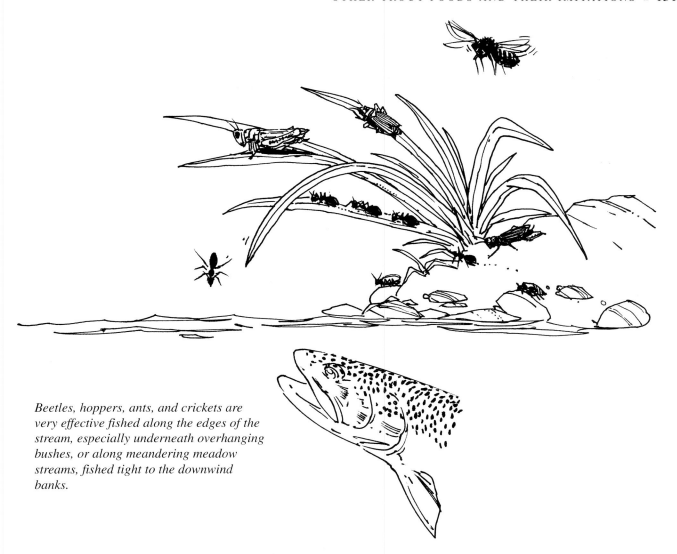

Beetles, hoppers, ants, and crickets are very effective fished along the edges of the stream, especially underneath overhanging bushes, or along meandering meadow streams, fished tight to the downwind banks.

Black ants fall off trees and willows and other streamside foliage. Trout riseforms are aggressive, often causing a boil or splashy surface disturbance. Stomach samples that I take prove that trout eat huge numbers of black ants. When I say "huge," I mean the black ants in the stomach pump outnumber all the aquatic insects, three to one.

I have enjoyed tremendous success nymphing drowned ant imitations around overhanging trees and bushes. How many times do you find ants crawling on your shirt sleeves when you are moving to a new hole or walking through the willows and bushes? A drowned black ant pattern is one of my go-to flies throughout the summer, especially on the Taylor and Blue Rivers. My favorite drowned ant is a size 20 thread-bodied black ant with black Krystal Flash legs.

Terrestrial Fishing Strategies

Ants may be fished on the surface, or drowned with a standard nymphing rig. If the trout are keying on ants heavily, I fish two ants at a time. I have success with both red and black ants, ranging in size from 14–20. With regard to surface tactics, I like to use foam ants with indicators so that I can spot them in shaded areas (under bushes and protruding logs) or in high-glare situations. Fish them tight to the bank, covering the water methodically.

I always fish beetles dry, searching the water methodically and casting to any risers. When blind-fishing, break the river down into a grid—fish the water foot by foot. Make three to five casts in each area and move on, spending more time around the weed beds and underneath overhanging foliage. Fish Chernobyl Ants, cricket patterns, and cicada imitations in a similar fashion.

Terrestrials are most effective during the latter part of the summer, but success varies depending on the drainage you fish. I have had tremendous success fishing beetles in March and April on the Green River below Flaming Gorge—not when you would expect to see a large number of beetles floating down the river. Cicada fishing varies depending on the tailwater. Anglers find some of the most reliable cicada fishing on the Green River. The best dry-fly fishing occurs between mid June and the first part of July. Anglers can sight-fish to trout positioned near the bank, or just pound them up by methodically covering the water. Cicadas are clumsy fliers

Some of the best terrestrial fishing in the West is on the Green River below Flaming Gorge Dam. Trout will eat beetles from March to October on the Green River. Beetles cast tight to the bank and around the weed beds, especially in potholes the size of a dinner plate, can be very effective. A good oarsman is key in these situations, keeping you tight to the bank, within a good casting range. Chernobyl Ants, crickets, and cicada patterns are also very effective here.

and often fall into the water, creating a small surface disturbance and an explosive rise. Opportunistic trout will move a foot or two to eat a cicada. When casting your cicada, make sure the fly creates a small splash when it hits the water to get a trout's attention.

Hoppers can be fished on the dead-drift or skated to impart action. I have mixed results with each technique. As with cicadas, the most important part of hopper fishing is creating a big splat when your fly hits the water. In most cases, you'll get a strike in the first 3 to 4 feet after the fly has hit. After that, continue to dead-drift your hopper, or skitter it to entice a strike as it floats downriver.

Some of the most aggressive strikes, however, occur after the fly has been skittered, which imitates the natural behavior of a grasshopper struggling to get off the water. The increased activity draws an explosive strike. The best hopper fishing is

on windy days. Concentrate your efforts on the downwind banks, or fish them tight to overhanging bushes and willows. Hoppers do fly, so it is entirely possible to find them floating at midchannel. Cover the water methodically when fishing hoppers. Hoppers also work well when fishing dry/dropper rigs. Any standard small beadhead pattern such as a Hare's Ear, Pheasant Tail, Prince, or Copper John fishes well as a dropper.

FLY RECIPES

PILATZKE'S COLORADO CRYSTAL BEETLE

Hook:	#10–14 Dai-Riki 305 or Tiemco 100
Thread:	6/0 UNI-Thread, black
Underbody:	Crystal Chenille, lime/black
Back:	2mm black foam strip
Indicator:	1/2-inch yellow foam indicator
Legs:	Black Krystal Flash

PILATZKE'S ICU FOAM ANT

Hook:	#8–18 Dai-Riki 300
Thread:	8/0 UNI-Thread, black
Body:	1/8-inch black foam indicator strip
Legs:	Krystal Flash, black

CARL'S FOAM FLYING ANT

Hook:	#12–16 Dai-Riki 730 or Tiemco 5262
Underbody:	8/0 UNI-Thread, black
Body:	Black foam, with three distinct segments
Wing:	Medium dun hen hackle tips
Legs:	Rubber leg material or Flexi Floss, small black
Indicator:	EVAZOTE foam, orange (clipped), tied with orange thread and colored with a black Sharpie on the bottom of the fly. The size of the indicator can vary depending on your vision.

AMY'S ANT

Hook:	#4–8 Tiemco 5263
Thread:	6/0 UNI-Thread, brown
Underbody:	Tan foam, 1/8-inch-wide strip
Overbody:	Brown foam, wider strip than underbody
Rear legs:	Rubber legs, brown, medium
Body hackle:	Brown, undersized
Body:	Crystal Chenille, olive
Wing:	Light elk hair over small clump of pearl Krystal Flash
Thorax:	Arizona peacock dubbing
Wingcase:	Overbody foam, pulled back and tied down
Legs:	Brown rubber, medium

B/C HOPPER

Hook:	#6–10 Dai-Riki 730 or Tiemco 5262
Thread:	3/0 Monocord, tan
Adhesive:	Zap-A-Gap
Body:	3mm foam, tan
Binder Strip:	3mm foam, tan
Rear legs:	Round rubber legs, tan
Underwing:	Web Wing, mottled tan
Flash:	Krystal Flash, root beer
Overwing:	Elk hair
Bullet head:	Natural deer hair
Front legs:	Round rubber legs, tan
Indicator:	McFlylon or Float-Viz, pink or chartreuse

DAVE'S HOPPER

Hook:	#6–14 Tiemco 5263
Thread:	6/0 UNI-Thread, tan
Tail:	Saddle hackle, red
Abdomen:	Wool yarn, pale yellow
Hackle:	Saddle hackle, brown
Wing:	Mottled turkey
Head:	Spun natural deer hair

Attractors are effective in pocketwater between early August and mid-September when the fish are accustomed to looking up. This small brown trout took a Royal Wulff during a nonhatch period.

ATTRACTORS

While matching the hatch is an important part of fly fishing, it is not always the only formula for success. Sometimes "unmatching the hatch," or fishing with large, bright, gaudy flies, commonly called attractors, is an important strategy for a successful day on the stream.

Early on in a hatch, the trout are not nearly as selective as they are during the height of the hatch. For that reason, attractors often work well during the initial phases of a hatch, but as the numbers of hatching insects intensify, attractors are less effective as the trout feed selectively. During the transition from opportunistic feeding to selective feeding, focus on matching the hatch with the correct size, shape, and color; otherwise, you may become frustrated with your inability to fool the rising trout.

I have sometimes been surprised, however. I remember one evening when a group of guide buddies and I were floating around in the Texas Hole during the last two hours before dark. Our primary objective was to catch the evening midge hatch. This piece of water may have more rising trout than any other hole, on any river, throughout the West. That's a strong statement, but I wholeheartedly believe it is true.

That particular evening, I was casting a Hi-Vis Matt's Midge and a size 26 Parachute Adams to fish that were "midging" every few seconds. The biggest challenge that evening was seeing the fly in the scum lines with the evening glare. Noses were poking up everywhere.

During the evening midge hatch, if you make a good presentation and can see your fly, the chances are pretty good you'll hook a couple dozen trout before dark. I was catching a fair number of trout, but my friend Clay Anselmo, who was in the next drift boat over, was knocking them dead. He was putting on a dry-fly clinic! Before long, I couldn't take it anymore. "What are you using?" I asked him. He told me his fly was a size 16 Limeade.

First of all, he could see the fly in the scum line, and second, the peacock herl body must have imitated a cluster of midges. I couldn't argue with his success, but sometimes things just don't add up. The San Juan is not known for its superb attractor fishing, but rather for its hard-fished, selective trout that scrutinize your presentation with a fine-toothed comb. In most cases, you'll need a size 24–26 thin, sparse, perfectly dressed dry fly to fool fish during the evening midge hatch.

Attractors are helpful when the water is blanketed with naturals. I have seen times in the Texas Hole when there were so many blue-winged olives that you could not find your artificial fly. This situation leaves only one option: an attractor or Hi-Vis pattern.

If you match your fly to the naturals, your imitation is just one of many for the trout to choose from. From the standpoint of sheer numbers, your odds drop dramatically. Sometimes just having a bigger fly than the naturals triggers an opportunistic feeding response from the trout. This can be effective during a dense caddis or mayfly hatch. Many anglers use a bright attractor in a two-fly rig to help locate their smaller fly when the surface is covered with naturals. Attractors are also effective when incorporating dry/dropper tactics with nymphs or emergers.

Attractors can be especially effective during the post-runoff period on certain rivers like the Blue, the Taylor, and the Yampa. As previously mentioned, several miles downstream from the dam, many rivers begin to resemble freestone rivers. With increased water temperatures, the trout are more active and the hatches are generally better. Some of the evening caddis hatches are nothing short of excellent.

If the trout have been exposed to good hatches throughout the summer, they'll get accustomed to feeding opportunistically on the surface. I have enjoyed attractor fishing clear into the autumn with Royal Wulffs and Renegades when the vast majority of the hatches were done for the season. Once the water temperatures dip below the 42–44-degree mark, start fishing smaller flies as the trout get selective again, feeding mainly on tiny mayflies and midges.

My favorite attractor patterns are Limeades, Royal Wulffs, Renegades, and H&L Variants. I encourage you to carry them in sizes 10–20—you never know when you might need them, and they just might save the day.

FLY RECIPES

DORSEY'S LIMEADE

Hook:	#10–18 Dai-Riki 730 or Tiemco 5262
Thread:	8/0 UNI-Thread, black
Tail:	Moose, two-thirds shank length
Abdomen:	Flashabou, green, with peacock herl
Wing:	Calf tail, chartreuse
Hackle:	Brown

ROYAL WULFF

Hook:	#12–18 Dai-Riki 305 or Tiemco 100
Thread:	8/0 UNI-Thread, black
Tail:	Moose body hair
Abdomen:	Peacock herl and red floss
Wing:	Calf tail or calf body hair, white
Hackle:	Rooster, brown

RENEGADE

Hook:	#12–18 Dai-Riki 305 or Tiemco 100
Thread:	8/0 UNI-Thread, black
Hackle:	Rooster, brown
Abdomen:	Peacock
Rib:	Monofilament
Hackle:	Rooster, white

H & L VARIANT

Hook:	#12–18 Dai-Riki 305 or Tiemco 100
Thread:	8/0 UNI-Thread, black
Tail:	Calf tail or calf body hair, white
Abdomen:	Stripped peacock quill and peacock herl
Wing:	Calf tail or calf body hair, white
Hackle:	Brown rooster

CHAPTER 14

Matching the Hatch and Reading the Rise

MATCHING THE HATCH

Fly fishing Western tailwaters is a tricky business. Heavily fished waters present the greatest challenge because intense fishing pressure has educated our trout, making them extremely difficult to fool. Anglers are now faced with fishing smaller flies on finer tippets, and using fluorocarbon and more exacting imitations. Fly fishing has reached a new level of sophistication with all recent gear advancements, innovative fly patterns, and many other refinements. CDC, snowshoe rabbit, and a wide array of synthetic fly-tying materials (i.e.,

Z-Lon, Loco Foam, and Thin Skin) have opened doors for creating lifelike patterns that fool even the most superselective trout.

Bruce Olsen, Dealer Relations Manager from Umpqua Feather Merchants, recently told me, "I'll know I've done my job when the Hare's Ear is no longer part of our catalog." While this is not far from the truth, we must be careful not to outthink ourselves with all the latest and greatest fly patterns. Many of the new, cutting-edge fly patterns catch as many fly fishers as they do trout!

In order to match the hatch, you need a fly of the right size, shape, and color—and you need to match the behavior of the natural. Brush up on your entomology by taking a class or consulting some of the resources in the back of this book.

The trout's primary goal is still to find feeding locations that provide it with the greatest amount of food for the least amount of effort. Second, these locations must also protect them from predation if they are to survive for an extended period of time. Though many anglers tend to outthink themselves, presentation should remain on the top of any fly fisher's to-do list. With good techniques, a number of patterns will fool fish during a *Baetis* hatch—so it is not so much the pattern that matters. Many anglers believe that they need to change flies frequently, rather than concentrate on the basics: the proper approach and a good presentation. If you're continuously changing flies, you're losing valuable fishing time.

Matching the hatch has two parts: First, you must decipher which species (midges, mayflies, caddis, or stoneflies) the fish are feeding on; and second, you must identify the actual stage of emergence. Are the fish keying on free-floating nymphs, emergers, adult mayfly duns, or spentwing, egg-laying adults? Solving this part of the puzzle is one of the most satisfying parts of fly fishing. In addition to matching the size, shape, and color of the insect, you need to match the behavior of the natural.

In time, you'll be able to look at a seine or stomach sample and identify a size 16 scud or a size 18 pale morning dun nymph. If you're not there yet, be patient—things eventually fall into place if you're willing to learn. Most important, you'll be able to take the information from the seine or stomach samples and choose the correct fly with a systematic approach. Once you overcome this hurdle, you're well on your way to mastering Western tailwater fisheries.

Size

Size refers to the length of your artificial fly or the natural food organism you are trying to imitate. For identification purposes, most anglers refer to hook size when referring to either the natural or the artificial fly.

Choosing the correct size fly can make or break your day. I carry several sizes of the same pattern for this reason. For example, you should carry Pheasant Tails in sizes 16 through 24, which allows you to imitate almost any mayfly nymph you encounter on a tailwater.

Because tailwater trout are extremely selective, they may refuse a size 16 *Baetis* nymph imitation based on unfamiliarity, but readily accept a size 20 because they see them on a regular basis. Many anglers believe that big flies will catch big fish. This is true under certain circumstances, but on the whole, you'll need to be in the ballpark with regard to size if you plan to catch tailwater trout.

If you're not getting strikes (and you know that the trout are actively feeding and that you have a good presentation) be willing to change, experiment, drop down one hook size, and see what results you may get. If you must err on one side or the other, go small!

Shape

Shape is the silhouette of your fly, whether it's on the surface, just below the surface, or bouncing along the stream bottom.

If you're trying to imitate a *Baetis* nymph, you'll need a thin, sparse, streamlined mayfly imitation. If you're trying to imitate a green drake, you'll want a much larger mayfly pattern, with a robust, boxlike thorax. If you're trying to imitate a midge larva, you'll need a thin, wormlike pattern. But if you want to focus on midge pupae, you need a pattern with a bulbous thorax. We could go on—these are only a few examples, but I think you get my point.

The shape of dry flies is critical. Trout that are keying on mayfly spinners will be less likely to eat a standard upright wing (dun) pattern than a spentwing mayfly pattern. Many anglers fail to detect the subtle switch from duns to spinners, resulting in fewer strikes. If you're fishing during a caddis hatch, you'll be more successful with a tent-wing silhouette than a standard hackled fly like a Royal Wulff, Light Cahill, or Adams.

If you encounter a difficult or superselective surface feeder, changing flies can be beneficial, especially if you are positive that you are getting a drag-free presentation. I have experienced several cases where switching from a standard hackled fly like a Blue Dun, Blue-Winged Olive, or conventional Adams to a No-Hackle or Compara-dun style fly has made a world of difference. The latter patterns sit flush, or "cleaner" on the water's surface, especially in glassy pools where trout have a long time to inspect your flies. This is where modern innovation coupled with the proper execution of technique makes a huge difference.

Color

The color phenomenon puzzles all anglers, because on some days the fish will key on one particular color, while on other days, fish could not care less. I have learned through experimentation that red, pink, and blue are important colors, so brightly colored flies often factor into my fly selection. I frequently use red midge larva imitations, and I have recently gained a tremendous amount of confidence in blue midge patterns. I tie a blue Mercury Brassie that has proven itself as a great trout producer—especially in low-light conditions.

I found this to be interesting: Gary Borger unveils in *Presentation* (Tomorrow River Press, 1995) that there is a natural loss of light and color as the water depth increases. Borger suggests that some of this is due to the colors being absorbed by the water molecules, algae, and other free-floating microsubstances in the water. This fact underscores the importance of having the correct shape to match the natural you are trying to imitate.

While an earthworm-brown San Juan Worm has caught more fish that any other color by far, hot pink, orange, and red San Juan Worms can be effective under certain circumstances. In my experience, stocked rainbows are more sensitive to color than wild trout. Pink San Juan Worms work well on some of the private leases we fish, where the trout are primarily Kamloops rainbows. I have been amazed with the results of using a purple San Juan Worm too. These trout are obviously opportunistic feeders, and for some reason the bright color triggers

Riseforms are often the telltale signs of what the trout are eating on the surface. Based on the riseform in the top right corner, an angler tries to match the hatch in Colorado's Elevenmile Canyon. It is not a bad idea to carry a small pair of binoculars to closely examine riseforms from across the stream.

correctly colored wings and abdomen. Choosing the right color scheme is often as important as choosing the correct size and silhouette.

Behavior

Imitating the behavior of certain food organisms is instrumental to your success on any given day. Behavior ranges from active skittering to a dead-drift, so you need to be observant and adapt your presentations to match what the naturals are doing. The gospel of the dead-drift is ingrained in most fly fishers, but active retrieves have their place and time as well. Swinging a caddis pupa or *Baetis* nymph imitation can be very effective when trying to imitate an emerging caddis or a swimming *Baetis* during the height of the hatch. Imparting action to a streamer is deadly when you're trying to imitate forage fish such as minnows, baby trout, and sculpins, as well as other large food organisms such as crayfish or leeches. Even though dead-drifting scuds and sow bugs is the most effective approach, a stripping motion can be effective too. Experiment with your retrieve, find what works best, and always be willing to change.

IDENTIFYING RISEFORMS

For the dry-fly angler, there is nothing more exciting than locating a fish, or pod of fish, that is feeding on or near the surface. The riseforms identify actively feeding trout, whereas fish feeding on nymphs are harder to spot. When a fish eats something from the surface of the water, its vibrant feeding action produces a pulsating set of wavelike, widening rings, commonly referred to as a riseform. Riseforms have fascinated anglers for ages because the surface disturbances are often the telltale signs of many hidden clues: whether the fish is feeding on, in, or just below the surface; what it might be eating; the amount of confidence a trout has in its food; its direction of travel; and even the fish's size—sometimes.

In the late Vincent C. Marinaro's book, *In the Ring of the Rise* (Crown Publishers, 1976), the author goes into great detail explaining the different riseforms of trout. Marinaro, one of the most respected spring-creek specialists of his time, wrote, "The riseform is the final act in what may be, many times, a very complicated process of acquiring a tiny bite of food."

Through his intense research and photographic essays, Marinaro concluded that trout rise to the surface to eat in three different ways: the simple rise, the compound rise, and the complex rise. All his studies were conducted in a natural environment, with wild trout, and with a natural blind. He admits, "It was not an easy thing to do."

Trout face into the current (which is not always upstream) in moving water environments. As a rising trout ascends in the current, the speed of the water gently pushes the trout downstream before it eats the food item on, or just below, the surface. After eating, the trout dips below the surface and swims upcurrent, repositioning itself behind a current-blocking structure, taking up what is commonly referred to as the holding position. Marinaro refers to the trout's holding

an aggressive feeding response. Time in and time out, trout will eat a pink San Juan worm—even in clear water.

Pink San Juan Worms are especially effective during spring runoff when the water is off-colored. I have fooled both stocked and wild trout in situations that my customers deemed to be impossible. I must admit that at first I had my doubts, too. But the proof is in the pudding—the power of the worm is amazing. At our shop, the guides call the pink San Juan Worm "Pink Death"—because it is one of the most effective patterns we fish. Don't let the simplicity of a San Juan Worm fool you—it catches trout. Last time I checked, that was the goal of fly-fishing.

We use a custom pink San Juan Worm that is very effective. Tie it with a size 14 Dai-Riki 075 hook (heavy wire, perfect for dredging deeper riffles and runs) for durability. Next, lash a 2-inch piece of hot pink chenille to the hook with 6/0 pink thread. Then wrap the shank of the hook with pearl Krystal Flash to give the fly some additional sparkle.

Aside from using bright colors to draw attention, matching the color of the natural aquatic insect is important too. During a pale morning dun or blue-winged olive hatch, you'll need to have the appropriate silhouette with the

SIMPLE RISE

position as the observation post. Marinaro concludes that by the time the circular rings are detected by the naked eye, the trout is already heading back upstream to the observation post.

With that in mind, it's safe to assume that the riseform is below where the trout is positioned in the current—unless, of course, the trout is cruising. Having some previous knowledge on the positioning of the trout, as well as its movement during the rising process, will assist you in delivering an accurate cast. Water speed and where the fish is positioned in the water column determine how far a trout will travel downstream to obtain its food. If the fish is positioned just below the surface in a slow, glassy pool, the trout may move only a few inches downstream. If a fish is positioned closer to the stream bottom, and the current is swift, the fish may be pushed 3 to 4 feet downstream prior to eating a food morsel from the riffled surface.

All three riseforms begin in a similar fashion, with the trout positioned facing into the current, in a strategic holding position. In each scenario, the trout closely inspects the food as it drifts downstream near or on the surface of the river. Each riseform is dictated by the "confidence level" the trout has in the food that is drifting overhead.

Simple Rise

A trout that is certain of its food generally makes a simple rise. You'll observe this type of riseform during a moderate to heavy hatch (i.e., blue-winged olives or pale morning duns), especially in slow-to-moderately paced currents.

The simple rise involves a quick decision on the part of the trout. After a trout identifies a food organism that is floating overhead, it rises in the water column while at the same time getting pushed gently downstream by the current. When the rising trout and the food rendezvous near the river's surface, the trout will either eat the food or refuse it, and return to its original holding position, regardless of its decision. In most cases, the trout eats the food floating overhead.

A simple rise is an efficient feeding pattern because it allows a trout to capitalize on a good meal with minimal effort. Typically the rising trout is in the upper third of the water column, feeding repeatedly on mayfly duns. I have watched trout eat in excess of 15 to 20 duns in a several-minute period, incorporating a simple rise.

Compound Rise

During a compound rise, the trout takes more time to closely inspect the natural food organism or artificial imposter. Generally the fish has some doubt about the food source; therefore, it drifts slowly downstream, carefully deciding whether to take or refuse the food floating overhead.

Marinaro concludes that midway through the drift, the trout will finally make a decision on whether or not to eat the natural or artificial fly. For that reason, the angler must have a long, drag-free float. If drag occurs, the trout will reject the offering (this is often termed a refusal) and return to its original holding position. The trout may or may not inspect your artificial offering again.

I have observed many occasions when a trout nudges the fly with its nose, with the end result being a refusal. My speculation is that the trout is trying to see if the artificial fly will move or skitter. I have sat there with amazement, watching this behavior during a green drake hatch on the Blue River.

Could it be that the natural behavior of the adult insect (i.e., a mayfly's fluttering or skittering action that occurs on the surface of the river as its wings dry out preparing for flight) entices a strike? In many cases, imitating the behavior of the natural food organism is as important as choosing the correct fly.

Complex Rise

As the name implies, the complex rise is multifaceted. A complex rise occurs when the trout has very little confidence in its food. As with the compound rise, the trout drifts downstream with the food organism, closely inspecting it, delaying its decision because of its uncertainty about the food source.

COMPOUND RISE

COMPLEX RISE

The inspection could end here—with the trout returning to its holding position—or curiosity may set in as the fly begins to float downstream. At this point in the drift, the trout chases the food as if it were getting away. Marinaro firmly believed that once a trout begins the downstream attack, he'll never refuse the fly. After the food has been consumed, the trout swings in the current, rotates 180 degrees, and returns to its strategic holding position.

I have observed this type of behavior many times on the Green River below Flaming Gorge Dam. It usually occurs when I'm fishing beetles or other terrestrials, like cicadas, from my drift boat, close to the bank or around the weed beds. I see the trout rise, follow the artificial fly, look at it carefully, and then finally strike the fly with a downstream attack.

This process will demand some patience on your part, because the whole rising process may take one to three seconds. Be careful not to set the hook prematurely; let the fish come up, eat your fly, and dip below the surface. Then gently set the hook.

Dealing with Refusals

If you get a refusal, the trout has considerable doubt about your artificial offering. This may be because of poor presentation. Other culprits could be fly size and tippet diameter.

First of all, make sure you are getting a good, accurate cast and precise dead-drift. Several inches to the right or left is not good enough, and can cause immediate drag, especially if the trout is positioned in a swirly seam or foam line. Many anglers cast beyond the seam, which results in immediate

BULGES AND BOILS

drag because the faster water pulls the fly as soon as it hits the water. You need to place your fly or flies several inches above the rising trout. You may need to use a reach mend or other specialty cast to offset drag (see the section on specialty casting in chapter 7). Many times, changing your angle of attack can make a big difference. If you're positive that your presentation is drag-free, then you need to change flies, or drop down your tippet diameter one size. In most cases, these alterations will entice a strike.

In most small-fly situations, I fish with 7X tippet from the beginning of the hatch to alleviate this problem. That will narrow down your options to changing flies. If you're getting refusals with a standard hackled fly, change to a No-Hackle or Compara-dun version. If that fails, go with a #24–26 Parachute Adams. In almost all cases, they'll eat a small Parachute Adams if they are actively feeding on small mayflies or midges. That, of course, hinges on an accurate dead-drift. If you're still getting refusals, cut the tail off the Parachute Adams.

Other Helpful Clues

Prior to casting to a rising trout, study the riseform and natural aquatic insects carefully. Don't rush—take an extra minute to carefully inspect the river for additional information that might help you determine what the fish are feeding on. Shake a willow tree or bush; look on the water's surface, or in the air, for any clues as to what food organisms the trout may be eating.

Anglers should rig their rods along the river's edge after taking a moment to glance around the river, looking for any evident hatches, inspecting the river closely for suspended or feeding trout subsurface, searching for dimples or rising trout near or on the surface. Speculate how the current conditions (flows and clarity) will affect fishing. Look around the streambank for any additional clues, inspect rocks closely, seine the river, look to see what's trapped in spider webs.

I have often watched a mayfly dun float downstream prior to getting eaten by a rising trout. Being able to identify whether it's a blue-winged olive, pale morning dun, or red quill is extremely beneficial. I have witnessed times when a slight breeze slowed down the progression of a natural mayfly, causing a refusal from the trout. Whether natural or imitation, the food must float drag-free.

When you can't see the food floating down the river, which is often the case with tiny midges and spentwing mayflies, or when trout are keying on emergers (especially with surface current and glare), there are some helpful clues to help determine fly pattern choice and presentation.

Bulges and Boils

A topwater disturbance doesn't necessarily mean a trout is feeding on the surface of the water. An uplifting of water near the surface of the river (something I think resembles a mushroomlike bulge) with no trout in sight is a good indication that a trout is eating emerging insects just below the surface.

As a trout rises toward the surface of the water to intercept an emerging insect, the trout's body mass pushes water upward, causing an upwelling near the surface. Bulges are common during the initial phases of a good midge or mayfly hatch. This behavior is common during a blue-winged olive or pale morning dun hatch, and in many cases, the trout will eat more emergers than duns. This can be a frustrating experience, especially if you do not have the right fly.

Boils are similar to bulges, but they are much more aggressive. I associate a boil with a good caddisfly emergence, where a trout actively chases a pupa, creating a swirly boil near the water's surface. This generally occurs during the first part of May and continues until the end of August.

Sippers

Sippers probably produce the most common riseform on Western tailwaters and spring creeks. The classic case is a trout, or pod of trout, feeding on small mayfly duns in slower pools, riffled currents, or scum or foam lines and fast/slow seams. Sippers produce the stereotypical ringlike rise—often referred to as a dimpling rise—that anglers associate with all surface feeders.

One of the greatest challenges is detecting a rise in riffled currents to begin with, because the riseform disappears quickly into the agitated currents. Countless anglers walk right past rising trout that are feeding in only a few inches of water. Many of these surface feeders are tucked tight to the bank in less-than-obvious places. Look carefully around protruding logs, partially exposed rocks, and moss beds. There is no substitute for careful observation when approaching a trout stream. You'll be amazed how many trout are rising if you really look for them.

SIPPERS

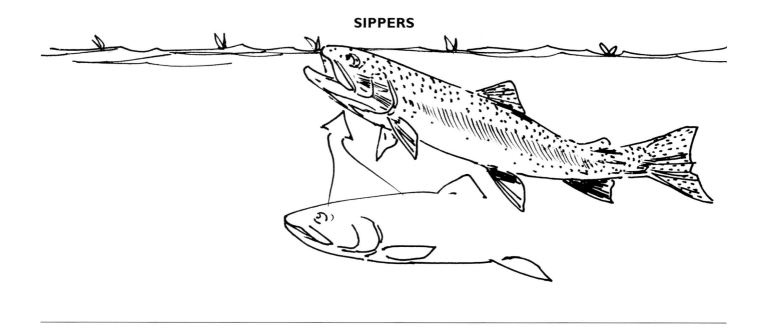

CRUISERS

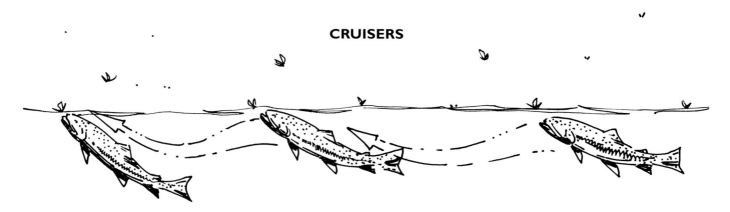

The sipping riseform can fool you, making you believe that the trout that are rising are very small. Don't be fooled by sippers—they are not always small trout. Sippers just poke their noses through the surface of the water causing very little disturbance. You'll hear a small snapping sound when the trout pokes it nose through the surface film and grabs a mayfly dun.

I learned a valuable lesson one day while I was fishing the Colorado River a few miles downstream of Granby Reservoir. My friend Don Hodgkin and I were driving home after fishing the lower Colorado when we spotted a pod of rising trout on the left side of the island directly downstream from Windy Gap Reservoir. We pulled over to take a closer look. The rising fish appeared to be very small, but they were feeding on the surface. It was about 3 P.M., and conditions were overcast and drizzly—the perfect scenario for a good blue-winged olive hatch. We had been nymphing all day, so it was hard to refuse a little dry-fly action.

Both Hodgkin and I set up dry-fly rods and hiked down the steep river embankment, carefully wading upstream into a strategic casting position. Upon closer inspection, the trout were indeed sipping tiny olive-bodied mayfly duns from the smooth, glasslike currents. The surface glare was harsh and it was hard to tell the size of the rising trout.

Hodgkin pulled some line off his fly reel and made a precise upstream delivery to a trout rising in the back of the pool. He immediately hooked a nice fish. He gracefully landed the 16-inch rainbow, admired its beauty, then released it. It was my turn now. Like all good fishing buddies, we alternated every other fish. I took a couple of steps forward and cast to another trout that was feeding steadily. The fish tilted its head back, and rose with confidence to eat my fly—but I missed him. I was so excited I set the hook too early! I took another shot at a different fish and managed to persuade a nice 15-inch rainbow to the net.

Hodgkin and I fished for nearly 45 minutes, eventually hooking and landing nearly a dozen fish. We were both pleasantly surprised at the size of the trout and glad that we hadn't passed on this opportunity simply because of the small dimpling riseform.

Cruisers

As if things weren't complicated enough, toss in a moving target, commonly referred to as a cruiser, and things get really

PORPOISING RISE

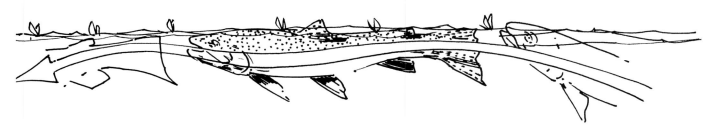

HEADLESS PORPOISING RISE

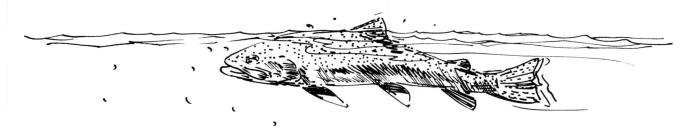

GULPERS

challenging. In slow, lakelike water and back channels, trout often cruise looking for food in both selective and opportunistic phases. I have watched a trout key on midge pupae just below the surface in these areas or glide from one blue-winged olive to another, sipping the tiny, sleek, olive-bodied mayflies with confidence. Your casting must be delicate, and accurate.

If it is overcast, determining the direction the trout is traveling can be difficult because the visual clues are lost in the surface glare. If the lighting is good, and the surface glare is not too harsh, you can try to second-guess the direction in which the trout is traveling, then make a delicate cast into its general feeding area. Don't be fooled by multiple cruisers. I have observed cases where there were two or three cruising fish feeding at the same time. In some cases, it works best to just place your fly in the general area where the trout is rising and wait for it to cruise by and eat your fly.

Porpoising Rise
The porpoising rise is one of the most graceful sights in fly fishing. The riseform is characterized by a head-to-tail rise

that may indicate the fish are eating on or just below the surface. The deciding factor is whether you actually see the head of the trout break the surface of the water, or if you see a back-to-tail rise. The most accurate way to see if a trout is eating on the surface, as compared to below the surface, is to watch an individual mayfly dun float downriver. If the natural disappears into a trout's mouth, you can assume the fish are feeding on the surface.

If the trout are focusing on emergers, you'll see the back of the trout roll, rather than a full head-to-tail rise. In this scenario, use an emerger pattern, like a Quigley Cripple or soft-hackle, or grease an RS2 in the film.

Gulpers
Gulping rises are associated with a heavy hatch such as a Trico spinner fall. Trout will eat five or six mayflies before they drop back underneath the water's surface. Gulpers swim slowly, scooping food from the surface, moving upstream slowly and methodically in a side-to-side, effortless fashion.

Trico spinner falls bring the largest and most wary fish to the surface. They have predictable feeding patterns which

SPLASHY RISES

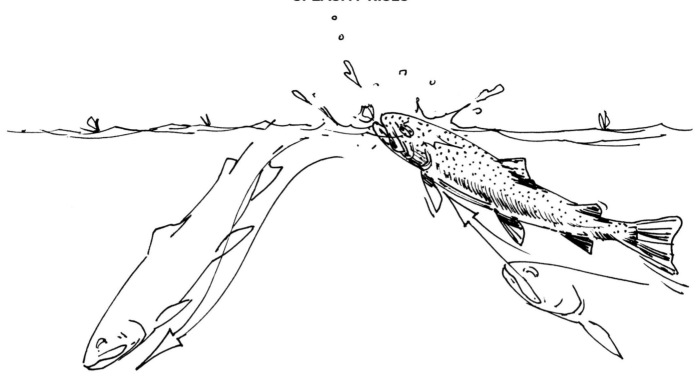

makes them fairly easy to fool. Repeated casts work to your advantage, but be careful—the trout are spooky because they are positioned just below the surface. Sometimes excessive false casting can put them down.

Splashy Rises

Splashy rises indicate that a trout is eating a fluttering insect of some sort. Likely candidates are caddisflies, Yellow Sally stoneflies, or adult crane flies.

Trout that are keying on these food organisms typically feed sporadically and opportunistically, as the hatch is not particularly dense in any given area. This is extremely challenging, yet rewarding, dry-fly fishing. Cover the water methodically, occasionally twitching or skating the imitation to impart action that makes the artificial behave in a lifelike manner.

Trout eating green drakes also make splashy rises. Watch the surface closely; it's not uncommon to have caddis, Yellow Sallies, and green drakes all hatching at the same time.

CHAPTER 15

Equipment and Knots

quipment is the foundation of the sport of fly fishing. If you want to catch trout, you'll need a rod, reel, fly line, terminal tackle, flies, waders, vest or waist pack, and a landing net. You can start with a minimal investment, you can purchase the best equipment money can buy, or you can settle on a middle-of-the-road philosophy with midpriced gear. All anglers will find their own equipment niche, based on how frequently they visit their favorite trout stream and, especially, what they feel is important.

Fly-fishing equipment ranges from the simple to the sophisticated. Whether you are budget-minded or like the best of the best, there is now a wide range of gear from which to choose. And never before has the equipment been so good. Rods are lighter and more responsive; advanced machining processes and higher tolerances have produced lighter reels with smoother drag systems; new designs and seam construction with Gore-Tex result in waders of increased durability and comfort; and highly advanced layering, WindStopper, and outerwear products make fishing in the elements, regardless of the weather, more feasible than ever.

While personal taste and aesthetic appeal come into play, stay focused on how and why each particular piece of gear was designed. Then make a careful decision based on your budget. I am a firm believer in purchasing good equipment

Choosing the appropriate equipment is an important part of fly fishing. Check with your local fly shop for guidance in selecting your gear.

There are many fly rod options to choose from, but a 9-foot 5-weight, is the most common for Western tailwaters. It performs well under a wide range of conditions, including fishing nymphs, dry flies, and streamers.

from the beginning. In most cases, if you purchase cheap gear, you'll need to replace it quickly, and it ends up costing you more in the long run.

FLY RODS

A 4- to 6-weight rod will fill most needs on Western tailwaters. While some anglers prefer 8 to 8¹/₂-foot rods, most favor 9-foot rods, which help manage their fly line more efficiently and reach farther across the stream channel, especially when high-stick nymphing pocketwater, smaller slots, and seams. A 9-foot rod allows hassle-free mending, which is very important when fishing larger tailwaters and when long-line nymphing transitional zones, gravel bars and midchannel shelves, or extending your drift in short-line scenarios.

Many anglers fish with 10- and 11-foot rods so they can reach even farther across the stream to offset tricky currents. These rods allow them to incorporate two-handed or mini-Spey-casting techniques into their bag of tricks. They are perfect for tight-line, high-stick, or Czech nymphing. Most of the 10-foot rods are single-handed, and the 11-footers are two-handed.

After choosing the weight and length of your rod, the flex index is the next major concern. Flex index—an Orvis manufacturer-specific term—is best defined as the action of the rod, or in other words, its stiffness or performance. It may also be

interpreted as how and where the rod bends. While some anglers like a fast rod, many prefer for slow to medium rods.

The two most common flex indexes are tip-flexes (fast and stiff rods) and mid-flexes (medium-fast rods). The vast majority of anglers prefer a tip-flex because it delivers the fly with defined accuracy, even in breezy conditions. The tip-flex gives you a featherlight feel and allows you to maximize your line speed. Tip-flex rods cater to anglers with quicker and shorter casting strokes. This can be extremely important on rivers like the South Platte, Green, San Juan, or Bighorn, where wind can be a big problem.

A mid-flex performs well under a wide range of conditions and casting styles. A mid-flex rod offers you the combination of a stiff butt for battling fish, while at the same time affords ease of casting. If you're the type of person who sets the hook aggressively, and frequently breaks off tippet and flies, consider a softer rod or mid-flex to absorb some of the power.

Anglers who fish out of a boat frequently rig up multiple rods: for instance, a 9-foot 4-weight for dry flies; a 9-foot 5-weight for nymphs, and a 9-foot, 6-weight for heavily weighted streamers. This allows the angler to be prepared for any type of situation, river condition, or hatch. You might also choose to have two nymph rigs set up: one with two small nymphs (i.e., one size 20 Mercury Midge and one size 22

RS2), and the second with an attractor pattern such as a scud or aquatic worm, trailed by a small mayfly or midge pattern. The small, two-fly setup will perform better in the slower stretches (see Slow-Water Nymphing in chapter 6) while the rig with a larger food patterns or attractors will function better in the quicker, riffled water where trout have very little time to inspect your flies. Switching back and forth is okay, but it takes a lot of time and effort—not to mention that if your flies are not in the water, you cannot catch fish.

Even on walk-and-wade trips I frequently rig two rods, one with nymphs and one with dry flies, or a dry/dropper rig to cover all the bases. If you carry only one rod for simplicity reasons, a 9-foot 5-weight is the best overall choice, because it performs well when fishing nymphs, dries, and streamers. There is no right or wrong approach. Figure out what works best for you.

Many anglers' preference is a four-piece rod for the sake of convenience when traveling. Two-piece rod cases are awkward and bulky and sometimes present problems with storage. There is a perceived benefit that two-piece rods are lighter and cast better because they have only one ferrule, but good four-piece rods cast and perform as well as two-piece rods. Four-piece rod tubes store nicely in your fishing bag, car, and under the seat of your drift boat or raft.

Many rod companies offer introductory rod packages that are appealing to novice anglers. Most starter kits include a rod, reel, fly line, and backing for as little as $150. This keeps the purchase simple and less confusing, and most important, affordable. Typically, rod companies include a low-end rod tube with the purchase, which you'll probably want to upgrade. Inexpensive rod cases have a tendency to break (which may result in a broken rod) or warp in extreme heat in the trunk or back of your car. You can also purchase a rod/reel case that keeps the rod and reel together. This is the safest way to carry a strung-up rod because the rod case is designed from rugged PVC material to prevent breakage. The reel is well protected too, with a padded, fully-zippered pouch for easy access.

If you're looking to compromise, midpriced packages are in the $300 to $400 range. If you're shopping for a high-end rod, prices run between $500 and $650. The top-of-the-line models incorporate a high-modulus graphite blank with superior rod components made from titanium and nickel silver. The rods are lighter and considerably more responsive when compared to lower-priced rods. As with many purchases, you get what you pay for.

Many rods now have lifetime guarantees. There is a nominal fee for shipping and handling, usually between $30 and $50, to get your rod replaced in the event of breakage or damage. Whether it gets accidentally stepped on, shut in a car door, crushed by a rock, or breaks while fighting a fish, simply take your rod back to your fly shop, and they'll handle the rest. Unfortunately, at some point, most of us will break a rod, and it's comforting to know that it will be repaired in a reasonable period of time. A good fly shop will issue you a "loaner" to use while your broken rod is sent off to the repair

The importance of a good fly reel cannot be overemphasized. Playing big fish on fine tippets requires a smooth drag system and a lot of finesse and skill. Landon Mayer prepares to release a South Platte beauty that he fooled on a size 18 Barr's Emerger with 6X tippet.

shop. If you break your rod at the height of the season it will take longer to get it back than in the off season. Most manufactures get rods back to their customers in four to six weeks.

REELS

There are many options available with regard to drag system, size, line storage and backing capacity, and material construction. First and foremost, you should be knowledgeable about the reel's manufacturing process and internal parts. Do you want a spring-and-pawl or a disk drag? Do you want a mid- or large-arbor reel? Do you want a reel constructed from die-cast aluminum alloy or a reel machined from bar stock? These are all important questions to ask before making this purchase.

While some rod companies offer rod, reel, and line packages, I recommend purchasing each piece independently, or upgrading the "kit reel" for a reel that is designed with the highest performance level in mind. Anglers who believe a fly reel's only purpose is to store line typically fight and play their fish by stripping fly line under the casting index finger.

There are many options to choose from when selecting a fly line. The two most popular choices are a weight-forward and double-taper lines.

Unfortunately, this leads to many frustrating days on the river, many lost fish, and tying lots of new rigs.

Under no circumstances should you ever play your fish by stripping the fly line under your index finger. All your fish should be played on the reel, whether the fish is 10 or 28 inches long. Get into the habit of playing all your trout on the reel. This is one of my biggest pet peeves when I am guiding customers. I am continually reminding them to "get the fish on the reel." There are many times, however, when a fish runs toward you, and it works best to keep the slack out by stripping the slack with your fingers as opposed to trying to reel up the slack. You cannot reel fast enough, so strip in line until you have the fish under control—then get the fish on the reel.

Your hookup-to-landing ratio is directly linked to a good, smooth drag system and, in theory, the smoother the drag the better your chances of landing the fish. Because much of the fly-fishing on Western tailwaters is done with minuscule 5X and 6X tippets, a smooth drag system is a must if you want to land big fish.

Reels range in price from $79 to more than $500, and their internal components and construction vary greatly, depending on the drag system. Lower-priced reels typically have some plastic internal parts. Metal parts are manufactured separately and then assembled later. These reels are built from a piece of lightweight die-cast aluminum alloy and are not as durable as other alternatives.

The other option is to choose a reel that is machined from a solid piece of bar stock metal. Believe it or not, you can purchase bar stock reels now for as little as $130. These reels are lighter, stronger, and much more durable than die-cast aluminum. Bar stock reels generally have higher tolerances than die-cast reels, which guarantees a more efficient and smoother drag system.

Reels are available in a variety of sizes depending on the weight of the rod, line specifications, and the amount of backing you desire. Follow the suggested guidelines of the manufacturer with regard to fly line sizes and backing capacity. It is important that the rod, fly line, and reel balance for maximum performance and casting distance. Balancing the fly line to the rod means fishing with the fly line that the rod was designed for. There are times when anglers opt to "overload" the rod by stepping up the line by one line weight. This can be beneficial in windy conditions, or assist in loading a rod that is extraordinarily fast and stiff.

Today mid- and large arbor reels are popular because they pick up line quicker than a standard reel. Because the arbor is wider in diameter, it reels in double, if not triple, the length of line with each turn of the handle than a standard-arbor reel.

DOUBLE-TAPER FLY LINE

WEIGHT-FORWARD FLY LINE

Double-taper line and weight-forward line

FLY LINES
Along with buying a reel, you will have to purchase a good fly line with adequate backing material. Fly lines range in price from $29 to $100. I follow the manufacturer's suggested guidelines with regard to backing material. There are many different varieties of fly line, but in most tailwater situations a weight-forward (WF) or double-taper (DT) floating (F) line will cover most of your needs.

Many anglers prefer a weight-forward line because it allows for easy casting, handling, and mending in a wide range of conditions. Weight-forward lines are the most versatile because the belly (weight) is concentrated toward the front end of the fly line. In theory, this allows anglers to shoot line farther with less effort, and roll-cast with ease when short-line nymphing.

Another viable option is a double-taper (DT), a fly line known for its delicate presentations, especially for dry-fly enthusiasts. Unlike the weight-forward line, the belly of a double-taper is in the center of the fly line, and tapers toward each end. This helps with a delicate presentation. One of the best features of a double-taper fly line is that is has two fishable tapers. If the front part of the line gets worn, cracked, or dirty (resulting in a line that sinks) simply cut it from the backing material and reverse it. In theory, you have a new fly line or fishable taper.

If you enjoy fishing streamers, especially in deep or fast water where a floating line, long leader, and split-shot won't sink your rig fast enough, explore sinking-tip options. There are welded loop-to-loop sinking-tip systems and intermediate and full-sinking lines available, depending on your needs. Carrying a separate spool with a sinking-tip line is a great idea and very cost-effective. Simply remove the spool with your WF or DT floating line and replace it with your sinking-tip line. Or you can purchase a separate reel, which is okay too.

Butt Sections, Braided Loops, and Welded Loops
Many anglers simply attach a piece of .021 monofilament (18–24 inches long), called a butt section, to the end of their fly line with a needle-nail knot or a standard nail knot. Many anglers use a piece of brightly colored (fluorescent green or red) piece of Amnesia for the butt section, which serves as a

Another advantage is that there is less coiling of the fly line when it has been stored on the reel for any length of time.

Spring-and-pawl reels employ a leaf spring that pushes against a triangular piece of metal or plastic, commonly referred to as a pawl, which in turn presses against a gear toward the middle of the spool. This tension creates drag or resistance on the spool. Most spring-and-pawl reels have an external adjustment knob, which allows you to tighten or loosen the drag. I keep my drag on a very light setting; however, you must be careful that the reel does not backlash itself while you're landing a fish.

Disk drag reels incorporate a disk and synthetic pad that creates the tension or resistance. When the drag system is tightened, the pad applies pressure to the disk. Once again, there is an external adjustment knob on the frame of the reel to keep your drag system finely tuned. Disk drag systems have a better range of drag settings—in other words, there is a noticeable difference between the lightest and heaviest settings.

Several reels on the market have drag plates or cones that reduce heat and provide a good drag system. Brass plates are used in the low-end reels. This is old-school technology that has been replaced with high-tech plastics such as Delrin or carbon composite. They do not require any maintenance and have a low start-up inertia. These reels usually have a sealed drag system that is engaged by some type of clicker or actual pins (feet) mounted on the spool, technology that was perfected in the 1990s and continues today. The conical drags provide more drag surface area in a smaller package. The Delrin plastic part usually sits inside a silicon-impregnated brass housing that lubricates the reel.

Another type of drag system employs a cork disk mounted on the spindle that is compressed against the anodized back part of the spool. Some companies place a plastic disk on the back of the spool for the cork to push up against. Cork drags are among the most effective, because you can really crank the drag knob down against the cork, giving you smooth stopping power. The spool is tightened against the cork disk when you turn the drag knob. This pulls the spool toward the frame along the spindle. There is usually a spring mounted on the spindle on the spool side to help the spool retract when pressure from the drag knob is released.

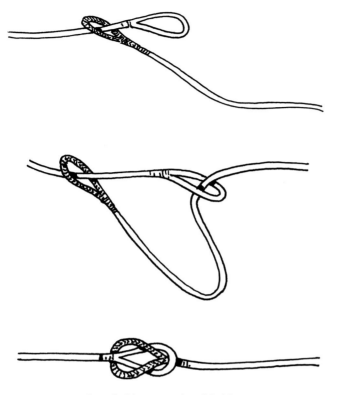

Braided loops and welded loops

strike indicator when tight-line nymphing or Czech nymphing (see Czech Nymphing in chapter 6). I strongly recommend carrying a Tie-Fast Knot Tyer in your vest or chest pack, or on your lanyard, to assist in tying a quick, secure nail knot.

As you replace or attach new leaders, the butt section becomes noticeably shorter; therefore, you'll need to replace your butt section from time to time. Many anglers prefer this method because the fly line–leader connection rarely gets hung up in the tip-top guide, which can break your rod. For this reason, most anglers use a blood knot to join their leader and butt section together.

Another way to attach your leader to your fly line is the loop-to-loop system, which allows for ease and convenience when changing or replacing leaders. Today, most fly lines have either a braided loop or a welded loop on the end of the line. Welded loops are becoming more and more popular because they prevent the wicking of water up the core of the fly line with a high-floating loop system. If you cut off the braided or welded loop, water will eventually seep into the Dacron core of the fly line, causing it to sink unless you seal the end with Super Glue or Zap-A-Gap.

Welded loops are radio frequency (RF) welded: the fly line is folded back on itself and fused into one solid piece, forming the loop. With this modern advancement, the tip rides high on the surface of the water, ending the previous problem of sinking line tips that had frustrated anglers for decades.

In theory, the welded loop doubles the microballoons (microspheres) by increasing the diameter of the tip of the fly

line with the welded loop. This increases the fly line's floatation and overall performance. A high-floating fly line allows anglers to avoid micro-drag, to mend line easier, and to cast more efficiently at farther distances. It also ensures a quick hook-set because the fly line is floating on the surface of the water, allowing for a clean pickup of the line. If your leader does not have a loop, create one by tying a perfection loop on the butt end of your leader. (See the knot diagram on page 182 for a detailed illustration of the perfection loop.)

To join the two loops together, thread the loop of the fly line through the loop on your tapered leader, then take the tag end of the tapered leader and place it through the loop on the fly line. The junction should look like a figure-eight, not a snug knot. To remove the leader, grab the fly line with your left thumb and forefinger and the leader with your right thumb and forefinger, and push the two loops together. Pull the tag end out, and replace with another leader. If you attach the two loops improperly, you'll have more difficulty getting the two loops separated, and potentially damage your loop.

Cleaning Your Fly Line
To maximize the performance of your fly line, you need to keep it clean and dressed. Every six to eight visits to the stream, clean your line with warm water, a rag, and a mild dish soap. Clean and dressed fly lines cast farther, float higher, and perform better, resulting in better line control. Keeping your fly line clean protects your investment and prolongs its life. Once the line is clean and dry, apply Agent X or Glide to help with its floatation and slickness.

LEADER AND TIPPET MATERIAL
To properly deliver your flies, you must transfer energy from the fly line to the leader by turning over your fly line, leader, and tippet material so that your fly lands delicately on the water. Inadequate turnover results in a poor delivery, drag, and refusal from the trout, even if you have the right fly. While the transfer of energy is critical in dry-fly fishing, turnover is not generally a major problem with "chuck-and-duck," or short-line nymphing tactics.

Choosing the right leader and tippet is an important part of successful fly fishing. A good rule of thumb is to fish with the largest diameter and shortest leader you can get away with and still get strikes. If you're not getting strikes, and you are sure you are getting a good dead-drift, switch to a smaller tippet diameter.

There are many options to choose from when selecting the proper leader or tippet material. Do you want to build your own leader, or use store-bought, knotless leaders? Do you prefer a 7$^{1}/_{2}$-, 9-, or 12-foot leader? Is your preference monofilament or fluorocarbon? What are the advantages of each? Carefully consider these options before you head to the stream.

Leaders
I strongly recommend carrying a leader wallet stocked with 7$^{1}/_{2}$- and 9-foot leaders with 3X, 4X, 5X, and 6X tippets.

Consider carrying at least two of each size. The 7½-foot leader is the most versatile for fishing Western tailwaters and can be altered easily simply by adding additional 6X or 7X tippet material.

My preference is to buy leaders from a fly shop. Knotted leaders collect moss and other debris, creating a maintenance nightmare, as you are continually picking debris off your leader. It's plain and simple: if you're constantly cleaning your leader, you're not fishing. Watch your downtime closely.

I add an additional 18 to 24 inches of tippet material to prolong the life of my leader. As I break off rigs or change flies, I am shortening the tippet material rather than my leader. If you damage or scar your leader, you can reestablish the original taper of the leader by simply adding tippet material. With this approach, repairs cost pennies, compared to replacing the whole leader, which costs about $4.

Tippet

Spooled monofilament or fluorocarbon with the same level diameter is referred to as tippet material. I suggest carrying tippet in 0X through 7X in standard monofilament, and 2X through 6X in fluorocarbon. Organized anglers keep their spools of tippet on a tippet bar or tippet spool holder, organized from the largest to the smallest diameter. These accessories can be clipped onto your vest, lanyard, or chest or waist pack for ease and convenience.

Many anglers believe that fluorocarbon is the only way to go. Fluorocarbon tippet is made from polyvinylidene fluoride (PVDF) rather than nylon, like conventional tippet materials. Fluorocarbon works well in clear water and caters to superselective trout: it is invisible to the trout, and sinks slightly in the film, reducing overhead shadows; it is more resistant to scars and abrasions than nylon; it is resistant to ultraviolet rays; and it has incredible knot strength.

Unfortunately, fluorocarbon is nearly double the price of standard nylon tippet. Fluorocarbon also takes considerably longer to break down, so it's important to dispose of used leaders properly. Cut your damaged leaders and discarded tippet material into small pieces before throwing them into a trash receptacle. This will keep birds, waterfowl, and other animals from getting tangled up in improperly discarded leaders and tippet. Fluorocarbon leaders do not perform well when fishing dry flies. As previously mentioned, fluorocarbon has a tendency to break the surface film quickly, which can be problematic when fishing small dry flies.

I use both monofilament and fluorocarbon as the need arises. In most situations, standard tippet works just fine. If the water is off-colored, or the fish are not leader-shy, by all means use standard tippet. If you're fishing a gin-clear stream or spring creek, fluorocarbon can make or break your day.

FLIES

There is no such thing as a "lucky" fly. Fly selection is important, but presentation is still the most essential aspect of catching fish. Remember: "It's not the plane, it's the pilot." Now, don't get me wrong. You have to be on the right page: if

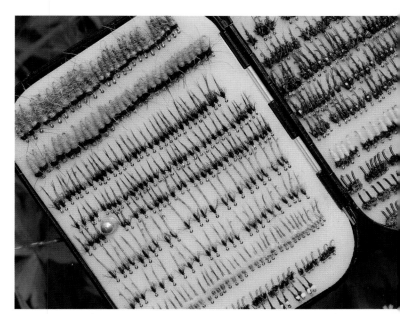

Having a good assortment of flies allows you to be prepared for any type of situation you'll find on our Western tailwaters.

you're using a size 10 Beadhead Prince Nymph during a blue-winged olive hatch, your results may be limited.

Confidence in a trout fly is a whole different state of affairs. If you believe in the fly that is tied to the end of your tippet, you'll fish it harder, concentrate on achieving better drifts, and focus better on the strike indicator. The end result is more fish. On the other hand, poor concentration may lead to this analysis: "The fish are definitely here, but they're not interested in what I have." I hear that comment all the time when I'm guiding a client on the stream. Fly-fishing success boils down to confidence and a good drift.

Fly tying is the next step in the fly-fishing addiction. Tying flies keeps you connected to the sport, even during some of the slower periods or less productive times of the year, such as winter. Keep in mind that tailwaters are fishable 365 days a year—so theoretically there is no off season—but there is considerably more downtime during the winter. Use this time to your advantage.

Between November and March you have the opportunity to restock and organize your fly boxes so that you'll be prepared for the upcoming season. There is nothing more frustrating than running out of a productive fly at the height of the season. It's much harder to "play catch-up" than to have an ample supply or backstock of the top producing fly patterns. There are certain flies like Pheasant Tails, San Juan Worms, scuds, Black Beauties, and RS2s that you should never run out of. Tie several dozen and backstock in them in a compartmental fly box to be used later in the season.

I don't tie flies as much as I used to when I was a commercial tier; nevertheless, I still tie enough flies for my own fishing and for personal enjoyment. I don't limit myself by fishing only flies that I tie. I have run across many situations

Myran fly boxes are excellent for storing your dry flies. This Myran fly box is stuffed with a variety of pale morning dun imitations.

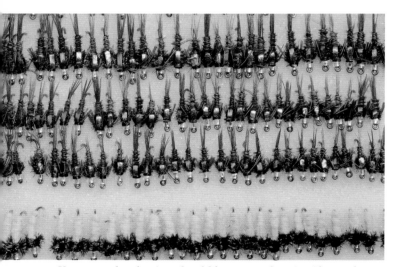

Your nymph selection should be comprehensive if you plan on fishing 365 days a year. Wheatley Swing Leaf fly boxes allow anglers to stockpile huge numbers of tiny nymphs.

where purchasing a certain fly (based on a fly shop's recommendation) made a big difference in the outcome of my day. If I go into a fly shop and ask a few questions, I always buy a few flies to show my appreciation for their local knowledge. Don't limit your success by being cheap—it will hurt you in the long run.

FLY BOXES

In the beginning, selecting a trout fly can an intimidating experience, especially when you walk into a well-stocked fly shop with over 1,400 bins to choose from. You might ask yourself, "Where do I begin?" The best approach is to spend some time with knowledgeable sales associates at your local fly shop. Bring in your fly selection so they can take a closer look at what you have. Discuss with them where you plan to do the majority of your fishing. They will help you decide whether you need nymphs, drys, or streamers, and the quantity of each you should carry.

As a rule of thumb, never buy one or two of a specific pattern. Buy at least six (or tie at least six), so that you don't run out. It's not uncommon to lose a dozen flies per angler on a routine visit to the stream. Running out of flies has an adverse effect on your day. Flies do not have a shelf life, so buy more than you think you'll need—they won't go to waste!

Once you get your core fly selection in place (whether you tie or buy them), filling in the holes is a much easier task. From the beginning, use a methodical approach, separating your flies into basic categories: tailwater flies, bead-heads, freestone flies, and streamers. Furthermore, you may want to keep your midges, mayflies, caddisflies, stoneflies, scuds, eggs, and aquatic worms in different fly boxes. You may choose to keep your dry flies separate from your nymphs. This allows you to think like an angler: carrying what you need—nothing more and nothing less.

Make sure you include all the appropriate phases of the life cycles of each aquatic insect that you are trying to match. Sometimes having the correct stage of the life cycle is as important as the fly itself. For example, if you're fishing in a Trico spinner fall, and you only have standard dun imitations (with upright wings), your results will be limited, compared to fishing a spentwing pattern.

Many anglers have a hodgepodge of fly patterns jammed into one or two fly boxes. Their organized chaos can make them dysfunctional on the stream. Below are a few ideas that have worked well for me over the years. You'll eventually come up with a system that works well for you.

Myran Fly Boxes

It's hard to beat Myran fly boxes for storing your dry flies. Myran fly boxes are highly durable, compartmented fly boxes with a brass pin hinge system, which allows anglers to open and close the fly box with ease. Plastic compartmented fly boxes protect your dry flies, reducing the chances of mashing down the hackles.

Ruining dry flies gets expensive—take extreme care not to damage them. Myran fly boxes are reasonably priced ($4.95 and up), easy to carry, lightweight, and take up very little space in your vest, waist pack, or chest pack. They fit nicely into a pocket of your fly-fishing shirt for ease and convenience.

I use Myran 6-, 12-, and 18-compartment clear boxes for my dry flies. They work well because you can easily see what's inside each box. That keeps you from fumbling around trying to find the right box of flies, especially during a good hatch when the trout are rising.

I keep my flies organized by each "hatch," i.e., I keep all my midge, blue-winged olive, pale morning dun, red quill,

C&F Design fly boxes are another great option for storing tailwater flies.

green drake, Trico, caddisfly, and stonefly imitations in their own separate boxes. You can label them (i.e., "caddisflies") to keep things simplified.

I keep all my flies in a waterproof gear bag, and only take the ones I need. (If you're float fishing, you can take along the entire bag.) This helps to reduce any unnecessary weight that might cause neck or back strain. If you're fishing in the middle of the winter, there is no need to imitate green drakes, red quills, Tricos, pale morning duns, stoneflies, etc.—leave them at home and only carry your adult midge boxes and a box or two of small nymphs (midges and mayflies).

Wheatley Fly Boxes

I use a wide assortment of Wheatley fly boxes for stockpiling my nymphs. My favorites include the Swing Leaf boxes ($3^{1}/_{2}$ x $2^{3}/_{8}$ x 1 and 6 x $3^{1}/_{2}$ x $1^{1}/_{2}$) because they allow me to stock huge numbers of tiny midge and mayfly nymphs in my fly arsenal. In effect, you have two fly boxes in one.

Wheatley fly boxes make a statement about your seriousness with regard to fly selection and fly boxes. They are quite an investment; however, they are worth every penny. The swing-leaf boxes start at around $40 and go up from there. The good news is that once you buy a Wheatley fly box, it will last you a lifetime. I have had many of my Wheatley fly boxes for nearly 20 years.

Wheatley fly boxes are available in silver anodized or black powder-coated finish. They are extremely durable, resisting breakage from being dropped, stepped on, or squashed. Replacement foam inserts can be purchased separately if you wear them out from continually removing and replacing your fly inventory.

Wheatley ripple foam fly boxes work well for larger nymphs such as large stoneflies, crane flies, caddis nymphs, and a wide array of bead-head patterns. They start at around $30. They also work well for streamers and dry flies.

C&F Design Fly Boxes

Scientific Anglers C&F Design Micro-Slit Foam fly boxes are another good option for keeping your flies organized. The special patented Micro-Slit Foam works very well to securely store flies in your vest, waist pack, or chest pack. Just slide your flies into the premade slits and you're ready to go. The biggest advantage to the Micro-Slit Foam is that there is minimal wear and tear on the foam inserts.

Depending on your needs, C&F Design has many options to choose from: waterproof fly boxes, streamer boxes, saltwater boxes, threader boxes (especially nice for your midge selection), compartmented boxes, and flip-page models (similar to the Swing Leaf Wheatley models).

C&F boxes come in many different sizes and designs with 8-, 10-, and 14-row layouts that cater to the small-fly specialist. The flip-page models are the most popular for tailwater anglers, because you can cram twice the flies into the same space.

Breathable waders keep anglers comfortable. I wear waders year-round because water temperatures can range between the low 30s to the high 50s, depending on the season. Waders also provide protection from biting insects, sunburn, thistles, poison ivy, and other skin irritations.

Ripple Foam Fly Boxes

If price is a major concern, consider a plastic ripple foam fly box. They are reasonably priced and come in three different sizes. Prices start at $6.95.

Anglers can put drys, nymphs, and streamers in the same box, if need be. The flat foam works well for nymphs and streamers, and the ripple foam performs well for dry flies. In theory, the hackle dips into the V part of the foam, protecting the hackle from getting mashed. Keep in mind that these boxes are not as durable as Wheatley or C&F Design fly boxes. You get what you pay for.

WADERS

Waders are another important part of your fly-fishing equipment. Many anglers base their needs on the time of year, water temperatures, and weather conditions. Comfort is the single most important thing to consider if you wish enjoy the whole experience of fly fishing.

Many anglers wet-wade during the summer months when the water temperatures exceed the mid-50s (wearing a pair of shorts, wading shoes, or sandals), especially when fishing from a drift boat. I must admit that wet wading is especially comfortable when fishing from a drift boat or raft. Make sure you apply an ample supply of sunscreen on your legs, because the reflection from the water will burn them quickly. I opt not to wet-wade in many areas because of the heavy patches of poison ivy.

Today, most waders are breathable (keeping out water but allowing perspiration to evaporate) and range between $130 and $700, depending on the manufacturer and design. Many companies offer a "satisfaction guarantee" against leakage, while others repair them for a nominal fee. In many cases, the first repair is free.

The first important consideration is whether you want hip boots, waist-high waders, or chest waders. Many anglers prefer chest waders over hip boots or waist-high versions because the latter two limit their ability to wade safely. Hip boots greatly increase the odds that you will get wet.

The next decision is deciding on boot-foot verses stocking-foot waders. Boot-foot waders are cumbersome and heavy, but they are convenient. Many drift-boat guides use boot-foot waders, especially throughout the winter months, because they provide better blood circulation to the feet. Once again, comfort is everything. Walk-and-wade anglers are constantly moving around. Walking along the riverbank and in the river increases circulation to the feet. However, an oarsman is stationary in the rower's seat, and the additional room of boot-foot waders allows better circulation and the ability to wiggle your toes from time to time.

Stocking-foot waders (the more popular design) require a separate pair of wading shoes in addition to the waders. What they lack in convenience—they take longer to get into—they make up in comfort and support. There are many price points in stocking-foot waders, from the low-end, two-ply version to a higher-end, five-ply models. There is a tradeoff between durability and breathability. I wear a three-ply wader in the summer, and a five-ply in the winter. The upper-end waders generally have gravel guards attached to prevent gravel, sand, and fine grit from getting into your waders.

Wading belts are made in a wide range of materials, from neoprene to nylon and other stretchable, elastic-type products that cinch up nicely around your waist. Keep the wading belt adjusted and tight at all times!

In the event you do take a spill, a wading belt can literally be a lifesaver. It will keep 90 percent of the water out of your waders. A properly adjusted wading belt can mean the difference between gallons of water or a quart or two entering your waders.

Wading a river is an important part of fly fishing. In order to catch fish, you must carefully position yourself in a strategic location that holds a lot of trout.

Wading Shoes

If you use stocking-foot waders, you'll need a comfortable pair of wading shoes. Prices vary from $59 to $225, depending on the materials, sole, and support features. Models vary depending on your needs, from a pack-and-travel version to a rigid and stiff sole wading shoe with solid leather construction.

If you do a lot of fishing in the winter, consider Simms Aquastealth studded soles because they help eliminate snow buildup on the bottoms of your wading shoes, especially when you are traversing a trail or hiking long distances. The accumulation of snow on the bottoms of your shoes is frustrating and it becomes a safety consideration, as you are prone to slip, fall, or twist an ankle.

Most anglers prefer felt soles with either ceramic or tungsten studs, which provide extra stability on the stream. But if you do any float fishing from a drift boat or raft, you need a pair of wading shoes without studs. Wading shoes are now available with interchangeable sole systems. Many anglers have two pairs of shoes—one felt sole with studs and one without studs—but I must admit that the convertible sole system is probably the way to go (for float fishing) as you'll never get caught off-guard with the wrong shoes. Simply keep the extra soles in your boat or fishing bag, so that you are prepared for any situation.

The construction of the boot varies from pack-and-travel models, to midweight versions, to heavy, durable guide boots. Many anglers prefer a rigid boot construction because it affords additional ankle support and added protection from sharp rocks and other protruding objects. The stiffer sole is considerably more comfortable and durable compared to the lightweight versions. Comfort is important, especially if you spend eight to ten hours a day walking on cobbled substrate.

Purchase your wading shoes one size larger than your street shoes because when they dry out they become stiff and tough to negotiate. This will allow you to add an extra pair of socks in the winter when water temperatures are icy cold, and the larger boot helps with good blood circulation.

HEADWEAR AND SUN PROTECTION

Twenty years ago, most anglers overlooked the importance of good headwear, but today more and more fly fishers are concerned with sun protection as skin cancer rates continue to escalate. More and more guides are now taking sun protection seriously. A good, wide-brimmed hat provides protection for

A wide-brimmed hat provides excellent protection from the excruciating sun.

your face and neck. For years I wore a standard fishing cap, but after many visits to my dermatologist, I wear a wide-brimmed hat during most of the year.

If you wear a cap, choose a long-billed cap, because it provides additional protection from the sun and helps reduce glare when spotting fish. There are saltwater caps that provide ear and neck protection with a stiff back flap that drapes over your ears and neck for added protection. A Simms SunClava provides excellent protection for your head and neck area, by incorporating a four-way-stretch, breathable fabric, which looks similar to a hood.

While on the subject skin protection, a pair of Sungloves gives you maximum sun protection (SPF-50 and UV protection) for your wrists and the backs of your hands. There is a small opening on the palm of the glove to help you handle the rod properly. To avoid burning or blistering your lips, apply SPF-30 lip balm frequently.

Wide-brimmed hats are sometimes difficult to keep on your head on windy days, so many anglers attach a hat clip (a tether that attaches the hat to the collar of your fishing shirt or vest). If the wind blows your hat off your head, it stays attached to the tether and dangles from your collar or vest.

During the winter or in wet, drizzly conditions, many anglers wear a waxed cap and/or stocking hat. When the temperatures are extreme, a Headsokz is another great option because it protects your neck, face, and head from the elements. Keep your head covered if you want to remain warm in the winter—80 percent of your body heat is lost through the top of your head.

OUTERWEAR

Choosing the appropriate outerwear is also important. Consider wearing a long-sleeved shirt to protect your arms from the sun, bushes, poison ivy and oak, and sharp objects, as well as biting insects such as mosquitoes, deerflies, horse flies, and ticks. I like a shirt with a lot of pockets to carry lip balm, small fly boxes, tippet, weight, a handkerchief, and other frequently used items.

Many fishing shirts have build-in sun protection (SP-30 protection). Look specifically for shirts with this sun protection built into the fabric, because it is possible to get sunburned through some lightweight materials. It's better to be safe than sorry. Most fishing shirts are lightweight and are manufactured out of materials that dry quickly in the event you fall into the river unexpectedly. Avoid wearing cotton shirts: their drying time is considerably longer if you take a spill.

Buzz Off Insect Shield shirts are designed with an odorless insect repellent in the fabric that helps repel mosquitoes that may carry West Nile virus, encephalitis, and other illnesses, and ticks that may carry Lyme disease. They also repel deerflies and horse flies, which can be a nuisance on the stream. Other Buzz Off products include socks, convertible pants, sweatshirts, caps, and bandannas. For maximum protection, incorporate several of the Buzz Off products together, i.e., shirt, pants, socks, bandanna, and cap.

Layering

Layers are critical for comfort. If you're cold and miserable, your fly-fishing experience deteriorates quickly. Dress warmer than you might need to, because it's easy to peel off a layer. There are products available to wick moisture, fight odor, and provide insulation properties to keep you comfortable and fishing year-round.

During the summer, a lightweight bottom or a convertible zip-off pant works well under your waders. Many models have stirrups for maximum comfort and performance. Midweight socks provide wicking performance and comfort. During the winter, add heavyweight fleece pants over your long underwear. Wearing a thicker pair of socks for increased insulation on cold and wintry days is mandatory. A pair of Liner Socks is not a bad idea, either, as these provide added warmth and moisture-wicking features.

For your upper body, a breathable fishing shirt performs well through the summer, but it's a good idea to carry a fleece vest for cool mornings or cold afternoon rain showers, which oftentimes produce a chill. Throughout the winter months, you might wear a midweight or heavyweight top in addition to your normal fishing shirt. These fabrics stretch in the shoulder area for unrestricted casting and body movement.

Preparing for Extreme Weather

Anglers should always prepare for the worst weather, or for falling into the water. Depending on the situation, always carry extra clothes, especially if your car is within walking distance. In a drift boat, you should carry a dry bag with several layers of clothing including extra fleece, WINDSTOPPER jackets and shells, raincoats, bandannas, hats, fingerless gloves, or foldover mitts and hand-warmers. On a walk-and-wade trip, carry extra clothes in a backpack or daypack. Wear fabrics that wick moisture, such as fleece, Capilene, and polypropylene.

I remember several occasions with my friends on the Bighorn, San Juan, and Green Rivers when the weather has turned for the worse, and thank God, we were prepared with a Thermos of hot coffee and extra clothes. Carrying a tarp and a portable propane heater in your drift boat through the winter is not a bad idea. Light the heater with a match or cigarette lighter, then drape the tarp over the bow and the front seat of the boat, making a tentlike structure. You'll be amazed how quickly you can warm your core body temperature when you're in an enclosed area, out of the wind. I recommend bringing extra bottles of propane in the event you need to use the heater for several hours, or in case of an emergency.

If you're fishing in remote areas, make sure you have extra food, water, and a survival kit with matches. I carry a Strike Master Survival Tool in my boat. It's the safest and most dependable tool on the market to light a fire. It performs well during inclement weather, cold temperatures, and at high elevations. For more information, call Charles Houtchens at 360-695-8561. Extreme conditions are rare, but it's always best to be prepared.

Comments on Hypothermia

Hypothermia occurs when your body temperature cools, and your ability to keep it warm fails. Signs of hypothermia include shivering, lack of focus, a blank stare, apathy, and a possible loss of consciousness. Contrary to what most people believe, the air temperature does not have to be below the freezing mark for a person to develop hypothermia. Hypothermia can happen during the summer months.

Once you notice any of the signs of hypothermia, immediately begin treatment. If at all possible, call 911. Carry a cell phone in your dry bag at all times for safety purposes.

If the victim is wet, remove damp clothing immediately. Get the victim into dry clothes as soon as possible. Warm the victim slowly, by lighting a fire and wrapping him or her in a blanket. Gradually give the victim some warm liquids such as soup or hot cocoa. Don't warm the victim too quickly because this may cause dangerous heart complications. Your main goal is to get the victim to a warm place as soon as possible.

Wading Staffs

If you're an aggressive wader, consider purchasing a wading staff. This will allow you to negotiate heavy currents and

Dressing in layers is important throughout the winter months. John Keefover is bundled up on a cold, wintry day while fishing on the Madison River.

cross rivers with confidence. Three of the most popular wading staffs are Folstaf, the Simms sectional wading staff, and the Orvis telescoping wading staff.

My favorite is the Folstaf. I have used it everywhere, from the San Juan River in northern New Mexico to the Quesnel River in Likely, British Columbia. It folds up nicely into a holster-type sheath that attaches to your wading belt. It springs open instantaneously if the need arises.

The Folstaf has a carbide tip that digs into rocks and crevices, and a cork handle that allows you to maintain a good grip. There is a lanyard that allows the wading staff to hang from your belt while you are casting. The lanyard floats on the surface of the river—be careful not to trip on it.

If you're in a bind, grab a large log from the bank of the stream. I cannot tell you how many times I have used a log as a wading staff. Test the log before you enter the stream to make sure it will not break while you are crossing heavy currents. Choose one that is waterlogged—it will sink to the bottom much quicker than a dry log, which is prone to floating. My dad taught me this trick a long time ago; I still use it today, and it has kept me dry many times!

I use my wading staff in fast water, especially in pocketwater, where the stream bottom is slippery and difficult to negotiate. Wading staffs can be purchased for about $125.

A wading staff is a excellent tool for negotiating tricky currents. Hunter Dorsey uses a wading staff to help his footing. A wading staff becomes a third leg.

Polarized glasses are a vital part of your fly-fishing gear. They protect your eyes from sharp objects found streamside and the harmful rays of the sun. Gary Bartell spotted this Cheesman Canyon rainbow before he hooked it.

Use the wading staff on the downcurrent side when walking across the stream. In essence, the staff becomes your third leg, increasing your stability and confidence to move about the stream.

Polarized Sunglasses and Magnification Aids

Polarized glasses are among the most important parts of your fly-fishing gear—both as a visual aid and for safety reasons. Glasses provide UV protection from the sun, as well as protection from obstacles found streamside such as branches, fly rods, flies, and other sharp objects. You should never enter a stream without some sort of eye protection.

Polarized glasses add to the whole experience of fly fishing. They incorporate a specially laminated film between two layers of glass, which creates a filtering process that helps eliminate surface glare. This allows anglers to see fish and river structure while wading. High-end glasses also filter UVA and UVB rays, which are very harmful to your eyes.

Prices range between $15 and $270, depending on the manufacture and composition of the glasses. There are many choices when it comes to selecting a pair of glasses, including clip-ons, polycarbonate (plastic) lenses, and glass lenses. Photochromic versions (lenses that get darker when it is bright, and get lighter when it is dark) are also available.

Glass lenses are heavier than plastic lenses, but the trade-off is well worth it. Glass lenses offer the best polarization, UV protection, clarity, and depth perception, as well as being highly resistant to scratching. If you're serious about fly fishing, this investment is worth every penny.

Additional options include side shields, which prevent light from entering from the sides. Some models are "wrap-around," offering a tight fit and reducing any light that may enter from the sides.

A net will expedite the landing process, ensuring a speedy release. Dave Stout prepares to release a 16-inch Blue River rainbow just above the Heeney Bridge.

Sidewinders are moldable side shields that help prevent side glare, UV rays, and annoying wind that can irritate your eyes. The only drawback is that sometimes they fog up when it is cold. A product called Kleer Vu Anti-Fog and Cleaner will prevent this from happening, even under extreme temperature variations.

Another important piece of equipment is a Croakies—it keeps your glasses tethered around your neck when you're not fishing, preventing them from getting scratched or sat on. In the event your glasses fall into the water, Croakies float— another safeguard from losing your glasses in the stream.

Landing Nets

A landing net is an essential piece of gear to ensure the safe and speedy release of trout. Nets range in price from $25 to $150. Landing nets are constructed from hardwoods such as maple and walnut, with four- or five-ply bow construction, which lasts longer in harsh Rocky Mountain conditions where the humidity is very low.

There are many shapes to choose from—oval, round, teardrop, and oblong—with each shape offering different bag alternatives. These include catch-and-release bags, deep bags, rubber bags, and rubber-impregnated bags. The rubber-impregnated bags reduce snagging the hooks of dropper flies. (Remember to always pinch down the barbs of your hooks with hemostats.)

If you're fishing out of a drift boat, you'll need a long-handled net or boat net to assist in landing your fish. Many anglers prefer a rubber bag, which allows for a quick release with minimal damage to the trout.

Many nets come equipped with French clips, which help keep your net free from bushes and other obstacles while walking streamside. A magnetic net holder with a coiled lanyard is another great option. It offers plenty of reach when netting a trout, and retracts when not in use. Most of these magnets have 5 pounds of pull strength to ensure your net stays attached to the aluminum split rings and out of the way.

VESTS, CHEST PACKS, WAIST PACKS, AND BOAT BAGS

A good vest varies in price from $49 to $200, depending on the material, design, and support features. Comfort is the number one factor—get a vest that has a good yoke and support system to reduce any muscle, neck, and back pain that can ruin your day.

Vests are manufactured in a variety of materials for year-round flexibility and comfort. Some models have superlight shell fabrics with mesh that perform well during the summer months in warmer climates. They are resistant to sun damage and fading, and dry quickly in the event of a rain shower. Other vests are designed more ruggedly, incorporating cotton and nylon fabrics for durability. As you might imagine, vests

You'll need a vest, chest pack, or waist pack to hold your net and store all your fly-fishing paraphernalia. Many anglers use a combination of a vest and a waist pack to reduce neck and back strain.

manufactured from these materials get hot during the summer. For that reason, many anglers have a winter vest and a summer vest so they can fish comfortably year-round.

It's important to look for a vest that has plenty of room for your fly boxes, terminal tackle, and gadgets, and has a cargo pocket for your raincoat. For that reason, purchase your vest one size larger than you think you might need. I prefer models with zipper pulls on the pockets rather than Velcro closures. With the latter, you run the risk of losing some of your valuable belongings. It is important to routinely check to see if your pockets are properly fastened. There is nothing more frustrating than forgetting to close one of your zippers and later find out you have lost a box of flies. It is not a bad idea to put a tether or zinger on your fly box to prevent this from happening. Also, it is not a bad idea to label your fly box with your address and phone number. There are still a few honest people out there who will call you if they find it.

Other alternatives to a vest are chest and waist packs. There is a growing demand to get away from a cumbersome vest, as anglers want to be thrifty and carry only the items they need. Many anglers use a combination of chest and waist packs. Typically, chest packs have a drop-down design, which provides a nice working surface when you are adding tippet or changing flies. With this approach, you can keep the vast majority of the heavy items in your waist pack, and keep the lighter weight and more frequently used items in your vest. Most waist packs have water bottle holders on the sides.

Another option is either a Tech Pack or a chest/backpack system. The Tech Pack is like a conventional vest, with a one-size-fits-all approach. With regard to brand names, Fishpond stands alone. Their products are durable and fully functional, withstanding the abuse that the Rocky Mountain region can dish out. These models adjust at the shoulders and waist, creating the perfect, lightweight design.

Chest/backpack systems incorporate the features of a backpack with those of a chest pack. Many include a hydration system, which allows an angler to stay on the river for hours. The 2-liter hydration unit has its own sleeve in the main pack. This vest is a good compromise, with more room than a typical chest pack, but it's not as awkward as a normal vest. These packs have a small backpack, rod tube holders, and fully padded, adjustable shoulder straps.

Boat bags are important if you do a lot of float fishing. This allows anglers to keep a full assortment of flies, leaders, tippet, and weights (sinking aids) in the bag at all times, and it keeps you from overloading your vest so that you carry only the items you need. This rationale is important from an organization standpoint. Keep the boat bag right next to the rower's seat for ease and convenience. Many boat bags have a "raincoat" or waterproof cover that protects your gear, and performs day after day, rain or shine.

A lanyard helps to organize some of your commonly used items. A good lanyard is padded in the neck area, and is adjustable. Most lanyards have several aluminum clips to

GADGET LIST

It won't take you long to figure out that fly fishing is a gadget sport. Below is a "bare-bones" list of the basic essentials to carry on the stream. By no means are all of these items mandatory to enjoy a day of fly fishing, but they are certainly items you might want to carry in your vest, chest pack, or waist pack, or in the boat bag.

- Zingers
- Nipper
- Tie-Fast Knot Tyer
- Split-shot
- Perizzolo's Mojo Mud (tungsten putty)
- Inverted floatant holder
- Dry-fly floatant
- Dry-Shake
- Leaders (3X–6X)
- Tippet (2X–7X), both monofilament and fluoro-carbon
- Leader straightener
- Strike indicators
- Forceps
- Scissors
- Stomach pump
- Cigarette lighter
- Headlamp
- Magnifier for tying on flies
- Seine
- Water purifier
- Stream thermometer
- Nymph box
- Dry-fly box
- Streamer box

Fishing from a drift boat is a great way to fly fish. Ginny Loman caught this Bighorn rainbow while nymphing a deep transitional area 5 miles below the Yellowtail Afterbay.

attach the bare essentials such as tippet, tungsten putty, dry-fly floatant, Dry-Shake, forceps, and a nipper.

DRIFT BOATS, RAFTS, AND PERSONAL WATERCRAFT

Many tailwater fisheries are nonnavigable. On others access is limited unless you float the river in a drift boat. Many Western tailwater fisheries offer both walk-and-wade and float access. In many cases, there is intermittent private water along the float—know where the public access points are. Maps and floater's guides are available to identify public access. The law varies greatly, depending on the state. For example, in Colorado, the landowner owns the streambed, and in Montana, you can wade the river up to the high-water line.

My first float trip was many years ago on the Bighorn River below Yellowtail Dam, and that experience is one I'll never forget. After that memorable day, I knew deep inside

that someday I would have to own a drift boat myself. At the Orvis Guide Rendezvous in Cody, Wyoming, my wife and I took a drift-boat class to familiarize ourselves with boating safety and rowing procedures. We spent the first part of the day on a lake, and the second part of the day on the Shoshone River downstream from Cody.

We were blessed to have Steve Hyde as our instructor. Since that day, the Hyde family has gained our respect and confidence. After we bought our boat, we had some trouble with the lights on the boat trailer. Steve Hyde personally picked up our trailer from our house, fixed the problem, and sent it back two weeks later—free of charge. I am now a "customer for life" of the Hyde Drift Boat Company.

Without a doubt, purchasing our boat was one of the best fly-fishing decisions we have ever made. My wife, Kim, and I have experienced some of the legendary fly-fishing waters in the Rocky Mountain West, logging countless miles each year

PERFECTION LOOP

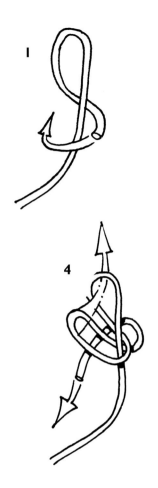

on the fabled Green, Bighorn, and San Juan Rivers. The vast majority of our family vacations revolve around fly fishing, and our drift boat is the key to enjoying our excursions.

Drift boats range widely in price, depending on the manufacturer, hull design, accessories, and whether you choose fiberglass or aluminum. Used drift boats are good option. Many guides trade their drift boats in for new ones on an annual basis: the manufacturer then reconditions them and sells the boats at nearly half-price. Many fly shops, lodges, or outfitters will rent boats for around $100 per day in the event you need one; however, each renter is thoroughly screened to make sure he or she is competent behind the oars to avoid any type of unforeseen accident.

I strongly recommend that any Hyde boat owner investigate the G4 bottom, which adds unbelievable strength, incorporating a totally shatterproof, virtually unbreakable bottom into your boat. Several of my coworkers and I saw our first G4 bottom at the Denver International Sportsmen's Expo in 2002, and we took turns using a sledgehammer to try to break the bottom of the boat. The G4 bottom was indestructible. We purchased our boat before the G4 technology was incorporated—therefore, we did an aftermarket G4 installation. Several friends have put G4 bottoms on their boats too; this has made a huge difference in the durability.

In certain situations, rafts and personal watercraft work better than "hard boats." Rafts are especially nice in low water, and in streams with an abundance of rocks (and pocketwater) to maneuver around. Prices start at about $4,000 and vary depending on the size and features you desire. I must admit that my preference is a drift boat, but there are times when you float unless you use a raft or pontoon boat.

Personal watercraft (small pontoon boats) offer another option for anglers who want to float their favorite trout stream or lake. They consist of a metal frame with two pontoons, which incorporate four air chambers into the design for extra stability and uncompromised safety. Complete with a set of oars, these boats can be used on larger Western tailwater rivers and they allow the oarsman to get into tight spots, which are key feeding areas for trout. These boats work well in windy conditions because of their low profile.

One word of caution: never get into any of the previously mentioned watercraft without taking a rowing class first. I have personally witnessed several boating accidents, and in most cases, the person behind the oars had very little experience. This is no joking matter: an accident on moving water can lead to serious injury, even death.

You can use your boat to fish out of, or to get from fishing spot to fishing spot. Many anglers simply float down the river,

DOUBLE OVERHAND SURGEON'S KNOT

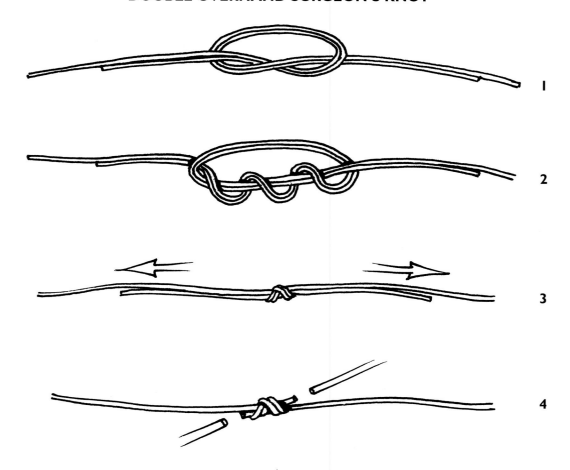

maneuvering the boat into the key holding areas, temporarily anchoring, or having the oarsman hold them in position to fish productive water. It is extremely important that you know which water is private and which is public, and understand the rules that govern each stretch. These rules vary from state to state. Many anglers wear normal street clothes such as jeans, shorts, and a pair of hiking boots while drifting, but it is my opinion that you limit yourself dramatically by doing so. I prefer to use the boat as a tool to get from one piece of productive water to another—fishing along the way, and getting out to slowly and methodically work the best runs.

KNOTS
Many years ago, a colleague referred to knots as the "administrative overhead of fly fishing." In our fly-fishing schools and on guided trips, he constantly stressed the importance of tying good knots, because there is a direct link between the number of fish you land and good knots. "You are only as good as your knots," he said. I cannot overemphasize practicing these knots before you get to the stream. If you have to go and sit on the bank to tie on a new fly, you're costing yourself valuable fishing time. Practice will increase your speed and proficiency.

The good news is that there are only a handful of knots you need to master before heading to the stream. These include a perfection loop, double overhand surgeon's knot (many anglers prefer a blood knot), and a clinch knot or improved clinch knot. These knots allow you to attach your leader to your fly line, add additional tippet to your leader, and tie on a fly, respectively. The latter two will be the most commonly used knots in your fishing rigs.

Perfection Loop
Used for connecting the loop on the end of your fly line with your leader, the perfection loop is a time-tested loop knot that is quick to tie, and strong.

Double Overhand Surgeon's Knot
The double overhand surgeon's knot is used to connect two pieces of fluorocarbon or monofilament together. Anglers frequently use this knot when adding tippet to the leader, or to repair damaged leaders, to reestablish the original taper. This knot is easy to tie, even when it is extremely cold.

Blood Knot
Like the double overhand surgeon's knot, the blood knot connects two pieces of leader or tippet. Of the two, I prefer the blood knot's strength and symmetrical, finished appearance. The blood knot is more difficult to tie, but in my opinion, it's well worth the extra effort.

BLOOD KNOT

1

2
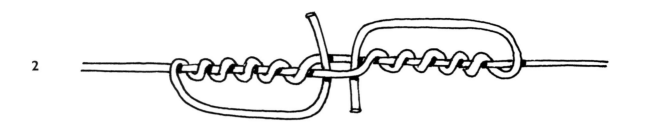

3
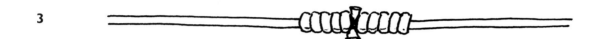

CLINCH KNOT

1

2

3
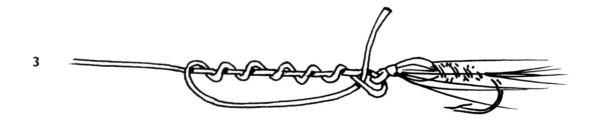

4
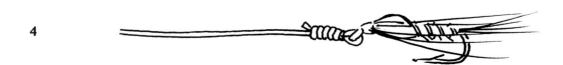

IMPROVED CLINCH KNOT

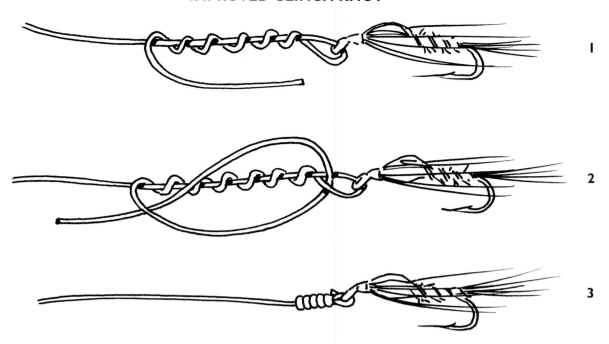

1

2

3

This knot works well for those who prefer a 0.21 butt section (with a nail knot tied to the fly line) without a loop-to-loop system. Double overhand surgeon's knots are bulky and do not slip through the tip-top guide as easily as blood knots.

Clinch Knot

The clinch knot will be your most frequently used knot. Whether you're nymphing, or fishing with drys, dry/dropper rigs, or streamers, you'll tie one or more clinch knots into your system. If you are using a two-fly tandem nymphing rig, you'll have three clinch knots (or improved clinch knots) in your setup.

I prefer the standard clinch over the improved clinch. I find it is too easy to have one of the wraps falls out of sequence when placing the tag end back through the loop created after threading the tippet through the opening near the eye of the hook, causing the improved clinch knot to fail.

Test your knots by giving them a couple of good tugs before you cast. It's better to have a knot fail in your hand than to lose a nice fish like this.

KNOT TIPS

- Practice your knots at home. To be a proficient angler, you must be able to tie a rig in a few minutes. Remember: if your flies are not in the water, you cannot catch fish.
- Keep your leader and tippet diameters as close in size as possible—no more than two tippet sizes apart. For example, you could join 3X to 4X, or 3X to 5X, but joining 3X to 6X may result in a poorly tied not. Take the time to establish the correct taper to ensure secure knots.
- Lubricate your knots before securing them. Moisten knots with saliva or dip them into the river prior to cinching them tight. The will reduce friction that may result in your tippet heating up during the tightening process, causing the knot or tippet to fail.
- Tighten your knots with slowly increasing pressure. Avoid snugging your knots too abruptly. Use even and steady pressure until you feel the leader material stretch slightly.

- If your knot doesn't secure properly, retie it. A poor knot won't magically fix itself. Take an extra minute to tie a good knot.
- Take care when trimming your knots. Don't cut the tippet too close or nick the knot with your nippers. Leave adequate tag ends to allow for slippage under maximum tension.
- Don't bite your tippet material with your teeth. This has the potential of chipping your teeth as well as getting giardiasis from the river water. Use your nippers to trim knots.
- Check your knots before casting. Give your knots several good tugs. It is better to have the knot fail in your hand than when you're fighting a nice fish. Your knots are the weakest links in your rig. Take an extra minute to check them carefully.

CHAPTER 16

Angler Responsibilities

Anglers have certain responsibilities when visiting a trout stream. These include fishing safely, acting as stewards of our environment, taking care of the fish that you catch, being cordial to fellow anglers, and following a set of streamside manners commonly referred as etiquette. You must also follow the rules and laws that govern the section of river you are fishing. This includes having the appropriate fishing licenses and habitat stamps, following special regulations such as slot limits or fishing barbless hooks, as well as understanding property boundaries and no-trespassing laws.

Before I joined Trout Unlimited in the mid-1980s, the preservation of our coldwater fisheries was the furthest thing from my mind. For some reason (like many other anglers) I thought there was an unending supply of trout, and Mother Nature would take care of things. If you're not a member of Trout Unlimited, you should consider joining.

Twenty-five years ago, many anglers based their day's success strictly on catching their limit. To this day, my great-uncle (he's in his mid-90s) still can't imagine going fly fishing without bringing a few fish home to eat. Nearly three decades ago, a full creel was the true test of an angler's skill. If they came up short, anglers were often discouraged, complaining they had a slow day.

I'm embarrassed to say that that's how I viewed fly fishing as a young man too. I based my day on filling my grandfather's hand-me-down willow creel. But I'm proud to say

Please consider catch-and-release when fishing our Western tailwaters. Catch-and-release angling protects trout populations and ensures that the trout will thrive in years to come.

187

STREAMSIDE ETIQUETTE

- Follow the rules and regulations of the national forests, state parks, Bureau of Land Management (BLM) lands, and state wildlife areas. It is important to familiarize yourself with each government agency's rules and regulations. It is your responsibility to know where the dividing lines are between public and private water. Do not trespass under any circumstances.

- Avoid confrontation at all costs. Communicate freely and treat others with respect. Work together to achieve the same common goal.

- Be a steward of the environment. Practice catch-and-release and pick up any beer cans, bait tubs, monofilament line or tapered leaders, strike indicators, or any other trash. If you build a fire along the river, destroy the "fire ring" before departing.

- Be considerate and courteous to others at boat ramps. Use the prelaunch areas to prepare your boat prior to floating. This will help alleviate any congestion at the put-ins. Upon the conclusion your float, use the nearby parking facilities to tidy up your boat (put the oars away, stow rods, remove gear, etc.). This leaves the boat ramp available for those who need it.

- Don't anchor your drift boat or raft in prime holes. There are certain holes, such as the Texas Hole on the San Juan, where it is an unwritten rule not to anchor your boat. Anchoring would disrupt the normal flow whereby anglers follow a clockwise rotation, allowing a large number of drift boats to fish a specific area. If some inconsiderate angler anchors a boat in the middle of the hole, it causes a lot of problems, and often

confrontation. Use your head, be courteous to others, and work with them to avoid problems. We're all in this together.

- When you're drift-fishing, respect walk-and-wade anglers and float behind them. Be careful not to disrupt their fishing hole. There's nothing worse than having a disrespectful boat angler float through your pod of rising fish.

- Be cordial. Greet your fellow anglers. Condescending attitudes only hurt our sport. Be respectful and generous with your knowledge, flies, and techniques.

- Drive slowly on gravel roads. There is nothing more frustrating than some jerk driving fast on a gravel road, kicking up a lot of dust when you are trying to put on your waders, eat lunch, or have a cocktail at the day's end. Use common sense—if you see someone near his or her car, slow down! Once again, treat others as you would like to be treated.

- Don't be a "hole hog." There is a honey hole or two on every river. Please don't fish the same run or hole all day. Catch a few trout and move on so that others may enjoy it too. I see this all time—this is simply being impolite.

- Be courteous to guides. Keep in mind that guides are making a living—give them a break and the benefit of the doubt. Guides continually educate anglers on proper methods, etiquette, fish-handling practices, the environment, and conservation. Guides are not the enemy—they help with the overall education process.

that things have changed! I have practiced catch-and-release for nearly 30 years. I believe it's important for all anglers to consider catch-and-release to preserve and protect the future of our pristine tailwater fisheries. Many tailwater fisheries have special regulations to protect them, so catch-and-release on these waters is mandatory. Poaching is still a big problem, however. If you see someone fishing with illegal methods, or keeping trout in protected areas, please call the state fisheries and wildlife officials, or simply dial 911.

Conservation efforts begin with proper education. I firmly believe in teaching our youngsters the importance of catch-and-release and protecting our coldwater fisheries. Kids are the future of our sport—we must begin now, if their kids are to enjoy our streams in the future. Please review the list below for the commonly accepted guidelines for releasing trout.

- Use barbless hooks. First and foremost, this is a safety precaution for all anglers. Purchase barbless hooks, or

mash down your barbs with a pair of micro-pliers, non-serrated forceps, or hemostats. This helps with a speedy release and keeps your flies from hanging up your net bag. Losing a trout because there is no barb on your fly is an invalid and poor excuse.

- Use a fine-mesh net. Avoid nylon-mesh nets—they scrape the body slime off trout. Choose a net with a soft bag with the trout's protection in mind. Catch-and-release net bags are preferred.

- Don't play a trout to exhaustion. Land the fish as quickly as possible, especially if water temperatures are above 65 degrees. If the fish is foul-hooked, point the rod tip at the fish and snap off your rig. If you're using barbless hooks, they will work themselves free quickly without any serious ramifications.

- Keep the fish in the water at all times. This is one of my biggest pet peeves. I routinely see anglers mishandling

Use available prelaunch areas to get your boat ready prior to entering the boat ramp. This helps alleviate congestion at the boat ramp.

- Don't stand on high banks and fish the opposite side of the stream. If another angler is present, fishing from a high bank on the opposite side of the river is not a good idea. This is especially frustrating for the angler who is stalking a rising trout near the opposite bank.
- If you see other anglers resting at a hole, gearing up, or eating lunch, ask them if they are planning to fish the hole before you just hop in. Don't just step into a hole: always ask permission.
- Anglers moving upstream have the right of way. Don't "short-hole" them—give them at least two runs or pools before entering the stream.

- Yield to an angler who is moving downstream while fighting a fish. Reel in your rig and step back toward the bank until the other angler has moved past you. The angler fighting the trout should be courteous and respectful of the other angler's water, trying not to disrupt his hole when wading through. Assist in the netting process (ask first), and offer to take a photo if he or she doesn't have a camera.

trout on the river by keeping them out of the water for too long. After netting the fish, please keep it in the river! Gill damage occurs rapidly if the fish are held outside of the water. Never place your fish in grass, rocks, or on the gravel next to the stream for a photo. If you want to take a picture, keep the fish in the water prior to taking the photo. Take a quick shot, and immediately put the trout back into the water. If you're by yourself, lay the fish into your net bag with the fish partially or completely submerged.
- Wet your hands before handling any fish. Dry hands strips away a fish's protective body slime, leading to fungus infections and other diseases.
- Avoid putting your fingers in the gills when handling any fish. Take extreme care when removing trout from your net.

- When a fish takes the fly deeply, carefully cut the tippet material as close as you can to the fly, and get the fish back into the water quickly. If you've used a barbless hook, the fish has a decent chance of survival.
- Don't squeeze the fish too hard. If possible, use hemostats or forceps to remove the hooks, or a Ketchum Release tool. For photo purposes, keep the palms of your hands behind the fish and hold it gently with your fingers.
- Face trout into the current prior to releasing them. Cradle your fish just under the surface of the river until the fish reorients itself and gets oxygen running through its gills. Make sure the water is free of silt, sediment, and other fine debris that may have been kicked up during netting. The trout will let you know when it is ready to swim away—cradle it until it wiggles and swims out of your hands. Make sure it does not turn belly up. If it does, repeat the process.

Kids and young adults are the future of our sport. Educate them about conservation, proper etiquette, and how to become stewards of our environment. Forrest Dorsey wet his hands prior to handling this fish, and kept it out of the water for only a few seconds to take a photograph.

PROPER ETIQUETTE

Streamside manners are an important part of fly fishing. If you treat others as you would like to be treated, the river will be a much more enjoyable place. In most cases, streamside etiquette is common sense, but I must admit that I see a lot of knuckleheads on trout streams. Unfortunately, there is no referee to put you in the penalty box for improper conduct on the stream. We must take it upon ourselves to behave well at all times.

The number of people on a stretch of river dictates proper etiquette. If it's crowded, be flexible. On the other hand, if there is only one other fly fisher in sight, give him or her the benefit of the doubt—don't fish right on top of them. Move several hundred yards upstream before entering the water.

Communication is the key for a nice day on the stream. Let's face it—conditions are more crowded than ever. Unless you book private water, your days of solitude are long gone. Such questions as, "Are you moving up or downstream?" or "Would you mind if I fish over there?" go a long way. In most cases, good communication will avoid confrontation. So enjoy your time on the water, and be sure to use your best streamside manners.

REFERENCES

Arbona, Fred Jr. *Mayflies, the Angler, and the Trout.* New York: Lyons & Burford, 1980, 1989.

Bartholomew, Marty. *Fly Fisher's Guide to Colorado.* Gallatin Gateway, MT: Wilderness Adventures Press, 1998.

Borger, Gary A. *Presentation.* Harrisburg, PA: Tomorrow River Press, 1995.

Dentry, Ed. *Blue Ribbon Rivers of the Rockies.* Denver, CO: Denver Publishing Company, 1994.

Dorsey, Pat. *A Fly Fisher's Guide to the South Platte River.* Boulder, CO: Pruett Publishing Company, 2005.

Engle, Ed. *Fishing Small Flies.* Mechanicsburg, PA: Stackpole Books, 2005.

Engle, Ed. *Fly Fishing the Tailwaters.* Harrisburg, PA: Stackpole Books, 1991.

Hafele, Rick, and Scott Roedereer. *An Angler's Guide to Aquatic Insects and Their Imitations.* Boulder, CO: Johnson Publishing Company, 1987.

Hafele, Rick. *Nymph-Fishing Rivers and Streams.* Mechanicsburg, PA: Stackpole Books, 2006.

Hill, Roger. *Fly Fishing the South Platte River.* Boulder, CO: Pruett Publishing, 1991.

Lawson, Mike. *Spring Creeks.* Mechanicsburg, PA: Stackpole Books, 2003.

Marinaro, Vincent, C. *In the Ring of the Rise.* New York: Crown Publishers, Inc., 1976.

Mayer, Landon. *How to Catch the Biggest Trout of Your Life.* Bothell, WA: Wild River Press, 2005.

McKinney, Dennis. *Guide to Colorado State Wildlife Areas.* Englewood, CO: Westcliffe Publishers, 2001.

Miller, Bob. *Tricos.* Allentown, PA: Rod Crafters Press, 1997.

Nichols, Jay. *1001 Fly Fishing Tips.* New Cumberland, PA: Headwater Books, 2008.

Obmascik, Mark. "Pushed to the Brink: The South Platte Battles Fire and Flood, Drought and Disease." *Trout* Winter, 2003.

Pobst, Dick. *Trout Stream Insects: An Orvis Streamside Guide.* New York: Lyons & Burford, 1990.

Rickards, Denny. *Fly-Fishing Stillwaters for Trophy Trout.* Fort Klamath, OR: Stillwater Productions, 1997.

Rosenbauer, Tom. *The Orvis Fly-Fishing Guide.* New York: Lyons & Burford, 1990.

Saile, Bob, and Blair Hamill. *Fishing the South Platte River and Reservoirs.* Parker, CO: River Bend Publishing Company, 1995.

Smith, Robert. *Native Trout of North America.* Portland, OR: Frank Amato Publications, 1994.

INDEX